Transnational
Sport

RACHAEL MIYUNG JOO

Transnational
Sport

GENDER, MEDIA, AND GLOBAL KOREA

DUKE UNIVERSITY PRESS

DURHAM AND LONDON

2012

© 2012 Duke University Press
All rights reserved
Printed in the United States of America
on acid-free paper ∞
Designed by Nola Burger
Typeset in Scala by
Keystone Typesetting, Inc.
Library of Congress Cataloging-in-
Publication Data appear on the last
printed page of this book.

To my parents
Han Pyung Joo and Un Suk Joo

Contents

Acknowledgments

In writing this book, I was supported by the generosity and enthusiasm of family, friends, colleagues, as well as strangers who sometimes became dear friends. Many people were very excited about this project, and this enthusiasm inspired me to continue to research and write. They have waited a long time to see this book.

I am truly grateful to the people in Seoul and Los Angeles who were willing to meet me, to be interviewed, and to hang out. Despite their terrifically busy schedules, they opened their lives to me and often demonstrated a great amount of openness and trust. I know I can never repay them for their time. I hold them in high regard, and I hope that my affection for them shows in this text.

My academic training has been shaped by teachers and mentors who generously shared their passion for intellectual engagement. Purnima Mankekar has been an inspiration as an uncompromising intellectual, a passionate activist, and a close friend. I have been welcomed into her family, and I am more grateful for her generosity and friendship than I can express. The Cultural and Social Anthropology department (CASA) was an amazing program to be a part of while it lasted. When I became a member of its first cohort, a spirit of newness and creativity became the hallmarks of my education. My dissertation committee members, Purnima Mankekar, Paulla Ebron, David Palumbo-Liu, and Gi-wook Shin, were incisive in their critiques and unwavering in their support. Faculty members Paulla Ebron, Purnima Mankekar, Miyako Inoue, Sylvia Yanagisako, Akhil Gupta, Gordon Chang, Renato Rosaldo, Nicholas DeGenova, Valentin Mudimbe, and David

Palumbo-Liu made their mark through their labor as teachers, mentors, and advocates. Ellen Christensen and Shelly Coughlan kept the department together and kept me from falling apart. Richard Yuen, Cindy Ng, and Shelly Tadaki at the Asian American Activities Center (A3C) at Stanford offered me opportunities to share my work with members of the Stanford community and worked tirelessly to sustain dialogues around Asian American issues on campus. During coursework at UCLA, John Duncan, Tim Tangherlini, and Gi-wook Shin welcomed me to Korean Studies and convinced me of the enduring significance of Area Studies.

My fellow graduate students could never have been more supportive. I have great admiration for Marcia Ochoa, who demonstrates the centrality of political engagement to significant and cutting-edge scholarship. Marcia Ochoa, Natalia Roudakova, Nejat Dinc, Jen Chertow, Tim'm West, Kyla Wazana Tompkins Fisher, Lok Siu, Cari Costanzo, Kutraluk Bolton, Celine Parrenas Shimizu, Timothy Yu, Lalaie Ameeriar, Kelly Friedenfelds, Soo Ah Kwon, and Yoonjung Lee were excellent interlocutors and supportive friends. Graduate school taught me to never underestimate the power of a coffee break with colleagues.

During fieldwork, I was assisted by Seo Young Park, who was a patient and supportive colleague. Kim Hyun Mee, despite her insanely busy schedule, found time to take me out to eat and chat about research, national politics, and academic politics. I also appreciated the intellectual and social companionship of fellow academics Jennifer Chun, John Cho, Doryun Chong, and Juni Kwon during research in Seoul.

My year at Duke was an enlightening one. The kindness and generosity shown to me by Orin Starn, Christina Chia, Diane Nelson, Anne Allison, Grant Farred, Ken Wissoker, Tahir Naqvi, Margot Weiss, Neta Bar, and Caroline Yezer made it memorable.

My colleagues at Middlebury College have been extraordinarily supportive, and they have made Vermont a wonderful place to live and work. Members of the program in American Studies, including Michael Newbury, Susan Burch, Roberto Lint Sagarena, Holly Allen, Jason Mittell, Kathy Morse, Karl Lindholm, Andy Wentink, Tim Spears, Will Nash, and Deb Evans, have been excellent colleagues. Renee Brown is an extraordinary force in the department who makes me look a lot more competent than I actually am. I appreciate the help and feedback of writing group sessions with Leif Sorensen, Rachael Neal, Folashade Alao, Holly Allen, Joyce Mao, and Ben Graves. I am also grateful for the amazing work done through the Center for the Comparative Study of Race and Ethnicity, especially Susan Burch, Jennifer Herrera, and Shirley Ramirez Collado. My students inspire me to produce relevant scholarship, and they challenge me to think about the ends and the ethics of research.

This book emerges from institutional support from the National Science Foundation, the Department of Cultural and Social Anthropology at Stanford University, the Center for East Asian Studies at Stanford University, the Clayman Institute for Research on Women and Gender at Stanford University, the Shorenstein Asia-Pacific Research Center at Stanford University, the Center for Comparative Studies of Race and Ethnicity at Stanford University, the Institute for International Studies at Stanford University, and the Fund for Faculty Research and Development at Middlebury College.

I have received valuable feedback on parts of this book from generous audiences at Stanford University, Duke University, Cornell University, Temple University, Middlebury College, and the University of Michigan at Ann Arbor. Some of the material that appears in chapter 5 was presented at a 2004 summer workshop sponsored by the Korean Studies Program at Stanford University for a special issue of the *Journal of Korean Studies*. Michael Robinson expertly ran the workshop and guided our papers into publishable articles. I would like to thank the Shorenstein Asia-Pacific Research Center and Gi-wook Shin for permissions to reprint "Consuming Visions: The Crowds of the Korean World Cup," which was published in the *Journal of Korean Studies* in the fall of 2006.

At Duke University Press, Ken Wissoker has shown a consistent enthusiasm for this project. He has been generous with his time and has offered amazing feedback. He has also offered invaluable professional advice. I also want to thank Mandy Early for her patient answers to all my questions—big and little. Without her help, this book would have never been put together. Kathy Chetkovich and Anitra Grisales offered editorial comments at different stages in this process.

My family members have always provided solid support and constant encouragement. My partner Jason Schwaber has been totally supportive and has always offered to help me get my work done by reading drafts, listening to lectures, and assuming the bulk of domestic responsibilities. He was my lifeline during our multiyear, bicoastal relationship. Our son Cyrus was born just before the submission of the first complete draft of my manuscript. Every day, he reminds me that wonderful things are rarely, if ever, easy. All my life, my sisters Miok Joo Snow and Grace Joo have offered tough advice and set high standards for me. They have showered me with generosity. My parents, Han Pyung Joo and Un Suk Joo, have supported me in my pursuits and have always thought that sport was a great topic. They remind me that a life of critical analysis is empty without compassion, generosity, and love. Their lives inspired this project, and I dedicate this book to them.

Note on Transliteration

I follow the McCune-Reischauer system of Romanization for Korean words, except for names and places that have their own conventions (e.g., Park Chung Hee, Kim Il Sung, Seoul). In discussing Korean figures or Korean authors, I follow the Korean practice with the surname first followed by the given name. In the case of Korean (American) authors writing or published in English, I follow the standard English practice with the surname last.

Introduction

A few days after I arrived to begin fieldwork, all of South Korea seemed caught up in the frenzy of the 2002 FIFA[1] World Cup. So many people were wearing red T-shirts that televised views from news helicopters made the thoroughfares of Seoul look like a network of arteries that pooled crimson at massive digital screens. Throughout the month of June, I gathered with tens of thousands of Koreans and watched digital projections of games in stadiums, on the street, and in bars. Traveling as part of the crowd, I was in constant contact with other bodies, brushing by some and squeezing between others. The restless waiting was interrupted by kinetic cheers that each began with a single tone—a tone that generated sonic ripples and waves and quickly spread. Sometimes, stray cheers would develop into a unison chant. At other moments, the sound seemed to swell and result in a single loud boom.

Around each South Korea team match, I spent hours talking to companions and strangers about their feelings and thoughts on the events of the month and the impact of those events on their lives. I found that this month-long event was not primarily about sport per se; it was a great opportunity to celebrate with millions of others under the aegis of supporting the nation. It was a great chance for Koreans to attend the party of their lives, to brush up next to warm bodies, to inhabit collective spaces, to express emotions publicly, and to experience the intimate pleasures of mutual recognition.

After the Korean victory over Italy in the Round of Sixteen, I went to launch fireworks over the Han River with women from our *kosiwŏn* (boarding house). As we drank *soju* and snacked on *anju* (drinking snacks), Chŏng

Chi-hye, the kosiwŏn manager, explained that she was being an appropriate nationalist by partying all night. As she took a drink from her paper cup, she offered a playful invitation to the rest of the group and stated, "We must. After all, the whole world is watching!" Although there was an element of sarcasm to Chi-hye's pronouncement, all the women joined her in the toast. Into the early hours of the morning, these women expressed their excitement at being part of an event that would go into the annals of South Korean and, quite possibly, world history. They were making their own inscriptions on a historical narrative that was in the process of being constructed. They could now claim that they had participated in the spectacular street scenes, and they could later reflect on their contributions to creating this incredible global spectacle. "Will there ever be another opportunity like this in our lifetimes?" whispered Lee Mi-sŏng. The scent of her drunken breath spread across the aluminum mat, and while no one responded to her question, her words created a sense of intimate connection.

The World Cup was memorialized in national history as it unfolded. The dies of nationalist history were cast prior to the event, and the sporting results greatly exceeded the expectations of memorialists. Due to the strong sense of anticipation prior to the event, a powerful feeling of nostalgia saturated the social interactions that occurred throughout the World Cup. This "nostalgia for the present" was not an effect of a postmodern lack of historicity (see Jameson 1989); rather, it was produced through the affective memories encoded through past nationalist spectacles that unfolded over the history of South Korean national development. Nostalgia was woven into the affective field generated by the crowds, and it was expressed in the attempt to capture every moment as a personal keepsake with camera phones, video recorders, and digital cameras. The ability to record (and review and delete) every moment digitally helped create a collectively edited memory that captured the "right" feel for the time.

The "intimate publics" that came together during this event captured what Lauren Berlant refers to as the "juxtapolitical" nature of mass culture. Berlant, in *The Female Complaint* (2008), explains that the affective spheres generated by mass culture operate to produce political potentialities. Indeed, both the embodied experience of mass(ive) mediation and participation in the World Cup crowds inspired the spectacular character of the large-scale protests against the U.S. military that took place in 2002 and were also recalled in the so-called "mad cow" anti-American protests that began in May of

2008.[2] The memories of movement, of proprioception, through the hundreds of thousands of emotive bodies that filled the spaces and streets around Seoul City Hall connected these large-scale sporting and political events (Massumi 2003). Proprioception entails the physical memories of bodily movement "of contorsion and rhythm rather than visible form" (179), and these physical memories of massive collective gathering, dancing, chanting, and gesturing during the World Cup were again evoked in the explicitly politicized domains of anti-government and anti-U.S. military protests. Korean subjects felt that they had helped construct this significant moment through their physical participation in the crowds and protests. This feeling was also shaped by mass-mediated images that reinforced ideas of community and connection among Koreans both within the geographic boundaries of the nation and around the world. This book proposes that the embodied participation generated through sporting events and sporting images contributes to the making of a global Koreanness. The text demonstrates how a Korean style of globalization, or *segyehwa*, is projected through media sport, and how the debates and contests around the meanings of global Koreanness can be understood through an investigation of media sport. By media sport, I refer to competitive sports that are structured by commercial mass media and manufactured for mass consumption (Hargreaves 1986; Jhally 1989).

The women with whom I sat that evening helped craft the national images that circulated around the world. They understood the significance of those moments through their own bodily sensations and the visual reinforcement of mass media that surrounded them. They clearly expressed their own sense of place within this global event. Was this a unique opportunity to lose oneself in the thrill of the crowd, or was it an especially spectacular demonstration of the everyday forms of self-fashioning that take place in the media-saturated context of the twenty-first century? Were the expressions of intimacy that evening presenting a feeling of global connection, or were they expressing a desire for recognition within the nation and among themselves as a group of young women? I sensed that they felt they would never again experience the immense pleasure of being part of such an ecstatic event. Indeed, I often asked myself whether there would be another opportunity like this in my own lifetime. This desire to reexperience the immense power of such crowds raises important questions about the emotional intensity of the event and how it worked to expand the realm of emotional possibilities around national belonging. It is from this place of longing and desire for another similar experience—one that tingles due to the size and intensity of the human convergence—that I approach the implications of sporting events and media spectacles from the perspective of cultural analysis and critique.

The World Cup framed my research on transnational media sport as it coincided with the beginning of an extended period of fieldwork about sport and Koreanness that informs this text. The World Cup demonstrated how hegemonic ideas of global Koreanness were generated through popular culture and how ideas of the nation were being shaped in significant ways through commercial media. Moreover, the event created dramatic social and political effects and left a powerful impact on Korean communities in both South Korea and the United States. Riding this wave of excitement, I investigated how subjective engagements with sport were woven together with the histories, political ideologies, economic circumstances, social realities, and everyday lives of South Koreans and Korean Americans. My research led to an analysis of how the social locations of subjects shaped their relation to the national discourses of media sport. The period surrounding the World Cup was used by many as an opportunity to express opinions about Koreanness and desires for representation within the national body. It brought attention to the representational practices of national subjects who were conscious of their role in shaping an idea of global Korea. It offered a framework to situate subjective responses along specific sites of global connection that cut across and intersect along local, national, transnational, and global vectors (see Tsing 2005). The subjective experiences of mass mediation and the embodied practice of crowd participation inculcated through the World Cup crowds were indeed ripe with political possibilities. Presence in these crowds shaped ideas of embodied citizenship that were later borne out in explicitly politicized terrains. Clearly, sport has played a powerful role in shaping the affective terrains of both Korean nationalism and Korean American transnationalism at the beginning of the twenty-first century.

Global Koreanness and Transnational Media Sport

This book investigates the role of transnational media sport in producing notions of Koreanness in the contemporary global era. Media sport plays a powerful role in shaping the mass media content of urban economies around the world, and the study of sport in contemporary communities offers important insights into the cultural dimensions of globalization (Martin and Miller 1999). In this book, I focus on significant sporting events and iconic athletes that have emerged in tandem with South Korean segyehwa (globalization) policies in order to demonstrate how media sport as an assemblage of institutions, images, and people produces ideas of global Koreanness and how these ideas of Koreanness are lived and experienced by Koreans in both Seoul and Los Angeles. Changing media technologies, the transnational expansion of sporting markets, and the processes of media globalization have expanded the role of transnational media sport in the everyday lives of Koreans in both cities.

The emergence of transnational media sport featuring Korean players and teams began in 1998 with the popular successes of professional female golfer Se Ri Pak in the Ladies Professional Golf Association (LPGA) and baseball player Chan Ho Park in Major League Baseball (MLB). Both athletes became national heroes in Korea after their spectacular and closely followed successes in U.S.-based sporting institutions. Their successes initiated the regular entry and growth of Korean players in U.S. professional sports and the subsequent development of Korean-language mass media productions of transnational sport. The number of Koreans watching baseball and golf grew rapidly, and fan cultures formed around individual players and their respective sports. The debuts of Pak and Park can be interpreted as historical markers indexing institutional transformations[3] that fostered the popularity of transnational celebrities and athletes and their continuous visibility through mass media within what is known as *Hallyu*, or the Korean wave of popular culture throughout Asia and beyond.[4] Since then, mass-mediated representations of Korean athletes performing in North American, European, and Japanese leagues have increased steadily, and they have become a substantial part of Korean popular culture in both South Korea and the United States. At the Vancouver Olympics of 2010, Kim Yuna won the first-ever gold medal for South Korea in ladies' figure skating and set off a national and commercial spectacle that brought her more money and media exposure than any Korean athlete before her. When this book was written, she represented the zenith in celebrity-athlete exposure. She was hailed as the new queen of Korean women's sport and, arguably, Korean popular culture. The growth of transnational media sport within and among Korean communities around the world offers an important context for investigating and tracking social changes in an era of neoliberalism, and it also reveals how the affective fields of mass culture offer an important context for understanding national discourses.

In tracking media sport to segyehwa policies in South Korea and to transnational processes in Korean America, this book details how Koreanness is evoked within the global assemblages of cultural power that shape ideas of nationhood in two specific sites, Seoul and Los Angeles. The emergence of transnational media sport featuring Korean athletes is situated within political and economic transformations in the public cultures of South Korea, including the expanding role of transnational media representations and cultural flows that shape national identities. The growing global circulation of South Korean popular culture, referred to as Hallyu, has depended on the spectacularization of individual movie stars, pop stars, and athletes as celebrities. Ideas of Koreanness in the United States are shaped, in part, by commercial mass media from South Korea, as demonstrated by the growing popularity of Hallyu stars in Korean American communities. This book offers insight into the movement of Korean people, goods, and images between Seoul and the United States. By regarding Seoul as a cosmopolitan center, this text presents an important narrative in Asian American studies that works to provincialize the United States in studies of Korean America. This text also brings attention to the narratives of nation, race, and gender that hail from mainstream U.S. institutions and shape ideas of Koreanness in the United States and South Korea. Though they may be critical of American power, investigations into the workings of U.S. hegemony in the transnational field too often focus exclusively on the United States as a defining force. I diverge from this tendency and argue that media sport exists as an important domain to demonstrate how Koreanness and Americanness are shaped in relation to each other and how these articulations of nation "look different" from different national locations.

Media sport exists as an important domain for tracking the ideologies of global Koreanness, as it highlights key components of South Korean segyehwa policies. By the summer of 1995, the government of South Korea, led by President Kim Young Sam, had developed a plan to promote globalization at all levels—politics, foreign affairs, economy, society, education, culture, and sport (S. Kim 2000a). National segyehwa policies were considered a way to promote economic liberalization and bolster a strong sense of Korean national identity. The economic aspects of liberalization eased financial regulations in the foreign ownership of banks, media companies, and other national industries; privatized many national industries; endorsed free trade over protectionism; and opened travel and a variety of consumer opportunities for everyday citizens. The state, however, wanted to emphasize the importance of national unity and a sense of national identity as a way to dictate the nature of these changes within a nationalist context. The statement "The most Korean thing is the most global thing" was often iterated to convey a sense of national significance to the promotion of policies that would further connect South Korea to the global economy. The use of the transliterated word *segyehwa*—rather than globalization—by policymakers, and my use of it in this text, indicates the nationalist tone associated with the policies of economic liberalization; South Korea needed to globalize in order to maintain its status as a significant player in the world of industrialized nations, but in the process of globalizing, Korea's uniqueness and distinctiveness would remain intact and work to influence the rest of the world.[5]

The economic liberalization policies expanded dramatically during Kim Dae Jung's presidency (1998–2002) due to the Asian financial crisis of 1997 and structural adjustment programs instituted by the International Monetary Fund (IMF) (Song 2009). The Kim Dae Jung presidency was also a time of expanding social freedoms. With the expansion of travel freedoms and the deregulation and privatization of mass media outlets, South Koreans were able to purchase a wider variety of non–South Korean consumer experiences. The timing of these economic, political, and social transformations coincided with the successes of Pak and Park, and they help to explain why these athletes emerged at that particular time and became such powerful symbols of Korea's globalization.

A central aspect of segyehwa policies included the attempt to highlight the significance of Korean ethnic identity across national boundaries by promoting the notion of a global Korean diaspora. The mass-mediated image of the Korean athlete operated within the context of nationalist appeals to travelers, students, workers, residents, and citizens who reside outside of South Korean territorial borders and are known as overseas Koreans. This discourse became part of the official state policy and was instituted in the founding of the Overseas Korean Foundation in 1997. Within this discourse, narratives of a shared Koreanness operate across borders to promote a focus on intra-ethnic interaction and social reproduction among Koreans who might be located in different national contexts. These discourses of national kinship pervade the arenas of athletic competition, and the notion of a blood connection among Koreans continues to shape ideas that Koreans, regardless of their country of residence, possess an innate and natural connection to one another (Shin 2006). According to this racialized blood-nation logic, overseas Koreans are expected to maintain a sense of loyalty to the South Korean nation and act on that loyalty as citizens of a global Korea. The athlete, as a gendered subject who travels transnationally, yet functions as a symbol of the nation, is easily absorbed into the discourse of the overseas Korean. There are increasing numbers of athletes who perform on a transnational circuit and possess Korean heritage but are citizens of nations other than South Korea, are biracial/multiracial, or claim dual citizenship. Nevertheless, Korean athletes continue to be presented primarily as ethnically and racially Korean. This focus on athletes' Korean "blood" works to connect Korean players and fans in ways that tap the emotions and passions of the sporting spectacle, and it uses feelings of national kinship to intensify the feelings of intimacy and obligation directed toward the athletes and their athletic abilities.

In this book, I attempt to offer an account of the complex lived experiences of global Koreanness. In order to do so, my analysis moves back and forth between Seoul and Los Angeles to describe how subjects located in and between the two sites comprehend transnational media sport, given their particular locations in two heterogeneous global cities. Going beyond a discussion that interprets this exchange as "cultural imperialism" or Americanization, I discuss the significance of media sport as it is constituted through connectivities between these sites (see Grewal 2005). These connectivities, or "transculturations" in Koichi Iwabuchi's figuration (2002), occur within and through asymmetrical relations shaped by the power differentials of nation-states, institutions, capital flows, and gender relations. As with other global flows, the "mediascapes" analyzed here are produced through the "differences and disjunctures" that exist between the subjective practices of production and consumption in South Korea and the United States (Appadurai 1996). Practices of media making and media consumption investigated in this text are characterized by uneven circulations of mass media and inconsistent practices of viewing and spectatorship. Obviously, not everyone is a sports fan, and each fan has his or her own subjective viewing practices. Furthermore, some people who are not fans might be interested in watching sports for a number of different reasons. Nevertheless, in this text, I establish that the realm of media sport exists as a significant domain for the distribution and circulation of ideas of Koreanness between South Korea and the United States.

For Korean American immigrant populations in the United States, the popular appeal of these "homeland" narratives can be explained as a response to the marginalization and invisibility these groups feel in political, economic, and media domains. This position assumes that a goal of Koreans living in the United States is incorporation into what Lisa Lowe (1996) refers to as "U.S. national culture." Although Korean Americans certainly face challenges as a racial and ethnic minority in the United States, many Korean migrants express strong Korean nationalist sentiments and remain invested in South Korea in political, social, economic, and emotional ways. These connections are structured through institutions that promote a shared Koreanness, such as churches, veterans' associations, business associations, school alumni associations, and regional community associations. The South Korean government also actively promotes a nationalist version of Korean culture and heritage in the United States by funding academic research, cultural events, and educational programs through institutions such as the Korea Foundation and the Overseas Korean Foundation.

One middle-aged, male Korean American respondent, Mr. Yoon, explained to me the essential superiority of the Korean nation as proven through the success of Koreans in professional sports. As he described the lovely hands of Korean female athletes and the fierce drive of Korean male athletes, his wife interjected by accusing him of an exaggerated sense of national pride and self-importance. She huffed, "You no longer live in Korea. Why do you pay so much attention to these Koreans? Why can't you pay attention to America?" Even though she was also invested in Korean athletes, her self-conscious reproach of such nationalist sentiments was a common critique of the narratives of Korean nationalism, as well as a commentary on the inability of many Korean Americans to involve themselves with so-called mainstream U.S. interests and culture. Of course, the entry of Korean players into mainstream U.S. sports has offered immense pleasure for many Korean Americans, as it has opened new collective spaces for shared interest and attention among Koreans. Although it is not clear whether these Korean athletes point to a new direction and position for Korean Americans in mainstream U.S. society, engagements with these athletes enable Korean Americans to articulate their relationships to Koreanness and what it means to be Korean/American in the United States. The slash between Korean and American references the slippery, contradictory, and strategic connections between the two identifications (see Palumbo-Liu 1999).

I do not measure whether it is marginalization in the United States or a sense of connection to South Korea that underlies the popularity of media sport among Korean Americans. Korean Americans maintain varying degrees of affinity and affiliation to the United States and South Korea. Their relationships to both nations are shifting, contextual, and strategic. Media representations of Korean athletes performing in the United States are conveyed through U.S., South Korean, and so-called global media outlets. South Korean athletes who perform abroad are situated within the narrative contexts of travel, exile, migration, and foreignness that resonate in some way with many Korean Americans. Many viewers in the United States relate to the challenges that athletes face as they struggle with language and communication issues, isolation, cultural misunderstandings, food cravings, and generalized feelings of displacement. Even while Korean Americans may see athletes as having similar experiences to themselves, part of the appeal of media sport for Korean Americans is connected to the relative invisibility of Korean Americans in other forms of mainstream media in both the United States and South Korea. Media sport operates as a highly visible context for the production and apprehension of multiple, often competing, narratives of nation, identity, and belonging.

For those located in South Korea, media sport productions offer representations of the nation that articulate a relationship between diaspora and homeland. When discussing athletes who perform in the United States, many of my respondents connected them to relatives, friends, or acquaintances who had immigrated, traveled, and studied in the United States. As Grewal, Gupta, and Ong explain:

> Media representations of migration, themselves shaped by the need to address diasporic markets, then significantly influence the reimagining of the nation and its inhabitants. Diasporic populations, because of the growing importance of emerging markets and of remittances and investment to newly liberalized national economies, create new categories of belonging. *Transnational media and capital reshape the nation while they are transforming the diasporic experience.* (1999, 657; emphasis added)

Mass-mediated forms of communication, such as television, Internet, and newspapers, have facilitated the political, intellectual, financial, and social interests and investments of migrants with their respective countries of origin. These connections have sparked debates about the nature of the relationship between different diasporic Korean populations. Korean Americans, especially those with U.S. citizenship or permanent resident status, are privileged representatives of the Korean diaspora in relation to other diasporic groups, such as Korean Chinese and Koreans from the former Soviet republics (Park and Chang 2005).[6] Clearly, financial, social, and political incentives shape formal state policies and commercial appeals to Korean Americans as privileged "overseas" subjects.

Transformations wrought by transnational media, markets, and migration have affected political notions of nation, citizenship, and identity, but these modes of political identification are constantly rearticulated. Within the processes of globalization, nationalism remains a powerful ideological force (Smith 1997).[7] As Roger Rouse (1995) points out, nationalism is unlikely to disappear, but it will most likely undergo transformations within transnational processes. Indeed, Gi-wook Shin, in *Ethnic Nationalism in Korea* (2006), details the resilience of Korean ethnic nationalism within the contemporary era of segyehwa. He discusses the embedded histories and enduring legacy of Korean ethnic nationalism as promulgated by changing political regimes throughout the twentieth century. Whereas the rhetoric and presentation have changed somewhat during the current era, Korean nationalism has demonstrated a capacious scope as it hails all those who share "Korean blood" around the world.

National discourses embedded in transnational media sport hail Korean viewers in both South Korea and the United States as subjects of the nation. Narratives of South Korean and U.S. nationalism structure meaning in productions of media sport that feature Korean athletes performing in U.S. leagues. These media representations interpellate Korean viewers as national subjects through their specific modes of address (Althusser 1971; Hall 1985). This book attempts to track and detail a variety of nation and gender narratives that are embedded in media sport as a way to demonstrate the complicated relationship between transnational texts and the subjects hailed by these texts. I incorporate ethnographic material to analyze the subjective interpretations and social significance of media sport in the everyday lives of South Koreans and Korean Americans. Rather than use ethnography as a means to make authoritative claims about the subjects of my research, I use it as an evocative narrative that indicates the human possibilities of reading and interpretation (Mankekar 1999b).[8] Using participant observation, I track national ideologies to their everyday effects. I acknowledge the existence of heterogeneous responses, but I draw attention to the ways that media sport frames events within highly structured narrative scripts. This book demonstrates the complex relationship of subjects to discourses of power, and it analyzes their negotiations with these discourses within the material realities that shape their everyday lives.

The Publics of Transnational Media Sport

New forms of transnational experience and subjectivity have been shaped by transnational mass media (Morley and Robins 1995). Following the influential work of Benedict Anderson, Arjun Appadurai (1996) emphasizes the work of the imagination in shaping contemporary ethnic and national subjectivities in an era of globalization. He points out that migrants can imagine themselves as connected to people in their "homelands" through mass media. The shared consumption of national mass media creates "diasporic public spheres" that are constituted through collective and simultaneous engagements by subjects located in different spaces around the world. These connections have specific routes, directionalities, and locations that reveal the specificity of these community-making practices. This book highlights the processes by which media sport works to generate a sense of national community, yet the affective contexts of media sport produce effects that that can hardly be limited to geographic spaces and nation-state agendas; indeed, they operate across porous boundaries with audiences that have complex identifications, which take place through a number of media productions (Berlant 2008).

Therefore, the audiences delineated throughout this book offer an important example of the contingent and emergent, yet fleeting, character of publics that are thrown together in an instance but disappear soon after. This book investigates characteristics of publics that respond to discourses of transnational media sport. Publics, as a "relation among strangers" (Warner 2002, 55), emerge in response to the circulation of mass-mediated texts around athletes and athletic events. Sporting publics capture the intimacy among strangers that has been described by Michael Warner as an "expressive corporeality" (2002, 57). In fact, the commercial genre of media sport depends on this very corporeality in its viewers and fans. Warner noted that publics are full of potentialities, but they are not inherently political. In this book, I attempt to demonstrate how the intimacies and affective intensities generated through the circulation of media sport connect to ideas of global Koreanness and work to highlight the debates around its meanings. These connections that constitute a public depend on the historical moment, the temporality of media circulation, and the nature of the collective participation. Media sport has the potential to draw together a crowd, and it also has the potential to inspire and intensify politicized affects.

In considering media sport as a genre, I borrow from Lauren Berlant, who understands genre as "an aesthetic structure of affective expectation, an institution or formation that absorbs all kinds of small variations" (2008, 4). Berlant goes on to point out that genres have "porous boundaries allowing complex audience identifications" (ibid., 4). Berlant's discussion of genre enables me to keep the category of media sport broad so that it includes performances, television, print media, and Internet sites that feature athletes, games, and teams. These are connected not by a uniformity of narrative or function but by an affective expectation generated around bodily sensations, feelings of belonging, and emotions around competition. Productions of sport absorb a great number of diverse viewers who watch for a variety of reasons—all of which involve the physical and embodied experience of sensing athletes' movements. The dramatic narratives of competition and personal triumph elicit visceral reactions to each game and rivalry. The loyalties and allegiances, as well as the emotions and passions inspired by sport, blend well with the emotional requisites for nationalism in the global era. The visual field of media sport also inspires powerful feelings of recognition conveyed through the spectacular image-saturated contexts of national public cultures. The genre centrally relies on narratives of gender and sexuality to produce its affective charge. In this book, I demonstrate how consumer desires are shaped and intensified through the discourses of gender and sexuality, as conveyed through sporting productions. As a highly commercial genre, media sport highlights the power of corporate media institutions and the commodification of national ideologies within the context of global media.

During the World Cup month of June, if I mentioned the dangerous politics of nationalism or the possible drawbacks of large celebrations, the response was largely unsympathetic. When I expressed concerns about the uniform nature of the crowd, I came to be perceived as a dour critic who couldn't understand the joy of Koreans on the streets (see H. Kwŏn 2002). Some pointed out that they felt my national and physical constitution as a Korean from the United States—a Korean American—explained my inability to fully immerse myself in the celebratory mood. At the beginning of the World Cup month, I was greatly moved by the massive human mobilizations. My enthusiastic participation, however, was tempered by outright fatigue toward the end of the month. At a viewing party with an Internet *moim* (group) during the middle of the World Cup, I failed to wear a "Be the Reds" T-shirt and was shamed by the eldest member of the group who ridiculed my pink blouse and asked whether I forgot my shirt. I was embarrassed about the public shaming, and I mumbled something about not buying one, even though the T-shirts only cost about 3,000 won (around $3 at the time, or the equivalent of a roll of *kimbap*), and they could be found easily in nearly any busy commercial area. In fact, I had intentionally rejected this expression of solidarity. My initial excitement was dampened by my research agenda and the concern of colleagues and friends outside South Korea who were worried by my enthusiasm for the national zeitgeist. Friends warned me to check myself as they watched events unfold with alarm, imagining me to be a lost red dot within a crimson sea of bodies where independent and critical thought were squelched. As a result, I began to think more critically about what it meant to be part of these extraordinary gatherings and why it was so easy for me to dive in and feel so good.

In my attempt to maintain a critical position that focused on the intellectual significance of the event, I was faced with many challenges: how to offer a critique of the nationalist character of the crowds while recognizing the political importance of the pleasure of women, children, and other traditionally marginalized groups; how to think of the crowds as a mobilization of the state and as a consumer response to state mobilizations; and how to recognize the various stakes involved in participation for people differently located within South Korea and Korean diasporas. In my discussion of the significance of this event and other productions of media sport, I am not interested in coming up with a conclusive depiction of how sport is experienced or with an exhaustive account of its social significance. Following Ien Ang's ideals for the field of cultural studies, I attempt to "[participate] in an ongoing, open-ended, politically motivated debate, aimed at critiquing our contemporary cultural condition" (1997, 134). The political importance of cultural studies resides in its ability to engage in a positioned and strategic critique of ideologies and institutions that sustain and reproduce relations of power and inequality (Mani and Frankenberg 1996).

Cultural studies have been especially important in demonstrating the power of mass media to shape political ideologies that have real social, material, and psychological effects.[9] Rejecting ideas of universal meaning and interpretation in mass media, I investigate the various ways that Korean subjects positioned differently in the nation interpret the narratives of nation embedded in media sport. Rather than forcing a single determined understanding, mass-mediated texts produce interpretations that are contingent upon contexts of reception and meaning making. My attempt to contextualize the interactions between media sport and Korean viewers does not, however, assume that the process is wholly democratic. It is, rather, an attempt to situate viewing within structures of inequality and to highlight the various stakes involved for different actors.

Instead of celebrating the subject's ability to resist dominant narratives in mass media, Stuart Hall maintains the importance of paying attention to the dominant ideologies that structure narratives of mass media "though [they are] neither univocal or uncontested" (1980, 134).[10] The dominant ideological discourses in mass media operate within contexts of power and knowledge to shape political subjectivities. There is, however, no necessary correlation between the discourses in mass media and the construction of subjectivities. Rather than an inescapable force of mind control or a factory of meaningless entertainment, the relationship between media sports and Korean subjects might be better understood as a site of negotiation between dominant discourses, resistant readings, contradictory interpretations, and intentional misreadings.[11]

Instead of concentrating on dominant readings that are imposed from without, I adhere to an approach that attends to the negotiations over meanings that take place within subjective practices of reception and production. David Morley states, "the meaning of the text will be constructed differently according to the discourses . . . brought to bear on the text by the reader and the crucial factor in the encounter of audience/subject and text will be the range of discourses at the disposal of the audience" (1992, 57). Morley here argues for an investigation into the range of discourses encountered by a subject without assuming that the process is one of limitless interpretation. He points to the fact that the production of meaning is framed by the structure of the text as well as the subjective and social contexts of reception. Ethnographic methods offer an opportunity to detail the various ways that meanings are limned by historical, social, and subjective factors.

By investigating the practices of reception, ethnographic studies of mass media offer an important perspective into how subjectivities are constituted through everyday practices of media consumption (Ginsburg, Abu-Lughod, and Larkin 2002; Mankekar 1999b). In attempting to detail how mass media constitutes subjectivities through ideological discourses, I draw from Althusser's notion of interpellation, which describes how individuals are hailed through ideology. Althusser understood ideology as the "imaginary relationship of individuals to their real conditions of existence" (1971, 162). Althusser explains:

Ideology 'acts' or 'functions' in . . . a way that it 'recruits' subjects among the individuals . . . or 'transforms' the individuals into subjects . . . by . . . *interpellation* or hailing, and which can be imagined along the lines of the most commonplace everyday police (or other) hailing: "Hey you there!" (1971, 174)

My ethnography aims to narrate this process—that is, the practices of recognition (and misrecognition) by Korean subjects of national and gendered ideologies. My study attempts to detail a multiplicity of ideologies embedded in mass media and the various ways that Korean subjects recognize and also fail to recognize these ideological discourses.

Clearly, reading practices are not as simple as identification or non-identification, recognition or non-recognition, acceptance or resistance. Hall draws attention to the unpredictability of these processes in his own work. Going beyond a binary reception theory, José Esteban Muñoz offers the idea of "disidentification" as a way to explain intentional misreadings that work as critiques of power and open possibilities for alternative readings of ideology (1999). Muñoz argues that disidentification brings attention to complex workings of ideology through the performative rearticulation of hegemonic ideologies by racial minorities and queer subjects. Although my own project focuses on hegemonic ideologies through what might be understood as readings of direct identifications to the ideologies detailed in this text, I do not want to preclude the possibilities for other kinds of readings, and, indeed, the ethnographic archive offers great possibilities in alternative and critical reading practices.

Martin and Miller argue that sport has the potential to offer new directions for research and intellectual investigation in the study of popular culture. They argue that sport can challenge "the very conception of the practical and popular as they have been understood in cultural studies more broadly" (1999, 1). In this book, I move from athletic icons to spectacular events as a way to demonstrate how media sport and transnationalism connect in a variety of ways. Sport has the ability to help us think about the connections among various fields of inquiry, including the social sciences and humanities (Cole 2001a). C. L. Cole points to the connections between bodies, mass media, political discourses, and structural conditions in her work on sport. Cole also points out that sport conjoins questions about the body and the socius; the local, the global, and the national; and the abject and the intimate (2001a). This text attempts to highlight—through specific case studies—the complex connections among nation, race, sexuality, generation, and gender by investigating how sport operates within a variety of sites.

Gendered Transnationalisms

Between 1999 and 2008, I traveled multiple times from the United States to Seoul, South Korea with sport on my mind. Each time I arrived in Seoul, I was reassured of the relevance of this research topic by the regular sight of large crowds gathered about television screens and watching sport programming. People would stop in the subway, linger in department stores, and stand outside the front window of electronics shops. Although the practice of watching televised sports in public spaces in Seoul is not something new, the athletes and games that are watched mark a new chapter of mass-mediated sport—that of transnational media sport featuring Korean players and teams. Mediated sporting events that featured Korean players produced moments when people in Seoul took regular breaks from work, and, within the otherwise frenzied pace of city centers, foot traffic would slow and stop in front of television screens.

During these moments, I would scan the crowd and circle around it to get a better sense of who had stopped and for how long. Most people in the crowd were men across a range of ages and dressed in a variety of clothing styles—suggesting their diverse class and status backgrounds. The small female presence in these spontaneous gatherings was overwhelmed by the male-dominated space constructed around the television screens. Expropriating space around the televisions, men would stand as if mesmerized or squat comfortably and enter into an all-absorbed focus on the action occurring on screen. This street scene seemed to reflect what Cho Han Haejong commonly refers to as the androcentric public sphere in South Korea (2000). Cho Han argues that until the late 1990s, a possessive investment in male privilege silenced women and precluded female self-expression in public contexts.[12]

Throughout the 2002 World Cup, however, the crowds of spectators on the streets were characterized by the highly visible presence of women and feminized practices of sport fandom (Cho Han 2002a; Hyun Mee Kim 2002). This was especially noteworthy in light of the nationalist mass mobilizations of the past half century in South Korea, such as nationalist parades, sporting spectacles, and pro-democracy demonstrations, which were characterized by their male-dominated political cultures (Moon 2005). The World

Cup marked a shift in the gendered characteristics of mass mobilizations and sport fandom that work through Korean national themes. This transformation was widely noted and discussed by commentators across social and political spectra. The changes were attributed to rights won by women's movements as well as to the increasing power of women—as laborers and consumers—in the economy (Moon 2005). Whereas this event did not radically alter the masculinist structure of media sport industries and the male orientation of its productions, it did signal a significant change in the range of actors, practices, and purposes involved in the consumption of sport. The gendered shift is related to the spectacular aspects of media sport as a global genre of popular culture, which is based in celebrity worship and consumer advertising (see Miller 2002; Cashmore 2006).

Women's practices of reception, though not entirely different from men's, should be situated in relation to their gendered locations within the nation. The overdetermined gendered domains of media sport (e.g., female golfers in the LPGA, the "queen" of figure skating Kim Yuna, male baseball players in MLB, and male football [soccer] players in the World Cup) present various articulations of the relationship between gender and nation (Kaplan, Alarcón, and Moallem 1999). Gendered ideas of nation are conveyed through the presentation of national athletes within the sex-segregated spheres of athletic competition and the gendered meanings embedded in sport discourses. These gendered ideas of nation are also produced through different interpretations of and attachments made with sport by male and female fans. Thus, an ethnographic reading of Korean male and female athletes and viewers offers opportunities for the critical reading of transnational connections among gender, sexuality, race, and nation (Eng 1997; Gopinath 2005; Povinelli and Chauncey 1999). Subjective interpretations of male and female athletes present various understandings of these connections and how ideas travel across borders and become a part of peoples' everyday lives.

Korean male and female athletes powerfully demonstrate the gendered dimensions of transnationalism and how transnationalism as a discourse continues to rely on and work through narratives of gendered and sexualized differences. This book approaches questions of gender, sexuality, race, and nation in media sport through readings of athletes as transnational icons. The transnational athlete acts as an important symbol of a global Koreanness —one that travels across borders, a figure caught up in circuits of corporate capital, and an idealized representation of the neoliberal Korean subject. The Korean athlete demonstrates how ideas of gender and sexuality are defined through the transnational movement of the athlete across borders. This analysis contributes to a body of work that points to the centrality of sexuality in transnational encounters (Gopinath 2005; Manalansan 2003; Mankekar and Schein 2004; Povinelli and Chauncey 1999). This line of research details how ideas of national sexuality travel across borders and how movements across nation-states become constitutive in the meanings of nation, gender, and sexuality.

The discourses of gender and sexuality in transnational media sport stimulate and sustain Korean and Korean American consumption of media sport and function centrally in viewing practices. Visual representations of Korean athletes act as generative sites in the production of national erotics for Korean/Americans (Mankekar and Schein 2004). The sexual desire and excitement generated around Korean national athletes operate as allegories of desire for the Korean nation. The erotic narratives in sport produce Korean nationalisms that emphasize the global reproduction of an ethnic Korean nation. These hegemonic Korean nationalisms privilege heterosexual intraethnic sexual relations that reproduce patriarchal family relations. They also operate through a discourse that treats the heterosexual family as a necessary context for staging capitalist success. In other words, the family acts as a primary justification for the accumulation of private wealth (see Ong 1999). Moreover, the discourses of sexuality in media industries promote and expand sporting and entertainment markets. The discourses of sexuality are easily commodified and packaged for sale in transnational commercial contexts of media sport. National sexualities operate through erotics that further promote national economic growth and commercial prestige in a globalizing capitalist world. Gendered icons convey ideas of a "global Korea" and a "powerful Asia"; in doing so, they appeal to Korean consumers within and across national borders.

Increasing female participation in sport and the rise of female athletes represented in media is understood by some as an indication of an advance in women's positions (see United Nations 2007). The idea of female empowerment, as conveyed through mass culture such as media sport, should be distinguished from transnational feminist practice. Though there have certainly been significant improvements for women in South Korea, important struggles for equality are not resolved by images of powerful and wealthy celebrity transnational athletes. Seungsook Moon argues that the "asymmetrical incorporation of men and women into the nation" has produced gendered differences and inequalities in citizenship for South Koreans (2005, 7). She points out that national projects of development and modernization have shaped very different relations to the nation for women and men. The developmental state has been depicted as pursuing a "hyper-masculine" approach to national economic growth, which treats men's work as being of central importance to nation-building. Women's work, on the other hand, is met with expectations of obedience and subservience to the nation's needs (Hyun Mee Kim 2001). As a result of democratization and the growing power of women's movements, there have been substantial gains toward gender equality in political and legal contexts. Although the rhetoric of women's equality has become a mainstream discourse in this era of glob-alization, structural barriers to gender equality remain, as evidenced by ma-terial disparities between men and women in the workplace, in education, and in the home (Hyun Mee Kim 2001). The national economy continues to structure distinct and unequal roles for most women and men within cur-rent neoliberal contexts (J. Song 2009).

Despite these inequalities, both male and female Korean athletes, as icons of global capitalism, represent Korean competitiveness in the global econ-omy. Their symbolic power has been connected to the intense commercializ-ation of transnational sporting productions in South Korea over the past decade. The national discourses that infuse these athletic contexts offer gen-dered narratives of national economic subjectivities. The MLB player repre-sents Korean masculine strength and competitiveness in the fields of global capital. The LPGA golfer signifies the flexible neoliberal subject of the trans-national economy. The dreams produced in this global capitalist system pro-mote particular class and gender fantasies through sport. The mythologies of the *chŏn nom* (country bumpkin) turned baseball millionaire or the lower-middle-class girl turned elite lady golfer constitute national dreams of capi-talist success within the context of global media.

Korean female athletes offer powerful representations of the ideal eco-nomic subject of neoliberal Korea. Through private initiative rather than state sponsorship, the female athlete demonstrates the ability of Korean female subjects to adapt to the flexible economic contexts of the new era of global competition. The Korean female athlete exists as a symbol of female empowerment and of the new Korean woman in the twenty-first century. She demonstrates that global recognition can be won without disavowing femininity. She is presented as a middle-class subject who represents the successful development of contemporary South Korea. In the context of globalization strategies of the South Korean state, she helps present the

Korean female as a respectable and sexually desirable subject across Asia, and she works to knit together ideas of biological and cultural essentialism to market the Korean female athlete as a distinct genetic type.

In the context of mainstream U.S. media, the Korean female athlete exemplifies a type of Asian/American female figure who is especially successful at adapting to White, middle-class norms. She is easily absorbed into the narratives of the good immigrant to the United States; her success as a migrant demonstrates the continued promise of the American ideals of opportunity and open access, despite disappearing opportunities for class mobility (see Honig 1998). Even though representations of Asian female athletes often fall into stereotyped generalizations of Asians as robotic and lacking individuality, the female athlete still demonstrates a relentless work ethic and quiet endurance that presents her as a model minority in relation to other minority subjects. Her model status extends to the realm of sexuality, as she helps to strengthen ideas of heterosexual femininity in sport and assuage anxieties around lesbianism and female masculinities. As a docile Asian female subject, she remains subordinate to men within the patriarchal institutions of commercial sport, and she remains dependent on men for her management and protection.

In contrast to the docile female subject, the hard body of the Korean male athlete represents South Korean nationalist discourses of global competition and economic development, as well as a masculine desire for geopolitical recognition. The military themes of loyalty, national honor, and a fighting "warrior" spirit often pervade sporting contexts. In this light, the Korean male athlete offers a kind of militarized masculinity; he can substitute mandatory military conscription with sporting success on the global stage. He also works as an index of South Korean national development on a modernizing scale of nations, and he offers a symbolic representation of how Korean men might compete within the highly competitive and overtly racialized contexts of global capitalist competition (Ling 1999). Even while the narratives of a newly liberated Korean woman pervade popular discourses in South Korea, male athletes continue to be privileged representatives of the national body. This might be understood as a reflection of an androcentric national culture, but male sport in general remains a privileged domain in global capitalist circuits of sport since male sporting productions continue to receive far greater media coverage and commercial investment than women's sport around the world.

Transformations in ideas of embodied manhood can be traced to the in-

creasing interest in the actual physical constitution of the Korean male athlete, especially his physical dimensions—his height, weight, and musculature. The recent change in the representations of male bodies and body mass
in South Korean media reflect changing ideas about the standards of sexual
attractiveness for men as well as the increased interest in presenting male
bodies for female consumption. The fetish for the hard athletic body can be
tracked to Hallyu and the increased media visibility of male athletes and
movie stars within a global context. It can also be tracked to the globalization
of commercial images of the male athlete's naked torso. The hard body of the
Asian male athlete offers powerful visual evidence of Asian males who have
overcome the emasculation of the colonial subject, which has its history in
modern geopolitical relations and racist eugenic theories. Yet, the use of the
physical body as visual evidence continues to depend on the logic of physical
superiority. This focus on the hard and large Korean body points to the
continued connections made between physical power and national power.

For Asian American men, the new representation of physically powerful
and successful Asian athletes offers a new narrative of masculinity within a
historical lineage of emasculating discourses around Asian male sexuality
(Eng 2001; R. Lee 1999). The abundance of Asian males in mainstream
venues of professional sport certainly presents new and highly visible images for consumption. The male athlete shapes transnational contexts for
Asian male sexuality in the United States that move beyond associations with
weak, nerdy, and impotent men, but the transnational dimensions of these
masculinized representations present limited contexts for recognition by
and with Asian American male subjects. The images of Asian athletes are
usually presented as "foreign" rather than "American"; this quality fails to
assuage—and might even heighten—anxieties around the perpetual question of foreignness that plagues Asian American subjects.

As gendered capitalist icons, professional athletes offer a powerful expression of the rare exception that operates as a justifying logic in capitalist
ideology. The athlete has "won" the unlikely gamble for success, wealth, and
visibility, and this becomes the basis for dreams of success rather than the far
more ubiquitous realities of failure. Interestingly, it is precisely this exception that offers the clearest contradiction of the athlete as national representative. In the casino economies of the late twentieth and early twenty-first
centuries, athletic success offers a highly appropriate demonstration of the
unequal terms of competition, the extremely limited number of opportuni-

ties available for obtaining success, and the inordinate level of obsession elicited by a highly visible few. The gendered and sexualized dimensions of these sporting narratives heighten the intensity and appeal of these capitalist fantasies.

Fields of Vision

My research investigated commercial media sport and athletes that circulate as celebrities within competitive media environments. Due to the power of commercial advertising and global media consolidation, there is grow-ing uniformity of athletic celebrity cultures and celebrity-based coverage of sport throughout the world (Amis and Cornwell 2005; Cashmore 2006). Although there is a degree of homogenization that occurs in productions of media sport, media environments continue to be characterized by national accents and expressions particular to local spaces. Through ethnographic fieldwork in Seoul and Los Angeles, archival research into the history of Korean sport and media, textual analyses of South Korean and U.S. media productions, and both formal and informal interviews, I engaged in multi-sited analyses to detail the distinctions and connections between subjective practices of reception to transnational media sport featuring Korean athletes in both sites.[13] As a result, I point to some of the social processes of globaliza-tion and to the unique place of media sport in shaping Koreanness at this historical moment. I also focus on how discourses of nation are interpreted by women and men in both places and how they respond to and shape ideas of nation. I am particularly interested in how the relationships between viewers and media texts are expressed in personal and subjective ways.

In Seoul, I paid close attention to the place of transnational media sport in the *segyehwa sidae* (era of globalization), which was officially initiated by the state in the mid-1990s (S. Kim 2000b). I investigated how productions of media sport shaped ideas of South Korea as a cosmopolitan nation, a com-petitive nation within the contexts of global competition, and a unified na-tion within and across national boundaries (notwithstanding the enduring legacy of the Korean War and partition from North Korea). I engaged in participant observation on the streets of Seoul, in public meeting places, in official conferences and meetings, in bars and restaurants, and in stadiums. All of my interviews and interactions in South Korea took place in the Korean language. I interviewed policymakers responsible for sport and cultural policy, sport reporters and news journalists, intellectuals and political activists, members of sport fan clubs, and "ordinary" women and men from a variety of age and class backgrounds.

During my time in Seoul, I lived in an all-female kosiwŏn. The kosiwŏn was originally considered to be a temporary boarding place for students, but it essentially operates as low-cost indefinite housing for young adults in a city whose cost of living ranks among the highest in the world.[14] The women in my kosiwŏn came to Seoul from various regions of the country to live and work. The boarding house consisted of tiny rooms (which were approximately 1 meter wide by 1.5 meters long and separated by thin particle board), group toilets and showers, and a shared kitchenette. At the time, the rooms cost between 200,000–300,000 won a month (about $170–250). Most of the women in the kosiwŏn were young adults from lower-middle-class households who made just enough money to survive through a variety of service industry jobs and some supplementary family support. I wanted to live with female residents of Seoul so that I could get a sense of their everyday lives, their aspirations, and their hopes at a time when significant transformations in economic opportunities and gender roles were said to have been occurring (see J. Song 2009). Even though I came from a relatively privileged position as a doctoral student from a well-regarded U.S. university, I felt that the boarders and I shared an ever-present sense of marginality in the city, as it was never quite *home* for any of us. I became close to many of my fellow boarders, many of whom offered immense hospitality and companionship. In many ways, this book is a testament to their friendship and help.

While in Seoul, I kept abreast of responses to media sport among Korean Americans through online media accounts and personal correspondences. In many ways, fieldwork in Seoul informed my understandings of and inquiries into the role of media sport in Korean America. When I went to Los Angeles in January of 2003, I planned to investigate the impact of media sports, including baseball, golf, and *possibly* football (soccer), on the Korean American community. Soccer, however, played a large role in my interviews as the memories of the World Cup remained vivid and inspiring. I attempted to replicate many aspects of the research I had done in Seoul by investigating the production and consumption of media sports by Koreans in Los Angeles. I investigated the organization of media sport institutions and the actors within these organizations. I focused on subjective responses to media sport that demonstrated their importance to the everyday lives of Korean Americans. My interviews took place in either Korean or English and sometimes a mixture of both. This decision was dictated by the comfort level of the interviewee. I interviewed journalists, fan club members, and other members of the community. I spoke with those who considered themselves to be a central part of Koreatown, such as business owners, residents, and community activists. Consumers, churchgoers, and occasional visitors to Koreatown also took part in my study.

While in Los Angeles, I lived in an affordable room in a shared apartment in west Los Angeles. I usually met interview subjects in Koreatown and engaged in most of my participant observation in institutions and consumer spaces centered in Koreatown. Like many other Koreans who spend time in Koreatown, I commuted there alone in my car. I listened to Korean-language radio on my way to and from research. I attempted to track how the idea of Koreatown as a location is produced through interactions among those who reside, labor, worship, study, recreate, and consume in "Korean" establishments. The space is produced as a disjointed network of streets, cars, buildings, and billboards. Therefore, Koreatown is constituted by those who drive and park between and around specific sites that are multisensory markers of Koreanness, including billboards, business signs, foods, smells, buildings, cars, and pedestrians, all of which signify the continuous block-by-block processes of boundary-making in Koreatown.

Unlike much of the literature on Korean Americans, which focuses on questions of immigration and citizenship, my research approached these questions in an oblique and indirect way. The details of immigration, regional origin, and citizenship status as conveyed by my subjects were often highly unreliable, unknown, or obscured. Of course, questions about immigration and citizenship status were included in my interviews and were critically important, since they offered some insight into the political location of subjects vis-à-vis the U.S. state. They did not, however, correlate with the sense of connection expressed by my subjects to ideas of Korea or Koreanness. Some so-called second-generation Korean Americans articulated a far more powerful sense of Korean ethnic affiliation than those who had just recently migrated. At times, my questions about Koreanness and Americanness puzzled my subjects, since they assumed a shared ethnic identity with me. Assumptions of shared politics and values were most problematic when questions of religion and politics were raised, and I attempted to engage these topics in as sensitive a manner as I could manage. My time in Los Angeles was colored by the War on Terror and the official beginning of the U.S.-led invasion of Iraq, and discussions regarding the United States were fraught with contention and emotion. The subject of sport often became an entry into difficult discussions around nation and belonging, and it often became an important context through which to assess the political opinions and feelings of subjects.

This discussion of methodology and my "sample" is offered to admit that my work is in no way representative of all Koreans and Korean Americans. This book treats the lives and narratives of my subjects as significant sources that demonstrate the subjective and contradictory nature of responses to mass media. They also helped to demonstrate the wide-ranging effects of ideologies of nationalism across many social categorizations and differences. I attempt to present their voices in a way that evokes the human and personal dimensions of this project. Though I do not pretend that this was a genuinely collaborative project, my subjects helped to shape my research questions and guided the directions of my research. The people I worked with inspired my work, offered me encouragement to go on, and challenged me with questions that were critical in shaping this book.

Overview of Competing Visions

The book is divided into three parts. In the first part of the book, I offer a historical framework that details the discourses of nation and sport that emerge throughout the text. I locate my study within historical narratives of mass media and sport as articulated in both South Korean and U.S. national narratives. The second part of the book presents analyses of gendered athletic icons and their importance in defining ideas of nation and transnation in contemporary mass-mediated contexts. The third part of the book details the production of national publics in the context of media sport and offers readings of the specific characteristics of transnational publics from a variety of vantage points. I conclude by discussing some of the political connections between media sport and public culture that emerged over the course of my research, and I look to possibilities for reimagining Koreanness through the lens of media sport.

I begin by investigating how South Korean developmental nationalisms and U.S. multicultural nationalisms offer frameworks for understanding the emergence of the South Korean athlete within transnational contexts of media sport. In the first chapter, I demonstrate how the development of the fields of modern sport and mass media are closely connected with state-nationalist modernization policies in South Korea. For most of the twentieth century, the practice of sport was strongly associated with national representation in international competitions, rather than with entertainment or leisure. The connections between sport and mass media have operated to produce national viewing subjects by combining practices of media consumption with powerful narratives of nation. Media sport continues to play a critical role in current nationalist discourses of segyehwa and a global Korea.

The historical analysis of U.S. media sport I offer in chapter 2 emphasizes how minority and foreign athletes in media sport have been represented within shifting U.S. discourses around race, especially in the context of multicultural discourses. I track media sport from the moment of Jackie Robinson's integration to the current multiracial figure of Tiger Woods. This chapter also details how Asian Americans in sport have contributed to the production of political discourses of race and nation. Rather than offer an exhaustive account of all Asian American athletes, this chapter attempts to point out how Asian Americans have been situated within racial rhetorics of integration, assimilation, and multiculturalism. These discourses of racial difference persist within transnational contexts of the U.S.-based sport-industrial complex. I argue that U.S. corporate interests continue to rely on a U.S. nationalist rhetoric of multiculturalism, even while these same corporations aim to expand global markets by exploiting transnational connections.

The second part of the book goes on to investigate the connections between and among gender, sexuality, and nation through the figure of the transnational Korean athlete. It looks closely at the production of ideas of nation through the discourses of masculinities and femininities in media sport. In chapter 3, I engage ideas around Asian/American and Korean masculinities by analyzing the body of the Korean/Asian male athlete. In the contemporary global era, Korean male athletes have emerged on the global stage to compete successfully with and against men around the world. In these highly mediated contexts, male athletes offer depictions of a muscular and competitive nationalism that operates within the terrains of global capitalism. They are represented as agents of the new Asian capitalism wherein East Asian males play an aggressive and central role. Male athletes are also situated historically within the colonial and racial relations of inequality that have marked the production of Asian/American masculinities.

In chapter 4, I discuss the importance of the Korean female athlete in gendered discourses of nationalism and in exemplifying neoliberal ideas around individualism and private initiative. Although the phenomenon of figure skater Kim Yuna relates to the analysis I offer, this chapter looks specifically at the emergence of female golfers in the LPGA. Over the last decade, a great number of Korean players have entered the LPGA's highest ranks. I demonstrate how Korean and U.S. nationalisms are embedded within the transnational contexts of production and reception of Korean LPGA golfers. In Korean media, patriarchal nationalist narratives characterize dominant discourses of golf. The mediated bodies of "lady golfers" convey ideas of femininity, middle-classness, and a cosmopolitan global nation. In U.S. media, Korean female golfers are treated with a high level of ambivalence. On one hand, they are represented as an Asian invasion—a cultural blight to the racially-exclusive traditions of golf. On the other hand, they are praised for globalizing the LPGA and revitalizing a discourse of dominant heterosexual femininity in women's sports.

The final part of this book focuses on the emergence of national publics through collective engagements with media sport. These three chapters detail publics that emerged in the context of the 2002 FIFA World Cup Korea/ Japan, and how they were interpreted in both Seoul and Los Angeles. These chapters offer possibilities of reading a mega-event to investigate the emergence of national publics and the political potentiality of these publics. They also focus on the gendered dimensions of publics and how these "intimate" publics operate to generate the affects of nationalism (Berlant 2000).

Chapter 5 discusses the 2002 World Cup as a significant moment in South Korean nationalist history. The event demonstrated the power of media sport to produce national publics. The crowds were characterized by new modes of spectatorship derived from women-centered modes of viewing and participation. The feminized crowds highlighted a new place for women within Korean national publics. Gender and sexual subjectivities, shaped largely by commercial mass media, were expressed in response to this mega-event, and they were widely interpreted as nationalist expressions. The lasting effects of these events, however, remain contested as the place of women in the nation continues to be debated in social and political contexts.

The World Cup also produced crowds in Los Angeles's Koreatown. Chapter 6 discusses the power of transnational media to shape notions of Koreanness in Koreatown. Within the social geographies of Koreatown, Koreanness is performed primarily through acts of consumption, celebrations of heritage, political activism, community-oriented activities, and churchgoing. In the context of media sport, Koreatown is produced as a transnational space and Korean Americans as a transnational community of national fans. I discuss the assertion of transnationalism with respect to the relationship between Korean Americans and other racialized groups, particularly Latinos, who comprise the majority residential population in the actual physical space that comprises Koreatown. This chapter pays close attention to the contexts through which people engage with the transnational in their everyday lives.

Chapter 7 details how Korean subjects in both South Korea and the United States describe their experiences of the World Cup and other media sport events through discourses of generation. In South Korea, the World Cup year of 2002 was considered a significant period that indicated a shift in national power to a younger generation. Youth took center stage in discussions of social and cultural change. Some even referred to the year as a generational revolution in South Korea (H. Song 2003). Among Korean Americans, members of the so-called second generation were said to have discovered their Koreanness through the World Cup and other media sport events. During these events, anxieties over generational difference were quelled, albeit momentarily. The discourses of generation in South Korea and among Korean Americans expressed significant connections that challenged linear kinship-based models of generational change. I demonstrate how media sport produces opportunities for the production of youth culture and ideas of generation across national contexts.

In the conclusion, I connect media sport and politics by discussing several events that have occurred since the 2002 FIFA World Cup. In response to the killing of two junior high school girls by a U.S. tank, large-scale protests were held against the U.S. military presence in South Korea. These protests came on the heels of the World Cup, and the crowds that converged around the "Tank Incident" shared many characteristics with the World Cup crowds. Even though there is a tradition of anti-Americanism in South Korea that dates back to the 1980s, there were clearly indications that the "Tank Incident" protests marked a shift in the tactics of organizers and participants, the social characteristics of participants, and their reasons for participating in anti-American protests. In 2008, the "mad cow" protests again recalled the large-scale sporting celebrations of 2002. Again, a major concern was the nature of the relationship between South Korea and the United States; this time, the protestors were upset with the terms of a renegotiated free trade agreement between South Korea and the United States, which lifted the import ban against U.S. beef. The conclusion helps to connect many of the questions raised in this book by highlighting the political stakes involved in understanding how sporting events connect to ideas of global Koreanness. It also looks at the multiple layers of Korean/American transnationalisms, including the governmental action and organized protests that might be considered in the context of media sport.

Going beyond the binational South Korea–United States perspective, the conclusion also includes the question of North Korea. During my fieldwork, there were several inter-Korean (North Korea and South Korea) sporting events that took place. These were significant moments of human interaction between people from these two states. For South Koreans, these events offered opportunities for the public expression of divergent and shifting opinions toward reunification and North Korea. They highlighted the ability of media sport to raise important questions and debates about the nature of Koreanness in an era of globalization. Notwithstanding their contrived nature, they also demonstrated the power of media sport to influence political opinion and open possibilities for change. Clearly, these moments were fleeting and did not progress in a cumulative way toward more exchanges, either cultural or political, but they did offer moments that demonstrated alternatives to the current dismal state of relations between the two states.

Transnational Meaning Making and Media Sport

As I demonstrate in this book, media sport offers an important demonstration of the interconnectedness and mobility of capital, people, cultural productions, commodities, and representations across global spaces in late capitalism (Grewal, Gupta, and Ong 1999). This book covers a number of instances that detail how the transnational dimensions of media sport connect Korean communities between South Korea and the United States. Following Tsing's discussion of globalization, this book understands transnationalism as a "set of projects with cultural and institutional specificities and limitations" (2000, 328). Nevertheless, there is a clear attempt to focus on the popular and the mainstream. As phenomena that take place through popular mass media, the representations of media sport are available to a wide range of subjects—not just elites or a subculture of fans. This book highlights the subject-positions of people located differently in relation to institutions of power.

I bring attention to the distinctive articulations of the transnational in Seoul and Los Angeles, but I also attempt to see where there are resonances and connections across differences. What structures of feeling inform Korean and Korean American viewership of transnational media sport? What power relations, asymmetries, and discontinuities shape these practices of viewing? How do athletes produce ideas of a global Korea? How do transnational Korean subjects and Korean Americans refigure notions of Koreanness, and how does transnationality redefine ideas of racial and ethnic difference in the United States? How does sport work to facilitate the movement of ideas about gender and sexuality across borders, and in what ways does sport operate as a site of connections between and among gender, sexuality, race, and nation?

Sporting contexts become sites for the emergence of intimate publics of nation (Berlant 2000). The engagements and interactions that take place within these publics are characterized by asymmetries of capital and power relations. They also operate as contexts for political possibility and often as stages for counterhegemonic action. With this book, I attempt to demonstrate the interconnected nature of media representations and political ideologies and reveal why transnational media sport exists as an important site for social and political critique. I bring attention to the specific and contingent meanings of the transnational and how the transnational is incorporated into meaning-making practices by all national subjects. Though the story I offer is essentially a critical analysis of the social relations of power, I hope to suggest possibilities for imagining coalitions and social change that occur through transnational interactions that are shaped in and through mass-mediated communications.

PART I

SITUATING TRANSNATIONAL MEDIA SPORT

To Be a Global Player

SPORT AND KOREAN DEVELOPMENTAL NATIONALISMS

Within this global era, state rhetorics of nationalism continue to inform understandings of sport, and the nation remains a central way of framing consumer practices of sport. A consideration of historical connections between media sport and nations helps explain the contradictions and connections between various narratives of nationalism that appear in Korean/American understandings of transnational media sport. Rather than offering an exhaustive history of the role of sport in both communities, I attempt to trace a "genealogy" of sport and national ideology in two national contexts —South Korea and the United States.[1] Popular forms of sport have been characterized in and produced through mass media within changing political, economic, and social contexts. They have been shaped by the intersections and disjunctures between the two nation-states. The visibility of South Korean athletes performing in the United States and beyond can be understood better when it is tracked across imbricated histories of national discourses in media and sport.

In offering several historical narratives, beginning in this chapter with a focus on South Korea, my work offers a corrective to a common assumption in European and American studies of mainstream media sport that foreground a standard response to commercial sport that privileges a Euro-American male subject. It also challenges the assumption that non-Western subjects have an easily predictable and simple nationalist reaction to sport. This study of sport can be situated within literature on cultural globalization that critiques staid ideas of center-periphery developmental models of globalization that reproduce the priority of the West and the derivative or dependent nature of the Rest, not only in the analysis itself but also in empirical content (see Condry 2006; Iwabuchi 2002). There are important nation-specific considerations in understanding the significance of global media sport. Furthermore, universalizing generalizations about sport do not convey the complexity of meaning-making around sport. Media sport becomes meaningful in different ways to subjects around the world, based on specific histories of engagement with sport, and these histories are not erased or transcended by the increasing globalization of media sport.

In this chapter, it is not my interest to investigate the systems of sporting competition and media distribution that are indeed becoming increasingly standardized and commodified within the global commercial markets of media sport.[2] Although popular sports and sport programming are being standardized, especially in the context of global media consolidation, there are still important place-specific responses to the narratives of global media sport. Rather than investigate the processes of homogenization in global sporting markets, this chapter discusses the meanings of nation and trans-nation that are conveyed through representations of sport in Korea at significant historical junctures throughout the twentieth and into the twenty-first centuries. This offers a framework for understanding the contemporary connectivities forged among corporate, national, institutional, and subjective interests in transnational media sport and how the discourses of nationalism inform the ideological force and intensities that enable these connectivities. The following discussion does not follow the development of an individual sport but instead discusses media sport as a genre constructed through a technological assemblage of people, television, Internet, daily sports papers, radio, images, consumer products, and advertisements.[3]

Historical contingencies underpin the growth of transnational media sport in South Korean and Korean American communities. The recent explosion of interest in media sport in contemporary Korean communities in Seoul and Los Angeles can be tracked to changes in the public and consumer cultures in Korean communities in South Korea and the United States. The following pages offer partial contexts to explain the significance of media sport in South Korean and Korean/American migrant communities. The historical genealogies of nation and media sport I present in the first two chapters are largely distinct and cannot be compared in a parallel way; they offer a sense of the imbricated terrain through which meanings of sport are encoded. The association I examine in this chapter—between sport and modern nationalist development in South Korea—offers an important his-

torical basis for the claims about connections between South Korean nationalism and sport that are articulated throughout the book. In a century
that was marked by nationalist media spectacles, an important connection
exists between the growth of commercial mass media, the rise of state nationalism, and the popular emergence of media sport. These connections
between state nationalist discourses and media sport continue in an era of
segyehwa (globalization).

By detailing the development of media sport in South Korea from the
introduction of modern sport to the current state of global sport, this chapter traces the historical connections among mass media productions, sport,
and their attachments to developmental nationalist narratives. Mass media,
rather than direct physical participation, are the primary means by which
representations of sport have been apprehended and consumed by most
Korean subjects. In South Korea, sport became a major presence in everyday
modern life due to the circulation of athletes, games, and stories in mass
media formats such as radio, newspapers, and television.

Developmental Nationalism and Media Sport in South Korea

In August of 2002, Professor Chang Han-sŏng, a professor of political science and a member of the Presidential Policy Planning Commission, framed
the recent success of the Korean national football team in the 2002 World
Cup within a nationalist narrative of South Korean history. In our interview,
Professor Chang kindly dictated his interpretation of the role of sport in
Korean society, although he fully admitted that he was not an expert on this
subject. Nevertheless, he told me he was happy to speak about his views on
the World Cup and other affiliated topics. We proceeded from his office to the
basement of his university's social science building in order to get some
chap'an'gi (vending machine) coffee. Professor Chang pulled the small paper
cups of instant coffee from the vending machine, and we sat down at an
empty folding table. With images of the World Cup fresh in his memory, he
discussed three influences the World Cup had on South Korean society:

First, the World Cup instilled national pride and personal pride. For a long
time, Korea has been oppressed and directed by more powerful countries.
In our economic and military affairs, we have been pressured by outside
forces. As a result of this World Cup, we gained the confidence to lead
ourselves. Second, we gained a new understanding of foreigners. It wasn't

until the latter half of the nineteenth century that we came into contact with the West. Until then, Westerners were treated with much hatred and suspicion. As we modernized, we took up Western rational thought and science. The great success of the World Cup was the result of Western rationality and science combining with the Korean people's inherent strength and sense of unity. Finally, the football players created new ways to succeed by putting into practice scientifically proven ideas in creative ways. A combination of the Korean people's dynamic strength and intelligence worked to promote a new way of doing things and thereby made a stronger team.

He later reminded me of Korea's development from one of the poorest countries in the world (at the time of liberation from Japanese rule in 1945) to one of the wealthiest industrialized nations. In his opinion, the success of the football team was a result of the unique properties of Koreans as a people and their own version of modernization—a process that combined the Korean national essence with Western rationality and science. In discussing sport, Professor Chang drew on nationalist discourses of *chuch'e* (self-reliance) that promoted a uniquely Korean form of modernization.[4] His comments also reflected state globalization policies that extend the goals of nationalist modernization by promoting a rhetoric of segyehwa (S. Kim 2000a). In Professor Chang's opinion, the performance of the national team proved Korea's potential for success by combining Korean and Western elements in a way that put Korea on top.

This classic nationalist narrative of South Korean history has little to do with sport, yet it still offers important insights into notions of Koreanness that were promoted through the World Cup. I'm sure that Professor Chang, if pressed, could relay a far more accurate history of modernization and sport. Clearly, this was not his goal. His explanation offered a kind of nationalist shorthand that evoked mythologies of the shared essence and strength of the Korean people. I mention Professor Chang's story because it was a common nationalist explanation for Korean sporting success in the World Cup and other transnational contexts. It also evoked historical narratives of Korean developmental nationalism to offer reasons for South Korea's World Cup success and to explain the significance of the moment to Koreans throughout the world (see Moon 2005; Shin 2006).

As a way to get a sense of the background to these discourses of modern nationalism and sport, the following section briefly details the history of modern sport in South Korea and demonstrates how sport functions as a vehicle for the articulation of nationalisms and transnationalisms. The trajectory of modern sport history in South Korean sport scholarship tends to follow major shifts in political regimes, and it is divided into five categories: the Introductory Era (1890s–1910), during which modern sport was introduced by Western missionaries; the Colonial Era (1910–1945) of Japanese rule in the Korean peninsula; Nationalist Modernization (1945–1979), which lasted from Liberation until the end of Park Chung Hee's regime as president; the *P'al-yuk p'al-p'al* period (1980–1988), which characterized the expansion of the role of sport in national public culture in preparation for the 1988 Summer Olympics; and the Era of Liberalization (1989–present), which has been marked by privatization and commercial media influence in sport (H. Lee 2003). This narrative presumes the powerful role of the state in shaping particular kinds of experiences of sport, and it also connects changes in institutionalized sport to nation-building projects throughout the twentieth century.[5] This story not only demonstrates how sporting narratives operate to naturalize teleologies of national development and progress, it also highlights the centrality of media sport in representing aspirations for national strength and global recognition.[6]

The Emergence of Modern Sport and Colonial Expressions of Nation

Representatives of foreign states introduced various forms of modern sport in the latter half of the nineteenth century when Korea was first beginning to actively engage in modern international political and economic relations.[7] Even though they were not formally representing state interests, U.S. and British missionaries set up educational institutions in the mid-1880s, which became the initial sites for the practice of modern sport (Hwa 2000; H. Lee 1985; 2003; T. Yun 1992). Sport constituted an important part of the missionaries' attempts to inculcate what they understood as "Christian manliness" through notions of bodily discipline, gentlemanliness, sportsmanship, and standardized rules (Mangan and Ha 2001).[8] Foreign missionaries also organized the first modern-style sporting tournaments in Seoul, and these tournaments functioned as a newly modern form of public gathering.[9] Soon after the introduction of modern sport by foreigners, Korean sporting associations organized public sporting events for domestic competitions.[10] Modern sport and Western education were not accepted wholeheartedly by Koreans; rather, they were sharply contested by people who perceived the encroachment of these new cultural practices as a form of cultural imperialism and a threat to "traditional" Korean ways of life (see Hwa 2000; Mangan and Ha 2001).

During the colonial era, when Korea was under Japanese rule, sport became popularized as a form of mass-mediated entertainment, and it operated to produce new understandings of the body and modern subjectivity. In his important text, *Sŏul e ttansŭ hol ŭl hŏhara* (Permit Dance Halls in Seoul) (1999), Kim Chin-song discusses the production of the modern subject in Korea through popular consumer culture. Kim tracks the changing understandings of the body in modern colonial society and associates these changing conceptions with the capitalist consumption of visual images, texts, and commodities. Participation in sport inculcated new forms of spectatorship and consumption and novel modes of experiencing pleasure for both men and women. Kim argues that sport offered new understandings of the body's function in the moral order of modern colonial society as a disciplined body, a commercial body, and a body for the expression of pleasurable pursuits (see James 1983). Modern sport shaped a unique phenomenology of subjective experience, and it offered a new physical understanding of what it meant to be a national subject.

Productions of sport during the colonial era functioned as popular news items, which were conveyed through newspaper and radio.[11] In the 1920s, domestic sporting events taking place in Korea were covered in two major Korean newspapers, the *Dong-A Ilbo* and the *Chosŏn Ilbo*. These publications also played an active role in sponsoring Korean sporting tournaments.[12] Beginning in 1928 and continuing into the 1930s, radio broadcasts of sporting events such as baseball, boxing, and basketball were among the most popular programs on the colonial Kyŏngsŏng Broadcast Corporation (KBC) (Ch'oe and Ch'oe 1998).[13]

Kim points out that sport operated as a form of cultural education that produced a modern capitalist sensibility in Korean subjects. In addition, media sport helped shape a new kind of national subjectivity in the colonial era. It can be assumed that sporting programs passed censorship by the colonial government, but some scholars have argued that mass media productions of sport were powerful forces in producing a modern idea of nation among Korean subjects (H. Han 2002; T. Yun 1992). According to this argument, sport produced a sense of an "imagined community" for Koreans who competed in games, attended sporting tournaments, talked about the competitions, read newspapers for sport-related articles, and tuned in to the radio to root for the Korean team (see Anderson 1991).[14] Sport also shaped affective terrains for the production of feelings of nationalism. The emotional sentiments of nation expressed within this "nonpolitical" context might have been considered, at some points during this period, relatively innocuous by colonial authorities and other Japanese subjects living in Korea.

As far as colonial policies were concerned, physical education was incorporated into the educational and military curriculum for a limited number of colonial subjects (H. Lee 2003). In 1931, the cultural policy of *naissen ittai* (Japan and Korea as One)[15] resulted in the inclusion of sport in education programs that emphasized incorporation and assimilation. Sport became a means to integrate Korean men into the Japanese empire, especially as military subjects. Korean subjects who excelled in elite sports were recruited to participate as part of the Japanese national team in international tournaments. In spite of these dimensions of incorporation, sporting events and practices also offered spaces of opportunity for the expression of various responses to colonial policies.

Historian Lee Hang-nae argues that sport became a critically important site of nationalist resistance and cultural nationalism during the years of colonial rule (1985; 2003). Sport also expressed the transnational character of the Korean independence movement. The YMCA functioned as a primary location for the education and practice of sport during this period.[16] The YMCA has also been well documented as a center for semipublic gathering and a space for independence activities throughout the colonial era (see No 1987).[17] Overseas Koreans from China, Japan, and the United States sent teams to engage in friendly matches (H. Lee 1985; 2003), and these matches became sites of contact between overseas Koreans involved in the independence movement.[18] At times, sporting events operated as spaces for the production of an anticolonial Korean national identity and as outlets for expressions of colonial resistance (Hwa 2000; H. Lee 1985). Thus, sport can be understood as having a double-edged potential as an institutionalized practice for incorporation into empire and as a site for resistance to colonization. Furthermore, sport exemplifies well the contradictory character of "colonial modernity," in which Korean national expressions within the mass culture realm exhibit varied dimensions of accommodation and resistance (see Shin and Robinson 1999).

One canonized moment in modern nationalist history is the gold medal triumph of Korean marathoner Son Ki-jŏng in the 1936 Berlin Olympics (H. Lee 2003).[19] Son Ki-jŏng, who competed under the auspices of the

Figure 1. Son Ki-jŏng published on the cover of the
Dong-A Ilbo on August 25, 1936.

Japanese national team, won the gold medal in world-record time, and a fellow Korean, Nam Sŭng-nyong, won the bronze.[20] Thus, two Korean marathoners were awarded medals in this pinnacle of Olympic events. Within a few days of the event, the *Dong-A Ilbo*, one of the leading Korean newspapers of the day, deliberately clouded out the *Hinomaru*, the Japanese flag, from the front of Son Ki-jŏng's uniform on its cover image, inciting a political furor known as the *Ilchang'gi malso sagŏn*, or the "Japanese Flag Erasure Incident" (T. Yun 1992). As punishment for these subversive anti-Japanese activities, the newspaper was severely censored, and several members of the staff were jailed (H. Lee 2003). The event resulted in an immediate crackdown on nationalist sentiment in mass media, and it may have contributed to the colonial government's resolve to suppress all expressions of Korean uniqueness during the period of "total war" after the outbreak of the Sino-Japanese

War in 1937. In the transition toward "total war," dramatic changes in colonial policy were enacted to suppress all cultural activities suspected of breeding anticolonial nationalist sentiment. Thus, all forms of sport were to be dedicated solely to the purposes of military training, and leisure sports were strictly prohibited (H. Lee 1985).

Developmental Nationalism and Modern Sport in South Korea

During the tumultuous period from Liberation to the Korean War,[21] several nationwide tournaments took place, many of which commemorated Liberation (T. Yun 1992). In 1947, a Korean named Sŏ Yun-bok won the Boston Marathon with a world-record time, inducing a nationwide celebration and public parade (S. Lee 2004). Three years later, in 1950, Koreans came in first, second, and third place in the Boston Marathon, prompting another national celebration that was broadcast live on radio (Ch'oe and Ch'oe 1998). These marathon victories are noted as particularly high moments in a period when the nation experienced highly fractious politics in the wake of Liberation (Cumings 1981).[22] These victories were facilitated through the financial support of the United States Armed Forces and affiliated U.S. charitable institutions in Korea. The largesse demonstrated by the U.S. military command attempted to shore up ideological support for a U.S. military and political presence in the country.[23]

In 1948, Korea was divided by the United Nations into two territories to be "protected and overseen" by the United States in the south and the Soviet Union in the north. After the division of the country and the brutal Korean War (1950–1953), modern sport in the Republic of Korea, or South Korea, became part of a nationalist project conducted within the arena of Cold War ideologies.[24] Although there were a few friendly tournaments between the North and South that took place during the period after division and prior to the Korean War, the Cold War context initiated a period of fierce ideological opposition and competition that was expressed through international sport. Sport in the North became a domain for military training and, eventually, an arena for the nationalist glorification of the North Korean leader, Kim Il Sung.[25] During the U.S. military occupation and the rule of Syngman Rhee, institutions in the South included sport in educational practices that emphasized military physical instruction (Tal-u Kim 1992). During this period, some Korean athletes from the South participated in international competitions through the sponsorship of U.S. military organizations. Since Division, there have been several important moments of intersection through sport between North and South Korea (H. Lee et al. 2007). However, sport in the North became increasingly limited in its international scope as a result of the regime's isolationist policies, in contrast with the increasing internationalization of sport in the South. This book focuses on the transnational connections between the United States and South Korea since Division as a way to understand how transnational media sport operates to shape ideas of global Koreanness. Thus, the remaining part of this chapter focuses on the history of sport in South Korea and draws attention to its transnational connections with U.S. sport.

It wasn't until the military dictatorship of Park Chung Hee (1961–1979) that sport became an official part of the state's domestic developmental aims (Chong-hŭi Kim 1999). For the first time, sport was included in nation-building projects. Park instituted the *Kungmin ch'eyuk chinhŭng pŏb* (Law for Improvement of Citizen's Sports) in 1962 to emphasize the need to maintain the physical health of the citizenry—particularly young men—thus reviving the colonial policies of physical education for military and national purposes (Chong-hŭi Kim 1999; P. Kang 2001). Using the slogan "*Ch'eryŏk ŭn kungnyŏk*" (Physical Strength is National Strength), Park's military regime established policies to promote the development of physical education for boys throughout the country as a way of strengthening the national body (Hwang 2002; Chong-hŭi Kim 1999). Sport reflected Park's obsession with creating a powerful nation based on the absolute dedication of a united citizenry to building the economy, to strengthening national military power, and to raising the status of the nation within the context of Cold War and international competition. Sport policies symbolized the kind of militarized masculinity that Park considered central to Korean national development (see Moon 2005). Through the *Mun'gyo-bu*, or the Ministry of Culture and Education, Park focused his sport policies on instilling sport in the educational system and creating sporting facilities in each regional province in the nation. The Park regime also instituted an "elite sport" system that focused on the education and training of promising athletes for international sporting competitions, such as the Olympics, the World Cup, and other large-scale tournaments (Chong-hŭi Kim 1999). Elite sport was treated as a way to encourage a consciousness of comparative national development in an international arena and to present the superiority of the South over the North (Hwang 2002).[26] The regime also sponsored international tournaments that became sites for the production of the sporting crowd as a nationalist spectacle (Tong-yŏn Lee 2002).

The consumption of media sport became a common leisure activity by the late 1960s (An, Chŏng, and Im 2002; P. Im 1994). Once in power, the Park government immediately promoted South Korean national television broadcasting by instituting the television division of the Korean Broadcasting Station (KBS) in 1961 (C. Ch'oe 1983; Hang-je Cho 2003).[27] Initially, television broadcasts of sport were quite limited, yet some important sporting tournaments were broadcast live.[28] Furthermore, the highly commercial nature of sport programming, especially around boxing and wrestling, became a major draw for the sale of televisions (C. Ch'oe 1983; Chŏn 1998).[29] The 1970s are referred to as "the Television Era," given the rapid increase in the number of households with televisions (Hang-je Cho 2003). Although the most popular shows were dramatic serials, the three domestic channels—KBS, MBC, and TBC—competed to cover sporting broadcasts (P. Im 1994; T. Yun 1992).[30] Televised broadcasts of sport, such as soccer, volleyball, basketball, Ping-Pong, and especially high school baseball, were popular and commercially lucrative (Ch'oe and Ch'oe 1998). During this period, an increasing number of sport-related articles appeared in major newspapers (P. Im 1994),[31] and the first sport dailies emerged in 1963 and 1969.[32] By the 1980s, sport and mass media converged to create an everyday consumer practice available to most South Korean citizens. Media sport offered commercial opportunities for corporations, and media productions of sport were also effective in instilling ideas of national unity and strength within an international field of competition.

The 3-*S* Policies of the Chun Doo Hwan Regime

The reign of Chun Doo Hwan in the 1980s has been referred to as the *Sŭp'och'ŭ Konghwaguk* (Sport Republic) or the *Sŭp'ochŭ man'gae ŭi sigi* (Era for the Blossoming of Sport) (Chŏn 1998; T. Yun 1992). After the assassination of Park Chung Hee in 1979, the military general Chun Doo Hwan came to power in 1980 through a military coup d'état.[33] In 1981, as a result of a powerful diplomatic push, the Republic of Korea was awarded both the 1986 Asian Games and the 1988 Olympics (both in Seoul), thus fulfilling a dream of former president Park (Pound 1994).[34] Whereas Park invested primarily in sport at the educational level, Chun's sporting policies focused on preparing the nation for the international games (Han and Kim 2001). As a way of preparing for unprecedented international exposure, a separate *Ch'eyuk bu* (Ministry of Sport) was instituted in March of 1982 with future president Roh Tae Woo as its first minister (P. Kang 2001; Tae-gwang Kim 2003).[35] The slogan of "*P'allyuk P'alp'al*" (Eighty-six eighty-eight) was constantly repeated in national propaganda to remind the national public of the impending international scrutiny.[36] As part of his sport-based cultural policies, Chun's regime instituted the first professional men's leagues for baseball (1982), football (soccer) (1983), and *ssirŭm* (a traditional Korean style of wrestling similar to sumo) (1983) (Tae-gwang Kim 2003). Professional sports were established to increase the understanding and popularity of sport by the general public and to expand the role of sport in everyday life.

The Chun Doo Hwan regime of the 1980s exists as a critical period in the development of media sport in South Korea, as sport played a central role in the regime's cultural policies. Commonly referred to as the 3-S policies of sport, sex, and screen, these policies have been heavily criticized as an ideological strategy to produce an ignorant and apolitical national public (Han and Kim 2001; T. Kwŏn 2003). Many progressive academics have noted the fascist character of these policies, citing a "culture industry" critique to describe their insidious role during the Chun regime (see Adorno 1991).[37] According to this critical perspective, Chun used sport and media to quell opposition to his brutal military policies and distract from the illegitimate basis of his power. The emotional energy of the public was diverted from anger about the conditions of inequality and corrupt military authority toward frenzy over televised sporting competitions, and the political consciousness of the Korean citizenry fell into a televised sport-induced torpor. In the minds of his many critics, the excessive attention Chun placed on sport plunged Koreans into a "*Sŭp'ŏch'ŭ ŭi Hwangp'yehwa*," or a "Wasteland of Sport" (H. Yun 1999; T. Yun 1992).

Although the role of sport as part of the cultural industries of the Chun regime has been clearly marked by its inclusion as one of the three Ss, cultural critics have been slow to recognize or thoroughly investigate its ideological and political power during this period. Kim Kyung Hyun, in his text *The Remasculinization of Korean Cinema* (2004), discusses the role of "sex" in cinema during Chun Doo Hwan's regime. Kim states:

> Sex is perhaps the only expression through which the Chun Doo Hwan regime's perverse strategy to rule can be critiqued. Perhaps the most unpopular leader in post-war Korean history, Chun tried to compensate his

low popular support by retaining the draconian censorship on political matters but offering clemency on erotic representations in publications and in cinema. (170–71)

To amend Kim's rather sweeping statement, I would argue that sport, along with other mass media publications and cinema, played a powerful role in capturing public attention by eliciting not only erotic but also bodily and emotional responses. Sport might be considered an even more powerful ideological arena than cinema, as it operated on a far more popular register (television) than the art cinema of Kim's analysis.[38] Kim does draw attention to the political function of erotic discourses in popular culture in general, just as I examine the association among narratives of sport, sexuality, and nation in the following chapters.

The professional team sports of baseball, basketball, football (soccer), and *ssirŭm* were instituted by the state in the early 1980s as genres of televised entertainment (Han and Kim 2001). In nationalist fashion, Chun Doo Hwan threw the first pitch at the inaugural baseball game, which was televised throughout the country on March 27, 1982.[39] This game was broadcast in color—an exciting new media format introduced by KBS in December of 1980.[40] In fact, Chun gave away free color televisions during his reign as a way to curry favor with the public (Ha and Mangan 2003). Sport programming on the three television stations—KBS 1, KBS 2, and MBC—increased dramatically during this period, rising from an average of 19 percent of total programming in 1981 to an average of 27 percent in 1982 and 28 percent in 1983 (Ch'oe and Ch'oe 1998; Song and Ch'oe 1999). The state ideology of *sŭp'och'ŭ palchŏn* (sports development) worked to encourage the development of sport and media in the formation of national public cultures (T. Yun 1992).

The 1988 Seoul Olympics functioned as the dominant national event of the period, and this event has been considered to be a critical turning point in South Korea's modernization. Within nationalist discourses of progress, the Olympics were depicted as the apogee of the development drive that began with Park Chung Hee. The runner in this official Olympic poster (figure 2) symbolizes the arrival of South Korea on the global scene as a masculine and athletic presence. The poster features a sole Korean male runner who evokes the lineage of Korean champion long-distance runners of the twentieth century. The poster represents an interpretation of this tradition as a kind of "fulfillationist" narrative that interprets past victories as a way to explain its contemporary accomplishments (Oppenheim 2008). It also represents the

Figure 2. Poster from the 1988 Seoul Olympic Games. International Olympic Committee, reprinted with permission.

"Race to the Swift," described by Jung-en Woo (1991) in her discussion of Korean national development, in which national policymakers considered the Olympics to be a way to accelerate South Korea's political and economic growth. The Seoul Olympics functioned as a critical marker of development for a country that emerged from being one of the poorest countries in the world after the Korean War to a major industrial player—a "little tiger" in the economic development rhetoric of the period.[41]

The physical restructuring of Seoul during this period offers a powerful demonstration of how a global sporting event such as the Olympics can permanently change the conditions of life for millions of people (Ok 1995; Yong-hwan Kim 1988). This event brought about the most radical urban development project in contemporary South Korean history. In preparation for the games, intensive environmental cleanup of air and water quality took place. Massive transportation measures resulted in the construction of roads and expressways and the improvement of public transit. Numerous public facilities, such as public parks and public restrooms, were installed (T. Chŏng 1999).[42] A number of large-scale cultural facilities, such as museums and performance halls, opened and were accompanied by an unprecedented international promotion of the traditional arts and national cultural treasures (Ok 1995).[43] As most of these improvements took place in Seoul, the Olympics greatly intensified the hyper-centralization of the nation. Even though the games resulted in the creation of thousands of jobs, major infrastructural development, and new housing in the city of Seoul, the Olympics and the subsequent development of the area south of the Han River heightened population problems and increased social polarization in the city (see Nelson 2000).

Given the specter of the Cold War, the Olympics represented a major triumph of the capitalist South over the communist North (Pound 1994).[44] The Cold War in Asia played an important role in shaping the Olympic Games for the second half of the twentieth century. Noriko Aso notes that the selection of Tokyo in 1964 as host emphasized the role of Japan in "containing Communism in Asia," and it provided the opportunity for Japan to prove "the viability of Western democracy and capitalism in an Asian country" (2002, 14). Indeed, the "tit for tat" boycotts of the 1980 Moscow Olympics by the United States and allied countries and of the 1984 Los Angeles Olympics by the Soviet Union and its allies reflected the role of the Cold War in shaping the Olympic Games,[45] and these themes continued to sound loudly during the Seoul Olympics (Pound 1994).

49

The Olympic slogan of "The World to Seoul, Seoul to the World" high-lighted the consciousness of the global gaze instituted by this event. Though the South Korean state was most certainly involved in bringing attention to the nation as an example of successful capitalist development, the Olympics can also be interpreted as a time when global media attention on the nation was strategically used by the democracy movement to demand democratic reforms (T. Im 1994; Yong-hwan Kim 1988).[46] The unprecedented inter-national media attention spurred student activists to stage massive demon-strations throughout June of 1987, eventually forcing the Chun regime to accede to democratic elections in the same year (J. Choi 1993). Chun mo-mentarily quelled the protests, thereby assuaging the International Olympic Committee, which was threatening to move the games to another site in light of political unrest. Thus, the awareness of the global exposure inculcated through the state rhetoric of *p'allyuk p'alp'al* was used by those in opposition to its policies and succeeded in enacting significant changes.[47]

During the 1988 Seoul Olympics, all major television outlets focused their efforts almost entirely on the Games (Ch'oe and Ch'oe 1998; T. Im 1994). Most other news items were crowded out by the Olympic broadcast efforts (Han and Kim 2001). The incredible national mobilization for the games and the intensive media coverage demonstrated the perceived importance of such global mega-events to national identity by the state as well as the mass participation of the citizenry in shaping this image. The state again worked to mobilize the nation in preparation for the 2002 World Cup by attempting to harness interest akin to this Olympic energy, although it did so on a far smaller scale (Y. Choi 2004).

Neoliberal Transformations and Media Sport in a Segyehwa Era

After the 1988 Seoul Olympics, sport policy became less explicitly state-driven. Media sport became more commercialized as a profitable form of media broadcast. An increase in leisure time and disposable incomes re-sulted in the growth of lifestyle sport for some middle-class subjects. A movement of "sport for all" was initiated by civic groups that demanded investments in athletic facilities for ordinary citizens (P. Kang 2001). Despite these efforts to democratize access to sports, the state-sponsored athletic infrastructure continued to promote elite sport, thus continuing to limit consumption of sport for most Koreans to mass media. There have been efforts to improve access to sport training facilities and recreation facilities for everyday people, but access continues to remain highly restricted due to land-use issues, environmental pollution, uneven development, high costs involved in pursuing leisure sport, and, perhaps most powerfully, the educational system (Han and Kim 2001).

The state approach to globalization—segyehwa—was announced by president Kim Young Sam in 1995 as a uniquely Korean way of integrating into the global economy (S. Kim 2000a). Associated with state segyehwa policies, liberalization policies outlined by the World Trade Organization (WTO), the IMF, and the World Bank, especially after the Asian financial crisis in late 1997, brought about significant changes in the South Korean economy. The restructuring of the sport bureau into the *Munhwa kwang'gwang bu* (Ministry of Culture and Tourism) in 1998 reflected a major change in the state approach toward sport as a primarily for-profit commercial activity that should be controlled in the private sector, rather than in the state realm. In a clearly neoliberal shift, sport was included in the same bureaucratic division that regulated mass media, tourism, and cultural heritage sites.

Recent years have seen major changes in media sport within the context of media privatization and globalization.[48] Until the 1990s, there was a virtual duopoly between KBS and MBC, both funded largely by the state (Hang-je Cho 2003). Under the pressure of the WTO, media liberalization began in earnest in 1995. Some of the changes in mass media included the introduction of cable television, the relaxing of ownership restraints, and the deregulation of advertising sales (S. Yoon 1996). The Integrated Broadcasting Law in 1999 ushered in the era of satellite television (P. Yun 2001). The privatization of media resulted in the proliferation and diversification of sport channels— both domestic and foreign (H. Han 2002; P. Yun 2001). Many transnational sport cable television channels, such as ESPN, Golf Channel, StarTV Asia, and BSKYB have been granted space on Korean airwaves. Productions of media sport are now conveyed through multiple forms of media, including television (broadcast, cable, and satellite), radio, dedicated newspaper sections, sport newspapers, magazines, films, video games, cell phones, digital billboards, and a variety of websites on the Internet.[49] The expansion of these media outlets has intensified the competition among various sources of media. This highly competitive context has contributed to the further spectacularization of media sport content in the twenty-first century.

The increase in transnational media and commodities in Korean domestic markets and the transnational movement of media and athletes abroad have produced media sport as a thoroughly transnational phenomenon. The U.S.

corporate entities of MLB and the LPGA have invested heavily in promoting their broadcasts and logo merchandise in the South Korean market. Korean players who perform in top-earning global commercial sporting markets are accompanied by sponsorships and advertising contracts from South Korean transnational companies and other globally marketed companies (see Joo 2000; Wang 2004). Rather than a waning of nationalism, athletes who compete abroad operate as mediated symbols of the global Korean nation. They promote the idea of a transnational nation that aligns neatly with the nationalist segyehwa policies of the South Korean state. For athletes who perform in the United States, their status as Korean national icons does not foreclose their ability to bolster ideas of U.S. nationalism, as I demonstrate in the following chapter.[50]

Some South Korean social critics see the current media sport context as a late capitalist version of the 3-S policies of the 1980s (U. Kwŏn 1995). The production of media sport stars drives the popularity of particular sports. For example, hypersexualized athletes, such Ahn Jung-hwan and Kim Nam-il, generated immense and unprecedented interest in football (soccer) prior to and during the 2002 World Cup (Chŏn 1998).[51] Another powerful example of the continuing 3-S cultural policies is the popularity and proliferation of sport dailies, which are essentially tabloids obsessed with featuring celebrities and their personal scandals. These daily papers feature sensational stories about wealth, prestige, sex, melodrama, and scandal in sport and other entertainment industries, such as film, music, and television (P. Im 1994). Beginning in the 1990s, sport newspapers began to incorporate large sections on movie stars and pop music stars in their attempt to survive in the increasingly competitive digital media environment. Filling the pages of sport dailies are very large full-color pictures accompanied by titillating stories and seductive images unrelated to sport, such as full-page seminude shots of female actresses, adult short fiction, and adult cartoons with explicit sexual content (Chu 1991; Tŭk-jae Lee 1995). Large images of scantily-clad pop music and movie stars—whose salacious activities are often mentioned in the accompanying text—characterize the content of these sport dailies.

Even though there has been a liberalization of content and a proliferation of spectacular media images, the relationship between sport and the state remains strong. Furthermore, as the case of U.S. sport shows, this relationship does not have to be written into official policies for sport to operate as a powerful ideological force for nationalism. Korean sport demonstrates how the relationship between sport and nationalism has been recast within current neoliberal contexts. Although the consumption of media sport is presented within the rhetoric of free consumer choice, media sport continues to be a powerful mode through which nationalist ideas about globalization (segyehwa), liberalization, and Korean identity are conveyed. Nationalist discourses embedded in the narratives of media sport remain effective in attracting and maintaining interested consumers, and the state message continues to constitute a large role in the context of sport.

During the 2002 FIFA World Cup Korea/Japan, in a manner similar to the 1988 Seoul Olympics, mainstream news outlets focused almost exclusively on the World Cup. Prior to the World Cup, many state-driven campaigns were set in place to prepare the national public for the event (Chŏn 1998; Horne and Manzenreiter 2002). During the World Cup, immense media coverage featured the *Korean* World Cup, diminishing the fact that the event was cohosted with Japan. Even though there has been a proliferation of news sources in the information era, stories about the Korean side of the World Cup saturated Korean-language media outlets. The millions of fans in red T-shirts in public spaces and on the streets during the World Cup were represented as a unified national body, and they became the most significant news item of the event.

A series of sport-related events during the World Cup year demonstrated the continuing power of sport to produce nationalist feelings. Earlier in the year, during the 2002 Salt Lake City Winter Olympics, there was a large-scale public protest in response to the controversial disqualification of South Korean short-track speed skater Kim Dong-sung. According to Olympic officials, Kim Dong-sung illegally blocked U.S. skater Apolo Anton Ohno from passing. When he realized that he was disqualified during his victory lap, Kim threw the *Taegukki* (Korean national flag) onto the ice. This incident spurred a nationwide "cyber protest"; a flood of electronic messages from South Korea jammed the U.S. Olympic server.[52] E-mails expressed outrage at the ruling, and many e-mails included death threats to gold medal-winner Ohno. Because South Korean media coverage focused heavily on events in which Koreans have formerly won medals or are expected to win medals, including short-track speed skating, a large proportion of the national television viewing public viewed this particular incident live, and it was broadcast repeatedly in the subsequent minutes and hours. In Korean public discourse, there was virtual agreement with the notion that Ohno had intentionally engaged in gestures that made it seem as though he had been cut off. Commentators referred to Ohno's physical moves as "Hollywood action"

Figure 3. Kim Dong-sung and Apolo Anton Ohno upon hearing news
of Kim's disqualification. Yonhap News, reprinted with permission.

performed in an attempt to throw the results of the race. Furthermore, Kim's
dramatic act of throwing the flag onto the ice was enough to spur nationwide
attention. The perceived injustice to Kim Dong-sung and the fact that Ohno
was a Japanese American ignited impassioned public protests and calls for a
boycott of U.S. goods. The incident was revived in June, during Korea's
World Cup game against the United States. Upon scoring a goal, the goal
ceremony of midfielder Ahn Jung-hwan and his teammates paid tribute to
Kim Dong-sung by mimicking what was referred to as the "Hollywood action" of Ohno. The coordinated goal ceremony was clearly premeditated and
rehearsed, and it was done in an attempt to avenge the past incident. The
response to the Ahn-led "revival" of the Kim Dong-sung/Ohno incident was
overwhelmingly positive in South Korean media, and it is said to have sustained and contributed to growing anti-American sentiment and subsequent
large-scale anti-American protests throughout 2002.[53]

One of my respondents was very active in the protest events around the Kim Dong-sung incident and informed me that he was part of the campaign to overturn the ruling. Twenty-six-year-old Song Chin-yŏng said that he had sent several e-mails in outrage to the Olympic site. Although he did not want to share with me exactly what he wrote in the e-mails, he did say that he felt he had to do something because he was so angry, and the Internet seemed to be the logical venue to express his anger. He clearly felt that the cyber protests were more effective than a boycott of U.S. products and that the results were measurable; they had crashed the servers. Though he did, in spirit, support the boycott, he did not personally boycott U.S. products, and he admitted to feeling guilty when he ate at McDonald's, Starbucks, TGI Friday's, and other U.S. chains. When I pressed him about whether he really thought that the Internet protests were effective, he looked at me askance and could not understand what exactly I was trying to ask. His confusion with respect to my questions reminded me of the difference between how the Internet was incorporated into everyday life in the United States and South Korea at the time. In 2002, Song Chin-yŏng and others like him in his generation used the Internet in a way that was constitutive of their identities as national subjects and in ways that were central to their everyday lives. Because South Korea is the most "wired" nation on Earth, the e-mail-based campaign was one that used the tools of everyday life to make a statement of protest that was, for participants, a significant and heartfelt way to engage in collective expressions of discontent. Their ability to crash the servers of the U.S. Olympic site demonstrated the material results of this cyber protest. Moreover, online/offline dynamics of these cyber social movements transferred sentiments shared online to a U.S. goods boycott and pickets outside various McDonald's chains. These online/offline connections demonstrated the self-conscious understanding of some very passionate protesters that online communications were not enough to demand substantial change, and they demonstrated the multiple dimensions of a cyber protest, given the mutually informative role of online networking and offline tactics.

The passion with which feelings of national loyalty were expressed by Korean subjects during these sporting events clearly demonstrates that sporting events, particularly international events, remain arenas for the production of nationalist emotions and the expression of national loyalties. Even though the diversification and liberalization of media have produced an immense amount of information that circulates rapidly and widely in a variety of formats, nationalist rhetoric continues to be powerfully conveyed through media sport, and it is naturalized through the narratives embedded in media sport. Throughout South Korean history, international sporting events have been opportunities for the production of national spectacles. In the contemporary era, productions of sport operate as contexts for the presentation of South Korea as a nation united in its desire to be global.

Global Visibility for the Nation through National Icons

At the turn of the twenty-first century, there was an exodus of talented Korean players to foreign sporting markets, particularly the United States, Japan, and Europe. This movement occurred as a result of many factors in South Korea, including a number of highly skilled athletes trained to "global standards" of excellence who have come of age, the liberalization of sport and media markets, the potential for higher salaries and income from playing abroad, and the promotion of globalization by state and corporate interests. Much media attention in South Korea is directed at athletes who compete abroad. Those with the highest *momgap* (body price) are those who play in top global markets. This *momgap* is determined not only by their salaries but also by their earnings through sponsorships and advertisements. These global stars are often referred to as *sŭp'och'ŭ chaebŏl* (sports conglomerates). They operate as what Appadurai (1996) refers to as "metacommodities" who promote a number of products from a multinational cast of corporations. South Korean corporations are eager to attach their brand name to Korean athletes who compete and win on a global stage.[54]

Athletes who play abroad represent the image of the newly globalized Korean subject who leaves the country to succeed yet continues to maintain a strong sense of Korean identity. As Koreans leave the country to work, live, study, and travel abroad, the Korean athlete is held as an example of the loyal overseas Korean.[55] Representations of highly successful Korean athletes convey the idea that Korean global success is indeed possible. In the increasingly corporate rhetoric used by the neoliberal state, athletes operate to spread the "brand name" of South Korea to other national media markets. They advertise the nation and help the South Korean state "market" an idea of Korea that competes on par with the most developed nations in the world. They also *opkŭreidŭ* (upgrade) the status of South Korea in the context of competitive global sport and offer important expressions of global Koreanness through advertisements that represent the financial and technological contemporariness of a digital Korea.

Some Koreans I spoke with did not particularly like the fact that the best athletes were leaving the country to play abroad. Many of those who were older than forty were especially disappointed about this exodus of players, but, at the same time, they felt resigned to the fact that these were inevitable changes. I had one meeting with a young, recently separated couple—Lee Bong-ju, a forty-two-year-old electrician, and Kang Su-kyŏng, a thirty-eight-year-old hairdresser. They met me in their tiny Seoul apartment in Chamsil-dong, which was being occupied by Kang Su-kyŏng and their eight-year-old daughter. Lee Bong-ju was living with a friend on the northern side of Seoul and had come to join us for coffee. As we discussed their relationship to sport, Lee Bong-ju proceeded to dominate our discussion. "I'm an ultra-nationalist," he half-joked. He continued, "I think that all Korean players should stay in Korea and build up our own system of sport." He went on to criticize several players for leaving the country, and he complained that the level of play in South Korea would never reach its full potential because the best athletes left. He stated, "We don't even have enough of our own men to play on our teams, and if you go to Chamsil baseball stadium, you'll see that our baseball teams have foreigners and even blacks."

At the end of our meeting, Lee Bong-ju explained that he had come to the meeting on behalf of their daughter, and he wanted to develop a working relationship with me. I left disappointed that I had let him dominate our discussion. As I asked the friend who introduced us why she had set up such an awkward meeting, she explained that the couple was interested in sending their daughter to the United States to learn English, to have the experience of learning in the United States, and to get out of the competitive South Korean educational system. They wanted me to help arrange a study abroad experience for their daughter. I was thunderstruck by this revelation, as it seemed like such a contradiction to Lee Bong-ju's "ultranationalist" approach to sport. Lee Bong-ju's statements demonstrated the contradictions between the discourses of national loyalty that arise through sport and subjective desires to access globality, even though it was putatively for the sake of his child and not himself.

A sense of ambivalence often accompanies subjective responses to athletes who go abroad. Though they may work to market South Korea, they often make those who can't leave the country feel left behind. They may bring national attention or national pride to some Koreans, but they also highlight a national sense of inequality and inadequacy in relation to other nations. They plant global dreams in the lives of many aspiring children, yet

they also bring attention to the extreme limitations to realizing these dreams, especially for lower-income and middle-class subjects. Although they expand the geographic reach of Koreanness, they also demonstrate the waning affective significance of narratives of homeland. For many older-generation Koreans who lived through years of state-driven nationalist development, the realization that national dreams cannot be totally accomplished within the nation results in a mixed response to the exodus of Korean players.

Deterritorialized Nationalisms

The discourses of nationalism that circulate around national sporting events often evoke war narratives and militaristic metaphors that evoke national histories. These narratives travel to spaces beyond the geographic boundaries of the nation to draw in diasporic populations. In fact, the rhetoric of performing in the sporting realm seems to be one of the few contexts in which one might hear the discourses of war and national resentment so powerfully articulated. Sport operates in the affective realms of mass media to intensify and embolden feelings of nationalism and competition. Due to their affective power, sporting productions remain potential sites of nationalist propaganda easily tapped in periods of crisis. International sporting competitions, such as the Olympics and the World Cup, work to stage the emotional feelings of competition, resentment, and jealousy among nations. They also create contexts for the production of powerful feelings of nationalism by diasporic subjects.

Male athletes are often presented as warriors for the nation within the context of international competition. The label of *T'aeguk Chŏnsa* (Korean Warrior), which was popularized during the 2002 World Cup and reemerged during the 2006 World Baseball Classic and the 2008 Olympic Games, demonstrated the commonplace nature of militaristic attribution in the sporting realm. "Korea fighting" is a common phrase that athletes use in their efforts to connect with male and female viewers and fans. This battle cry demonstrates their self-understanding as national representatives. As they raise their hands in a *V* or a closed fist, they look straight into the camera and state, "*K'oreya hwa-i-t'ing!*" On camera, the players almost always express the idea that love of country and duty to fellow countrymen motivate them to play harder. During the 2002 World Cup and the 2006 World Baseball Classic, athletes repeatedly struck a patriotic tone when they referred to their role as athletes. These players earnestly stated that they were determined to play on behalf of their country, in the same way that soldiers might express their dedication to nation and fellow countrymen.

The World Baseball Classic (held in San Diego in March of 2006) offered a stage for the narrativization of competitive geopolitical relations on the baseball field. Although the event took place under the terms of U.S.-dominated professional baseball (Major League Baseball, U.S. mass media, and the MLB Players Association), the U.S. media sport establishment could not totally determine or mediate the sentiments felt between players and fans of various countries (J. Kelly 2006). The Korean-language media coverage of the three games played between Japan and South Korea was particularly intense. The large numbers of Korean fans in attendance were both male and female. Korean/American fans displayed their immense sense of emotional investment by traveling relatively long distances (most commonly from Los Angeles to San Diego) to watch the games and purchasing Korea-related fan T-shirts and thunder sticks.[56]

Although South Korea beat the Japanese team twice during the round-robin portion of the tournament, the two national teams met again during the semifinal, and by the sixth inning, it became clear that South Korea would not be able to beat Japan a third time. During the final few innings, Koreans who filled the stands chanted, "*kaench'ana*" (It's okay). John D. Kelly (2006) argues that South Koreans felt they had already won by beating Japan twice in the tournament. In my interpretation, these expressions of *kaench'ana* were preempting the disappointment of a loss. Rather than a genuine feeling of goodwill and sportsmanship toward the Japanese national team, the chants were public statements to console players and fans and to paper over feelings of deep disappointment. There was also a sense of bitterness about the other factors that may have contributed to the loss. A general feeling that the terms of the tournament were flawed and that they disadvantaged the South Korean team marked Korean/American sentiment. How could the Korean team beat Japan twice and still not make it to the final? Why did they have to play Japan three times? Why was their path to victory so difficult?

A friend who attended the game reported that, after the game, there was almost a fight behind the stands between a despondent Korean fan and a cheering Japanese supporter who was waving the imperial Japanese flag. The angry Korean man flew into a rage with arms swinging, while his friends restrained him from making contact with the Japanese fan. As I watched the game on television, my brother-in-law remarked in disbelief that the imperial flag of the rising sun was being shown uncritically on network television. He raised the question about whether the Nazi flag could ever be celebrated with such vigor. The image of Japan's imperial flag flying with fervor is bound to evoke strong visceral reactions in most subjects who possess even a minimal knowledge of Korean colonial history.[57] Furthermore, during the 2009 World Baseball Classic, the Korean and Japanese teams met five times, and the last match-up occurred during the finals. During these games, there were numerous Korean-language and English-language banners proclaiming the Korean possession of the contested Eastern Sea island known as Dokdo to Koreans.[58] Clearly, the cameramen did not understand the deep-seated resentment around this issue, and every time these banners were shown on the jumbotron, many Koreans in the crowd would break out in loud cheering.

These anticolonial nationalist sentiments continue to characterize international competitions, even in an era of globalization in the Korean diaspora. They were revived during the competition between Kim Yuna and her Japanese rivals throughout the ice skating competitions of the 2010 Olympics.[59] These historical memories heighten the level of investment by Korean/American fans. The fans seemed to revel in reviving bitter colonial memories as a way of raising the competitive stakes. During the game, "fighting words" were said under people's breath. The event became a moment for expressing the colonial back talk I grew up hearing in Korean American circles where slurs and derogatory statements often pepper any emotional mention of Japan as a nation. The affective force of the competition offered a context for the emergence of Korean fighting words drawn from the history of Japan–Korea relations.[60] They also raise the level of emotional investment by the competitors. Athletes themselves become the fighting subjects who stand in for the nation, who become the objects of national desire, and who become the subjects that point to the nation's success.

Within the context of media sport, Korean Americans are able to participate in the emotional worlds of Koreanness and experience a sense of belonging to the nation as fans. Clearly, their feelings about these players differ from those who live in South Korea, since they are subject to different national responsibilities and expectations, especially with reference to military service (as I discuss in chapter 3). Although the emotional investment by Korean Americans might remain high throughout a tournament or a game, it remains to be seen whether this feeling of connection then translates to action or some sense of responsibility to the nation—besides a feeling of obligation to prefer the Korean player or the team with a Korean athlete.

Koreanness in America

The historical narrative detailed throughout this chapter plays a critical role in understanding the transnational dimensions of Korean media sport in the United States, as its current popularity among Korean Americans has important connections with the histories of media sport on the Korean peninsula.[61] The Korean American population at the turn of the twenty-first century was still considered to be a largely immigrant population, and the most popular sports in Korean America have been those that feature South Korean national players. The apparent Koreanness of athletes and the associated Korean-language, transnational media coverage explains the consistently high level of interest from Korean Americans in sports that feature Korean national players. The popularity of these players can be attributed, in part, to the large number of Korean Americans who maintain material, social, emotional, and psychological ties with South Korea.[62] In chapter 2, and throughout the rest of this book, I establish that Korean media sport plays a powerful role in shaping ideas of Korea and Koreanness for Korean Americans. For many Korean Americans, the primary sources of news and information are Korean-language media outlets, such as radio, television, and the Internet.[63] Rather than function as a nostalgic genre, productions of media sport feature Korean Americans as central actors as they produce contemporary notions of a global Korea.

Of course, the subjective associations that individuals have with sport are far broader than a mere nationalist interest. Many of my Korean American subjects, particularly those who were born or educated in the United States, professed to follow their local U.S. sports teams, such as the Los Angeles Dodgers and the Los Angeles Lakers. Some lionized star players on U.S. teams, such as Derek Jeter from the New York Yankees or Kobe Bryant from the Los Angeles Lakers. Their appreciation of these athletes often emphasized their athletic skills and talents rather than nationality, ethnicity, or race. This rhetoric of "pure sport" fandom assumes that athletes perform simply for the "love of the game," and it also assumes that fans watch for the same reason. It is also regularly rehearsed within the contexts of U.S. sport and, to a lesser extent, Korean sporting forums. No doubt, many fans believe there are no factors besides their love of sport or the accident of their birth and geographic location that shape their own fandom practices. Clearly, the idea of pure sport fails to convey the historically contingent emergence of sporting icons, the political nature of sporting industries and events, the power of image advertising, and the role of money in sport. Moreover, the sporting realm continues to rely on and profit from social differences such as nation, race, gender, class, sexuality, and region. Nevertheless, elisions of these differences and a reluctance to speak openly of politically significant differences are themselves important expressions of sporting fandom. In addition, it is important to note that a few of my subjects expressed no interest in sport or sporting events whatsoever.

Notwithstanding these differences, the significant rise in Korean American interest in U.S. sport directly connects to the expanding number of South Korean nationals performing in the United States. Due to this heightened interest, many Korean Americans who previously had no interest in U.S. sport now consider themselves sports fans. Many Korean American spectators have been educated in U.S. sport with the aid of cultural translators such as Korean-language media, friends, colleagues, or their children.[64] Korean Americans are also encouraged to watch through the fanning of nationalist sentiment by Korean-language media discourses and Korean fandom practices that draw on discourses of (post)colonialism, anti-U.S. sentiment, and ethnic solidarity (see Joo 2000). For some Korean Americans, the practice of watching Korean athletes is characterized by a great deal of ambivalence, and there are those who offer interpretations of sport that are critical of the highly nationalist rhetoric expressed in sport. This chapter and the following one situate the viewing practices of South Koreans and Korean Americans who express varying degrees of interest in Korean players and teams competing in global media sport; there are indeed hegemonic and politically significant responses to these sporting productions.

Korean/American spectators who watch Korean athletes playing within U.S.-centered sporting leagues are also affected by the discourses of U.S. nationalism. Productions of mainstream U.S. media sport produced and conveyed in the United States are generally represented as "American," rather than as transnational or international. Even though many Korean Americans continue to receive their news through Korean-language media sources, the sporting contexts in which Korean athletes perform are portrayed as firmly U.S. national spaces.[65] Individual Korean players perform within an "American" cultural sphere that is dominated by representations of Americanness, such as the U.S. flag, national anthem, patriotic music, and frequent military displays and tributes. Most coaches, umpires, managers, owners, agents, and broadcast commentators are white Americans, and they are represented as essentially American. The explosion of U.S. patriotism in sporting events after September 11, 2001 made it clear that the genre functions powerfully to support U.S. national interests, especially in times of national crisis, as represented through the proliferation of corporate, military, and corporeal spectacles of nationalism in media sport.[66] However, despite the hegemonic U.S. nationalisms that are conveyed through most U.S.-based media sport, the presence of Korean players and Korean/American spectators changes the character of these representations of the United States as a nation.

As a way of situating Korean spectators within the sphere of U.S. sport, the following chapter analyzes how the discourses of U.S. multiculturalism have operated in mainstream media sport. Discourses of U.S. multiculturalism have functioned as hegemonic modes of discussing racial, ethnic, and national differences within the U.S. sporting realm. At times, the national differences of athletes have been sublated into racial categories, as with the category of "Latino" players in baseball. A newer focus on transnationalism, however, tends to maintain the national distinctiveness of players, so that South Korean and other Asian athletes are characterized primarily as foreign nationals. These ideas of foreignness work alongside representations of players as immigrant racial minorities who make up multicultural America. The Korean athlete can be presented within an integrationist narrative as an immigrant figure absorbed within the U.S. sporting complex, but he or she might also be seen as a temporary worker who does not change the essentially American cultural dimensions of sport.

In this chapter, I've attempted to demonstrate the social significance of media sport in generating ideas of Koreanness by articulating its relationship with political, economic, and technological developments in South Korea. The relationship among the state, media, and audience has shifted with historical changes, but, clearly, the state continues to be actively invested in promoting nationalism through national sport icons and sporting events. Throughout South Korean history, media sport has been associated with national development schemes. Today, media sport promotes neoliberal visions of the nation in an era of globalization. As in the colonial era, media sport continues to operate as an affective context that enables and intensifies national feelings. Kim Chin-song (1999) argues that cultural productions operate as sites around which Korean subjects enact what it means to be a modern national subject, and these subjectivities can be tracked through political economic changes that connect to media sport. Furthermore, the changes in media sport offer clues to how subjective bodily experiences of nation have transformed over time. Media sport connects Korean populations in South Korea to those beyond by offering a context for simultaneous and transnational practices of viewing and fandom. South Korean populations are connected to Korean American populations in the United States through media sport productions. Not only does this work to produce the idea of a Korean diaspora brought together through a sense of global Koreanness, it also means that ideas of Koreanness themselves are shaped by narratives of America and the U.S. nation.

A Leveraged Playing Field

U.S. MULTICULTURALISM AND KOREAN ATHLETES

Korean athletes performing in U.S. leagues symbolize particularly powerful narratives of both South Korean and U.S. nationalisms for viewers in both sites. This chapter examines the centrality of multicultural nationalism in U.S.-based sporting discourses, and it works to situate Korean/American athletes and viewers within the narratives of racial, ethnic, and national difference that constitute the discourses of multiculturalism. In the previous chapter, I traced the historically embedded processes that situate Korean nationalist interest in Korean athletes. Whereas Koreans and Korean Americans are largely drawn to these players by a shared sense of Koreanness, responses to athletes are mediated within and between nation-specific contexts. In this chapter, I focus primarily on the production and reception of Korean athletes in the United States. Although I assume that the significance of Korean players in Korean American communities draws largely from direct and indirect experiences of South Korea, as well as from connections to an idea of Koreanness, the consumption of Korean athletes playing in the United States by Korean Americans takes place largely through U.S. national productions of media sport. Korean and other minority athletes within the U.S. sporting complex are located within the United States and subject to the ideological force of its national productions.

The influence of multiple nationalisms and national discourses is not limited to Korean Americans, as Korean athletes in the United States also operate as representations of "Americanness" to consumers in South Korea and beyond (see Grewal 2005). Commodified ideas of America are accessed through the circulation and consumption of media sport and related products in South Korea. Korean athletes can also operate as sites for the expression of anxieties about the perceived Americanization of South Korean popular culture. Thus, the narratives of Koreanness and Americanness are complexly entangled in media sport that features South Korean athletes in U.S. sporting contexts. Nationalist discourses of multiculturalism offer an interpretive framework to understand Korean American reception to media sport.

New corporate policies of major U.S. media sport businesses, such as the National Basketball Association (NBA), LPGA, and MLB actively promote the growth of markets overseas (Maguire 1999; Tomlinson 2006).[1] Although transnational expansion is certainly underwritten by corporate capital, the absolute growth of transnational media sport has been enabled by the convergence of many factors, including emerging athletic talent abroad, media liberalization processes, and increased consumer spending on leisure activities in developing countries such as South Korea and China. U.S. nationalist commentaries often attribute the growing number of international players to the exceptional status of U.S. sport in the world. South Korean players performing in the United States strengthen a rhetoric of corporate multicultural nationalism and embolden the logics of U.S. capitalist expansion abroad. In other words, U.S. capitalist expansion abroad can be interpreted as just and equitable through the success of international athletes in the United States. The continuous entry of players from different countries is offered as proof that the United States continues to represent a space of opportunity for talented athletes around the world. For U.S. subjects, the success of international players works to demonstrate that the American dream remains alive and available and that lessons on how to attain that dream might be drawn from the success of these athletes (see Grewal 2005; Honig 1998).

The historical formation of media sport in the United States elicits a different kind of historical genealogy from the one outlined in the previous chapter. In contrast to the state-driven narrative in the South Korean case, the following narrative traces media sport in the United States as an almost entirely commercial, privately funded endeavor.[2] Even the sponsorship of Olympic athletes throughout the history of U.S. participation in the Olympic Games has been largely through private funding and commercial sponsors (Keys 2006). However, even with the role of private capital, sport has operated powerfully to convey ideas of national community and feelings of nationalism. Within this largely market-driven arena, I trace the changing understandings of racial difference in media sport within the context of multicultural nationalism. By multicultural nationalism, I refer to a "culturalist" notion of diversity that erases material differences and power inequalities between and among groups, as well as one that sees racial, national, and ethnic differences as essentially the same.[3] Lisa Lowe (1996) critiques the nationalist uses of multiculturalism and argues that this discourse operates to homogenize, aestheticize, and incorporate signifiers of ethnic difference. Lowe states, "Multiculturalism levels the important differences and contradictions within and among racial and ethic minority groups . . . while simultaneously masking the existence of exclusions by recuperating dissent, conflict, and otherness through the promise of inclusion" (ibid., 86). Lowe foregrounds the role of multiculturalism in perpetuating racial hierarchies, asserting that "multiculturalism is central to the maintenance of the present hegemony [in the United States]" (ibid., 86).[4]

Rather than a wholesale rejection of multiculturalism, I recognize the importance of a nuanced perspective on multiculturalism, given its history in radical social movements of the 1960s and 1970s (see Palumbo-Liu 2002). However, as Lowe points out, it is important to take note that the character of multiculturalism itself has been transformed within an era of transnational capital flows and diasporic politics. My critique focuses on neoliberal nationalist appropriations of the rhetoric of multiculturalism as discussed in Lowe's critical view. Multiculturalism has operated within corporate contexts of media sport to promote the expansion of sporting markets to variously defined consumer segments while still working through a U.S. nationalist rhetoric. In media sport, multiculturalism has operated as a hegemonic nationalist rhetoric that works to commodify differences while erasing the existence of enduring inequalities and ideological differences.

In the following pages, I discuss how nationalist multiculturalism operates through the commodification of racial and national difference in U.S. commercial sport. In mainstream media, celebratory stories about the integration of minorities and the assimilation of immigrants accompany the incorporation of minority athletes into the business plans of media sport corporations. The pre–Civil Rights era of integrationist discourse was marked by the introduction of a few token minorities who were carefully considered within the business contexts of sport. In the wake of Civil Rights movements, the racial integration of professional sport continued to follow closely the business calculations of team owners and media corporations. In the late 1960s, ideas of racial integration in sport came to coexist, albeit uneasily, with a rhetoric of multiculturalism that drew from progressive politics of ethnic nationalisms and racial pride. By the 1980s, in mainstream media sport, the rhetoric of multiculturalism took on a largely commodified form by promoting racial, ethnic, and national differences in an increasingly diversified marketplace. This marketing of difference worked well for commercial interests that catered to variously defined markets of viewers and consumers of media sport. Toward the end of the century, discourses of multiculturalism functioned within transnational contexts as a corporate rhetoric used by media sport industries to expand markets around the world (Martin and Miller 1999; H. Yu 2000). Both racial minorities and foreign athletes have been absorbed into U.S. nationalist discourses of multiculturalism that continue to promise equal opportunity for all groups while expanding "target" markets for media sport corporations. These discourses of multiculturalism highlight racial and national differences to varying degrees in a strategic attempt to appeal to U.S. mainstream audiences, U.S. domestic minorities, and viewers in foreign countries.

The history of racial integration in U.S. sport often follows a trajectory of famous African American male athletes who have integrated individual sports. This chapter rehearses this Black–White narrative, but it does so in order to highlight how racial, ethnic, and national differences have been understood and narrativized within hegemonic discourses of racial difference in media sport. This chapter also attempts to complicate this Black–White narrative by raising the case of several Asian American athletes and teams that fall outside of a Black–White depiction of race relations (see Bloom and Willard 2002; Burgos 2007). By presenting a number of Asian American narratives in sport, I demonstrate how mainstream discourses about Asian American athletes work within and challenge the hegemonic narratives of Black–White racial difference that are often raised in discussions of race relations in mainstream media sport. I understand the pitfalls of projecting a racial category (Asian American) that emerged during the Civil Rights movement onto diverse and variously affiliated Asian-heritage groups throughout U.S. history, but Asian athletes in the United States have now become part of the narratives of Asian American history and Asian American Studies. The racial representations of Asian/American and Asian Pacific American athletes throughout the twentieth century remain largely consistent with representations of Asians in other forms of popular culture, and the depiction of Asian athletes in U.S. sport has reflected time-worn orientalist stereotypes of the Asian American as perpetual foreigner, immigrant threat, enemy infiltrator, Communist threat, and model minority (see R. Lee 1999). The case of Asian Americans in sport also exhibits how transnational connections shaped Asian American communities prior to the contemporary era of globalization (see Chan 2005; Hsu 2000).

This chapter goes on to discuss how sport reveals the workings of multiculturalism within an era of transnational media and migration. Ideas about racial and ethnic differences in the United States have been intimately connected with transnational migration, imperialist endeavors, and the circulation of global capital throughout U.S. history. As Palumbo-Liu notes, "multiculturalism, while usually understood within the United States in terms of 'domestic' minorities, has always had an important international dimension" (2002, 110). The existence of the transnational within the context of U.S. multiculturalism is not unique to the contemporary era of globalization, but the character of transnationalism has changed with respect to the intensity, character, and scale of internationalism involved. An emphasis on the national differences of athletes does not erase the significance of race in U.S. sport; rather, it raises important questions about how national distinctions work alongside ideas about race within the shifting articulations of U.S. multicultural nationalism.

Discourses of liberal multiculturalism operate across the transnational terrains of media sport and interpellate both Korean American and South Korean subjects. An investigation into the relationship between transnationalism and discourses of multiculturalism highlights the complex relationships among race, sport, and nation in an era of transnational media sport. This chapter concludes by discussing the contradictions of multicultural nationalism. I focus on the case of Korean American athletes Toby Dawson and Hines Ward, both of whom claimed their Koreanness after highprofile athletic victories. Reading across Korean/American and U.S. mainstream media, it is clear that the actions of these athletes were interpreted in different ways. U.S. multicultural discourses conflated their expressions of Koreanness with desires for individual fulfillment and expressions of charity on the part of racial minorities who "give back to their communities." Korean nationalist discourses, however, praised their expressions of Koreanness as a kind of a "return-to-homeland" narrative that brought glory to the nation. Their interpellation by Korean nationalist discourses highlights the limits of multiculturalism as a way to explain racial and national differences in the United States. The transnational locations of Korean athletes produce unique contradictions and contestations over the meanings of race, citizenship, and nation, and they demand a nuanced and multisited understanding of how differences work within and across borders.

Commodifying Racial Diversity in U.S. Media Sport

In media sport throughout the twentieth century, racial, ethnic, and national differences were heightened and explicitly commodified to increase the popular appeal of commercial sporting events. The integration of minorities into the Whites-only field of media sport has almost always been associated with capitalist business interests. Rather than perceiving this as diminishing what some might think of as the "true" political purpose of integration, the hegemonic narratives of racial inclusion in U.S. media sport have valorized the economic utility of minority players and used assertions of their economic value as an important justification for integration itself. Furthermore, as Bloom and Willard argue, the integration of minorities into U.S. sport has been used to "prove the fairness of the system" of sport when compared to other institutions (2002, 2). Sport has also been used to demonstrate that a sports system (based in capitalist principles) exists as a meritocracy that, in its purest form, does not discriminate against any particular race. Although discourses of integration and multiculturalism have undergone a number of iterations, capitalist logics that prioritize profit making continue to influence the production of racial and national differences in the contemporary multicultural contexts of media sport.

Racial segregation and discrimination characterize the history of all professional sports in the United States. For the first half of the twentieth century, most forms of organized sport were racially (and ethnically) segregated, as were most institutions in U.S. society (Bloom and Willard 2002).[5] It is important to note that there were vibrant leagues and events that catered to communities of color during the Jim Crow era, such as baseball's Negro Leagues, Mexican American leagues, and Japanese American leagues; boxing tournaments in Filipino American communities; and basketball tournaments in Chinese American communities (Bloom and Willard 2002; España-Maram 2006; Franks 2000). There were also well-known minority competitors in individual sports, such as boxing, track and field, and swimming and diving.[6] In the early part of the twentieth century, a few select athletes of color were allowed to compete for the U.S. Olympic team. Even though most minorities were excluded from Whites-only sporting venues and leagues, and even though they experienced racial discrimination in many other aspects of life, the participation of the exceptional few was often publicized in ways that praised the nation. Successful African American, Native American, and other minority athletes were often hailed as "tributes to their races." Athletes such as African American boxer Joe Louis were presented as national representatives in the ideological fight against fascism and communism.[7] Furthermore, many non-White athletes were integrated as part of a management decision based on commercial interests of individual teams and owners. Adrian Burgos Jr. points out that some Latino athletes were integrated into Major League Baseball in a way that would "secure new sources of labor without disrupting the color line" (2007, 3).

The arrival of Jackie Robinson in 1947 as the first African American in Major League Baseball now exists as the most valorized moment in the narratives of racial integration and advancement in U.S. sport (see Rampersad 1997; Tygiel 1997). This moment has often been hailed as a precursor to legislation mandating general societal racial integration brought about by the 1954 U.S. Supreme Court ruling in Brown v. Board of Education. A common U.S. folk saying asserts that "Jackie opened the door" for the integration of other social institutions. The racial integration of MLB is often largely attributed to the business decisions of the aggressive general manager of the Brooklyn Dodgers, Branch Rickey. Integration into this formerly all-White league is said to have been a result of league managers and owners who hoped to increase profits by bringing in new talent and larger audiences.[8] Interestingly, this business motivation was clearly expressed in the film The Jackie Robinson Story, which starred Jackie Robinson as himself (Green [1950] 2001). This film, produced in 1950, offers a capitalist integration narrative that implies business interests, as represented by the character of Rickey, were the key factor in Robinson's entry into baseball. Rather than producing a skeptical view of the motives behind racial integration, this narrative promotes the idea that free enterprise and individual men who possess an entrepreneurial spirit operate as the greatest forces for social change.[9] As the business interests of baseball worked to rid themselves of the market distortions of racism, integration proved to be a boon for the system of baseball and, eventually, the political system of the entire country.[10] The film presents a Cold War narrative that sees the promotion of the ideals of capitalist democracy as an important logic for racial integration and draws an explicit connection between the Civil Rights movement and the Cold War (see Dudziak 2000).

This focus on business motivations suggests that racial integration was a

Figure 4. Branch Rickey convinces Jackie Robinson to testify before the U.S. Congress in *The Jackie Robinson Story*.

result of the entrepreneurship, courage, and foresight of capitalists. An exclusive focus on the business and geopolitical explanations behind integration diminishes the significance of social movements that operated to shift hegemonic racial ideologies of the period. Michael Omi and Howard Winant (1994) argue that notions of race underwent a paradigm shift during the 1950s and 1960s that was due to collective struggles of dedicated students and other progressive groups who demanded social equality for all races. Civil rights and international social movements demanded radical changes to systems of class oppression, racial inequality, and sexual inequality. Many movements were allied with anticolonial and anti-imperial movements taking place throughout the world. By the 1960s, those who developed more radical sentiments rejected the idea of gradual racial integration as failing to change the material, ideological, and structural conditions of inequality faced by minorities. Notions of multiculturalism were often contrasted with the tenets of integration, since integration connoted gradual change and eventual absorption into existing institutions controlled and defined by White men. Multiculturalism, on the other hand, implied respect for differences and diversity, and it called for an entirely new way of thinking about race relations: one that did not privilege a dominant race or racial tradition.[11]

By the 1970s, most large-scale media sports in the United States were in the process of integrating their athletic personnel. However, by the end of the decade, there was a turn away from narratives that pointed to racial disparities or previous racial exclusions as the sporting establishment argued that integration had been successfully accomplished. Omi and Winant (1994) point out that in the 1970s, the New Right began to promote a racial rhetoric that supported individual rights, opposing what they deemed as special rights for racial collectives or special interest groups. Mainstream media sport promoted these neoconservative ideologies by valorizing individual talent and rejecting radical critiques of racial inequality in sport and society (Johnson and Roediger 2000). The rising star of O. J. Simpson was a good representation of the neoconservative racial ideologies of individualism and meritocracy that were common during this time period. Simpson's story (before his legal exploits in the 1990s) rehearsed the narrative of a poor and crippled African American boy who, through individual effort, overcame physical, social, and economic difficulties to rise to the top of college and professional football (Johnson and Roediger 2000; Morrison and Lacour 1997). His status as a media favorite throughout the 1970s and early 1980s was tied to representations that reinforced his extraordinary drive. He was known as a politically safe African American man who refused to engage in controversial or politicized discourses about racial inequality, and he was able to market his amiable image as a spokesperson for corporate America. Of course, his former status as a neoconservative icon has been largely forgotten, given the infamous legal trials around the murder of his ex-wife Nicole Brown Simpson and her boyfriend Ron Goldman, which transformed Simpson's image from clean-cut African American success story to one of unrepentant and lifelong criminal (Morrison and Lacour 1997). Media coverage around the 2008 conviction of O. J. Simpson (in which he was charged with stealing sports memorabilia) highlights the continuing fascination with his life in mainstream media and sporting contexts.

The neoconservative ideologies of race that characterized hegemonic attitudes toward race relations in the 1980s offer a context for interpreting contradictions of racial representations within contemporary commercial sport. As athletes themselves may work to diminish the significance of their own racial differences, corporate interests in sport often exploit these differences to market players of color. Although the focus on racial difference by corporations is certainly geared toward appealing to a racially segmented consumer market, racial differences are also highlighted to point out that equal opportunities exist for people of color in sport and the United States more broadly. This is especially true for individuals who possess the drive for success. Michael Jordan's rise to the top of national and global media stardom in the 1990s has often been interpreted as an American success story. David Andrews (2000) asserts that the color-blind racial ideology of the Reagan era underpinned Michael Jordan's astonishing commercial success. Andrews argues that Jordan's astounding rise to wealth and global fame symbolized the Republican ideals of "open class structure, economic mobility, racial tolerance, [and] individualism" (172). Jordan's refusal to engage in race- and class-based discussions further cemented his status as a safe representative for corporate interests (Cole 2001b). The role of race in the production of the icon of Tiger Woods took cues from the contradictory approach to race presented by Jordan's image makers. Despite the self-proclaimed racial neutrality of figures such as Jordan and Woods, they continue to be absorbed in racialized narratives of integration and racial uplift that capitalize on their Blackness (Cole and Andrews 2001; H. Yu 2002). Michael Eric Dyson (1993) argues that the commodification of Blackness through their style, bodies, and exceptionalism as wealthy and heroic African American men makes these sporting figures extremely popular commodities. Although individual athletes and their sponsors profit from this commodification of Blackness, the social issues that make Blackness a liability for many African Americans are conveniently erased from their commercial representations. The rhetoric of a "raceless" individuality accompanies the presentation of self, whereas commercial success continues to depend on these marked racial differences.

The racially marked athlete continues to be marketed in commercial sport as an embodiment of racial difference. In most discussions of African American athletes, their Americanness is typically not in question,[12] but in the case of Asian American athletes, racial differences are clearly connected to questions about national difference. The following section discusses how the multicultural narratives of race in the context of Asian American sport have focused on the presentation of the Americanness of Asian Americans as a way to assuage concerns of foreignness. However, as I show later in this chapter, the recent emergence of high-profile Asian players in U.S. sport has complicated the question of nationality in Asian America, and the transnational dimensions of Asian players raise important questions about the relationship between Asia and Asian America both historically and at the present moment (Palumbo-Liu 1999). Asian transnational athletes demonstrate how the Asian American racial category is continually transformed in an era of transnational flows.

Asian Americans in Nationalist Narratives of Sport

As I have argued, the integration of media sport in the United States has been explicitly tied to business interests. Corporate logics in sport promote notions of racial integration and immigrant assimilation as ways to recruit players and fans from their affiliated racial, ethnic, and national groups. In mainstream media accounts, star athletes embody the myth that individuals can raise themselves out of poverty, racial oppression, and foreignness through individual effort and hard work.[13] Mainstream media sport coverage often peddles human interest stories that focus on the unparalleled opportunities for sporting success among minority and migrant subjects, and it features these upward mobility stories in a number of variations. The standard trope of minority athletic success usually charts the movement of an individual from a disadvantaged background or poor country to his or her rise to star status in the United States and around the world with the associated wealth, fame, and recognition. The minority athlete then becomes the embodiment of the American dream for people in the United States and in the athlete's country of "ethnic" origin.

For most Asian American athletes, this narrative of success situates them within a broader racial presentation of Asian Americans as a model minority. The athlete offers the image of the patriotic immigrant subject who asks little or nothing of the nation and simultaneously praises the nation for the opportunities bestowed upon him or her. Asian American star athletes not only overcome obstacles that range from overt nativist discrimination to low expectations of their athleticism; they also conquer these barriers in a way that is humble, quiet, and safe. For the most part, Asian/American athletes are praised for assimilating within the contexts of U.S. sport by being "team" players, behaving as obedient students of their coaches and agents, and avoiding negative or excessive attention on their personal lives. They offer unquestioning support for the institutions of sport and the nation. The following examples of Asian Americans in sport demonstrate how some of these narratives have worked over time. Rather than offering an exhaustive account of Asian/Americans in U.S. sport or of Asian/American athletes, I include several high-profile cases as a way to draw attention to the connections between historical cases of racial representation and the contemporary examples offered throughout this book.

The high-profile Asian and Asian American athletes who entered the U.S. media sporting realm in the 1990s were often mistakenly described as the first Asian athletes to play in U.S. sport. However, there were important instances of Asian American and Pacific Islander sporting success during the pre–Civil Rights era. Duke Kahanamoku, champion Olympic swimmer and popularizer of modern surfing, offers an important demonstration of how the non-White Hawaiian competitor for the United States functioned as a colonial exception to the Black–White color line (Willard 2002). Swimming for the United States in the 1912, 1920, and 1924 Olympics, Kahanamoku won three gold medals and two silver medals. As a native Hawaiian, he was clearly not White but was still able to compete with Whites in segregated venues that banned other minorities. In the same way that Jim Thorpe and other Native American athletes came to represent the United States in their feats as Native American athletes, Duke Kahanamoku, as a native Hawaiian, came to symbolize America's colonial beneficence and, eventually, its "indigenous" greatness (Deloria 1996; Willard 2002). His life story as an American athletic hero worked to naturalize and praise Hawaiian colonization by the United States and Hawaii's eventual statehood in 1959. Kahanamoku operates as an example of the ideal native subject—one who expresses the indigenous uniqueness of the U.S. territories and also demonstrates the positive outcomes of U.S. colonial policies.[14] He also helped to promote tourism to the Hawaiian islands through his appeal as an exotic native who commodified his body by surfing for White American consumers (Willard 2002). In this way, the case of Kahanamoku demonstrates the connection between sport and empire, and it shows how a sporting icon became part of the presentation of Hawaii as an exotic site for U.S. consumption in the early part of the twentieth century.

Kahanamoku's case demonstrates how the diverse narratives included in the former racial categorization of Asian Pacific Islander (which has, since the 2000 U.S. census, been divided into two separate categories of Asian American and Hawaiian Pacific Islander) have shaped the politics and discourses of Asian American Studies. This story also offers important connections to other former colonial subjects and the role of empire in the shaping of Asian America, as in the case of migrants from the Philippines, Guam,

South Korea, Tonga, and Samoa (the two latter sites being significant in American football). Furthermore, the story of Kahanamoku demonstrates the limits of understanding the racial integration of sport as a Black–White racial story that begins with the entry of Jackie Robinson in baseball.

The cases of Japanese American baseball has often been framed within narratives that attempt to highlight baseball as an essentially American prac-tice (see Natividad and Gall 2004). The Japanese American leagues are often held up as an example of the first truly Asian American sporting league. Until recent years, research on the Nisei leagues was largely absent from Asian American cultural histories. However, with the growing interest in minorities in baseball history (see Burgos 2007),[15] there was a surge in research on the Nisei leagues of the early twentieth century and on the place of baseball as a community-building event in various Japanese communities throughout the United States (see Regalado 2002). Most of the narratives that discuss Japanese American baseball highlight the success of the Japa-nese American community in producing a unique public culture in the context of overt discrimination and economic hardship (Regalado 2002). Though many historical investigations point to Nisei baseball as an example of the Americanization of the Japanese American community, the sport was also quite popular in Japan, as exclaimed in the 1911 book, *America's National Game*, by Albert G. Spalding.[16] Nevertheless, in the narratives of Japanese American assimilation, the transnational connections between baseball in Japan and the United States for Japanese Americans are largely diminished.

Perhaps most famously, the practice of baseball in Japanese American communities was used to attest to the loyalty of Japanese Americans around World War II (Mochizuki and Lee 1995). In his photo book of the Manzanar internment camp, *Born Free and Equal* (1944), American photographer An-sel Adams includes a photo of a baseball game in the camp as one of many images that together construct a story of the essential Americanness of Japa-nese Americans and their model status as U.S. citizens. The photo carries the caption "ALL LIKE BASEBALL AND OTHER SPORTS." The photo shows a game in play while casually dressed observers watch from behind a backstop made of two-by-fours and chicken wire. Beyond left field are rows of barracks-style housing, and the Sierra Nevada mountains rise dramatically in the distance. Adams uses the image of a baseball game on a makeshift field, along with the other images in the series, to assert that life in the camps was conducted in a manner much like the normal everyday lives of Americans outside the camps. Baseball is assumed to be a form of Americanization for Japanese Americans, and it is also praised as proof of the loyalty and dedication of Japanese Americans to the "American way of life."[17]

A Korean American story of sporting success from before the Civil Rights era also demonstrates how racial exceptionalism worked to promote U.S. nationalism.[18] Sammy Lee was born in the United States in 1920 to Korean immigrant parents. His father labored as a railroad worker and a greengrocer in Los Angeles. In stories of his early training as a diver, Lee was limited to using public pools on the one day of the week they were open to "colored" people, and during his competitions, he endured the racial prejudice of teammates, spectators, and sporting officials. He stated in numerous interviews that, rather than expressing his rage, he responded with silent anger (Franks 2000). In an interview with ESPN, Lee states, "My father told me to never, ever use your color as an excuse." He continues, "There were several times I used to think I was being screwed, but I bit my lip and kept my mouth shut. I used it as motivation. I wanted to show them that I could be better than them, that I could be the best. So I became the one who tried the most difficult dives."[19] This attitude of "silence" toward the enemy contributes to his later self-representation as a quiet, model minority whose exceptional sense of self-control amidst immense pressure proves that injustices might be overcome by individual effort and self-mastery. Furthermore, rather than contributing to a collective movement against racial injustice, his narrative emphasizes that, through hard work, proof of one's own value will eventually prevail.

Although he trained to enter the Olympic diving competition, Lee was unable to compete in the 1940 and 1944 Olympics, due to the suspension of the games. During this time, he completed a professional degree as a medical doctor and served in the U.S. Army medical corps. Lee eventually won two gold medals in diving during the 1948 and 1952 Olympics. After he won his first gold medal, he became a popular figure in both Korean American and South Korean communities. This connection was most likely heightened because of his family's close associations with Syngman Rhee, South Korea's first president who was backed by the United States. In interviews, Lee often points to the connection between his sense of South Korean national pride and his sense of national loyalty to the United States. He has remarked that when he won his first gold medal, he thought of the 1936 triumphs of Jesse Owens and Son Ki-jŏng, the first Korean gold medalist.[20]

Lee made a clear transnational connection between his status as a racial minority in the United States and a diasporic Korean subject. He went further to connect his experiences as a person of color and his experiences with racism to his own sense of anticolonial nationalism and desire for Korean independence.

The cases of Duke Kahanamoku, Japanese American baseball, and Sammy Lee all present various dimensions of pre-1965 experiences of sport in Asian Pacific American communities. All cases have been "recovered" in recent years and used as examples of Asian American sporting experiences that occurred before the large-scale entry of Asian immigrants to the United States (which was prompted by the Immigration and Nationality Act of 1965). Although these narratives of recovery are primarily celebratory, they also tend to situate Asian American athletes within the model minority narratives of the post-1965 era. According to heroic accounts, these Asian American athletes are clearly patriotic subjects who never once questioned their dedication to the U.S. nation. Their heroism is heightened by the fact that they, as individuals, were able to perform and thrive in the face of overt discrimination and prejudice. Despite overwhelming odds, their participation in sport enabled them—as minority subjects—to "prove" their worth to the United States. These cases were and continue to be used to assert that the sporting system itself is essentially a meritocracy. Ideally, it is race-blind, but at the very least, it is more liberal and progressive than mainstream society.

Even though these Asian Pacific American athletes are hailed as all-American competitors, all three examples demonstrate transnational connections of Asian American athletes with sites beyond the United States. Duke Kahanamoku competed for the United States while he was a subject of a U.S. territory, and he brought a Hawaiian tradition of surfing to the U.S. mainland. Japanese Americans in baseball were held up as examples of the Americanization of Japanese American communities, although there were clear transnational connections with baseball in Japan. Sammy Lee saw his own victories as connected to his own sense of Korean nationalism and with his identification as a person of color in the United States. These cases demonstrate the transnational connections that shape racial difference in the United States. They also demonstrate how ideas about the racial differences of Asians shift according to the national origins of the athletes and the relationship of each of these nations to the United States. The sporting contexts of these three examples highlight a cosmopolitan dimension to sporting contests in the pre–Civil Rights period that raises questions about how and why notions of American exceptionalism and insularity in sport get reproduced in popular and academic accounts.

After the Immigration and Nationality Act of 1965, the images of Asian athletes competing in the United States represented Asians and Asian Americans as model citizens within the context of the Cold War. Even the seemingly anomalous work of Sammy Lee as a coach for the United States, South Korean, and Japanese diving teams in 1964 can be understood in light of the fact that Asia was considered the primary battleground against the growth of communism (Aso 2002). The Olympics occurred just one year before the normalization of relations (at the urging of the United States) between South Korea and Japan in 1965. Clearly, Lee's nationalism and anticommunism inspired his work as a representative of three Republican presidents to the U.S. Olympic committee. C. L. Cole (2008) notes how the Cold War shaped media coverage of Taiwanese immigrant runner Chi Cheng, who dominated elite women's mid-distance running in the United States during the early 1970s. Cheng, as a runner from Taiwan, functioned as a feminized symbol of Asian/American support for U.S. power in Asia during the Cold War. Cole also points out that Cheng operated as a figure of racial quiescence at a time of Black power and social radicalism, thus demonstrating the political dimensions of the model minority as a safe and docile subject (2008).

Toward the end of the twentieth century, a number of high-profile Asian and Asian American athletes emerged within a few select sports. This period was also a time when a new kind of pan-ethnic Asian American consumer identity began to emerge in the public sphere (see Nguyen and Tu 2007). A few "second-generation" Asian American athletes, including Kristi Yamaguchi, Michelle Kwan, and Michael Chang, exhibited success within the capital-intensive sports of ice skating and tennis. These sports require immense private investments in children, and the result of these investments was the emergence of several star athletes who supported stereotypes of Asian American children as highly disciplined and single-minded in their pursuits. Accompanied by overprotective parents, these athletes were supported by the private resources of their families. The model minority myth emphasizes the close-knit family and its values, rather than the opportunities afforded by class and educational status, as the primary reasons for the success of Asian American children. This neoconservative discourse works to vilify other minorities who have not demonstrated such success. This stereotype works in contrast to the representations of failure in Black and

Latino communities, with respect to educational achievement, wealth, and patriarchal two-parent heterosexual families. The model minority myth also emphasizes the capitalist success of the Asian American family that draws on its own private sources of wealth and demonstrates the opportunities available to minority subjects in the United States.

In the 1990s, Asian American female ice skaters Kristi Yamaguchi and Michelle Kwan gained a great deal of name recognition in the highest-rated televised sport, ladies' figure skating. Yamaguchi won a gold medal at the 1992 Winter Olympics. Her triumph was attributed to her hard-working approach to the sport and her precise execution, yet her win was overshadowed by the highly publicized class drama that took place that year between two other White figure skaters, Tonya Harding and Nancy Kerrigan (Feder-Kane 2000). Following Yamaguchi, Michelle Kwan soon became the new Asian American skating phenomenon who remained among the top ranks of international ladies' figure skating for over a decade. In Asian American sporting narratives, Michelle Kwan functions as a tragic figure of near triumph but ultimate failure. Even though she stands as one of the most decorated female skaters of all time, her failure to win a gold medal in the Olympics has always marred her legacy. Two newspaper headlines, which immediately followed two separate Olympic competitions, added a sense of injury to the feelings of loss felt by many Asian Americans who rooted for her as a representative of Asian America. Using these slights to demonstrate the resilience of stereotypes of Asians as perpetual foreigners, historian Gary Okihiro remarked,

> During the 1998 Winter Olympics, an internet news site carried the head-line, "American Beats Kwan," referring to the American Michelle Kwan, an "LA (though not valley) girl" to the core. The "American" who beat her, of course, was Tara Lipinsky, whose surname wouldn't have conjured up the nationality "American" in another age or even the racialization, "white." And in déjà vu all over again in 2002, the Seattle Times sports headline proclaimed, "Hughes As Good As Gold: American Outshines Kwan, Slutskaya in Skating Surprise." When Asian American readers flooded the paper with their outrage, the editors apologized for having repeated the same error of four years earlier, explaining how their "dis-belief turned to deep embarrassment" over their mistake. "Ironically," the paper noted, "one of the most memorable aspects of these Winter Olym-pics was the rich diversity of the U.S. athletes. . . ."[21]

Okihiro demonstrates that the headlines inferred that Kwan, as an Asian American, was not *really* American and did not constitute what an American was *supposed* to look like. Okihiro also highlights the assumed connection between Whiteness and U.S. nationality. Finally, he points out the vacuous rhetoric of multiculturalism that accompanied the event. The active and near-immediate response of Asian American advocacy organizations, academics, and activists condemning these headlines was connected to Kwan's high profile in Asian American communities. Concerned Asian American organizations took up this cause, yet Kwan attempted to avert any negative attention by responding with clear displays of patriotism and heartfelt statements about her love of the United States.

Although these journalistic slips of the tongue were rightfully criticized, increasing numbers of athletes from Asia, especially those in MLB and in the LPGA, NBA, and Professional Golf Association (PGA), have contributed to a generalized confusion by many commentators about the difference between Asians and Asian Americans in U.S. sport. Of course, this is not an excuse for ignorant statements and a lack of research on the part of so-called professional journalists. It is also not to say that these statements are harmless. These misrepresentations continue to injure, and they continue to associate Asian America with foreignness.[22] Given the important work of Asian American scholars and activists who have clearly outlined the historical uses and political consequences of stereotypes about Asians as perpetual foreigners, there is a well-founded anxiety around proving one's U.S. nationality. The experience of being asked "Where are you from?" with the connotation that the one being asked is a foreigner is familiar to almost every Asian American, regardless of how long his or her family has lived in the United States.

The critical Asian American responses to the mistakes around Kwan's national identity, though justified, also highlight the anxiety around policing the boundaries of Asian America. The increasing role of transnational interactions in U.S. popular culture has worked to intensify the anxieties around defining Asian America. The association between Asian-looking players and foreignness is becoming increasingly dominant as the non-U.S. national origins of these players constitute a key part of their marketing and commercial image. However, it is quite possible that a newer generation of Asian Americans, who do not have the same orthodoxies around identity politics or national origins, can sit comfortably with the contradictions. For instance, most online fan lists of Asian American athletes include players who were

not born in the United States and players who would not consider themselves American. My own analysis of Korean athletes includes both Koreans
and Korean Americans, because they reflect the realities of Asian America
and the communities from which Asian American subjects hail. These communities are made up of U.S.-born Asians, Asian students, Asian workers,
new immigrants, undocumented immigrants, dual citizens, and those who
travel back and forth between Asia and North America. My concern is to
delineate the narratives of race and multiculturalism in the United States
that characterize the experience of Korean transnational sport for both Korean American and South Korean subjects, knowing that the distinction
between Korean American and South Korean is often blurry, as indicated
by the slash between Korean and American that I strategically deploy (see
Palumbo-Liu 1999). The narratives of race and multiculturalism are themselves transnational, and the following section highlights how U.S. multiculturalism absorbs ideas of transnationalism and how discourses of U.S.
multiculturalism are reframed within contemporary transnational contexts.

Immigrant America in a Transnational World

Rather than offering a clear distinction between Asian American athletes and
Asian athletes, I point out that foreign athletes demonstrate the capitalist
promises of the United States to a broad transnational audience. Athletes
who enter the United States often become symbols of the American capitalist
dream for immigrants and those who remain in their homelands. In mainstream media discourses, sport is often hailed as a progressive institution
that offers opportunities for immigrants, the working class, and the poor
to pull themselves out of marginality and squalor to fame and fortune.[23]
According to journalist David Margolick, the foreign athlete as immigrant
subject opens the way for the acceptance of those of his or her own ethnic group.[24] The assimilation of each immigrant group might be enabled
through the success of a spectacular hero. Paralleling the impact of Jackie
Robinson, athletes such as Fernando Valenzuela, Chan Ho Park, and Sammy
Sosa operate as icons for their racial minority and respective immigrant
groups.[25] These typical sporting narratives emphasize the movement of the
poor and unknown player from developing nations to wealthy cosmopolitan
success in the Western world. Athletes function as testaments to the continuing salience of the American dream both in the United States and in other
places around the world. As immigrants, these athletes choose to come to the

United States and operate to solve "America's problems of democracy" by proving that the dream of immigrant America endures despite persistent structural barriers to its achievement (Honig 1998). They prove to be the appropriate kind of citizen; they are not a burden on the state welfare system since they succeed in generating and spending their own individual wealth. The success of foreigners in sport reminds American subjects that the promise of the United States as a land of economic opportunity remains alive. This narrative of immigrant America focuses on the story of the individual athlete rather than on the interests of the sporting and media corporations, which benefit from the "opening" of new markets that work through the athlete's celebrity. Like the commodification of the African American athlete, the foreign immigrant athlete often represents unexplored or underexplored opportunities for growth. In contrast to the African American athlete, the foreign athlete is never represented as "fully" American; he or she must maintain a distinct foreign national identity. The athlete becomes a national representative from his or her "homeland" and functions as a conduit through which entire national markets might develop.

While maintaining an essentially American exterior, media sport industries have attempted to spread to increasingly global markets. Although some scholars have rejected the idea of hegemonic Americanization to describe global expansion, Maguire (1999) points out that the Americanization argument does help describe the ways in which U.S. media shapes the content and style of sports programs conveyed around the world. This "structure of common difference" produces a similar format of competition and commodification across borders (Wilk 1995). Others have argued that an investigation into the corporations involved in global sport is more significant, given the lack of borders and boundaries in many professional leagues (Tomlinson 2006). Well-endowed U.S. leagues mine the world for stellar athletes, promote their own private interests, and sap donor countries of their best talent (Klein 1991). Despite this full-fledged promotion of a transnational multiculturalism, U.S. sport continues to be characterized by a national imperative. In relation to European professional football leagues, the U.S. sporting system remains relatively isolated from the rest of the world (Markovitz and Hellerman 2001). Though foreign nationals have significantly changed the population of athletes in U.S.-based media sport, they have not changed the hegemonic ideologies or organizing principles of U.S. sport. Juffer (2002) points out that even though over 25 percent of the professional baseball players based in the United States are of Latino origin (primarily the

Spanish-speaking Caribbean), the essential Americanness of baseball continues to be reproduced as a hegemonic myth in the sport.

In the current transnational contexts of sport, most players emphasize their national differences in ways that do not compromise a U.S. national imperative. This tendency is apparent in the recent changes to Major League Baseball. Japanese, Korean, and Dominican players in U.S. baseball continue to assert their national identities for the crowds back in their countries of origin, encouraged by Major League Baseball. This approach is exemplified by the establishment of the World Baseball Classic. The celebration of national differences operates to promote the globalization of U.S. sport while continuing to bolster the sense of American exceptionalism produced through sport. The idea that players from abroad come with an entire nation of viewers is enthusiastically mentioned by commentators and sports writers who often employ hyperbolic generalizations about their national relevance. It is quite common to hear comments that suggest that the entire nation of China watches NBA basketball player Yao Ming or that all of Mexico adores golfer Lorena Ochoa. Through these suggestions, easy associations between nation and athlete are produced in U.S., transnational, and foreign national media outlets.

The multiculturalism of Tiger Woods traveled across borders and made him appealing as a global commodity (H. Yu 2000). He was the racialized hybrid figure who broke into golf, the bastion of White male privilege and exclusive private property. Woods was marketed as the progressive vanguard—someone who burned a path to brighter opportunities for individuals around the world who looked like him and related to him. His African American father and his Thai mother offered an important "biological" connection with a number of continents. For Nike, Tiger Woods emerged as the next global superstar who would follow in the "shoes" of Michael Jordan (Cole and Andrews 2001; H. Yu 2000; 2002). Even though Tiger Woods and Michael Jordan have been marketed as universal and global sporting icons, global marketing in sport continues to be most effective when it is tailored to a national audience. The strategies of U.S. media sport attempt to capitalize on national distinctions by assuming an innate connection between a player and his or her homeland.

The continuing significance of national affiliation to fandom practices is demonstrated through the emergence of Asian athletes in U.S. sport since the mid-1990s. The increasing presence of foreign athletes has boosted the number of fans of particular ethnic and racial origins both domestically and abroad. The Korean/Korean American fan base has increased considerably with the entry of Korean nationals into MLB and the LPGA in the late 1990s. In this attempt to appeal to foreign national markets, the most seductive fan market remains the China market. The "opening" of China to the NBA has been represented by the figure of Yao Ming (Wang 2004). In many ways resonant with the discourses of China's "opening to the world" during the Nixon era, Yao Ming has been marked as a radical force in shaping cultural and consumer interactions between the United States and China. The frenzy with which the NBA has attempted to market itself in China demonstrates the asymmetrical nation-specific attempts to expand global markets.

The terms of the arrangements across national markets are marked by power asymmetries. Even though individual stars from developing nations make millions of dollars, most economic benefits remain in the United States and Europe, which exist as the bases for most transnational media sport conglomerates (Maguire 1999). The increased number of players from South Korea has helped to increase profits for U.S. media sporting industries, including media companies, agents, and teams. Although these players have produced various national and minority markets for goods and services around particular sports, the globalization of intellectual property rights and the ability to determine the so-called market value of these players indicates that control continues to rest in the hands of transnational corporations based largely in the United States and Europe.

Reading across Global Koreanness and U.S. Multiculturalism

In this and the previous chapter, I have attempted to demonstrate the significance of Korean developmental nationalism and U.S. multiculturalism to situate how Korean/American subjects are positioned in relation to media sport. Clearly, disparities exist between South Korean and Korean American audiences, and national location makes a considerable difference in the ways that athletes are understood. However, transnational athletic subjects often complicate these national distinctions. Two U.S. athletes, Olympic skier Toby Dawson and National Football League (NFL) player Hines Ward, asserted their Koreanness and challenged both the limits of U.S. nationalist multiculturalism and Korean nationalist discourses of global Koreanness. Both athletes used their media visibility after high-profile victories in their respective sporting realms to assert investments in Koreanness. The players challenged the national limits of U.S. multiculturalism by demonstrating their explicit nation-specific goals, which were tied strategically to institutions in South Korea. Rather than engaging primarily as U.S. nationals, they directed their interests to personal histories within South Korea and used these stories as the grounds for their claims to Koreanness. In doing so, they also challenged the limits of the discourses of overseas Koreanness. Although both players appealed to ideas about the blood ties that bind the nation, they did so in a way that exposed the contradictions and limits to national community that are embedded within ideas of Korean ethnic purity. These players bring attention to the constructed nature of national community, and they work to expand ideas about what the Korean nation might look like.

Toby Dawson won a bronze medal in mogul skiing for the U.S. Olympic team during the 2006 Winter Olympics. Dawson was adopted at the age of three from a Korean orphanage by White American ski instructors who raised him in Colorado. Using his visibility as a world-class skier, Dawson called out to viewers for help in finding his birth parents. Prior to the Olympics, Dawson posted twelve photographs of himself as a child on the NBC Olympic website.[26] After his Olympic victory, a South Korean media frenzy ensued as many people came forward to claim they were his biological parents. As part of a deal struck with the Korean Ministry of Culture and Tourism, specifically the Korean National Tourism Organization (KNTO), Dawson agreed to assist South Korea with its Olympic bid for the 2014 Olympics if state organizations would help him find his birth parents. Eventually, DNA tests verified one claimant, Kim Jae-su, as his biological father. About a year after his bronze-medal winning run, he was reunited with his biological father on February 28, 2007.[27]

The U.S. media latched onto this story as an especially compelling human-interest story about an American competing in the Olympics. Clearly, NBC was interested in circulating this narrative by agreeing to post his childhood pictures on their website. U.S. media coverage highlighted the openness of his adoptive parents and their support for their adopted child in his Olympic pursuits and in his quest to find his birth parents. The generosity of his American parents was contrasted with connotations about the corruption of the adoption process in South Korea, as many individuals emerged to claim Dawson as their son.

In a South Korean context, Dawson's account can be absorbed easily into a nationalist reading of a lost national son who returned home. According to his biological father's account, rather than being given up by his parents, he had gone missing while at a crowded Pusan market with his mother, and he ended up at an adoption agency. Dawson's intense desire to see his biological parents and to understand the circumstances of his adoption provoked him to use extraordinary measures to find his birth parents. In nationalist narratives about the purity of Korean blood, Dawson was compelled to return to the country of his birth to be rightfully reunited with his biological father. He agreed to play a role in supporting South Korean state projects, and he even had a Korean wedding ceremony staged in Pusan six weeks after meeting his biological father. This narrative of Dawson's supposed return to his origins fits nicely with nationalist narratives of national purity and in the efforts of the state to encourage all overseas Koreans to recognize their connection to the country and contribute to the growth of a global South Korean nation.

The media genre of biological parent/adoptee reunions has been a significant narrative within South Korean national media for at least two decades (Eleana Kim 2001). These reunions operate as allegories of national division and eventual reunification that are expressed within the context of the reunion of biological kin. The live television staging of the moment of reunification involves viewers in a national melodrama that follows a trajectory of division, loss, reunification, and public mourning. When Toby Dawson offered a public call for his birth parents, he inserted himself within these existing adoption narratives. Dawson, as Olympic athlete, became a context through which these national narratives were mediated. The narratives of adoption reproduce ideas of Koreanness that are tied to the purity of Korean blood and myths about the homogeneity of the Korean nation. In the case of Korean adoptees, those who return to South Korea are often considered to be people looking for their true roots and their "real" selves.

Dawson's case raises important questions about the national and institutional conditions around his adoption. His account is riddled with questions about the role of his biological mother and the adoption agency, the lack of regulation by the state, the immense number of false claims of parenthood around the 2006 Olympics, and even his own feelings of intense ambivalence about the whole process. The South Korean state offered Dawson a quid pro quo, which assumed that he help the South Korean state bid for the 2014 Olympics in exchange for its assistance in finding his birth parents. Dawson also used his global visibility to find his birth parents, and his account points out how ideas of global Koreanness might be appropriated for a variety of interests. The complicated trajectories of Dawson's quest for his parents cannot simply be reduced to the narrative of a search for homeland. It is also important to note that the efforts to reunite with his family came from Dawson himself, rather than from a call by South Korea to claim him as one of their own. It was only after he had established himself as a top-level competitor and Olympic medal winner that he was hailed as a Korean subject and attended to by the state.

The case of Korean-born Hines Ward raises further questions regarding the contradictions of global Koreanness. Ward, who was chosen as the most valuable player (MVP) on the 2006 Super Bowl–winning Pittsburgh Steelers team, used his increased visibility during the NFL postseason to bring attention to the plight of biracial children in South Korea.[28] Ward's parents—an African American GI, Hines Ward Sr., and a Korean native, Kim Young Hee—met when Ward Sr. was stationed in South Korea. They married and moved to the United States when Ward was one, and soon after, they divorced. Ward's mother raised him alone while holding working-class jobs, including a long-term position as a school cafeteria worker. Her story of hard work and dedication to her son became a popular news item in U.S.-based media. She exemplified the model minority who worked hard, despite immense adversity, to provide an education and brighter future for her son. Furthermore, she continued to work even after her son became a success, demonstrating her commitment to supporting herself through her own labor.

Around the time of Ward's Super Bowl appearance and victory, he became a popular news item in South Korea. A month after the event, mother and son returned to South Korea for the first time since they left, and Ward met President Roh Moo Hyun and received an honorary Seoul citizenship granted by then governor Lee Myung Bak.[29] He was embraced by the South Korean media, and his message of inclusiveness for other races, especially mixed-race African American–Korean children, was praised as bringing a voice to disenfranchised mixed-race children. He also inspired a law banning discrimination against mixed-race Koreans. During his stay, he arranged a series of "hope-sharing" meetings on behalf of mixed-race children, and on April 30, 2006, he established the Hines Ward Helping Hands Foundation. He endowed it with $1 million to help mixed-race children in South Korea.

The eager embrace of Ward came after his recognition as the MVP in the most-watched media sport event in the United States. By no means a popular sport in South Korea, American football was thrust into the media spotlight after the game, and it was only then that Ward was embraced as a Korean American with Korean roots. Liberal discourses that condemned racism in South Korea focused on Ward's personal interest and investments in

Figure 5. Hines Ward, In Sik Kim, and Chan Ho Park at the 2006 World Baseball
Classic. Yonhap News. Reprinted with permission.

improving the plight of mixed-race children. Some went on to condemn the
history of mistreatment of Korean women who married American GIs, and
they called for the rethinking of national attitudes toward these women.[30]
The voluntary dedication by Ward demonstrated the genuine nature of his
position, as it was founded on his own struggles and on his desire to change
conditions for those who were similar to himself. Rather than asserting that
the issue of racism is a problem for the state to fix, or one that is connected
to nationalist ideologies based on blood purity, Ward dedicated himself to
changing conditions for mixed-race children without expecting the state to
do so. Thus, he demonstrated how South Korea's social problems might be
resolved through the use of private capital and the commitment of individuals who have a personal dedication to a specific cause. Through these
actions, Ward was able to establish himself as a worthy national hero, and his
popularity was further revealed in Korean and Korean American circles during the 2006 World Baseball Classic.

In the United States, both Dawson and Ward were praised as dutiful
American citizens who represented the multicultural diversity within U.S.
sport. As an Olympic promotion, Dawson was featured as the "2006 U.S.
Olympic Team Hopeful, Moguls and Dual Skier" on a Kellogg's Frosted

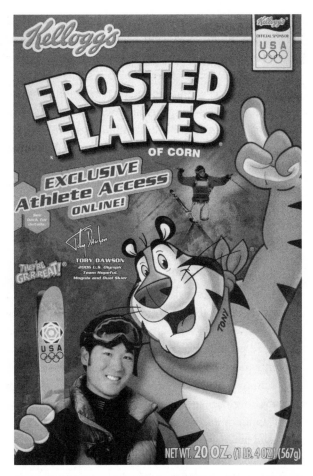

Figure 6. Toby Dawson on the cover of a box of Frosted Flakes in 2005.

Flakes box, which highlighted his own all-American appeal. The "collector's box" shows Dawson in two poses. In one pose, Dawson stands in full ski gear beside cartoon character Tony the Tiger who has one arm around Dawson and is indicating "number one" with his other hand. There is also a smaller image of Dawson demonstrating an acrobatic jump during a mogul run. An appearance on a cereal box cover presented commercial visibility for Dawson, and it highlighted his appeal to a U.S. national audience. It also demonstrated the growing multiculturalism surrounding commercial images of athletes.

During this period, Dawson became a symbol of U.S. skiing—an over-whelmingly White sport—and Ward was presented as an Asian American/multirace/foreign-born figure in American football, which is largely defined by U.S. Black–White distinctions. Their symbolic status as Asian Americans in U.S. sport was enough to merit recognition in the national media. Furthermore, the personal stories around their respective successes were interpreted as highlighting the social value of sport. They were both praised as athletes with a social conscience who were driven not by special political interests but by their own personal life experiences. Although their quests for change involved places beyond the borders of the United States, they were facilitated by the opportunities provided within the United States through sport.

Consuming Transnationally

The differences between South Korean and Korean American interpretations of Korean athletes were apparent in conversations throughout my fieldwork. While in Korea, not once did the South Koreans with whom I interacted perceive Korean-heritage athletes as anything other than South Korean nationals. These athletes were understood as South Koreans on foreign soil. In other assessments, they were seen as national representatives working to globalize the nation. I was interested in what South Koreans might think of Korean American spectators and fans, but in South Korea, many did not make a distinction between South Koreans and Korean Americans, as they assumed that shared ethnicity bound South Koreans and Korean Americans (see Shin 2006). Korean Americans, like the athletes, were considered to be overseas Koreans—Koreans in a foreign land. A few made a clear distinction between South Koreans and Korean Americans, but they were mostly uninterested in acknowledging any distinct significance for Korean Americans.

An episode of the HBO comedy series *Arli$$* lampooned the differences between South Koreans and Korean Americans to conclude that, in the final analysis, an immutable genetic essence connects these groups.[31] The show is based on the idea that differences between Koreans and Korean Americans might exist, but they can be overcome if shared roots are discovered and exploited. In one episode, sports super-agent Arliss Michaels is presented with the challenge of adding the first Korean Major League Baseball pitcher, Ja Ahn Kim, to his illustrious roster of clients.[32] The episode begins with

Arliss and his colleague, Rita Wu, celebrating Ja Ahn's new three-year, $15 million contract with the Los Angeles Dodgers in Ja Ahn's mother's nail salon. Ja Ahn's mother, Chŏng-ŭn, offers Arliss and Rita some kimchi during the celebration, but Rita, a Korean American, refuses to eat it because it "gives her heartburn." Rita offends Chŏng-ŭn by demonstrating a lack of Korean manners, and Chŏng-ŭn refers to her as a "banana" (yellow on the outside, white on the inside).

A crisis at the agency ensues when it is revealed that Ja Ahn has been drafted into the Korean army. Arliss tries to get Chŏng-ŭn to help him get Ja Ahn out of the service by stating that he can be of more service to Korea by fighting its wars on the pitcher's mound, but Chŏng-ŭn refuses to help. She has decided that he must serve in the military because "he is a Korean." Rita also attempts to change Chŏng-ŭn's mind by visiting her at the salon. This visit doesn't start off well, but Chŏng-ŭn decides to educate Rita on Korea. Incidentally, Rita and Chŏng-ŭn discover a shared history of trauma—that Rita's grandmother and Chŏng-ŭn's mother were both sex slaves during the Japanese occupation. After a cathartic cry, Chŏng-ŭn and Rita are bonded as fellow Korean women, and Chŏng-ŭn helps Rita "rediscover" what it means to be "really" Korean. After this life-changing experience, Rita comes to support military service for Ja Ahn and has decided that his national duty is more important than his baseball contract.

Meanwhile, Arliss calls a special meeting with the minister of the South Korean embassy in Los Angeles to try to convince him to offer Ja Ahn a military exemption. Rather than giving in to Arliss's demands, the diplomat settles on a wager. If Arliss loses the wager, then Ja Ahn will have to serve in the military, but if he wins, Ja Ahn will be given a military exemption. They agree that if Ja Ahn pitches in the Asian Games and helps South Korea beat Japan, he will be offered a military exception. The last scene of the show has Ja Ahn in trenches with Arliss ducking enemy fire.

This sitcom pokes fun at how notions of cultural authenticity and cultural difference work within a U.S. context of consumer capitalism, and it also demonstrates the humor in the notion that an American capitalist enterprise could intervene in the state policy of another country without any mutual political or economic interest. Rita fails at her performances of Koreanness, which seems to point out the ridiculous nature of the assumption held by Arliss that Rita could help finesse the deal. However, the narrative cynically reproduces the idea of cultural authenticity by presenting the notion that if one taps deep enough, there are bound to be compelling connections among fellow ethnics. Rita had not yet "discovered" what it means to be Korean until she meets Ja Ahn's mother, who represents a more authentic version of Koreanness. For Ja Ahn's mother, Rita's family history of suffering legitimizes her claims to Koreanness. The female bonding narrative evokes the collective mourning of the nation for its violated mothers, and it unifies the Korean family through the acknowledgement of a shared national and family suffering. In the superficial world of *Arli$$*, the analogy is made that sex slavery is to Koreanness as the Holocaust is to Jewishness. This story of ethnic discovery is then sublated within a narrative of essential national difference.

Clearly, Ja Ahn Kim is a thinly disguised version of Chan Ho Park, as Ja Ahn Kim is hailed as the first South Korean pitching phenomenon in Major League Baseball. Furthermore Ja Ahn signs with the Los Angeles Dodgers. Given the emergence of several Korean MLB players during the late 1990s, the "problem" of mandatory military duty became a liability around their recruitment. The representation of this issue in a 1999 episode of *Arli$$* hints at the kinds of (surely bungled) negotiations of cultural difference that took place within U.S. media sport as it attempted to globalize. The show demonstrates the hilarious assumptions of a sports agent who clearly has no understanding of racial, national, and ethnic differences but who still attempts to negotiate a diplomatic deal for his client based on faulty assumptions about the nature of these differences. He offers a very shallow view of multiculturalism and international diplomacy as tools for capitalist expansion. He also represents the somewhat false sense of power and privilege felt by U.S. capitalists to essentially ignore cultural differences in the name of free market fundamentalisms. The show presents the idea that personal freedoms are not as readily available in "other places around the world" and that national differences create challenges to smooth capitalist globalization. The complex issue of mandatory military conscription for Korean male athletes is resolved through a wager. Nevertheless, the show does highlight the inability of U.S. commentators, fans, and viewers to understand the politics behind the issue of Korean military recruitment and the seriousness by which these military exemptions are understood, as I discuss in the next chapter.

The potential of sport to shape ideas of belonging and community is not determined by the nationalist narratives outlined above. The discussions about Korean athletes by both Korean and Korean American respondents came to reflect many subjective ideas and opinions about the United States,

South Korea, and the relationship between the two countries. The subjective experiences of sport might be shaped within national contexts, but these national contexts produce a number of responses. Media sport might also be understood as a space for expressions of survival and pleasure for minority groups. When speaking with Korean Americans, or with South Koreans who had close friends and relatives in the United States, a narrative of immigration often accompanied their discussion of Korean athletes, who they saw as struggling in a foreign land to succeed in an exceedingly difficult and competitive field. Athletes were battling racism and discrimination, enduring cultural differences and misunderstandings, and facing extreme loneliness and alienation, yet they were bringing a new kind of entertainment to the often difficult and lonely immigrant lives of Koreans in the United States.

This narrative of immigrant survival and pleasure was, however, critiqued in an interview I had with a prominent sports reporter for a major Korean television network. Chŏn Mi-sŏng discussed her experiences covering MLB for the South Korean audience. She traveled in the United States throughout the baseball season, moving from city to city to cover games that featured high-profile South Korean players. She discussed her position as a sports journalist with a great amount of professionalism, refusing any notion that being a woman affected her reporting in any way. She wanted to make clear that her reports were directed to a South Korean national audience and not a Korean American one. When I suggested that she discuss the importance of these players to the Korean American community, she balked. "I wish they [Korean Americans] would leave them alone. They always expect Chan Ho to do something for them: Come to their restaurant; help them advertise for their business. They are just baseball players." This outburst was surprising, and I felt myself implicated in her distaste for Korean Americans. In this exchange, I was able to sense that Korean Americans were seen as getting in the way of baseball players' professional responsibility, which was to play sports. They were also getting in the way of her reporting. In Ms. Chŏn's opinion, Korean Americans made excessive demands of these players—demands that the players could not fulfill. South Korean players were not in MLB to save Korean Americans from their sense of discrimination and marginalization. They were not in MLB to perform some outmoded sense of Korean nationalism or community for Korean Americans. To Ms. Chŏn, they existed essentially for a South Korean national television audience, and they should be expected to do their jobs well—that is, to win games.

Ms. Chŏn's negative reaction to what she saw as a Korean American obsession with Korean players failed to take into account the position of many Korean Americans who might see these players as especially significant to their lives as diasporic and immigrant minority subjects. Instead, she herself had taken a view that privileged a "pure sports" attitude that contradicted her own assignment as a traveling journalist primarily covering South Korean players in Major League Baseball. Her own status as a transnational sports journalist allowed her to transcend issues of immigration, foreignness, and racism when discussing the sporting performance of South Korean athletes.

The consumption of minority players by minority subjects raises critical issues of citizenship and belonging. Some have argued that Joe Louis, Jackie Robinson, and Muhammad Ali offered hope to African Americans and other minorities during periods of struggle (Farred 2003; Rampersad 1997). The emotional pleasures of consumption offered a psychological lift and opportunities for cultural expression within periods of stark oppression. Minority athletes have given voice and visibility to oppositional and critical perspectives (Farred 2003). Even today, the popular appeal of media sport in African American communities raises critically important questions about the politics of representation and the variety of interpretations for differently located communities (see Dyson 1993). What kinds of pleasures are produced through the powerful and heroic minority athlete? How do minority viewers negotiate various messages within media broadcasts, refusing some while relishing others? How do minority athletes give voice and presence to otherwise invisible populations?

As Juffer (2002) points out, Major League Baseball is the most visible mainstream venue for Latino representation in the media. Likewise for Korean Americans, representation in mainstream media venues is concentrated in the LPGA, PGA, and MLB. These players operate as sites around which diasporic and minority communities coalesce with others in a nation of viewers imagined across discontinuous geographic locales (Anderson 1991). The convergence of South Korean media and people around these athletes produces a temporary "Korean" space within a sporting context represented largely as American. These mainstream representations offer a powerful sense of place and belonging for Korean Americans. The feeling that one is watching with thousands of others as a community only intensifies the drama of the event. Through sport, Korean Americans have the opportunity to feel part of the mainstream, and these mainstream moments are achieved through marvelous spectacle.

It became clear through my fieldwork that the kinds of investments that South Koreans and Korean Americans had with Korean athletes were situated within narratives of both South Korean and U.S. nationalisms. These narratives locate the desires of Korean and Korean American subjects with respect to Korean athletes. Though the contexts I offer in Part I of this book are limited, they still point to the complex field of interpretation that situates South Korean and Korean American responses to media sports. I also attempt to draw attention to the critical political stakes involved in this field of interpretation as a way to limit the endless commutability of signification within politically significant contexts (Hall 1985).

The narrative of Koreanness that runs through media sport offers a spectacular example of how discourses of race in the United States are being reworked within the context of transnationalism. Mainstream media sport conveys a number of U.S. mythologies around race and nation that promote ideas about a multicultural America. These mythologies are reproduced through the everyday engagements with the spectacles of media sport. As Guy Debord argues, "the spectacle is not a collection of images; rather, it is a social relationship between people that is mediated by images" (1995, 12). The social relations of race are mediated by and through spectacular images of media sport, and the case of Korean transnational athletes offers important examples of how such spectacles reveal shifting social relationships of race in the United States.

PART II

READING MASCULINITIES AND FEMININITIES THROUGH
TRANSNATIONAL ATHLETES

Playing Hard Ball

THE ATHLETIC BODY AND KOREAN/AMERICAN MASCULINITIES

A new kind of male body has emerged in Korean visual cultures—the hard-muscled athletic body. A transformation of the Korean male physique in popular culture is evidenced through the full exposure of the naked upper body. This focus on the chest in Korean mass media is a recent phenomenon, which is exhibited in the celebratory stripping of the jersey during soccer goal ceremonies, the shirtless images of pop stars such as *Bi* (Rain),[1] the frenzy around Olympic swimmer and gold medalist Park Tae-hwan, and the undressing and dressing scenes of film and television *Hallyu* stars.[2] The naturalistic, yet muscled, torso reveals and proves a kind of masculinity that is based on notions of physical strength and power. This gym-sculpted figure exists as a visual expression of Korean masculinity, and it demonstrates how athletic masculinities help produce ideas of global Koreanness. These built bodies produce desires and affects that maintain the interests of subjects within South Korea and its diaspora.

Korean male athletes embody the contradictions of *segyehwa* rhetoric; they function as nationalist icons yet ultimately remain invested in their own private accumulation of wealth. Korean male athletes not only operate as symbols of Korean national strength in an arena of global capitalist competition but also operate as transnational representations of Asian/American masculinity. Though these athletes represent a kind of globality, the state continues to be invested in the symbolic importance of male athletes, as athletes can literally substitute athletic success for military duty. Korean male athletes highlight the multiple and contradictory ways that Asian masculinities are produced and consumed within the transnational circuits of media sport.

The masculinized Korean sporting body—as the athletic body, the disciplined body, the large body, the wealthy body, the powerful body, and the virile body—has become an object for consumption by transnational audiences with varying degrees of interest and investment in these representations.

An investigation into the discourses of masculinity that circulate around South Korean male athletes reveals a variety of complex and historical factors that challenge any simple connections made between sport and masculinity in an era of globalization. This chapter investigates how discourses of masculinity work across a number of national and racial discourses. It first discusses the emergence of Korean male athletes within the South Korean contexts of national development and, especially, segyehwa policies. This chapter also discusses how ideas of sexuality are central to understanding the significance of male athletes by interpreting male athletes within transnational erotics of Korean nationhood. Even though male athletes are hailed as emblems of a global Korea, they are also managed by the state, which is highlighted most clearly by mandatory military duty. In order to understand the significance accorded to male athletes by the state, this chapter discusses the policy of military exemptions for successful athletes. Military exemptions offer an example of the "graduated sovereignties" that the state places on the media sport industry (and the players within it) and exist as part of the story of global media sport (Ong 2007).

Masculinities in transnational media sport also offer new ways of thinking about the enduring debates around Asian/American masculinities (see Eng 2001; R. Lee 1999; Nguyen 2002). Celebrations of new masculinities in Korean/American and Asian/American contexts often reproduce nationalist imperatives that link masculinities with national strength. The transnational dimensions of Asian masculinities present possibilities for thinking about Korean/American and Asian/American masculinities beyond the limits of the nation, and they also reveal the transnational dimensions of race. The chapter concludes by interrogating the possibilities for imagining a new Asian/American masculinity that refuses to reproduce a homophobic and xenophobic approach in calling for representations that redress the histories of racism against Asian men.

Body Development

The emergence of the Korean male athlete has helped shape the popular emergence of the naked male torso. The bare and muscled torso functions as a technology of the self that attests to the achievement of Korean masculinity within an era of global competition. Richard Dyer, in his reading of male pin-ups, argues that muscularity acts as a "*sign* of power—natural, achieved, phallic" (1982, 68). Dyer suggests that the male pin-ups' muscles attain power because they seem biological, and it is in the "natural-seeming" quali-ties of the muscles that "male power and domination are legitimized" (ibid., 71). Far from being considered a "natural body," the Korean athlete's body has been built from its "natural state" through disciplined physical exercise, long periods of strength-building workouts with extensive weight training, dieting, and supplements—or what is casually referred to in gym circles as *yak* (medicine). Within the capitalist contexts of mass culture, the fit body has been understood as a productive body, not one of leisure, but one that is the result of "work" within a national discourse about productive laboring sub-jects (Gremillion 2003). Therefore, in U.S. gym culture, for instance, the idea of "working out" is tied to ideas of economic productivity. However, the body reference in this discussion is also shaped through a process of self-commodification that produces the body for mass consumption. The body is not simply functional; it is a hyperreal representation of physical possibilities for Korean men.

This body requires an immense amount of time and disciplined labor dedicated to physiological transformation, which can be seen as a kind of self-fashioning practice.[3] In contrast to the "salaryman" or the office worker, the hard body demonstrates a new kind of Korean masculinity—one that turns away from the homosocial environments of work and after-work enter-tainment to the still homosocial, yet ultimately self-focused, environment of the gym.[4] The ultimate goal of working out lies not only in peer recognition of the achievement of physical transformation but also in the projection of the body as a public consumer object available for visual consumption by others. There is little discussion of self-transformation as a kind of spiri-tual quest. The reward for the effort lies in the physical evidence of self-transformation through the growth and hardening of muscles, the gaze of both male and female spectators on the flesh, and the erotic and visceral fantasies elicited in oneself and others by the experiences of feeling and viewing the hard body (Klein 1993).[5] The intensification and circulation of images work to generate desires for the male body within a variety of publics.

The emergence of this masculine, hard-bodied athletic figure connects closely with the changes in visual representations of both masculinity and femininity in South Korea since the 1990s. Dyer points out that "the celebration of the body in sport is also a celebration of the relative affluence of Western society, where people have time to dedicate themselves to the development of the body for its own sake" (1982, 68). Similarly, the development of the new aesthetic for male bodies might be charted along a Korean developmental narrative written onto the body. If a visual presentation of hegemonic representations of manhood were mapped onto a developmental schema, it might follow this pattern. The poor and diseased bodies after colonialism and the Korean War were disciplined through military dictatorship. Male bodies were then dedicated to the cause of nation building through industrialization. During the period of economic growth throughout the 1970s and 1980s, the organizational man—the office worker, student protestor, or union member—was presented with an efficient, slim, and highly disciplined body garbed in a uniform or relatively standardized dress. With new industrial wealth in the 1990s, men could focus on activities that were no longer directly linked to economic and political activities, and, on a basic level, Korean men had the proper nutrition to grow tall, strong, and muscular. The ideal Korean male body in an era of globalization is a cosmopolitan figure that can compete in the global marketplace and be at home anywhere in the world. Furthermore, this body is a source of national pride, as it continues to feature a Koreanness that is easily recognizable.

A significant figure who successfully accomplishes this new idealized representation of Korean manhood is Olympic swimmer Park Tae-hwan. Park displayed his broad and muscled chest as he lifted his arms in excitement after his gold medal victory during the 2008 Olympics. His chest was flanked by lateral muscles that fanned out from his rib cage, and his bulging arms created a solid trunk for his clenched fist. Park, also known as Marine Boy or *Daebak* (which means "big win"), became a high-profile athlete because of his success in the international arena of swimming (in which South Korea had not previously been competitive and where the vast majority of top athletes have been Whites from industrialized Western countries). Swimming is also understood to be a sport that requires height and a largeness that was previously seen as limited to a particular type of Anglo physiology.

Park's appearance contributed greatly to his emergence as a hugely popular commercial icon. His size, especially his height and broad chest, his thick and spiky hair, and his open and relaxed face factored into his image as a sexualized celebrity athlete throughout his late teens. Following his gold medal–winning swim, Park displayed a relaxed poise that seemed to indicate he expected to win. At various meets, he demonstrated camaraderie with his White competitors, including Australian Grant Hackett and American Michael Phelps, and showed a new kind of national masculinity—one that is not at all anxious or threatened by White, Western men. He was totally comfortable on the global stage and understood that his ability to gain endorsements had as much to do with his appearance as with his athletic performance.

The popularity of South Korean male athletes in professional baseball, soccer, golf, and other high-profile global sports lies in their depiction as representatives of the nation in the context of global competition. Their placement in U.S. leagues, such as MLB and the PGA, has produced a U.S.-accented masculinity that emphasizes size, strength, athletic talent, and individualism. The entry of baseball players in U.S.-based sport demonstrates that Korean men can achieve parity in terms of talent and physical size with not only U.S. athletes but also athletes from all around the world. This idea of being "just as good" is particularly important in the context of South Korean development, as national identity has been based in assessing the comparative level of Korean economic strength (J. Woo 1991). The existence of Korean men in these global sports exists as a representational context for assessing the level of national strength and capitalist development.

For the athletes who emerged in the mid- to late 1990s, particularly baseball player Chan Ho Park, the interest in and focus on their lives was especially intensive, since these athletes had the role of "announcing Korea to the world."[6] By competing in the American game of baseball, which became the most popular sport in South Korea, Chan Ho Park functioned as a national icon of visibility who represented his country and its global status. The success of Chan Ho Park during the late 1990s occurred as South Korea was reeling from the Asian financial crisis, and his popularity was connected to the symbol of national resilience he represented during this tumultuous period. Furthermore, his own status as a "metacommodity" was enabled by the economic changes that occurred in the neoliberal reforms that followed the crisis, including media liberalization (Joo 2000). South Korean sporting heroes, such as Chan Ho Park, could be seen as facilitating the processes of globalization for the benefit of a nation going through a financial crisis. These athletes demonstrated how a Korean might be successful in global competition and still remain a national hero.

Athletes demonstrate how Korean subjects might succeed in a neoliberal world economy through privatized forms of wealth accumulation. South

Korean national athletes who were previously understood primarily as functional representatives of state interests are now portrayed as cosmopolitan consumer subjects.[7] The shift of Chan Ho Park's image from a *chŏn nom* to a global superstar was well documented through his consumption habits (Joo 2000). The Korean-language press covered in great detail the baseball player's purchase of a multimillion dollar home in Beverly Hills. Through his relationship with the infamous sports super-agent Scott Boras, he demonstrated his ability to master not only the athletic demands of Major League Baseball but also his skill at maximizing opportunities for profit through aggressive contract negotiations. His actions as a skilled consumer and capitalist contributed to his national significance.

Star athletes such as Park are subject to the hyperexposed tabloid cultures of South Korean and Korean American mass media. Beyond their performances, they appear in Korean variety shows, television shows, advertisements, and public events. Furthermore, the heavily scrutinized bodies of athletes have helped shift the standards of sexualized beauty to emphasize bodily discipline, strength, athleticism, and physicality. Their popularity draws, in part, from their commercialized sexuality. While the 3-S cultural policies of sport, sex, and screen of the 1980s was largely a state-led policy, private media and corporations with an advertising stake continue to rely on connections between nationalist discourses and erotics.

National Erotics and the Commercial Athlete

An advertisement featuring Korean football player Cho Jae-jin presents an explicit sexuality. In the image shown here, Jae-jin's torso is well oiled and tanned to highlight its hard definition and smooth skin. The contours of his flesh are exaggerated by sharply angled lighting. He is posing in a sexualized position of active undress. His shirt is zipped down and thrown back. With one engaged thumb, he is gripping his saggy jeans. With the other, he is pulling down his underwear and threatening to expose his genital area. His expression seems to connote a kind of confidence that lacks self-consciousness about his nudity, as though clothing is an optional accessory to his body. The name of the clothing retailer, ASK Enquired, and the British flag across the front of his shirt also indicate a transnational or global aspiration, whereas the national signs evoke the sexualized fashion icon status of the celebrity footballer David Beckham. However, these symbols do not necessarily refer to a desire to mimic the West. Cho's physiognomy clearly demonstrates his

"조용하고 쑥스러움을 많이 타지만 끼가 많은 사람이다. 모델이나 연예계 쪽에서
욕심을 낼까 걱정이 될 정도였다. 사진을 많이 찍어보지 않았다는데도 카메라에 대한
두려움도 없는 데다 본능적으로 어떻게 해야 멋있어 보이는지를 아는 것 같다.
'조재진'은 축구를 잘하는 선수일 때 모델로서 가치가 있다는 사실을 잊지 말았으면 좋겠다.
아직도 초보 수준인 스포츠 마케팅의 성공적인 사례가 되길 바란다.
그에겐 그럴 가치가 충분하니까." 조선행<사진작가>

Figure 7. Footballer Cho Jae-jin in a 2006 ASK
Enquired print advertisement.

Asianness, and another explicit sign of his nationality might seem redun-
dant or too overtly nationalistic. His thick and straight black hair, dark
eyes, lean arms, and smooth pubic region distinguish him from other un-
dressed athletes. Furthermore, his lack of tattoos or decorative scars also
distinguishes him from many of his Western counterparts. This image offers a kind of negotiated take on the transnational, as he relies on so-called
Western markers for a cosmopolitan cachet but continues to represent a
kind of national possibility.

Global capitalist fantasies involve both female and male stars, but the powerful forms of capitalist masculinity conveyed through male athletes are closely connected to national status on a geopolitical scale. L.H.M. Ling (1999) discusses the East Asian male agent of capital as a kind of "global sex machine" who is hypersexualized through his extravagant wealth and global mobility, connecting masculinity to the practices of capitalism. Ling depicts the Asian businessman as a kind of mutant monster of Western capitalism. He has succeeded at the game so well that he poses a threat to its traditional ruling subjects. This image of the hypermasculine male evokes the century-old stereotype of the morally ambiguous and excessive Asian businessman who has no real moral compass and lures (White) women through extravagant gifts. Unable to attract White women through "natural" means, he seduces them through wealth and trickery. Although Ling connects Asian male sexuality to Western representations, the Korean athlete in the contemporary transnational period comes to represent national erotics significant to the production of Korean nationalisms in the segyehwa era. The Korean athlete functions as a national agent of capital who is sexualized through his wealth but who also succeeds because of his perceived loyalty to country. He is a fierce competitor in a global market, but he is one who remains essentially tied to representations as a patriot.

The Korean athlete becomes a site for the sexual desires of Korean subjects to be directed toward properly national men rather than male athletes from other nations (Hyun Mee Kim 2004). During the 2002 FIFA World Cup, the masculinized bodies of Korean players were closely scrutinized by South Korean and Korean American fans. Throughout the tournament, there were widely noted public displays of female sexuality through the dress and body language of female fans who offered public expressions of love and desire for members of the national team. Kim Hyun Mee argues that the masculinized narratives of sport and competition during this international event were superseded by feminine narratives of romance, fantasy, and desire. In the mainstream press, however, this unprecedented public display of female sexuality was interpreted as an acceptable form of adoration for the national team and for the nation.

One South Korean national team player became particularly famous for his torso. The defensive midfielder Kim Nam-il's naked torso became a common sight in media coverage of the team, particularly in the coverage of the team member's off-the-field exploits. Kim's flesh was exposed on the covers of sports tabloids, and images of his shirtless body were often accompanied by statements mocking women's desires to see and touch his body. Articles mentioned his musculature, especially his defined abdominal muscles, and his seemingly limitless energy for both football and off-the-field entertainment. Online female-dominated fan groups that focused on Kim charted his every move. A popular activity was to post "star sighting" accounts and swap fan images of his body. He became a surprising sex symbol during the World Cup, given the overwhelming popularity of midfielder Ahn Jung-hwan prior to the games. While Ahn could be seen as a *kkot mi nam* (translated literally as a flowery beautiful man) with the focus of attraction on his facial features, including his straight and high nose, narrow face, smooth skin, and long and permed hair (he advertised a line of beauty products), Kim offered a rugged, working-class masculinity. Kim Nam-il cultivated his *tôp'ŭ* (tough) guy presentation with an irreverent attitude and a rugged body. His short, spiky hair was dyed light brown and contrasted with his deeply tanned skin. His body became the focus of a haptic gaze that highlighted the firmness and contours of his flesh. His fans anticipated the moment of his undressing, and they watched closely for this money shot.

Sitting around the kitchen table with four young women from the Seoul *kosiwŏn* in which I stayed, I asked them about the athletes they favored. Twenty-six-year-old Sŏ Sŏn-mi told me that she liked Park Ji-sung because he seemed sincere and uncorrupt. He seemed like an earnest and hard-working player who treated the Dutch coach, Guus Hiddink, like a father. Her statement was met with eye rolling by the younger women in the group, who labeled her an *ajumma* (adult woman) for liking Park, and they likened her tastes to a middle-aged woman's desire for a pure and boy-like or son-like figure. The other three women, who were a few years younger, debated the merits of Ahn Jung-hwan and Kim Nam-il as objects of romantic fantasy. Though they uniformly thought that Ahn was better looking, they felt that they would want to date Kim. They seemed to think that a guy who looked like Ahn would be too difficult to keep for themselves, as other women would be constantly trying to steal him away. (Indeed, he was married to a former Miss Korea.) With Kim, one had to witness him play and see him undress in order to understand his true qualities. As nineteen-year-old Kim Chŏng-ŭn put it, Kim Nam-il seemed to be more like an everyday guy with skills and attributes that weren't immediately apparent. With a guy like him, there would be no competition with other women, but if he was your man, he would probably satisfy you better than Ahn Jung-hwan. To this, the rest of us squealed in laughter. Twenty-two-year-old Lee Hŭi-ju playfully reminded

Kim Chŏng-ŭn that she had a boyfriend, and the rest of the conversation focused on the gossip surrounding Kim Nam-il's extracurricular activities, especially his penchant for cavorting in trendy clubs in the chic neighborhood of Ch'ŏngdam-dong. Lee Hŭi-ju wondered aloud whether it was possible for a woman to achieve a stomach similar to Kim Nam-il's. For this group of women, the interest in male athletes was promoted by commercial investments in luring female consumers to the World Cup, and as I elaborate in chapter 5, it became a major way to understand the event.

Male athletes function as generative sites in the production of national erotics not just for Koreans but also for Korean Americans. Erotics are generally defined as narratives that "arouse sexual desire and excitement," and they are most often understood within the context of private sex acts (Mankekar and Schein 2004). Going beyond private sex acts, the sexual desire and excitement generated around Korean national athletes operate as allegories of desire for the Korean nation. These erotic narratives are constituted as transnational narratives that connect Koreans across nation-state boundaries through the shared consumption of sexualized images. Purnima Mankekar and Louisa Schein, in the introduction to a special issue of the *Journal of Asian Studies* on media, transnationalism, and erotics, discuss the centrality of sexuality in understanding how ideas of nation are generated through transnational media. Mankekar and Schein understand erotics as public discourses that extend "beyond sex acts or desires for sex acts, as enmeshed also in fantasy, everyday practices, social relationships, and political institutions" (2004, 359). Erotics are experienced in a number of domains—from sex acts between subjects to the love of citizens for nation to the capitalist fantasies produced in consumers through representations of athletes. Rather than seeing Korean American and South Korean viewers as having uniform interpretations of and responses to these images, erotics actively produce multiple notions of sexuality through active engagements with these images (ibid., 357).

Sexualized representations of Korean athletes forge a new kind of erotic relationship between Korean Americans and ideas of Koreanness. They operate as sites for the projection of sexual desire toward objects that represent Koreanness as a commodity. Following Louisa Schein, I understand media as a "key agent in both the erotic and the transnational subjectification of Asian Americans" (1999, 361). Schein emphasizes the production of "homeland erotics" through narratives of sexuality that are represented in and conveyed through forms of media produced by Hmong subjects in the diaspora. Schein effectively demonstrates how the narratives of homeland romance featured in diasporic films connect to material realities shaped by gender inequalities, geopolitical relations, and economic asymmetries. They also offer the opportunity for viewers in both the homeland and the diaspora to comment on these relations of inequality. In contrast to the narrative of Hmong diasporic media, the representations of Korean athletes in media sport are not connected to *homeland* erotics but to erotics of the global commodity image. Mass-mediated athletes exist as the location for the production of discourses of Koreanness. Their mass-mediated bodies operate as the site upon which desires are inscribed and through which fantasies are experienced.

Due to the traveling nature of sporting productions and the movement of athletes among various locales, Koreanness is not fixed to one homeland or a single geographic site in either South Korea or the United States. Instead, images of athletes offer temporary and deterritorialized commercial representations of Koreanness that are circulated through mass media in advertisements, live performances, and public sightings. This sense of dislocation makes athletes particularly emblematic of a global Koreanness—one that moves between South Korea and the United States. Korean athletes do not stay in one place; rather, like the transnational capitalists discussed by Aihwa Ong (1999), they maintain a flexible approach to their residence in various nation-states and maximize the financial, educational, and legal benefits offered within each site. Yet, as Ong points out, this doesn't mean that the nation-state and nationalism disappear. In fact, discourses of national connection become powerful ways to connect coethnics. Many nations, including South Korea, have now developed policies and institutions to tap these national loyalties.

The athlete acts as a figure through which intimacy with the nation can be felt. Korean Americans read Korean male players within a specific affective field generated within the context of sporting matches. For example, the baseball player becomes a site around which media publics emerge. These media publics enable viewers to experience a deep sense of connection while viewing the event. The activity takes place in a stadium where people gather to watch as a collective and interact with other people. Korean bodies, Korean athletes, mass media, and everyday forms of communication among people come together to create a sociality around Koreanness. A "we" emerges when the Korean athlete comes on the field, and his personage resonates with Korean/American viewers and spectators. His energy vibrates through the bodies of fans who have come to watch him precisely because of his Koreanness. These fans are eager with anticipation for his performance and wonder how many other Koreans they might see or recognize in the stands. They come for the feelings of connection they might have when they follow his body and its movements with their traveling gaze. They hope to witness moments of virtuosity, hilarity, and conflict. They want to feel the intensity of moments of immense tension and release. They come to be with others and to see others like themselves in the stands. They want to sense these feelings of connection and these moments of pleasure together as a collective. They also understand that their bodies might be mediated through television or the stadium screens to other viewers who are watching intently and looking for material signs of collective interest.

A particular form of erotics develops through feelings of recognition and intimacy. This narrative of erotics privileges heterosexual desire for the Korean nation and intraethnic sexual relations. The focus on male athletes privileges intraethnic sexual reproduction in an era of anxieties around reproducing the "pure" Korean family.[8] The anxieties about and social critique of out-marriage and interethnic marriage have existed since the colonial era but especially after the U.S. occupation of South Korea. These anxieties have been compounded with worries over sex-ratio imbalances, the increasing migration of non-Korean women as brides for South Korean men, and the possibility that South Korean women will leave the nation to marry non-Korean men. Korean male athletes who achieve a state of global desirability bolster a kind of androcentric nationalism that praises Korean male desirability within the contexts of increasing numbers of interethnic, interracial, and transnational families.[9]

The state has appropriated this growing interest in male players, and although it may not stem from an acknowledged recognition of sexuality as a significant form of nation formation, state policies have perpetuated this link nonetheless. The desirability of the athletes to a national audience explains, in part, their exemptions from military service. The following section examines how sexuality, masculinity, and nation have become embedded in a controversial state policy of granting exemptions for military service to male athletes who demonstrate a spectacular level of success in an arena of international competition. It discusses the contradictions of segyehwa policies as they relate to male athletes by highlighting the significant role the state continues to play in regulating the careers of male athletes with South Korean citizenship.

Korea Fighting: Military Exemptions and Korean Men

Although the practical effect of athletes in commercial sport seems to out-weigh the effect of the everyday soldier on the public imagination, sporting discourses also work to connect nationalisms, masculinities, sexualities, and sport through metaphors for war. Universal histories of sport often interpret sporting competitions as a supplement to or substitute for war.[10] Commercial, linguistic, and filmic representations often merge ideas of war, militarism, and sport. Through state institutional practices, sport has regularly been used to produce military-like discipline in young boys. As stated in chapter 1, this relation underpinned the role of sport in South Korea's educational system during the 1960s. The charge *"ch'eryŏki kungnyŏk"* (physical strength is national strength) was an educational motto that emphasized the importance of physical strength (of boys and young men) in defending the nation from communist aggression (Chong-hŭi Kim 1999). Even though sport no longer operates as a direct proxy for Cold War competition, the connections among sport, masculinity, and national security continue since athletic competition can be seen as presenting the comparative strength of the nation in the realm of global capitalism. National strength becomes interpreted through the sporting successes of a few who are engaged in private accumulation.

The heterosexual desirability of athletes is intensified, due to the ability of male athletes to transcend military service and continue to maintain a high level of national importance. Sexuality connects to their exemption since their value to the nation is measured in terms of their ability to bring global visibility to the country and elicit national desires among subjects. By current standards, if the South Korean national baseball team wins a bronze medal in the Olympics or a gold medal in the Asian Games, in addition to generous prize money, the victors are exempted from South Korea's mandatory military conscription of all able-bodied men. As a teenager, swimmer Park Tae-hwan won three gold medals in the 2006 Asian Games, and this victory cemented his status as a national hero. It also bolstered his status as an object of desire, as he had won his exemption even prior to being old enough to enter the military. Thus, even prior to adulthood, he completed his national duty through athletic achievements and would be free to engage as a private citizen without further extraordinary obligations to the state. During the first-ever World Baseball Classic held in the United States in March of 2006, the South Korean government quickly moved to offer the members of the national team a military exemption after they had defeated Japan twice and established the strongest record in the tournament. This demonstrated that the standard for exemption might shift according to the perceived national value of a particular international sporting event (as well as the nationalist excitement of politicians).

Male athletes are often presented as warriors for the nation within the context of international competition. The label of *T'aeguk Chŏnsa* (Korean Warrior), which was popularized during the 2002 World Cup and reemerged during the 2006 World Baseball Classic and the 2008 Olympics, demonstrated the commonplace nature of militaristic attribution in the sporting realm. "Korea fighting" is a common phrase that athletes use to connect to male and female viewers and fans. This battle cry demonstrates their self-understanding as national representatives. As they raise their hands in a peace sign or a closed fist, they look straight into the camera and state, "*K'oreya hwa-i-t'ing!*"[11] On camera, the players almost always express the idea that love of country and duty to their fellow countrymen motivate them to play harder. During the 2002 World Cup and the 2006 World Baseball Classic, athletes repeatedly struck a patriotic tone when they referred to their role as athletes. These players earnestly stated that they were determined to play on behalf of their country in the same way that soldiers might express their dedication to nation and fellow countrymen.

The project of making Korean men has been connected closely to mandatory military duty, and the discussion of military exemptions necessarily becomes a discussion of Korean masculinities. Even though the South Korean government has recognized the successful performance of male athletes as a legitimate exchange for military duty, a large group of Korean men feel that victories in international sporting tournaments do not equal actual participation in extended military duties. Every Korean man with whom I spoke who had served in the military felt that these athletes should not be offered an exemption, whereas the young men who had not yet served in the military and all the women with whom I spoke felt that it was an appropriate exception for mandatory conscription. One nineteen-year-old respondent who expected to enter the military in three years, Lee Sŭng-min, explained why he felt that more athletes should be given the exemption: "It is their time to perform at their peak, and it's the same time they are supposed to be in the military." He went on to explain that athletes who have their sporting careers interrupted lose momentum, and many athletes who had not yet proven themselves are unable to develop their talents. Lee Sŭng-min challenged me

Figure 8. Chan Ho Park suited up in military clothing.
Yonhap News, reprinted with permission.

to think about the loss of potential from what he believed were outdated policies. When I asked him what he thought about going into the military himself, he stated in a matter-of-fact way that of course he didn't want to go, but, like most others, he would have to do his time and hope for the best.

Twenty-six-year-old Ryu Kyŏng-hyŏn had just returned from his service a few months prior to our meeting. When asked about whether athletes should serve in the then twenty-four-month military service, Ryu Kyŏng-hyŏn stated, "Definitely! All men must go to the military." He continued, "I went as a citizen of the Republic of Korea, and so all male citizens should have to go." "No exceptions?" I asked. "No exceptions," he asserted. I pointed out that athletes might lose their peak athletic years during their service, and thereby weaken South Korea's chances in international competitions. Ryu Kyŏng-hyŏn responded emphatically, "I don't care! What about my peak years? Everyone must go." Rather than reflecting on the actual national importance of one's service to the nation, he deployed an argument that rested on an idea of individualism: As equal individuals under the law, all able-bodied men should be expected to serve in the military, and since athletes are individual citizens, they should also be expected to serve. Ryu Kyŏng-hyŏn's statements also seemed to imply that Korean-born men were not fully men until they had served in the military.

I first believed that Ryu Kyŏng-hyŏn and Lee Sŭng-min reflected the range of opinions on this issue, but after a serious conversation with three other men, I realized that feelings on this topic varied greatly. I found that many men were highly ambivalent about their feelings regarding the military. Most men agreed that they were forever changed by their experiences in the military, but individual men's stories complicated the idea of the military as a necessary rite of passage between adolescence and manhood. On a chilly fall night in 2002, I met Shin Chŏng-u, a twenty-seven-year-old neighbor in my kosiwŏn, and three of her old high school classmates from her hometown in Kwangju. Like Shin Chŏng-u, the three male classmates were also single, twenty-seven-year-old college graduates. They were also staying in temporary living arrangements in Seoul for an indefinite period of time. Kim Sŏng-yun was working at an Internet advertising sales company, Yun Wŏn-kyun was employed part time in electronic retail sales at a booth in a large electronics mall, and No Byŏng-chŏl was just trying to make ends meet with occasional gigs in what he referred to as Internet consulting. All three men had gone to college in Kwangju and had completed their mandatory military service prior to moving to Seoul to look for work and begin careers.

We first talked as a group over a pitcher of beer in a fairly inexpensive pub, and then I followed up by doing individual interviews with each man. The men informed me that, as residents of Kwangju, they were obliged to be fans of the baseball team OB, now the Doosan Bears. They were also fans of the Haitai Tigers, now the Kia Tigers. Beyond that, they were particularly proud of their high school, which produced a number of famous baseball players.

This first-order level of loyalty to region differed from many other people with whom I spoke, especially those who considered themselves from Seoul. These expressions of regional loyalty demonstrated that their own place-specific understandings of baseball went far beyond global icons and the national team. Regionalism played a central role in popularizing baseball when it was first introduced as a professional sport in 1982 and their expressions of loyalty reflected the continuing significance of region, despite a waning interest in these regional divisions by many scholars (H. Yun 1999).

Although none of these men felt that athletes should receive military exemptions, each offered an important critique of how the debate over exemptions becomes about the value of the athletes and not about the expectation that all men have to serve in the military. They critiqued the idea that military service was necessary for national security, and they argued against the notion that they had to go to the military to become Korean men. They reflected a widespread belief that the military recruitment system itself was rife with corruption, as it gave the worst positions to those who had the least money and status, whereas the easiest positions and even exemptions were given to those who were from families of status. It seemed to me that being men, for these three, did not result in an affinity for male athletes who represented the nation in international competitions. They seemed to refuse to recognize that these athletes were exceptional, given that they were also male subjects of the nation. Yun Wŏn-kyun, in a one-on-one interview, even admitted that he hated the large crowds that are typical of sporting events. He didn't go to cheer for the national team; he would rather watch games from home and cheer for whatever team he liked (instead of feeling forced to cheer for only the South Korean team).

All three felt that they had put their lives on hold, and they explained that the military had taken a toll on them. Coming back to college, they felt that they were not as intelligent as when they had left. They had lost two years that could have been spent building their own careers, and military service did not provide any benefits in an era of fierce competition for skilled jobs and increasing sexual equality in the workplace. No Byŏng-chŏl asked why the state only recognized athletes and not those who excelled in other contexts, such as intellectuals, artists, video gamers, or computer scientists. Being in the military made him feel as if he were behind in computer science—a field that changes very rapidly—and he felt that he was at a great disadvantage when he got out of the military. When he brought this up, his two friends nodded their heads in agreement. This discussion of lost economic opportunities reflected a sense of compromised masculinity; their ability to succeed in the job market had been compromised by military service.

Military service is understood as a formative period in the life course of South Korean men. Many South Korean men divide their personal histories into two periods: prior to and after military service. The debate over athletic exemptions (though not as heated as when they were first distributed) continues to indicate the contested role of military duty in shaping the lives of Korean men. Among the men I interviewed who had served in the military, their statements revealed an impassioned opposition to exemptions. The government uses extraordinary standards of success to recognize the national importance of a few international sporting matches. It is also understood that the possibility of exemption works as a great incentive for players to push beyond their normal level of play.

Seungsook Moon (2005) points out the role of militarized masculinity in producing state nationalist discourses, yet, paradoxically, the period of military service might be better seen as a time of emasculation or desexualization. Men complain about their girlfriends cheating on them or leaving them during their tenure in the military, and most are certain that their intimate relations will change after their time in the military. Rumors of rape by career military officers abound. Although masculine privilege has been seen as legitimized through military service and its national importance, these privileges did not seem to be felt or noted by the young men with whom I spoke, given the transformations in women's roles that have occurred within the last few decades. Successful athletes achieve hypervisibility as national heroes, whereas young men in the collective realm of the military remain largely invisible, especially to women. The capitalist masculinity represented by athletes actively involves women in the national fantasy of global competition, but the military continues to exclude women, except in the context of the abstract family in need of protection and of mothers who sacrifice their sons to the state. Even though the rhetoric of female empowerment and female equality now permeate public discourses about a new feminism or a postfeminist era in South Korean society, mandatory military conscription exists as proof that men continue to deserve privileges (in the workplace and at home) because of their national "sacrifices." Some men jokingly mentioned that women should also be required to go into the military, but it was never a serious assertion by anyone (man or woman) with whom I spoke.

When told of the military exemption, a few of my Korean American respondents, especially younger men, noted that the opportunity to get out of military duty must work as a great incentive for players to push beyond their normal level of play. The performance of Korean players in the United States allows Korean Americans to participate in a Korean national event without the added responsibilities of South Korean national citizenship. Korean male athletes demonstrate how a Korean male subject might achieve a level of national success without having to serve in the military. They also demonstrate how Korean American men might potentially come to represent a global Koreanness as fighting warriors for the global Korean nation.

My discussions with Korean American men tended to elide the significance of the South Korean state, which, by incentivizing sporting victory, continues to play a major role in the success of Korean male athletes. The contingencies of the military exemption highlight the "graduated sovereignties" of the athletes themselves (Ong 2007). They may be global stars, but they continue to have obligations (that the state might or might not waive) as South Korean able-bodied men. In addition, Korean men who serve in the military demonstrate the limits of ideological representation. Although many who have not yet served assumed that the state policy was appropriate, the men with whom I spoke raised important concerns about equity for all citizens and about the lack of recognition for their own service and sacrifice to the nation.

Asian American Masculinities

Although the popularity of Korean male athletes draws primarily from their status as South Korean national icons, they are racialized as Asian male athletes in the United States. Given the history of Asian male images in mainstream mass media, they represent a new kind of Asian male body. Asian and Asian American players have become a regular presence in MLB and in the NBA and PGA. Considerable numbers of Pacific Islanders, especially Samoans and Tongans, compete in the NFL.[12] These athletes present new dimensions of Asian American masculinity, and they complicate stereotypical narratives of Asian male emasculation and perversity that have characterized the history of Asian male racial representations throughout the nineteenth and twentieth centuries. Korean athletes, as well as other Asian athletes, also bring attention to the role of transnational movement and migration in the production of Asian American masculinities in the twenty-first century.

This section situates Korean athletes within the context of Asian American critique and foregrounds Asian American reception to representations of Korean and Korean American athletes. The power of this new sporting figure is situated in the context of past anxieties about Asian male racial representation. Rather than resolving the anxieties of Asian American masculinity, this new transnational Asian/American masculinity points to the privileged position of heterosexual masculinity in defining national and transnational subjectivities, and it suggests that White privilege continues to shape dominant representations of masculinity. Although the Korean athlete may offer new ways of representing Asian/American masculinity, the interpretation of these masculinities continues to be informed by national and transnational histories of race.

Masculinity has been a popular subject of Asian American critique, and it constitutes an especially fraught dimension of Asian American cultural politics (Eng 2001; Nguyen 2002).[13] As scholars point out, the history of racism has been sexualized through the pseudoscience of eugenics, legal prohibitions against intermarriage, and representations of Asian men as a sexual threat (Koshy 2004; Shah 2001).[14] Indeed, throughout U.S. history, there exists a meager corpus of images of Asian men, which is dominated by representations of Asian men as emasculated, effeminate, subservient, shifty, cunning, and alien (Eng 2001; R. Lee 1999). In popular images of the late nineteenth century and throughout the twentieth century, Asian male characters in mass media were often conveyed as sexual deviants. A popular narrative cast them as sexual predators who threatened the White American family by using cunning and deception to lure White women into depraved lifestyles (Lui 2004).[15] Within these narratives, the Asian male is considered biologically inferior to the White male, and the Asian male can never be a figure who would "naturally" attract a White female. Therefore, it is only through force, deception, bribery, or purchase that the corrupt Asian male is able to express his perverse sexuality.

The images of Asian threat have been an important part of the repertoire of Asian male sexuality, yet a great number of caricatures of Asian men throughout the nineteenth and twentieth centuries present the feminization of Asian men in relation to White men. Images of Asian men as effeminate and physically inferior to other races are drawn from orientalist stereotypes of Asian men as colonial subjects. According to this rather sweeping colonial logic, as subjects of decadent and effeminate societies, Asian men were not able to rule themselves, and they needed to be reformed and ruled by White men from the West (Said 1978). In the United States, Asian men, when represented at all, were often portrayed as submissively engaging in "women's work."[16] Popular depictions of Asian men as coolies, servants, laundry men, or service employees functioned to present the image of a docile and subservient Asian male figure. After the Immigration and Nationality Act of 1965, the image of the Asian "geek" in Hollywood films presented a new image of desexualized Asian manhood in the figure of the middle-class Asian immigrant.[17] Within popular representations, Asian men were presented as docile, hard-working, and family-oriented, and they were essentially unthreatening to White masculinity (Nguyen and Tu 2007).

It is difficult to make sweeping generalizations about the global satellite television era, but by the turn of the twenty-first century, there were more images of Asian American male actors in mainstream U.S.-based roles. Defying stereotypes, a few Asian men have emerged as central figures in commercial mass media productions and been given complex characterization. Beyond film and dramatic television, reality television and televised competitions emerged as a context for Asian male characters who defied stereotypes. There has also been an increase in images of transnational Asian male stars, including martial arts film figures such as Chow Yun Fat, Jet Li, and Jackie Chan, as well as athletes such as Yao Ming and Hideki Matsui. The emergence of these representations has generated new narratives, if not a significant shift, in depictions of Asian men in mainstream mass media.

Shaping Asian American Masculinities through Sport

The Korean athlete emerges within the context of this proliferation of images of Asian masculinity within the landscape of mainstream mass media.[18] Media sport differs from other forms of mainstream media since it is anchored to live sporting competitions. Sporting news, commentary, and advertising certainly play a large and connected role, but the power of media sport is based on the unpredictable and undetermined outcome of a live competition. This competition relies on the idea of fair play during each match, as mandated by the rules and regulated by the referees. According to the idea of fair play, the better performing team or athlete in any particular match should win. Clearly, these are ideals (ideologies) behind sport that come with many caveats, but the assumptions of fair play and indeterminacy of a competition form the implicit agreement made between fans/viewers/consumers and the commercial producers of media sport. These ideals also become the basis for explaining the significance of Asian athletes within the history of Asian male stereotypes.

In athletic competition, bodily skill is expressed relative to other racialized bodies in a structured yet largely undetermined media production. Unlike bodies in other media genres, sporting bodies depend not only on the representation of the body but also on the very workings of the body itself—its power, movement, responsiveness, and agility. An authenticity is accorded to an athlete's body mastery that is not given to other celebrities' gym- and supplement-built bodies. Although the celebrity status of the athlete in Korean/American mass media might seem to blur the boundaries between athlete and pop star, the star status of the athlete originates from his athletic skill and proven success. The bodies and the associated performance offer evidence of the size, strength, and power of the Asian male. This image conveys a new image of Asian masculinity—a powerful, competitive, physical, large, wealthy, disciplined, traveling, and sexualized masculinity.

Prior to the regular emergence of Asian athletes in the late twentieth century, the figure of the martial arts star exemplified by Bruce Lee emerged as an exception to the rule of Asian male emasculation (Hamamoto 1994; Prashad 2003; Tasker 1997). The body of the martial arts figure has been seen by Asian American critics as a particularly distinct type of Asian masculinity that emerged in the context of the Cold War and the Vietnam War, and the figure of Bruce Lee has been hailed as a symbol of radical Asian American politics.[19] Darrell Hamamoto argues that Bruce Lee had an important effect in Asian American communities by offering Asian American men a new kind of athletic representation. He states, "For most Asian Americans, Bruce Lee struck a blow against white racism with each high-velocity punch he delivered" (1994, 61). Lee's body represented the tight and small, yet powerful, male who stood up to "Western" men—both White and African American—and succeeded in body-to-body competition.[20]

Yvonne Tasker (1997) discusses Bruce Lee as a martial arts figure who represented a kind of "oriental" asceticism and anticolonial resistance through his hidden strength, quiet approach, and wise cunning, despite his smaller size. She also points out that Lee was presented as having only one real weapon, his body, and through the hardness of his body, he was able to defeat his enemies. Tasker's depiction does, however, note that this depiction continues to depend on stereotypes of Asians as small, quiet, and cunning individuals. Nevertheless, the new Asian body represented by athletes is not one of "hidden strength" or "surprising power." Rather, the new Asian ath-

lete exists as a large man who has the strength, height, and muscles to prove
his masculinity. He has commercial sponsors, media coverage, and wealth.
He offers a mainstream, highly visible commercial representation of Asian
male power. The wealthy, powerful, commodified, and large Asian male
athlete functions to create an Asian version of the visible "global body."

In a rather basic way, the bodies of Korean male athletes disprove theories
of biological inferiority that are based in a history of scientific racism. Korean
male athletes are able to compete as physical equals on the global stage. Athletes quell national anxieties about size as their bodies are shaped and condi-
tioned to the modal standards of elite, White athletes.[21] Size might be considered a South Korean national fetish, making players' body height and weight
more interesting than their level of play or professional success. The biological statistics of various athletes—weight, height, age—operate as an objective
statement of their physical power and virility. Their vital statistics are flashed
on screen as objective and hard "data." Their strong bodies are witnessed in
motion through the television screen or live in the stadium. Their bodies are
also analyzed in sporting magazines and newspapers that break down their
body parts into various segments for analysis. These moving bodies operate
as visual evidence of these athletes' physical strength, and they evoke a visceral reaction in viewers who are well rehearsed in the practices of viewing.

The image of the Korean male athlete involves the Asian American viewing subject within narratives of transnational desire.[22] Asian male sports
stars force Asian American viewers to confront the transnational as a fact
in the production of racialized images within the United States. Although
mainstream media outlets continue to convey U.S.-Chinese relations as dubious at best (Chuh and Shimakawa 2001), basketball player Yao Ming's
entry into the U.S. market was legitimated by his capitalist profit potential.
As China's "national treasure," Yao's nickname—"The Dynasty"—was seen
as appropriate in describing his appeal to commercial interests in the United
States as well as in Asia, China, and its diasporas. Mainstream U.S. newspapers hailed him as a Chinese national who came from the "world's biggest
country, untapped market of 1.3 billion, including 12 million from his hometown of Shanghai."[23] There was much skepticism about Yao when he first
entered the NBA, but he silenced his initial detractors with his success in both
athletic and commercial arenas. He is now considered the new 7-foot-5-inch
"walking marketing machine" and the "face of globalization" in basketball
and U.S. sports.[24] As "metacommodities" (Appadurai 1996), sports players
such as Yao Ming appeal to audiences around the world and operate within

multiple markets through privatized telecommunications channels to sell everything from credit cards and computers to food products and sports paraphernalia.[25]

These players exemplify what L.H.M. Ling (1999) refers to as a "global hypermasculinity" in their roles as symbols and agents of global capital of and for East Asian nations. To prove the internationalism of U.S. sports, the foreign national identities of these players are vigorously maintained. In some cases, this identity is legislated and regulated by a foreign state, as in the case of Yao Ming's tax obligations to China and in the case of military obligation and exemptions for South Korean players. In other cases, the commodification of athletes is encouraged and emphasized by corporate and national interests that are bound to profit through this commercial promotion of national pride and loyalty. This transnational display of nationalism benefits the sport industrial complex in East Asian countries and the United States by shoring up new television and commercial markets through the production and strategic assertion of national desire.

With Yao Ming's initial popularity, many NBA arenas used Chinese-sponsored promotions to attract local Asian/American populations. However, given the significance of transnational connections, there seems to be minimal attention given to an Asian American audience by commercial interests. Instead of shaping a kind of Asian American racial connection, representations of athletes shape an ethnonational identification with viewers in the United States. In other words, Korean Americans do not necessarily see Yao Ming as a hero or an icon. Chinese Americans do not necessarily feel an affinity for Hideki Matsui. Moreover, tensions between nationally identified groups shape national identifications with athletes. I never heard a Korean American of any generation speak with admiration for Japanese or Japanese American athletes. Nation-specific identification in Asian American communities challenges the notion of an Asian American panethnic audience. Although scholars have pointed out the political roots of the Asian racial category in the United States, sport and other forms of popular culture also play a significant role in shaping attitudes about race, and these attitudes may offer hints about the limited political potentialities of the Asian American category.

Cross-racial Identifications

There is an assumption (or wish) made on the part of corporations and the South Korean state that all or most Koreans, regardless of nationality, support

Korean players, but the responses of many Korean Americans, especially Korean American youth who identify as American, seem to demonstrate a variety of investments in sport and challenge any simple assumptions regarding racial or national identification.

Twenty-four-year-old Lawrence Kim discussed his love for sport with me in a café in Los Angeles's Koreatown. He had attended University High School in Irvine, California, he went to UCLA for college, and he was currently working as a bank clerk in the Park La Brea area very close to Koreatown. As we talked about sports, he stated that his true interests were not in Korean players but in "the best players" in any sport. He truly believed that the best sports in the world were played in the United States and that the best players in U.S. sports were the best players in the world. He thought football (soccer) was boring and did not want to discuss the World Cup with me, given his lack of interest in this global sport. As a self-proclaimed sports fanatic, he was offended that I would assume that he followed Korean soccer players simply because of their background. Kim had sporting loyalties that were based in regional loyalties to both Orange County and Los Angeles teams. He grew up in Orange County, but he also felt strongly affiliated with Los Angeles teams, especially due to his love for the Lakers NBA team. Though he was willing to discuss Korean players, he didn't think there was a particular need to discuss them separately from their teams or their contribution to their particular sports. As the child of immigrants, he did admit that his parents were heavily invested in Korean athletes and that he was probably more in tune with their status than the average American, yet he wanted to make it clear that he tried to steer clear of Korean nationalist interests in his sports fandom. During the Olympics, he rooted for the U.S. national team because he was American, and he seemed rather upset that I might have assumed otherwise.

Kim represents views shared by many of my Korean American male respondents who considered themselves sports fans. Many of them played sports themselves and often participated in basketball, softball, or volleyball leagues that were organized through Korean American churches. Most hung out with fellow Korean American friends regularly and watched major sporting events together, such as the NBA Finals and the Super Bowl, but they did not express a close identification with Korean male athletes as role models or as "representatives of the (South Korean) nation." Instead, I sensed that their identifications were stronger with the icons who played their favorite sports and on their favorite teams.

One day, I observed a pickup game between Korean American men in a park in a suburban subdivision of Hacienda Heights. The six young men on the court played basketball using a kind of "street slang" drawn from African American speech represented in commercial basketball and hip hop culture. They cursed incessantly and also likened their moves to talented basketball players who were primarily African American, such as Dwayne Wade, Paul Pierce, and Kobe Bryant. Clearly, the racial identifications of Korean Americans were not limited to identifications with Korean or Asian male athletes. The Korean American men were mimicking hegemonic modes of representation in basketball largely determined by a Black popular aesthetic.

There have been many critics who have commented on hegemonic Black masculinities in U.S. sport, yet the modes of fan and viewer identification with African American athletes are complex and contradictory. The global superstardom of figures such as Michael Jordan and Tiger Woods demonstrates the complicated relationships between racial representation and sport. Scholars point out that the "raceless" qualities of these stars stem from their commercial brand marketing and the disconnect of sport with history and politics (Andrews 2001). Although no athlete or fan transcends race, fan affinities for athletes are far more complicated than simple affiliations that connect fans of a particular race, nationality, or ethnicity with athletes of the same identification. Fan affinities are often based in institutional, regional, or familial associations. They are based on a particular athlete's style, looks, biography, and personality. They also draw from the commercialization and branding of particular players.

The self-styled modeling of Korean American golfer Anthony Kim seems to be based on the HBO television series *Entourage,* which is a show based around the everyday life of a Hollywood actor and his loyal friends who accompany him to social events.[26] After turning pro in 2006, Anthony Kim became known as the PGA's wild man who drank heavily, womanized, and hung out with a crew of loyal friends who acted as his "wingmen." He came to represent a new kind of golf superstar who embraces a reality show–like celebrity through conspicuous consumption and tabloid attention. Biographical features on Kim often mention his well-publicized split with his controlling father and their eventual reconciliation. By distancing himself from his overbearing father, Kim invented himself as his own person and thereby disconnected himself from a kind of stifling patriarchal Koreanness.

In a *Sports Illustrated* special feature, Anthony Kim is presented as a party boy living with his three best friends and his dogs in a Dallas mansion.[27] He comes across as a young buck who enjoys the company of attractive women but still maintains his single status. Kim is presented as a "raceless" celebrity athlete who has welcomed media attention in his personal life. In contrast to the pre–sex scandal celebrity of Tiger Woods, Kim embraces cameras, discusses his game openly, and flirts with the media gossip about his personal life. His presentation of himself blurs the boundaries between athletic success and reality television boorishness. This kind of personality-based celebrity offers a new kind of narrative of Asian/American masculinity through its ability to go beyond the anxieties around representation to an unselfconscious presentation of his life off the golf course.

Kim can be said to represent a kind of frat boy White male masculinity that rejects the significance of race or class and presents a narrative that is based on a work-hard/party-hard ethos. Media coverage focuses on his individual talent in addition to his self-indulgent, consumption-fueled pursuits of pleasure. He is rarely grouped together with other Korean players, unlike most of the other Korean nationals. Without the burden of representing the nation, which is often imposed by U.S. mass media, Korean mass media, and the Korean state, Kim can be seen as a minority athlete who is now able to go beyond race as a primary mode of identification. Nevertheless, he continues to be covered in South Korean and Korean American media as a Korean athlete, and regardless of his own position on identity politics, he continues to be followed as a Korean American.

These cross-racial identifications highlight the problematic relationship of contemporary representations of Korean male athletes and Asian American identity politics. Cross-racial identifications seem to suggest that Korean American men are able to pick and choose their own self-representation from a confusing mix of racial signifiers that are disconnected from history. However, previous stereotypes and their limitations continue to haunt Asian American male representations, and the expectation of minority representation continues to play a role in the lives of minority athletes.

Claiming Asian/American Masculinities

In relation to the past history of limiting stereotypes, the new representations can be seen as opening possibilities for reading Asian American masculinities in a number of ways, but in this conclusion, I would like to suggest that moving beyond the limitations of stereotypes requires dealing with their harmful effects. Some effective ways of countering Asian male stereotypes might be found in the popular films *Better Luck Tomorrow* and *Harold and Kumar Go to White Castle*. These films aggravate anxieties around Asian male masculinities by presenting Asian male protagonists who directly engage their own racial emasculation and are thereby able to overcome the limitations of racial expectations to express masculine power in surprising ways. The performance of stereotype in these films operates as racial parody, and these racial parodies work precisely due to their rootedness in history (see J. Jackson 2008). The iteration of these stereotypes might help the Asian American viewer "disidentify" with the stereotype (Muñoz 1999). However, the question remains whether there can be ways to imagine Asian American masculinities beyond or outside these stereotypes. Furthermore, the masculinity of the characters depends to a troubling degree on homophobic humor as a way to express heterosexual anxieties.

David Eng (2001) demonstrates the importance of situating Asian American masculinities within the historical contexts of their emergence. As in the images of the past, the most recent images of Asian men are not of Asian Americans' choosing.[28] The emergence of Asian sports stars is more a result of the attempts by sporting industries to expand into global capital markets than it is a push for more inclusive racial representation within a domestic market. Even though these images are not a product of Asian American self-representation, I would still insist on claiming them as Asian American. It is difficult not to see the Asian sports star as an improvement from the persistent images of the weak and submissive Asian male, but the desire to reproduce essentialist notions of race and heterosexist notions of gender and sexuality through "revised" images continues to exist as a dangerous one. In attempting to think of the significance of these images to Asian American men, I find the following questions to be particularly important:

What is psychically required of the Asian American male subject who desires to be part of dominant mainstream society? How is the Asian American male subject encouraged or coerced to see himself in a social order governed by race and racism? How does he unconsciously or unwittingly contribute to the perpetuation of his already contested existence? (Eng 2001, 22–23)

Eng points out that the "psychic salvation for the Asian American male cannot be the monopoly of a masculinist compulsory sexuality" (2001, 136). As players such as Yao Ming enter mainstream U.S. sports, they reproduce the ruling ideologies of global capital that erase the past histories of colonialism and imperialism, diminish the unequal relations of labor between Asia and the United States, and make invisible the unequal terms by which these relations are structured. Emergent discourses of Asian and Asian American masculinity are dangerous if they are part of an attempt to recuperate Asian American men from a past history of emasculation in favor of a present that prioritizes the accumulation of wealth above all else. Asians may be hypervisible within the transnational realm of commercial sports, but these images do not make up for the loss that comes from an erased Asian American history—one of imperialism and war, labor exploitation, homophobia, racism, exclusion, internment, and anti-Asian violence.

Can we interpret the emergence of representations of masculinized Asian males as symptomatic of a growing well-educated middle class of Asian American men who are in the process of reclaiming their masculinity through their pocketbooks? Certainly, this could be one audience. Nevertheless, beyond the few individual Asian athletes, Asian American men as complex individuals continue to remain largely invisible in most realms of mainstream media. Although Asian athletes as individuals represent a diasporic elite, they exist as media sites around which transnational ideas are apprehended by mainstream audiences.

The rise of Asian male athletes seems to present anxieties for the Asian American critic/observer who has relied heavily on U.S.-based racial identity politics, but this does not seem to haunt Asian American youth to the same extent. I am thinking about a younger generation of Asian Americans who log on to transnational websites to read about their favorite Asian/American sports players and entertainers, share anime with youth in other countries, and create cyber friendships within and across borders. It seems they have a greater ability to accept the transnational as part of their racialized experiences. Those who have fought long and hard through civil rights struggles based around U.S. racial political histories, student fights against discrimination and dehumanization, and the battle for Asian American Studies may feel dismayed at what might seem to be a lack of a historical understanding of racial formation in the United States, as well as a lack of commitment to racial justice through existing political channels by so-called "transnationalists." In the face of diasporic nationalism, it may be more difficult to build an Asian American political solidarity, but this may signal the need to move away from U.S.-focused, race-based identity politics to the "kung fu politics" of polyculturalism (Prashad 2003)—one that doesn't insist on definite iden-tity categories and is dedicated to struggles for justice and equality across gender, sexuality, nation, and race.

Whereas this chapter focuses on various ways of reading the figure of the Korean male athlete, the next chapter analyzes the Korean female athlete and how the figure of the female athlete offers an important demonstration of the ideal neoliberal subject of South Korea's globalization through the im-age of the hyperfeminine Asian/American global subject. As R. W. Connell (2005) and many others have pointed out, masculinities and femininities are articulated in relation to each other, and a relational understanding offers insight into the negotiations of power that take place in the articulations of meaning. In both of these chapters, I evoke the heterogeneous and unstable terrain of masculinities and femininities that are expressed within media sport through a number of different readings of the discourses of gender and sexuality in sex-segregated contexts. I highlight the contested nature of these masculinities and femininities within and across national borders. I also demonstrate the centrality of narratives of masculinities and femininities to political projects that take place around global Koreanness and Asian/American transnationalisms. The viewing subject relates to masculinities and femininities through identifications, misrecognitions, and disidentifica-tions that demonstrate the impossibility of stating for certain how these representations will be interpreted. I offer readings that highlight what I understand to be "everyday" understandings of these narratives of gender and sexuality and how these everyday meanings work to shape hegemonic ideas about nation and transnation. A gendered reading is particularly im-portant since discourses of gender and sexuality expressed through media sport contribute to the ideological power of global Koreanness and play a constitutive role in shaping the character of transnationalisms.

Traveling Ladies

NEOLIBERALISM AND THE FEMALE ATHLETE

The climax of the South Korean blockbuster monster flick *Koemul*[1] presents a final human confrontation with the so-called "host," a mutant amphibious creature that has been terrorizing Seoul by consuming human victims along the banks of the Han River.[2] When the monster bounds into the scene, the U.S. military attacks it with a biochemical weapon called "Agent Yellow." Clearly compromised, it writhes in a yellow chemical haze. Meanwhile, unemployed college graduate Pak Nam-il and a homeless man he has met under a bridge conspire to end its life. The homeless man pours a canister of gas over the monster while Pak Nam-il throws Molotov cocktails. Despite his substantive experience hurling these firebombs, he can't seem to hit the gas-doused creature, and his last burning green *soju* bottle slips from his hand and shatters at his feet. In an instant, Pak Nam-il's sister, Pak Nam-ju, who happens to be a champion archer, pierces a burning cloth that is lying amidst glass shards with her arrow. She confidently shoots the blazing arrow straight into the monster's mouth and lights it aflame. Turning from the monster, she calmly walks away in slow motion, her hair dancing before a fiery backdrop. The disciplined skill of the female athlete, who remains cool and in control, is able to accomplish the task that cannot be completed by other parties, including U.S. and South Korean military forces, peaceful "civil society" protestors who have gathered to oppose the use of biochemical weapons, and her college-educated brother.

The character of Pak Nam-ju, as a transnational female athlete, exemplifies a new kind of national hero in an era of neoliberal social and economic transformations. As an alternative to the tactics of authoritarian military

Figure 9. Image from *Koemul* (*The Host*).

regimes and democracy movements, she presents new ways of accomplishing the challenges set forth by global competition. She pursues the task of national rescue through her disciplined poise amidst immense pressure and her self-focused will that stands apart from entrenched institutions. The success of the female athlete works to circulate feelings of national accomplishment that resolve contradictions of neoliberal globalization. Korean female athletes are held up as examples of how South Korean subjects might engage in global competition yet avoid serious engagement with domestic crises, such as increasing social inequality, conflicts around gender roles, vast generational differences, and disappearing economic opportunities. Representations of the female athlete work to suspend these social anxieties not by offering real solutions but by working through affective attachments to the national family.

Anthony Lane, in his glowing review of *Koemul* for the *New Yorker*, finds the figure of the female archer as fantastical as the monster itself.[3] Lane sees the film as a science-fiction flick that evokes a glorious past of the genre that doesn't take itself too seriously. On the contrary, I would argue that the unmatched appeal of *Koemul* as the highest-grossing film in South Korean history has to do with much more than its "camp" value.[4] The popularity of *Koemul* can be partly attributed to the narrative, with its biting critique of U.S. power in South Korea and its portrayal of the apocalyptic state of a nation in crisis; its high production values; and the popularity of the actors. However, it is important to note that its widespread popularity with a South Korean national audience is closely connected with the affective "realness" of the film. *Koemul* is articulated in an affective context that is shaped within dramatic neoliberal transformations, including widespread privatization of media industries, changing gender roles, and the increasing ideological emphasis on self-reliance and individual competition. As a representation of the female athlete as national hero, the character of Pak Nam-ju as champion archer feels quite plausible and "real" in a Korean affective context. Archery remains one of the most popular female-dominated sports in South Korea, especially in the Olympic Games. The scene described above offers a recognizable view of national anticipation and success in the moment she hits her target.

Koemul presents a spectacular demonstration of the place of the Korean female athlete as neoliberal subject par excellence. Just as representations of masculinity in media sport shape ideas of global Koreanness, the figure of the female athlete works as an agent in conveying ideas of Koreanness in an era of neoliberal transformations. Part II of this book attempts to demonstrate a variety of ways in which Korean athletes function as sites for the production of gendered discourses of Korean and U.S. nationalisms and how they operate to (mass-)mediate relationships among gender, consumption, and nationalism within transnational contexts. Going beyond a consideration of athletes as simply reflecting socioeconomic changes in South Korea and Korean America, I am interested in how representations of athletes work to shape understandings about the nation. In this chapter, I explore how the female athlete generates and circulates the affects of neoliberalism. Sara Ahmed argues, "In affective economies, emotions do things, and they align individuals with communities—or bodily space with social space—through the very intensity of their attachments" (2004, 119). The representations of athletes in media sport produce some of the most intensely affective frames for shaping and producing national emotions.

Korean female athletes demonstrate how contemporary discourses of national identity are shaped through the gendered, classed, racialized, and sexualized narratives of transnational media (Grewal 2005; Mankekar 1999a; Schein 1999). As I argued in chapter 3, transnational mediations of the athletic body produce gendered ideologies of the nation in professional media sport, which proliferate through the media-saturated and celebrity-centered worlds of South Korean and Korean American public cultures. Although the narratives of masculinity and femininity work together, the meanings around male and female athletes differ in important ways. In this chapter, I detail the discourses of nation and gender that inform media coverage of Korean female athletes who compete in international contexts. I demonstrate how ideas of Korean womanhood and nation intersect in the processes of national and transnational meaning-making around these female athletes. I track their emergence as important neoliberal transformations and detail not only how Korean female athletes are a result of these transformations but also how they shape understandings of the economic and social changes that began in the late 1990s.

The emergence of female athletes in archery, the LPGA, and figure skating all work to constitute a particular media genre that presents a particular kind of relationship between nation and gender. By genre, I draw from the definition offered by Lauren Berlant, who refers to genre as an "aesthetic structure of affective expectation" (2008, 4). As a way to evoke this media genre, this chapter focuses primarily on the LPGA as the most visible context for the transmission of media images of Korean female athletes. The LPGA constitutes an important part of the media landscapes that connect South Korea and Korean America. Korean female golf icons function as translocal symbols of Koreanness that travel both physically (as athletes on a professional touring circuit) and digitally (through transnational media networks). Young Korean golfers materialize fantasies of neoliberal subjecthood by fashioning themselves as productive laboring subjects in the global economy through narratives of discipline, competition, and flexibility as they pursue golf-centered dreams underwritten by private capital. In transnational mass media, their sexuality is presented in contradictory ways—as daughters to be protected within the patriarchal Korean family and as hypersexualized Asian women to be marketed in transnational capitalist contexts.

An important reason to focus on the LPGA lies in the fact that the intensely affective attachment to female athletes began with the incredible success of golfer Se Ri Pak. As the first successful South Korean national in the LPGA, Se Ri Pak won two out of the four major tournaments on the LPGA tour during her rookie year of 1998. Her performances saturated Korean and Korean American media coverage, and by the end of the golf season, she was deemed a national hero by President Kim Dae Jung. Her initial successes occurred while the nation was reeling from the trauma of the Asian financial crisis, and, clearly, her importance was intensified during this period of immense social anxiety. She came to symbolize how South Korea might pull itself out of the crisis through global competitiveness, individual drive, and private capital.

Her wins at the U.S. Open and the McDonald's Championship were particularly significant since they occurred on a U.S.—some might say international—stage. She became a figure of national triumph, like a phoenix rising from the ashes of a collapsed financial system. Her win at the U.S. Open induced a burst of national emotion, and this feeling of intense national victory became a highly commodified national feeling that circulated through commercial media and advertising. In a television ad for Samsung's Anycall cellular phone, images of Se Ri Pak playing golf, including images from the 1998 U.S. Open Championship, are superimposed with the following text:

Uri ka ŏryŏul ttae, kŭ nyŏ nŭn uri ŭi him i toe ŏtda. / Uri ka chich'yŏ issŭl ttae, kŭ nyŏ nŭn uri ŭi miso ka toe ŏssŭbnita. / Tasi, kŭ nyŏ ŭi miso rŭl pogosib sŭbnida. Chigŭm aenik'ol ŭl ha seyo. [In our difficulty, she became our strength. / In our weariness, she gave us a reason to smile. / We want to see that smile again. Please use Anycall now.]

At the end of the commercial, evocative black-and-white photographs recount the emotional ending to her U.S. Open win, and a female voice whispers, "Tangsin ŭi han madi ka him i toebnida. Pak Se Ri hwa-i-t'ing!" (One word [of encouragement] can make a difference. Se Ri Pak fighting!). The ad ends with a photo of Se Ri Pak in tears of joy with an image of two cellular phones and the text ŏnje ŏdisona Han'gugin ŭn aenik'ol (whenever or wherever, Koreans use Anycall).

Samsung advertisements linking her golf victories to the country's economic woes helped shape her commercial image and reinforced her representational status as a national hero. Since Pak's success, these feelings of national emotion are eagerly sought by mass media and state interests, and they are reflected in the investment in and anticipation of success in such spectacular events. A decade after Pak's debut, the LPGA continued to inspire global capitalist aspirations in young Korean females. In 2009, the number of Korean women in the LPGA soared, and Korean-identified teenagers and women comprised more than one-tenth of the active players in the U.S.-based tour.[5] The explosion of Korean female golfers in international competition raises important questions about the social, political, and cultural contexts that have enabled the extraordinary growth and now ubiquitous presence of female golfers who hail from South Korea.

This chapter establishes the multidimensional significance of the Korean female golfer as a way to connect the emotional power of the Korean athlete with narratives of nation and transnation. First, I detail the place of the Korean female golfer as a powerful symbol of the relationship between the

Figure 10. Samsung Anycall television commercial
with Pak Se Ri, 1999.

Korean nation and transnational capital. The icon of the successful Korean
female golfer symbolizes the competitive place of South Korea in the global
economy. Furthermore, golfers operate to represent the gendered labor that
characterizes the workforce in developing nations. The disciplining of the
female golfer's body resonates with the disciplining of the Asian female
laborer in the transnational global economy.[6] Hegemonic discourses that
describe the athletic practices of Korean female golfers conjure visions of
the disciplined Asian female body as mechanized labor for transnational
corporations. Associated with the production of gendered forms of labor are
the patriarchal relationships of familial reproduction represented by female
players. Patriarchal kinship relations are reproduced on a transnational stage
through the hegemonic representations of Korean women as daughters of a
male-headed family and nation. The production of female golfers as daughters operates to assert notions of tradition (read: gender inequality and subordination to men) within diasporic contexts (see Mankekar 1999a). I argue
that a Korean patriarchal nationalism is rearticulated through these transnational routes.

The chapter then focuses on the Korean female golf star as she is represented within U.S. national contexts. Korean female golfers are situated
within the U.S.-based industry of the LPGA. The corporate multiculturalism
promoted by the LPGA demonstrates how racial and national differences are
sublated into the corporate contexts of the LPGA. The commercial successes
of Korean and other international players have been actively encouraged
through the targeted circulation of media productions and related commodi-

ties throughout the world. Korean female players have "revitalized" the LPGA by offering opportunities for growth heretofore untapped. I also look at the flap around an English-only policy that was proposed by LPGA management and how this controversy highlighted the complicated negotiations of nation and multiculturalism that take place within a globalizing sport in the United States.

Finally, this chapter investigates the production of compulsory heterosexuality in the figure of the female golf star. The LPGA, as a media sport industry, has emphasized the sexuality of female golf stars as a way to increase fan interest. The hyperfemininity of Korean female golfers promotes a hegemonic heterosexuality in women's professional sport, as their "look" caters to the imagined gaze of heterosexual men. The emphasis on the sexualized "straight" female body operates to assuage corporate anxieties over perceived lesbianism and lesbian aesthetics in golf and, more broadly, organized women's sport. The discourses of sexuality around these players are now produced in and through transnational contexts.

The following analysis attempts to convey the polyvalent discourses of nation and gender that constitute the array of meanings mediated through the Korean female athlete. It attempts to understand the global connections that might be read and understood through the figure of the female athlete. The golfers of the LPGA operate as sites for transnational connections among sports fans, aspirational middle classes in South Korea and the United States, media sport industries, media consumers, and professional and leisure golfers. These connections reveal the complicated ways that mediated images and ideas are transferred across spaces and bodies, creating powerful feelings of national belonging.

Korean Ladies in Global Competition

As of July 2011, 43 of the 123 international players in the LPGA were South Korean.[7] The list of international players did not include the increasing numbers of Korean-born players who have become naturalized U.S. citizens or dual citizens and Korean Americans born in the U.S., including Christina Kim and media darling Michelle Wie.[8] This accounting of current Korean players did not indicate the large numbers of Korean and Korean American professionals, juniors, and amateurs vying for a spot in the LPGA. Though this may seem almost naturalized, the visible presence of female players with Korean heritage[9] began a little over a decade ago with Se Ri Pak in

1998.[10] In 2004, the *Los Angeles Times* reported that "Pak is credited with almost single-handedly changing the face of women's golf."[11] Pak has been followed by a great number of South Koreans and Korean Americans who have now established a visible Korean presence in golf tournaments and have indeed reshaped the cultural landscape of the LPGA.[12]

Golf in South Korea is connected to colonial histories, as the sport was first practiced by the Japanese colonial military elite and U.S. occupying forces (Kim and Joo 2004).[13] Consumer desires for golf might be traced, in part, to these indelible historical pasts. Chungmoo Choi (1993) argues that consumer desires for particular "foreign" commodities demonstrate the internalized effects and enduring significance of postcolonial political and economic asymmetries. Though the political history of golf in South Korea offers significant insight into its elite foundations and symbolic importance, the contemporary expansion of golf and golf-related commodities must be situated within the processes of economic liberalization, the rapid emergence of an urban middle class, and the global production of consumer desires through transnational mass media (Kendall 1996; Nelson 2000).

Golf has become a status symbol in South Korea because of the associated meanings of wealth, privilege, and power that accompany the sport. During the past decade, there has been a frenzied explosion of golf with a reckless construction of golf courses; the purchase of elite club memberships and greens fees; the sale of golf-related goods and services; golf television programs and cable channels; golf educational institutes; golf-related websites; and visual, digital, and print media coverage on and about golf. Golf has now become one of the most popular stated reasons for leisure travel abroad as South Koreans travel to the Philippines, China, and Indonesia for the express purpose of playing golf. The expansion of golf has dramatically changed the landscapes of South Korea, filling sightlines with golf courses, rooftop driving ranges, and golf-related advertising.[14]

An expanding segment of elite and upper-middle-class consumers has fueled the growth of golf-related sales in South Korea. Shin and Nam point out,

> The average member initiation fee for country clubs in Korea is nearly U.S. $170,000. Daily green fees for members are on average [$50] and for nonmembers $100 on weekdays. Weekend fees are roughly $30 higher than weekday fees to both members and nonmembers. Golf in Korea is lavish. (2004, 236)

These costs are truly astounding, given the fact that the average annual household income is less than $20,000. The growing markets for golf point to the particular trend toward overconsumption in aspirational middle classes. As anthropologist Laura Nelson (2000) argues, there is a great concern about these trends toward *kwasobi,* or overconsumption, in South Korea by policymakers and government officials. From the 1990s to the present moment, *kwasobi ch'ubang* (prevention of overconsumption) campaigns have attempted to curtail excessive spending, conspicuous consumption, and credit card debt and default (Nelson 2004). The "national obsession" with golf, however, seems to indicate that these campaigns are having limited success. Government directives toward consumer restraint are contradicted by the valorization of professional golfers as national heroes and by the entrepreneurial and consumer dreams they inspire.

The production of female golf stars as national heroes has turned mass-mediated golf into a national pastime. Mass media have, in some ways, worked to proletarianize golf. Although the actual practice of golf on the greens is largely understood as an upper- and upper-middle-class pursuit, national media represent golf as a sport that can be accessed and consumed by anyone through television, the Internet, magazines, and newspapers. Furthermore, the now mythic narrative of Se Ri Pak, a lower-middle-class girl who rose to global sports celebrity, seems to convey the idea that golf might become a way to climb in class status. Representations of golfing success have become national symbols of citizen participation in a global economy. Consuming golf through media enables Koreans and Korean Americans to participate in these dreams of personal and national economic success in meaningful ways.

As national icons, successful Korean female golfers demonstrate how Korean subjects should adjust to the neoliberal contexts of a globalizing Korea. Rather than the products of state-funded elite sports directed toward international competitions such as the Olympics, Korean female golfers achieve their training through private capital and individual initiative. They demonstrate how free-market rewards can be appealing incentives for private investments and personal efforts. Se Ri Pak is described as a *sŭp'och'ŭ chaebŏl* (sports conglomerate), a transnational metacommodity who has endorsed a number of U.S.- and South Korea–based companies, including Adidas, CJ, Samsung, Maxfli, Taylor Made Golf, and Upper Deck. Even though these players may depend on private wealth and capital, the success of Korean and Korean American athletes remains a victory for the South Korean nation.

The success of nationalism within this privatized context demonstrates how subjects can remain appropriate symbols of the nation while they accumulate private wealth for themselves. The golfers and their private wealth are represented as the pride of the nation and, possibly, its future potential for success.

With the successes of Se Ri Pak and other Korean female golfers, the question of why such a large number of Korean female golfers were so successful in such a short period of time became a hot topic of discussion in international golf. Generally, it was stated that the sheer number of Korean golfers had to do with a Korean cultural propensity toward hard work and competition. In mass media accounts, individual players' successes were attributed to natural Korean tendencies, such as a strong work ethic, self-discipline, mental strength, and steady family support. Rather than simply repeat these uncritical and problematic iterations about "Korean nature," I am interested instead in understanding how cultural ideologies produce particular narratives of possibility (while limiting others) for Korean women. These essentialist ideas have a constitutive power, and they have played a large role in promoting golf among young Korean women.

In South Korea, the dominant discussion about golfers assumes that their success is due to their talent, their hard work, and the sacrifice of their families.[15] Shin and Nam (2004) believe that the intense training of Korean female golfers is based in the testing and examination culture of South Korean society. They state, "This relentless cycle of mental preparation for a single examination on which students are given only one chance per year translates well into the single-mindedness and never ending practice sessions seen in the Korean golfers" (ibid., 231). Despite its obvious exaggeration, their statement highlights a socially sanctioned attitude toward extreme forms of mental and bodily discipline for children and youth. Whereas educational practices certainly play a large role in producing subjects that are able to engage in high-stakes competition, an examination culture does not enforce competition for its own sake. An examination culture is situated within broader social and economic contexts that produce particular kinds of working subjects.

Revealing an essentialist pose, Shin and Nam perpetuate the stereotype prevalent in South Korean and Korean American contexts that Korean women are naturally well-suited to forms of sport that require extreme precision and concentration, such as archery, billiards, and golf. For example, there is a general societal expectation that Korean women will win medals in Olympic archery competitions. From 1984 until 2004, Korean women won all available Olympic gold medals in archery, and they won the 2008 team gold medal.[16] The national mythologies of the Korean female athlete have resulted in targeted financial investment and educational opportunities in particular fields that require precision, mental acuity, and dexterity. These myths materialize in the bodies of Korean female athletes through their high success rates in these particular fields during international competitions. These nationalist narratives also motivate and mobilize private capitalist investments in the potential athletic achievements of Korean girls and women.

One of the dominant themes about Korean female players in non-Korean media is their robotic character—the idea that they lack emotion, creativity, and individuality. Shin and Nam remark, "Korean golfers are entirely focused and devoted to the game of golf and their training" (2004, 231). They quote extensively from a thoroughly orientalist feature written by Michael Bamberger for *Sports Illustrated*. Bamberger describes Pak's golf swing as "hypnotically robotic, thoroughly repeatable and extremely beautiful" (quoted in Shin and Nam 2004, 230). Bamberger continues to state that Pak was the "closest thing yet to a human version of Iron Byron, the ball-testing machine . . . a golfing machine—no brain, no emotion, automated excellence" (ibid., 231–232). Rather than critique the implicit stereotypes embedded in the statement, Shin and Nam do nothing but confirm these orientalist descriptions and follow enthusiastically, "Yet this cool single-mindedness displayed by Korean golfers may be the secret to their success" (ibid., 232)!

The language of U.S. media sport (and, in some cases, academic analyses) used in describing Asian golfers often perpetuates orientalist stereotypes of the Asian female body as robotic, rote, detached, unemotional, and single-minded. These descriptions follow closely the language of the Asian / American female as worker in transnational capitalism (L. Kang 2002; Ong 1987). The language detailing women's work devalues their labor as "unskilled labor," which requires mindless repetition rather than complex thinking. Ong points out that "unskilled" work has been discussed as "biologically suited to the 'oriental girl' due to her feminine traits" (1987, 152). Laura Hyun Yi Kang notes that the Asian/American female body, within the transnational capitalist contexts of assembly line manufacturing, military prostitution, and sex tourism, is "often described with the inherent characteristics as childlike innocence and docility, digital nimbleness, physical stamina, keen eyesight, sexual largess, and muscular flexibility" (2002, 165).

Even though there are increasing numbers of Korean female golfers in the

LPGA, the conditions for Korean women in the the South Korean labor force remain highly unequal to men, particularly when compared to countries at an equivalent stage of economic development.[17] Rather than empowering women, the contexts of golf reproduce gender ideologies that maintain female subordination in economic spheres. Golfers are valorized for disciplining their bodies and demonstrating economic results. The female golfer strengthens the economic ideologies of segmented labor markets that specify tasks as gender-specific and age-specific and constrain definitions of what is possible for men and women. These narratives of female labor question whether golfers raise new opportunities and possibilities for women since they are so easily appropriated into the patriarchal capitalist narratives of subordinate female labor.

Patriarchal Nationalism

As Aihwa Ong (1999) notes in her study of Chinese capitalists, the mechanisms of transnational capitalism are facilitated through kin relations, which are structured through gender inequalities. The narratives of LPGA golf reproduce ideas of patriarchal family relations in transnational contexts. Korean nationalist discourses of LPGA golf represent the golfer as a daughter who is subjugated to her father, family, and nation. Within the ideology of the successful Korean golfer, the work habits of female golfers are inculcated under the authoritarian watch of dedicated parents who push their daughters to practice excruciatingly long hours and who encourage their daughters to compete to win. In some cases, it is reported that Korean parents invest everything they have—their money, resources, and personal lives—into their daughters. Often, they move from South Korea to the United States and Australia to raise their daughters in golf-centered environments, to send their children to golf academies, and to live in areas where golf can be played year round. While on tour, South Korean golfers reportedly travel with their families, who operate as support staff and take care of all non-golf-related details.

This family support has been noted as a particularly salient cultural advantage for the Korean female golfer. Beginning with the visibility of Se Ri Pak's father, Pak Joon-cheol, U.S. mass media has focused its attention on the idea of a Korean family model headed by a father.[18] In this family narrative, fathers are perceived as the primary motivating force behind their daughters' education and training. Many Korean players, including three of the first

Korean players in the LPGA—Se Ri Pak, Mi Hyun Kim, and Grace Park—acknowledged their fathers as the strongest influence in their careers.

In this Korean father–daughter LPGA narrative, successful daughters act as the conduits through which their fathers' efforts and dreams are realized. Obviously, this narrative impacted Ty Votaw, the former LPGA commissioner, who apparently believed that Se Ri Pak "gave the entire country of Korea the motivation and inspiration for fathers and daughters to say, 'Hey, if she can do it, we can do it.' "[19] Whereas the actions of the father are the basis for the daughter's success, the mother's labor is peripheral or entirely erased. The mother remains an invisible woman who is relegated to the domestic labor of nurturing and cooking. Shin and Nam perpetuate the myth of the female golfer by stating the following:

> Their fathers are their caddies, coaches, and confidantes. Their mothers are bulwarks of support and familiarity, sacrificing their marriages and family lives to pick up and move to the states [sic] to care for their daughter's needs. It is this never ending devotion of parents to their children's needs that plays a heightened role in these players' victories. (2004, 233)

In a transnational sporting context, the father–daughter narrative often trumps the narrative of the aggressive mother–child relationship, which emphasizes the critical importance of the Korean mother who dedicates all her energies to send her children to the best colleges (H. Cho 1998).[20] This emphasis on the child's athletic training rests on the shoulders of the father, who accompanies his daughter in public and redirects his own interests to discipline and perfect her performance.

The father's obsession with his daughter enables him to assert his masculinity in a transnational context. Within ladies' golf, patriarchal family relations appear to grow stronger as they are conveyed as essential to the success of a female golfer. In this media narrative, father and daughter must bond to fight competitors in a foreign land. This interest of Korean fathers in their daughters is often described as a borderline pathology in the U.S. media, as Korean fathers are often seen as aggressive and overzealous. Se Ri Pak's father reportedly forced her from a young age to repeatedly walk up and down fifteen flights of stairs day and night and to sleep in graveyards to overcome her fears (Shin and Nam 2004). Korean fathers also have been accused of violating rules such as coaching from the gallery and encouraging cheating, as with the father who was accused of cheating by kicking his daughter's golf ball out from behind a tree to give her a better lie.[21]

The contradiction between the celebration of the individual as a competitor and the Korean female as a member of a family is often explained away as a cultural difference—as an essentially different approach to the world by Korean people (Shin and Nam 2004).[22] In this orientalist discourse, Korean female golfers are not adult subjects who can, of their own accord, enter into social, labor, and sexual relations. They remain children in a patriarchal family context. The young nubile female golfer is sexualized yet still virginal and out of the reach of young foreign admirers. She remains in her father's "house" and protected by his watchful presence. Grace Park, often discussed as one of the most attractive and stylish Korean female players, was appointed in 2004 to be an international representative of the LPGA as a nonvoting board member. She stated that she would live with her parents until she was married because she is Korean.[23] Any relations beyond those between father and daughter are obscured and understood as supplementary, and even harmful, distractions.

Shin and Nam state, "Se Ri Pak enjoys the guidance of her father who keeps her focused on her dream. In regard to movies and boyfriends, Pak's father once said to her, 'Ten years from now. Golf now, that later.'" (2004, 234).[24] Although Shin and Nam are convinced that this is beneficial to the success of Korean female players, they fail to critique the system of gender inequality that enables such patriarchal control. They do not mention how the Korean media exposure of Se Ri Pak's Chinese boyfriend in 1999 demonstrated how her personal relations were not considered her own by Korean media and its imagined publics. As a "national hero," she was soiling the purity of the nation by mixing with a Chinese man, and she was violating the father–daughter pact and jeopardizing her own future success as a result.

The discourses that surround Korean female golfers demonstrate the exceptional success of this patriarchal father–daughter narrative within transnational contexts. Rather than being a process that undermines the authority of the father, the movement between South Korea and the United States for the golfing family becomes a process that strengthens these hierarchical relationships. Some scholars point out that, by migrating to industrialized countries, Korean men undergo an emasculating process that is due to the loss of male privilege protected within South Korean contexts (Kim and Choi 1998; K. Park 1997). Immigration to Western countries is said to result in downward mobility for Korean men as they experience the loss of cultural signifiers of status and respect accorded to middle-class men and have difficulty getting an equivalent level career because of language and cultural barriers.

In the United States, Korean men are also subject to the racialized and sexualized stereotypes of Asian men that have traditionally conveyed them as emasculated, subordinated, and inferior to dominant White men (see Eng 2001).

Scholars such as Kyeyoung Park (1997) argue that processes of Korean immigration center around female networks, but the golf narrative of migration focuses on the actions and decisions of men. In the still White-dominated and English-speaking context of golf, the loss of a dominant Korean masculinity is ameliorated by the success of one's daughters, who act as surrogates through which the father comes to assert his control and maintain his patriarchal dominance. Nationalist narratives operate through this patriarchal male dominance over daughters. The father comes to stand in for the national interest as he protects the progeny of the Korean nation in foreign contexts and ensures its enduring success. The national interests that ride on the success of female golfers depend on the patriarchal investment of the father who ties the nation and its daughters.

The connection between patriarchal nationalism and this father–daughter narrative in golf is exemplified by a television advertisement for Samsung's Anycall cell phone. The title of the ad, *Him ŭl chu nŭn sori* (the sound that offers strength), plays off the closeness of Se Ri Pak's name to the word *sori*, or sound. Playing off the idea that Pak gave strength to the nation, the commercial suggests that her father is the source of her strength. The commercial begins with several video clips of Pak playing golf alone on a verdant and isolated course. Pak then narrates, "*Kotog i naege k'ŭn kot'ong ŭro taga ŭl ttaemada na rŭl irŭk'yŏ chun sori ga itda*" (Whenever I am struggling with isolation, there is a sound that picks me up again). A cell phone rings, and a man's voice on the line states, "*Seri ya, hŭndŭllimyŏn andwae*" (Seri, you must not be shaken). Back in narration, Pak states, "*Na ege him ŭl chu nŭn sori ga itda*" (There is a sound that gives me strength). Finally, an announcer's voice states, "Anycall."

This ad works through the assumption that the Korean national public understands the role of Pak's father in her golf career. It is clear that the man's voice is supposed to be her father and that his authority gives her strength. Her isolation stems from the fact that she is far away in a foreign country and playing an isolating sport, yet she maintains her connection to her family, national public, and homeland through her cell phone. The ad, along with a number of others that highlight Pak's contribution to the nation, suggests that even though Pak might give the nation strength, her personal strength relies on her father.

Figure 11. Samsung Anycall television commercial with
Se Ri Pak, 1999.

In the case of transnational movement and migration, this patriarchal
narrative is not an innocuous one, but it has tangible consequences as to how
Korean subjects imagine the nation and their place in relation to it. The
dominant narratives of patriarchal nationalism in sport have enduring consequences as they produce an acceptable space for the iteration of gendered
ideologies that might otherwise be rejected by feminist opinions that are
iterated in discrete national contexts. As Purnima Mankekar (1999a) argues,
the nation in diaspora often remains a domain where patriarchy and male
dominance remain free from criticism. This is particularly true within the
spectacular contexts of media sport. The national family, as represented by
the golfer's family, becomes the symbol of the nation in an era of globalization, and it highlights the significance of maintaining the ties of blood kinship, despite interactions with diverse groups and movement across borders.
The narratives of Koreanness in these transnational contexts often reinforce
ideologies of nation, gender, and class that produce social relations of inequality in both South Korea and Korean America.

The Promise of America

The visibility of Korean players has encouraged the growing popularity of
golf among middle classes in South Korea. Korean female players have also
aided in the promotion of golf as a Korean national pursuit (see Kim and Joo
2004). The Korean television market garners the highest revenue for the

LPGA in sales of broadcast rights outside the United States, and most LPGA tournaments are broadcast on network television in South Korea. The Republic of Korea is also the country that purchases the most LPGA logo merchandise.[25] Since the turn of the millennium, the LPGA has seen a significant increase in fan attendance at tournaments, in U.S. television viewership, and in web traffic on lpga.com. This growth is largely attributed to South Korean and Korean American fans.[26]

Inderpal Grewal discusses the relationship between the state and corporate strategies and the production of consumer desire within transnational regimes of neoliberal governmentality. In discussing the incorporation of "American" commodities in Indian national contexts, Grewal cautions against a simplistic cultural imperialism model to explain the production of consumer desire:

> Since "American" goods and geopolitics circulate across transnational connectivities, they absorbe [sic], utilize, and rework the notion of "American" into particular agendas and strategies within which states and nations play uneven and heterogeneous roles. As various market segments rework and recreate the "American" lifestyle, the emergence of consumers with both national and ethnic specificities indicates a very selective and changing incorporation of Americanness. (2005, 95)

Grewal explains that a major factor in creating the demand for American products in India was the nonresident Indian, who operated to translate and mediate consumer practices between the United States and India. The nonresident Indian was central in the production of consumer desires for a particular class segment of Indian nationals who had cosmopolitan dreams.

The idea of transnational connectivities detailed by Grewal describes well the case of Koreans and the LPGA. Instead of locating the production of desire for golf in those who have experience in highly developed nations (in this case Korean Americans), I locate the distinctive cultural desire for golf in Korean communities as reproduced at the site of the mass-mediated bodies of Korean golfers. Their images saturate Korean-centered news media broadcasts to diasporic subjects around the world. Their popularity with Koreans in both South Korea and the United States draws from their perceived Koreanness and the national sentiments they inspire.

The golfers are represented as originating in the Korean homeland and moving out to the rest of the world. The national significance of these players is also produced through representations of Korean Americans (including

Korean foreign nationals in the United States) as spectators. Representations of Korean American spectators and fans play an important role in conveying the lady golfer as a Korean national hero. Korean Americans often wave the *Taegukki*, the South Korean flag, as they line the galleries at golf tournaments. Their physical bodies evidence a new kind of fandom that exudes new kinds of smells, the use of *Hankungmal* (Korean language), aural expressions of excitement and disappointment, and new kinds of physical bodily interaction in the crowded spaces of the galleries that line the golf greens. The visibility of Koreans and Korean Americans at tournaments demonstrates an eagerness to consume Korean-inflected commodities and engage in Korean-related activities on U.S. soil. Their practices of consuming golf media and commodities endorsed by Korean players demonstrate a continuing desire to connect to a sense of Koreanness.

Until the late 1990s, the LPGA remained largely a sporting context for White Northern Europeans and Anglo-Americans,[27] with a few notable exceptions, including Althea Gibson and Nancy Lopez.[28] In the last decade, however, there has been a fundamental shift in the racial makeup and, arguably, the cultural tenor of the professional women's game, due to the rapid entry of competitive tour players from Asia, particularly South Korea. Korean female players have been accompanied by journalists, spectators, fans, and commercial sponsorships and endorsements from companies (such as Korea Telecom and CJ) that hail from their "places of origin." The clothing of Korean female golfers is punctuated by logos from Korean companies that have little or no recognition in U.S. consumer markets.

In an effort to capitalize on the popularity that has followed the entry of Korean golfers, the LPGA has revamped its marketing strategies to promote itself as an exciting, contemporary, international, and sexy sporting organization. Though there have been detractors who decry the loss of the White, bourgeois "traditions" of golf, the LPGA website proudly displays its efforts to embrace multiculturalism through a "celebration" of international non-U.S. players who hail from places such as Australia, Mexico, Scotland, Japan, and Sweden. Koreans and other non-Anglo players now play a central role in globalizing the golf market by producing interest in golf and its related media and merchandise in places where golf exists as a relatively new or newly popular phenomenon. The dramatic changes in the LPGA are connected to the entry of Korean players and the growth of a consumer middle class in both South Korea and Korean America.

The influx of Koreans to the LPGA has not been without detractors, many of whom exhibit protectionist and racist attitudes as they decry the loss of the "essence of golf" and its traditions. In a 2003 issue of *Golf Magazine*, Australian LPGA player Jan Stephenson remarked, "the Asians are killing our tour—absolutely killing it. Their lack of emotion, their refusal to speak English when they can speak English. They rarely speak." Stephenson's now well-known and oft-cited remarks were promptly and summarily dismissed by the LPGA, as they were in direct conflict with their policies on diversity and interests in global expansion.[29] The professional golf establishment in the United States, spurred by the popularity of Korean and other international golfers, has shifted its commercial strategies to accommodate and promote international and racial diversity. The sport of golf has been slow to incorporate the tenets of multiculturalism that have been the hallmark of other highly profitable media sport industries (as discussed in chapter 2). One could make the argument, however, that golf has followed a familiar narrative of racial incorporation since it took a successful minority player to "open" the sport and prove the worth of the minority to the majority.

To global corporations, Korean golfers offer a high level of marketing potential because of the consumer connections between golf and nation. As of 1999, there was no active recruitment scheme on the part of the LPGA for foreign players; nevertheless, Korean players became part of a new expansionist business plan of the league.[30] Nike's global sports marketing director Kel Devlin stated that South Korea presents more potential for growth than the United States does since 30 percent of its 2.5 million golfers are women.[31] In a high-profile investment in Korean markets, Nike offered a lucrative multimillion dollar sponsorship to Grace Park in 2003 as the first athlete to represent their newly formed LPGA division.[32] Michelle Wie, another Nike acquisition, has been highly touted as a "marketer's dream."[33] Although Michelle Wie is marketed as American or Hawaiian in the United States, she is considered an overseas Korean in Korean markets.

The position of Korean female golfers as national media stars has changed the entire marketing strategy of the LPGA, which has been plagued with low ratings since its television debut (Crosset 1995). In an attempt to shore up profits, the LPGA attempted to institutionalize what it perceived as the essential components of these profitable practices. In 2004, Commissioner Votaw acknowledged the primary impact that Asian players have had in increasing the profitability of the LPGA.[34] "We're thriving," he stated. "Competitions have been enhanced by the presence of Asian players."[35]

Korean players work well within the corporate multicultural contexts of the LPGA since they demonstrate how foreignness operates to prove the continuing economic promise of the United States (Honig 1998). According to this myth, immigrants attain economic success through their hard work and self-sustained effort. Honig states, "In the capitalist version of the myth the immigrant functions to reassure workers of the possibility of upward mobility in an economy that rarely delivers on that promise, while also disciplining the native-born poor, domestic minorities, and unsuccessful foreign laborers into believing that the economy fairly rewards dedication and hard work" (ibid., 1). They are also celebrated as demonstrating appropriate foreigner behavior. They help U.S. corporations make profits by expanding markets abroad. They do not request government assistance since they rely on their own private capital. Korean golfers offer outside praise for the United States that its own citizens so easily forget. Grace Park has said, "This country offers so much more than anywhere else. That's why we come here. This is where the best courses are, the best teachers, the best competition. I think that I will stay for a long time."[36] It is no doubt due to such obsequious praise that she was initiated as an "international ambassador" for the sport. As a player who came to the United States at the age of twelve, she is fluent in English but maintains her Korean nationality. She has said, "I can be both. I can be Korean and American. If I'm tired of being Korean, I can just flip a switch and be American and vice versa."[37] This ability to choose—to have "flexibility" in her cultural identity—is enabled through her class status and experiences living in both countries. Although she does not exemplify the flexible citizenship discussed by Ong (1999) in her study of Chinese capitalists,[38] Park demonstrates the class associations between the flexibility of capital and subjectivity.

LPGA golfer Christina Kim, who was born in the United States to Korean immigrant parents, is interpellated as both Korean and American. She has stated that she is "damned proud of being an American," yet she is often targeted as a representative of Korean golfers by the U.S. media due to her fluency in English and her outspoken nature. She asserts, "I can understand both sides because I'm of both cultures."[39] She has used her own Korean "expertise" to make overarching statements about all Korean golfers, stating that Korean golfers' discipline is "an instinct that's bred into the Korean people and passed down from one generation to the next."[40] In this case, she used her position as a Korean American subject to speak with authority on matters of Koreanness, and her comments worked to perpetuate essentializing myths about Korean biological homogeneity and an innate Korean talent for golf.

Figure 12. Sony Cybershot print advertisement featuring Michelle Wie,
2006.

A 2006 ad for Sony Cybershot digital cameras, featuring Michelle Wie,
suggests that Korean and Korean American players do not necessarily choose
their own representations and that, within a U.S. context, Korean players
continue to be racialized as Asian. The orientalist print advertisement features Wie sitting in a cross-legged position with a golf ball in one hand and
a digital camera in the other. As a sixteen-year-old, she is dressed in velour
yoga pants and an orange jersey camisole decorated with an Asian bird motif.
She is seated on a lotus-leaf-styled golf green, and behind her is a mandala
made of fanned out 7-iron golf clubs. This embellished photograph approx-

imates Buddhist iconography (mixed with some Hindu) in a tongue-in-cheek way through its colors, iconography, and the positioning of the central body. Beyond its mockery of the Buddhist religion, the image erases the national distinctiveness of Michelle Wie and strategically evokes orientalism in an attempt to shape her into an icon that represents a generalized Asianness. Although athletic skills are hinted at through the golf motif, Wie is not wearing golf gear; rather, she is barefoot and dressed in yoga gear that looks like pajamas. This "oriental girl" image belittles Wie's success at golf by placing the main focus on her race and sexuality rather than her athleticism.

In U.S. media, Korean players operate as agents through which national and racial differences are understood. Korean players often critique the essentializing narratives that attribute their success to some innate Korean nature, which is characterized by discipline, stoicism, focus, single-mindedness, and drive, yet they continue to be lumped together as an entire group through discourses of absolute cultural difference. Korean players also express resentment at being lumped together with fellow nationals, even though they are intensely competitive individuals who strive to beat one another on the tour. Clearly, the decision to announce the English-only policy on August 20, 2008 demonstrated that the LPGA sees the rise in the number of South Korean players as a threat to its future.[41] The policy stated that players who had been on tour for two years had to pass an oral evaluation of their English or they would be suspended from tour play. By announcing this tour-wide policy in a special meeting with South Korean players prior to announcing it publicly, the LPGA sent a message to players that they would be evaluating their "cultural" capacity to remain on the tour. It was clear to many players that the sudden announcement of the policy was a desperate attempt to reduce the number of Korean players on tour and address the perception that these players were changing the racial composition of the tour and making the LPGA a Korean tour by speaking to one another in Korean. After a few days in the sports news media spotlight, the controversial policy was dropped by the tour as the legality of the policy and its implementation were in question.

One result of the change in leadership from Ty Votaw to Carolyn Bivens is that there seems to be an attempt to create a bifurcated tour—one that continues to appeal to the Anglo heritage of golf by presenting young, new, blonde talent (which represents a glamorous and primarily White tour) and one that attempts to maintain the pace of international growth for the LPGA.

In the attempt to present both images, the LPGA has both praised and targeted Korean players, yet it continues to fret about the growing number of Korean players on the tour. The treatment of Korean players in the LPGA presents the limits of multiculturalism within an institution that is based on a heritage of racial and class exclusivity.

The Anti-butch Campaign

As a way to further promote their newfound growth, the LPGA in 2002 created a five-year plan for financial growth. This plan featured the "Fans First" initiatives, which pushed all athletes to be mindful of what they devised as "Five Points of Celebrity." The five points were performance, approachability, passion and joy, appearance, and relevance. These points were understood to place a large emphasis on the appearance and personalities of the players rather than on their performance as athletes. In response to the announcement of the Five Points of Celebrity, there was criticism from feminist critics of sport and Title IX[42] advocates who protested against the implied sexualization of female athletes. Opponents of the five points argued that these guidelines reflected the crass corporate interests of the LPGA. Representatives of the sporting industry, however, argued that these changes were made on behalf of fan interests and desires. The industry, they argued, was essentially an entertainment industry where the viewer-spectator-fan was placed first in all decisions.[43] According to the new LPGA initiative, players were encouraged to increase their media savvy through bold athleticism, public personas, and appearance (read: sex appeal).

In 2004, Votaw said, "Asian players embody the Five Points of Celebrity perhaps better than some do here."[44] It was clear that the LPGA believed Korean golfers were national celebrities in South Korea, and some might venture to argue that the five points were inspired by the celebrity they were already enjoying in the Korean market. These guidelines, however, operate as a double-edged sword for Korean players. There have been criticisms that Korean players lack proper golf etiquette and that they only care about their own success while they ignore other professional duties such as pro-am tournaments and sponsor receptions. In response to these accusations, Votaw reminded Korean golfers that "performance is only part of the package."[45] Essentially, the Five Points of Celebrity are used as a way to tell all players they aren't doing as much as possible to make enough money for the corporation, since there is always some "part of the package" for players to improve.

Todd Crosset (1995), in his ethnography of professional women's golf, describes the LPGA as an institution controlled by manufacturers and advertising interests (as is the case with many other sporting leagues). As such, the institution's marketing division has always attempted to manage the image of its players by encouraging them to present themselves in an appealing way—to be friendly, dress well, and respond to the press. Furthermore, the commercial interests in professional women's golf have always used the public image of heterosexual femininity to appeal to a male market. This emphasis on femininity has been interpreted as a not-so-subtle attempt to enforce a compulsory heterosexuality in the LPGA. Abigail Feder-Kane, in her study of women's figure skating, argues that gender differences between women and men are reproduced less through the absolute physical differences between genders but more through the stylistic emphasis on the appearance of the players. She states, "When physical capabilities no longer distinguish men and women, femininity is overdetermined to keep female athletes from being labeled as masculine or lesbian" (2000, 208). In the case of figure skating, femininity is produced "by 'hiding' all signs of labor such as sweat, muscles, and grunting" (ibid., 208). This attempt to hide the physical labor of golf also marks professional women's golf with its emphasis on the appearance of players. In other words, celebrities do not sweat.

Marketing to heterosexual men has not precluded the emergence of a lesbian market for the LPGA. A substantial lesbian fandom has existed for several decades; some consider the presence of lesbian players and fans an "image problem" for the LPGA. Crosset states, "lesbian fans will often follow players they believe to be lesbian. The LPGA is a source of pride for many in the lesbian community" (1995, 127). Nevertheless, he points out that most lesbian-identified players have been wary of publicizing their sexuality. Rather than an outright rejection of lesbianism, the LPGA engages in a policy of silence toward homosexuality by failing to acknowledge the lesbianism of its players and their attendant fans. This policy of silence demonstrates the ambivalence of the LPGA in its attempts to maintain a collective base of lesbian fans and focus on the stellar play of lesbian golfers on the tour. An overt critique of lesbianism is avoided for commercial reasons; the LPGA does not want to lose its lesbian fans. For example, in 2004, tour player Rosie Jones announced her lesbianism to little controversy, even though there was certainly no praise from the LPGA establishment (see Starn 2006).

As the pinnacle of lesbian LPGA fandom, a major "lesbian event" is held in conjunction with a major golf tournament, the Kraft Nabisco Championship. This lesbian "spring break," which is held in Palm Springs, California, is also known as "The Dinah" after the original name of the tournament— the Colgate/Dinah Shore Winner's Circle Golf Championship.[46] The first official corporate Dinah Shore Weekend was produced in March of 1991 by Mariah Hanson, a lesbian club and party promoter.[47] It has since become one of the largest lesbian parties in the world. It attracts tens of thousands of mainly White, middle-class lesbian women who come to participate in large pool parties, concerts, outdoor clubs, and nighttime events. Though these events have no official affiliation with the Kraft Nabisco Championship, they demonstrate the connections between a particular middle-class lesbian aesthetic and the LPGA.

Nevertheless, by promoting a heterosexual femininity, the LPGA attempts to manage the "image problem" of the LPGA as a lesbian domain. The LPGA has promoted the use of female athletes' sexualized bodies as marketing images, such as the pinups of Jan Stephenson in the early 1980s and the recent 2005 swimsuit calendar of professional player Natalie Gulbis.[48] On the LPGA website, there is a link to advertisements featuring LPGA players (as feminine and glamorous athletes) for luxury watches, athletic clothing, portable electronics, and women's golf equipment.[49] The hyperfemininity of Korean players works to emphasize gender differences between women and men by erasing any sexual ambiguity. The form-fitting tailored clothes of Grace Park, the dangling chandelier earrings and wide belts of Michelle Wie, and the pixie girlishness of Kim Mi Hyun provide a primary focus of media attention. In contrast to the idea of the asexual robotic worker, the sexualization of the Korean body appeals to the target market of the LPGA, which continues to privilege heterosexual male viewers (see Crosset 1995).

Within the transnational contexts of golf, the sexual valence of players must take into account different national sexualities, religious understandings, and cultural attitudes toward women's bodies. Susan Brownell (1995) cautions against an automatic reading of the muscular bodies of Chinese female athletes as butch or lesbian. During her fieldwork in the late 1980s, Brownell found that the ideologies of sport in China refused the idea of sport as a male preserve. She argues that gender and sexual differences were diminished in the discourse of the national athlete, as both men's and women's sport focused on producing athletes as national subjects in the service of state goals of modernization and socialism. Brownell offers an important caution against comparative analyses that fail to situate athletes within specific national contexts of sexual meaning-making.

Since Brownell's study, there has been a considerable shift in ideas of public sexuality in both China and South Korea (see Farquhar 2002; Rofel 2007). This shift can be read in the changes to the public appearance of Se Ri Pak. She was transformed from a dowdy twenty-something golfer at her debut to the tidy player of today through a national makeover. The masculinity of Pak—her broad shoulders, strong legs, dark tan, baggy shorts, and flat short hair covered with ill-fitting baseball caps—did not detract from her initial national fame. Pak was probably the most popular athlete in South Korea at the end of the twentieth century. Over the years, her public image has been transformed through a wardrobe redo and the use of heavy makeup. She is often featured in women's magazines in tailored designer sportswear with highly stylized hair and makeup. In the photos, she strikes poses that emphasize her "feminine side"—taking a stroll in the woods, relaxing on a couch, playing with her dogs, or cooking in her kitchen. The transformation of a tomboyish national icon to the womanly figure of today demonstrates that, although femininity was not a requisite for her national importance, she was normalized into public femininity through the transnational circuit of images of professional golf.

In the current media climate in South Korea, female golfers are often sexualized through sport tabloids, fansites, and advertisements. These images are meant to appeal to the consumer desires of both women and men in South Korean publics. Though these images promote a hegemonic heterosexual femininity, there are no indications that this process operates out of a fear of lesbianism in South Korean golf contexts. This does not, however, preclude the likelihood that changing notions of sexuality will move beyond current heteronormative conceptions.

It is important to understand the production of sexualities within national contexts of meaning-making, but these national contexts cannot fully explain the production of the Korean golf icon between and among national spaces. Cyberspace operates as a context for the production of sexualities and expressions of desire that move across national boundaries. One powerful example is the website www.seoulsisters.com, a fansite dedicated to Korean female golfers in the LPGA.[50] This website includes photographs, biographies, and tournament coverage, as well as feature articles, gossip, and obscure trivia about Korean players. This not-for-profit website has now become a source of information about Korean female golfers for fans, journalists, and other golf industry researchers in South Korea, the United States, and beyond. The site was considered the first of its kind in English, and it is popular with both South Korean and American users. The website's creator, Eric Fleming, has been featured on South Korean television a number of times.

A glance at the guestbook for August of 2004 reveals an overwhelming number of positive responses by fans located in both South Korea and the United States. The site allows fans to make comments on the "happyfan bulletin board," and some of these commentaries include explicit sexual statements by guests. A post from "James" on May 3, 2004 reads:

> Woo hoo. The Seoul Sister rock! Intelligent, fun loving swm avid golf fan/player seeks saf on lpga tour for long conversations on and off the course. Engineering/Legal background. Able to fit in at any social event.

This somewhat upbeat posting is followed by a rather insidious one from a fan whose username is "Big***k." It states, "Thanks for the interview with Grace! She is so sexy." Within this context, fans can reveal and joke about their romantic fantasies about these players. In the first posting above, the writer is explicit about his race as an swm (single White male) and expresses a desire for an saf (single Asian female) partner. Here, nationality (Korean) is conflated with race as the swm requests an Asian on the lpga tour on a site dedicated to Korean golfers. The next posting does not indicate the user's race or gender, although the username indicates the writer's interest in producing a hypersexualized masculine aura. Big***k, which ambiguously refers to either "Bigfuck," "Bigdick," or "Bigcock," posts an example of "locker-room talk" within this context. This post produces homosocial contexts for straight male interaction since it assumes that other men are readers and consumers of this site.

Even though seoulsisters.com is a fansite dedicated to lpga players, it might be easily misread as a porn/mail order/dating site that features Asian women (see Constable 2003). The postings mentioned above could be pointing to the irony of the parallels between these fansites and other eroticized sites that feature commodified Asian women. The site is not meant to directly facilitate the production of sexual desires, but it features photos and commentary about Korean female celebrity players who are already sexualized in both Korean and U.S. mainstream media. It is important to note that this fansite operates within broader historical and social contexts that feature Asian/American women as objects for sexual consumption and that have real consequences for the social relations of Asian/American women. The production of Asian/American women in cyberspace continues to reiterate orientalist fantasies of Asian women as objects of sexual consumption (see Lee and Wong 2003). On a website trafficked by Korean, Korean American, and non-Korean users, postings such as these raise important questions about just how particular shared modes of consumption do and do not reflect shared registers of understanding between so-called "happy fans."

The Future of Korean Women through Sport?

To conclude, the figure of the Korean female golfer demonstrates how national discourses of gender and sexuality operate in powerful ways through representations of athletes. In this case, I detail how ideas of gender and nation are projected through the figure of the Korean female athlete and how the discourses of Korean womanhood and femininity intersect with ideas of nation across national contexts. I argue that the figure of the Korean female athlete offers an ideological representation of how Korean subjects might succeed in the neoliberal social and economic contexts of the twenty-first century. The ability of some Korean female athletes to thrive as individuals within the contexts of private capital in transnational contexts results in their projection as ideal cosmopolitan subjects of the nation. The argument could be made that unmarried Korean women are, in fact, better suited than Korean men to adjusting to speedy transformations in the global economy because they are not burdened by the traditions and hierarchies, such as military obligations and duties to family legacies, that prevent men from easily adapting to new economic transformations. The female golfer symbolizes the opening of possibilities for Korean women in the transnational workforce during the two last decades and their ability to adapt rather quickly to the opportunities presented to them in a globalizing context.

Contemporary myths about a "new woman" in South Korean society work to conjure the image of a global Korean woman who is capable of traveling, learning languages, adjusting to new contexts, and pursuing her own interests. In 2008, twenty-nine-year-old Yi So-yeon became the first Korean astronaut in space after the first Korean candidate, a thirty-one-year-old man named Ko San, was dismissed from a Russia-based team to the International Space Station due to a rules violation. The frenzy around Yi So-yeon as the first Korean astronaut and as a female was emblematic of the discourses around the transformation of ideas about female capability within a global context. She displayed a disciplined and ethical approach to her responsibilities, and she proved herself to be an appropriate and enthusiastic representative of the nation. She was featured in mass media and advertisements as the representative of the global future of the nation.

The media frenzy around figure skater Kim Yuna is unprecedented. Kim skated to a gold medal at the 2010 Winter Olympics and beat several well-known Japanese contenders in the process. The competition constituted a national media event, and her record-breaking score elicited a national celebration. U.S. media picked up on this national pressure to win the first-ever Korean gold medal against a Japanese competitor as a "hook," and the story of Kim Yuna as a national icon and hero became a central part of coverage on the skating competition.[51] She has since become a metacommodity that represents a slew of products and services. Her win drew comparisons to the amazing year in which Se Ri Pak won two majors, and her win was said to offer hope in a time of economic struggle. The intensity of the response to Kim Yuna's victory is associated with her personality, the sport of figure skating, and the transnational character of the sport, yet it comes at a time when the foundation for her celebrity was already well laid by other high-profile female athletes.

Myths about the new Korean woman continue to be overlaid with discourses of patriarchy and male dominance, however. In golf, female athletes are still characterized by notions of diligence and docility within patriarchal contexts of work and family. Within the LPGA, Korean female golfers are rarely presented as individual adults outside the contexts of their families and their fellow nationals. Furthermore, in the United States, Korean female golfers are subject to prevailing myths around exotic Asian sexuality. As in the case with Korean male athletes in the United States, centuries-old stereotypes around the Asian body continue to emerge within contemporary contexts to perpetuate ideas about the essential differences among races. Korean female athletes are also positioned within an athletic media sport complex that subjects them to forms of sexualization that highlight their ultrafemininity and desirability to middle-class male consumers in both South Korea and the United States. Female golfers are world-class athletes whose athletic skills are often diminished as they are expected to present themselves as desirable and sexy marketers for the association and its sponsors. As Feder-Kane (2000) points out, athletes in these feminine sporting contexts are presented as ladies who do not sweat.

Throughout part II of this book, I present the case for how Korean athletes operate as gendered and sexualized icons of nation. As traveling images and bodies, they present multiple meanings of gender and nation that can be read differently from a variety of national positions. I have attempted to demonstrate how the significance of these icons resides in their connections to social and economic transformations in both South Korea and the United States and how the national affects that continue to surround them explain a great deal about their popularity and relevance. Their symbolic significance lies in their ability to evoke national narratives in the contemporary contexts of transnational media and capital flows. Although a Korean or Korean American might not be a fan of sport per se, the media coverage of these sporting icons has produced regular representations of Koreanness and Americanness in both South Korea and the United States. The ideas of Koreanness, as conveyed through athletes, become ways in which the Korean diaspora produces deterritorialized nationalisms. In the case of these athletes, Americanness itself is produced in relation to ideas of Koreanness.

I have also demonstrated the differences between the discourses that inform representations of male and female athletes and how ideas of gender and sexuality are shaped within national and commercial contexts that go far beyond assumptions about biological differences. Rather than a "natural" difference, the ideas of male and female gender and sexuality are framed within the political, economic, and social contexts of nation and transnation. In the following chapters, I build on these ideas about gendered difference and gendered forms of reception to investigate how sporting contexts that feature Korean players and teams work to shape gendered national publics. I investigate how the intimacies of nation are produced through sporting events and how ideas of gender, generation, and kinship work to shape national and transnational publics.

PART III

THE TRANSNATIONAL PUBLICS OF THE WORLD CUP

Nation Love

THE FEMINIZED PUBLICS OF THE KOREAN WORLD CUP

On a wet June morning, I left my *kosiwŏn* to meet my World Cup cheering partner, Kim Chang-ho, and his Internet *moim*.[1] I first met Kim Chang-ho, a twenty-year-old student from Inchon, a few days earlier. We were introduced through a moim member, Ch'oe He-mi, a friendly twenty-two-year old woman who lived in the room next door in our all-female kosiwŏn. Since she had to work at her bar on the evening of the first South Korea match against Poland, Ch'oe He-mi offered me her ticket to watch a live broadcast of the game in the Chamsil Olympic baseball stadium. The match was being shown for a crowd of thousands on two enormous stadium screens. Using our cell phones as guides, Kim Chang-ho and I met up amidst a crowd dressed almost entirely in red T-shirts. Prior to the game, we impatiently sat through the performance of a then unknown performer, Bi, who lip-synched a few songs while gyrating on the baseball field. Although we were total strangers prior to meeting, we quickly became friendly acquaintances as we shared the emotional experience of watching the first-ever goal and victory by the South Korean team in World Cup history.

Having shared such a great experience, we planned to watch the U.S.–South Korea match at Kwanghwamun, an area in the center of downtown Seoul. Kwanghwamun is also the location of the U.S. embassy and adjacent to City Hall. On the day of the match, I crawled out of the packed subway on the coattails of an aggressive *ajumma*. I dialed Chang-ho over and over again only to get a busy signal (apparently his phone had broken in the rain). I eventually slipped through the packed entrance to join tens of thousands of fans dressed in red T-shirts. For hours prior to the match and throughout the duration of the game, I sat shoulder-to-wet-shoulder with strangers on piles of soaked newspaper laid on Kwanghwamun's main street, Sejŏngno. I strained my eyes in a futile attempt to watch the football action on the digital mega-screens attached to high-rise buildings along the thoroughfare.

For hours prior to the game, the wet crowd seemed to maintain high spirits; people sang and repeatedly chanted the same cheers in unison: "*Taehan Min'guk! Tchak-tcha-tchak-tchak!*" "*Arirang!*" and "*Oh, P'ilsŭng Korea!*"[2] The crowd continued to sing and chant throughout the game. The U.S. team scored early and led for the majority of the game. Then, in the last few minutes, star midfielder and heartthrob Ahn Jung-hwan headed-in the tying goal. This ignited an extended high-pitched screaming frenzy, and everyone in the crowd seemed to jump to their feet and thrust their arms in the air. Strangers embraced, girls screamed, and women and men cried. Minutes after the goal, the game ended in a tie score of 1–1. The crowd quickly dissipated as hundreds of thousands of people left in an orderly fashion, walking to the next available subway stop a kilometer or two away. Many stayed around to clean up the area by collecting and throwing away trash and scraping wads of wet newspaper off the ground.

Hours after the game, wet and tired, I returned to my tiny kosiwŏn room on the other side of the Han River and turned on the television to MBC (Munhwa Broadcasting Channel) to watch news coverage of the World Cup. Well beyond the games themselves, there was extensive coverage of the crowds of spectators throughout South Korea. The crowd at Kwanghwamun was commended for exhibiting ethical crowd behavior and persistent endurance through the rain—being orderly (not crushing one another), being peaceful (not attempting to vandalize or protest in front of the U.S. embassy), and being considerate (cleaning up the area by picking up trash). Effusive praise by the news media was directed to "our country's citizens" as best represented by the impressive fans at Kwanghwamun.

Throughout June of 2002, the millions of spectators clad in red T-shirts poured onto the streets of South Korea. The crowds of the 2002 World Cup constituted a historically distinct articulation of public culture in South Korea. Described as unified, feminine, youthful, energetic, orderly, and playful, the crowds raised important issues about how nation, gender, and consumption operate to produce Korean national publics (Kendall 1996; Nelson 2000). Through a discussion of the character and practices of crowds engendered by the World Cup, this chapter begins the final section of this book, which focuses on the making of South Korean and Korean American publics during a period of so-called liberalization, democratization, and globalization (Armstrong 2002; S. Kim 2000a).

The World Cup offers a context for investigating the emergence of national and transnational publics as media around such sporting mega-events address a broad audience of viewers as national subjects. The crowds that formed during the World Cup were a kind of public that emerged from their "common visibility and common action" (Warner 2002, 50). As I point out in this and the next two chapters, the sporting publics during the World Cup functioned to create national publics that transcended borders, and they presented affective contexts for the production of global Koreanness. Within the global event, a strong sense of intimacy generated a feeling of connection among strangers, and this feeling indicated how the privatized realm of media sport generated a sense of national belonging for the South Koreans and Korean Americans who participated in the event.

This final section of the book shifts from reading the symbolic dimensions of sporting icons to investigating the discourses of address and the practices of reception that characterize Korean/American consumption of sport. In other words, part III focuses primarily on the audience response to productions of media sport. Michael Warner (2002) points out that publics are constituted when an audience is addressed by a discourse that has its own temporality of circulation. Prior to, during, and after each game throughout June of 2002, a set of discourses directed to a national audience maintained the energy around the event and sustained interest by a great proportion of South Koreans and Korean Americans. The kinds of publics I discuss in these chapters connected through the shared consumption of media images, collective gathering, acts of material consumption, and commodity display that took place around the event. The World Cup's massive crowds brought attention to the significance of media fandoms and fandom culture in constituting national publics in South Korea and Korean America.[3] This chapter, in particular, begins by discussing many of the practices displayed within the World Cup publics by detailing the acts of consumption, expression, and gathering that came to define the event as a national event.

Although the World Cup public can be understood as a kind of national public, it would be a mistake to say that the emergence of this national public was entirely state-driven. Michael Warner (2002) argues that publics are self-organized, rather than being organized by the state. Of course, this doesn't mean that the state does not attempt to appropriate the energy and intensity of the crowd toward its own gain, and in this chapter, I point out that the

South Korean state did try to harness the energy of the crowds toward national developmental and economic aims. Though I agree that there is no necessary state involvement in the production of publics, the shape and form of the World Cup publics offered inspiration for direct political applications, which I discuss briefly in the conclusion to this book.

Publics, by nature, are ephemeral and episodic (Warner 2002). Therefore, particular historical contingencies—in this case, the World Cup as global mega-event hosted in South Korea—played a large role in shaping responses to and experiences of the event. Local and historically contingent factors included the efforts of citizens' groups, the unanticipated success of the South Korean team, and the modes of sociality produced through traditional mass media (radio, television, print) and new media technologies (cell phone, Internet, digital billboards). The relative impact of each factor can be debated, but the crowds were mobilized through mediated narratives that operated to inform and inspire participation by millions of individuals. This chapter focuses primarily on the impact of how national discourses, practices of consumption, and gendered assumptions about sport played a role in shaping the event. As I have argued throughout this book, in the contemporary period, political subjectivities are informed and expressed through specific consumer practices, particularly those that take place through and in response to mass media (Ginsburg, Abu-Lughod, and Larkin 2002; Mankekar 1999b).

The publics that were generated during the World Cup could be seen as a kind of "creative worldmaking" that generated new possibilities for thinking about national subjectivities (Warner 2002, 82). One major hallmark of this creative worldmaking could be seen through the feminized practices of fandom that characterized the World Cup crowds. The event was distinguished from previous national mobilizations by the large number of women and girls who were active participants in the cheering crowds. The densely populated public spaces around City Hall and Kwanghwamun were filled with young women in their teens and twenties, and it was reported that females constituted well over half of the participants in street celebrations (H. Kim 2002). This chapter again addresses questions of female representation but through an analysis of the behaviors and statements of participants and viewers. Moving from the discourses of nation and gender symbolized through female sporting icons of the previous chapter, this chapter engages in a discussion of how female practices of fandom helped to naturalize the connections among practices of consumption, mass media, and discourses of nation. As Korean women emerged to dominate representations of World Cup crowds, nationalists and progressives (not necessarily opposed categories) seemed to hail the feminized crowd as a marker of societal progress. The visibility of women and girls on the streets came to be viewed by some as proof of a kind of female empowerment.

Due to the international significance of this large-scale sporting event, the representations of women worked to highlight the female-accented dynamics as unique and noteworthy. The feminized crowds were also seen as evidence of a kind of global status achieved by South Korean national public culture. The high proportion of women to men in the crowds raised questions regarding gendered assumptions in Korean society about sport spectatorship as a male-dominated sphere. The participation of women in this media sport event was historically significant, but the event also could be seen as an extension of feminized practices already common in the context of popular culture events. The publics were shaped through consumer and media practices that were popular for years with South Korean youth, including online discussion forums, online group membership (i.e., "netizenship"), Internet-based communities of consumer-participants, and pop music fandoms.[4] Women participated as particularly effective consumer subjects during the World Cup, and these consumer practices saturated mass media coverage of the event. They played a constitutive role in producing the spectacle of World Cup publics by demonstrating their ability to interpret media texts, shape fan behavior, and effectively display themselves as appropriate fans to the nation and the world.

An important aspect of the feminization of the crowd was the public expression of female (hetero)sexual desire (H. Kim 2002). This chapter discusses the erotics of the crowd by focusing on notions of sexuality and female desire expressed through the discourses and actions of sports fans in relation to male football players. Although many of these expressions of sexuality might have been deemed inappropriate by nationalists if directed toward self-desire or desire for a non-national subject, within the context of the event, sexual desire for Korean national players was interpreted as desire for the Korean nation (H. Kim 2002). The discourses produced about the female citizen-viewer vis-à-vis male athletes highlight how media practices contribute to and influence notions of nationalism, sexuality, and gender in this contemporary transnational era (see Mankekar and Schein 2004).

The World Cup as National Event

The 2002 World Cup is widely regarded as an important historical monument in South Korean nationalist history. The South Korean team had done shockingly well in the world's most popular sporting match, reaching the Round of Four through a series of dramatic victories over the course of the tournament. The surprising success of the South Korean football team fueled a "World Cup fever" throughout South Korea and the Korean diaspora, dominating conversations between South Koreans who were within its interpellative reach. As the South Korean team entered the Round of Sixteen, then-president Kim Dae Jung announced, "Since *Tangŭn* [the founding of the nation], this is the happiest day in our nation's history!"

For the duration of that month, the World Cup seemed to be the only topic of discussion for all Korean-language media outlets affiliated with the Republic of Korea. The South Korean national football team had done exceptionally well in strict sporting terms by reaching the Round of Four, although they were 40th in the official FIFA rankings. However, the crowds are what generated the most interest from the media, critics, and observers of South Korean society. Millions of spectators drew widespread attention both domestically and internationally. The most important news topic was the crimson sea of fans in the stadiums and on the streets. This stunning visual image engendered visceral emotions in viewers within the country and around the world, ranging from ecstasy to fear.

According to celebratory accounts, the World Cup heralded a new era in Korean public culture. In contrast to state-mobilized and state-controlled public cultures (Koo 1993), the World Cup seemed to signal a different moment when the public expression of national pride was voluntary and spontaneous. This argument diminished the role of the state and mass media in producing the event and foregrounded the voluntary dimensions of civil society. Well-known progressive academics claimed that the rhetoric of nationalism was unchained from official state discourse. According to this celebratory view, emotional expressions of nationalism were not considered evidence of ideological indoctrination but, rather, cathartic explosions of pent-up stress accrued through the oppressive demands of modern and urban life. To some social commentators, the crowds reflected a new national reality shaped in a postideological era (Cho Han 2002a). Media images of World Cup crowds were said to have offered representations of new ways of being a Korean national subject. Koreans were able to celebrate the nation in a lighthearted manner and treat once-sacred national symbols, such as the flag, with playfulness and irreverence (see Huh 2004; Whang 2004). Korean subjects, especially young women, were said to have indulged in the individualistic pursuit of personal pleasure (H. Kim 2002). Unshackled from patriarchal tradition, youth and young women came out onto the streets to inhabit previously adult- and male-dominated public spaces. The insouciance of the crowds indicated important changes in the political atmosphere of South Korea, from repression and censorship to openness and freedom.

These celebratory reviews of the World Cup were especially surprising since many were authored by progressive academics and leftist social critics who had previously expressed deep suspicions about collective mobilization around state-sanctioned national events.[5] The celebrations of the World Cup also demonstrated the nationalist tendencies of many progressives and social critics in South Korea. Though I acknowledge the event as an immensely pleasurable experience for many different groups, I also argue that such expressions of pleasure were not intrinsically liberating or politically progressive. Clearly, the World Cup crowds did indicate important shifts in Korean society, just as they demonstrated new forms of public expression. I understand that many of these changes were hard-won through difficult political struggles, but Stuart Hall (1986) reminds us that no position is always already politically progressive.

Most people I observed were not asserting a politically progressive position by participating in the crowds; rather, they were responding to the hegemonic narratives of mass media. In fact, most people in the crowds were swept up in the collective actions and emotion of the unique spectacle. It would be dangerous to assert that millions of people acting collectively out of a desire for national victory in a commercial sporting event constitute a politically progressive movement; the participation of women, youth, children, and the diversity of the crowd did not make the crowds de facto politically progressive. Furthermore, the actions of the crowds were sanctioned and encouraged by the state, corporate media, and commercial entities. Dominant political ideologies operate through popular forms of cultural production that are spectacular by nature, such as popular music, sport, and public festivals (see Hall 1997; Lipsitz 1994). These popular events have the potential to create gendered consumer publics that promote hegemonic discourses of nation. Within the discourses of mainstream media, the crowds were interpellated by the discourses of national unity and the seductive images of collective pleasure. Some might venture to argue that the fascist tendencies of nationalist mass mobilizations operate through the affective dimensions of pleasure, which are created through a sense of unity, uniformity, and mutual recognition. Not determined by the state or a completely spontaneous emergence, the crowds can be understood as containing immense potential that can be harnessed in a number of political directions.

Mobilizing the Crowds

Commentators focused on civic participation during the World Cup, yet the powerful role of the neoliberal state in producing the event was underplayed. After winning the bid in 1996 to cohost the 2002 World Cup with Japan, the South Korean state took responsibility for preparing the nation by building stadiums, sponsoring events, and promoting national interest through various local and national campaigns. As Yoon Sung Choi (2004) demonstrates, the National Council for a Better Korea Movement was instituted to prepare South Korean citizens for global exposure by educating them in "global standards" of public behavior. These included campaigns on how to smile, the proper way to queue, and the so-called civilized use of public toilets. During the event, the state enacted national security measures, which included special antiterrorism protections for the U.S. team and transportation provisions, such as blocking roads, extending subway hours, and limiting car traffic by banning half the passenger vehicles during specific hours. The state's power was demonstrated when, with only a few days' notice, it instituted an official national holiday on July 3 to commemorate South Korea's success during the event. All government offices, such as administration, banks, and post offices, were closed to commemorate the historic success of the team.

The collective behaviors expressed within the context of the global event did not stray from the stated aims of the *segyehwa* policies of the state. A central feature of these policies has been to advance the economic position of the nation in the world. After the World Cup, the phrase "*Wŏltŭ k'ŏp sagang, kyŏngje p'algang*" (World Cup the Round of Four, Economy the Round of Eight) expressed the desire to harness the human energy expressed during the tournament toward state economic goals by raising the status of the nation to the eighth wealthiest nation in the world (S. Kang 2002; Tong-yŏn Lee 2002). Clearly, the competitive nature of international sport was seen as a direct corollary to capitalist competition among nations. There was rarely an hour of football (soccer) coverage on television that did not include the statement "The whole world is watching" to remind the South Korean people of their responsibility to present and to *opkŭreidŭ* (upgrade) the national image to the world (see Gitlin 2003). This "name branding" of the country was based on the notion that success in a major sporting event would function to produce a positive recognition of all things Korean, especially commodities and people around the world, thus legitimizing the expense and distraction brought to the nation by a private, for-profit multinational organization. The discourses of national development as a competition among nations characterized the Korean state response to this global event, and this state response connected the event to previous national sporting spectacles (see chapter 1).

The outpouring of human energy evoked prior periods of mass mobilization. Throughout South Korean history, large-scale national celebrations and demonstrations have occurred in Seoul's city center. During the Cold War, crowds were mobilized to produce national spectacles in massive human displays of state power. State parades through the center of Seoul often followed the victories of Korean athletes who succeeded in international contexts (see Ch'oe and Ch'oe 1998). The Asian Games and the Olympics, with its attendant *p'allyuk p'alp'al* rhetoric, assembled the public to create national spectacles planned around the events. At other times, crowds were mobilized in opposition to the state. Demonstrators famously filled the streets of Seoul to demand state reforms during the student revolution of April 19, 1960 and the democracy movement of June 1987 (see J. Choi 1993). In fact, during the 2002 World Cup, allusions were made to the June 1987 movement as the last time such a massive civic mobilization took place (see Cho Han 2002a).[6]

Interestingly, images of the crowds as a uniform crimson mass resemble the Red Parades in North Korea. Throughout the Cold War, mass-mediated images of such parades were used to stir up communist anxieties in the South Korean populace. The "Red Complex" that was directed against communism and its representative color produced a negative connotation to the color red. Thus, the use of the color red during the World Cup and the imprint on the T-shirts—"Be the Reds"—is said to have rearticulated the meaning of the color red in South Korean society. Although the event was, in the opinion of some, a revolution in color, the powerful use of this politically charged hue passed without an official political response, giving the impression that the red crowds constituted a rather ahistorical and somewhat accidental political message.

Figure 13. World Cup crowds around Seoul City Hall, June 22, 2002. Yonhap News, reprinted with permission.

Bearing important similarities to prior crowds that were mobilized by and in opposition to the state, the crowds of the World Cup presented important historical distinctions. They were not responding to an authoritarian call from the state to participate in a national spectacle. Neither were they "counter publics" that formed in opposition to hegemonic institutions (Fraser 1995; Warner 2002). Rather, these national crowds were produced through a collective response to media discourses produced in neoliberal fashion by the interaction of civic, corporate, and state entities. The crowds exhibited historical distinctions in terms of their scale and scope, media usage, and commercial nature. First, a massive number of people poured out onto streets throughout the country and beyond. The global reach of media images worked to connect communities in discontinuous spaces. Korean communities throughout the world, especially in the United States and Japan, mimicked the behavior of those in Seoul to create an imagined national community (Anderson 1991). Second, the widespread access to live media about the event bolstered the idea that participation was voluntary, democratic, spontaneous, and universal. Through media technologies, almost all were able to participate in the spectacle by joining the crowds, communicating with people in the crowds through cell phones, or actively watching the crowds on television or the Internet. Third, the commercial nature of the event constituted the crowds as consumer subjects. Successful participation in the crowds required particular practices of media consumption and commodity display.

In contrast to the idea of a forced mobilization by the state, people elected to participate in the event with enthusiasm. They displayed a consciousness that the event was being presented to the world by mass media, and they participated enthusiastically in producing national representations. Those who participated in the crowd understood that national, possibly even global, history was being written through their actions. By participating in the crowds, they included themselves as part of that history. They would be inscribed in world historical memory as helping produce a unique and distinct national response to an important global event.

Media and the Crowd

The massive World Cup crowds brought attention to the social significance of new media technologies, especially as they operate through media fandoms and fandom cultures (see Lewis 1992). The behaviors that came to characterize the crowds were initially produced through the Internet-based cultures of fandom. As the most influential fan group, the Red Devils Supporters Club attempted to create a specific culture based on Internet membership and event participation. Over the course of the tournament, the behaviors that emerged through these participatory Internet fandoms were conveyed through mainstream national media. Traditional forms of media, such as television, print, and radio, reproduced representations of fandom practices that enabled members and nonmembers alike to consume and participate in the behaviors promoted by the fan club. The Internet-based cultures of football fandom became a mainstream expression of collective national unity.

The Red Devils Supporters Club played a critical role in shaping the fan culture of the World Cup.[7] From the outset, their goal was to promote the growth of football appreciation in South Korea. There was a concerted effort on the part of the Red Devils to produce a uniquely Korean form of sports culture that did not attempt to copy societies that were more established in twentieth-century narratives of football lore.[8] They were often praised as the "12th man" of the South Korean team by creating an environment of universal support for the national team in stadiums and throughout the country. The sporting culture promoted by the Red Devils was characterized by the appropriation of what were understood as native and distinctively Korean symbols. Their chants emphasized the use of *Hankungmal* (Korean language). Elements of traditional folk culture were incorporated into the cheering practices, such as folk songs (*"Arirang"*), traditional dress, and Korean drums. Designs included the *tokkaebi* (traditional goblin) as the group's mascot. The *Taegukki* was also an essential aspect of their fan culture. During the games, giant South Korean flags were draped across entire sections of stadium seats supported by the extended arms of thousands of spectators. Youth, who were said to have previously expressed ambivalence and even embarrassment about the flag, wrapped their bodies with it and tattooed it (albeit temporarily) on their skin.

The Red Devils and other online chat groups promoted good civic behavior because, they claimed, the "whole world was watching." Korean fans were exhorted to clean up after themselves, and many did, in fact, pick up after themselves on the streets following massive gatherings. Images of such orderly behavior were broadcast around the world and featured in the international media as a quaint curiosity. They were held up by the South Korean national media as examples of good civic behavior. Beyond the resolute condemnation of hooliganism by national media, there was an attempt to demonstrate South Korea's exceptional behavior by representing to the rest of the world the peaceful, safe, and nonthreatening nature of South Korean football crowds. Through these methods of self-policing, the crowds worked to defy the naturalized associations of national sports with violence, football with mayhem, and sports fandom with hooliganism (Dunning 1988; Williams, Dunning, and Murphy 1984). Though there were some reported incidents of vandalism, particularly to cars and buses during all-night post-victory celebrations, the event remained, for the most part, amazingly nonviolent and orderly. Throughout the nation, there were very few reported incidents of violence and injury during the month-long tournament.

Due to wide exposure in the mainstream national media, the influence of the Red Devils went far beyond those who had officially registered online for membership. The organization stated that the only real criteria to be a Red Devil were a true love of football and dedication to the South Korean team. Membership was free and only required a *chumin tŭngnok pŏnho* (resident registration number) and a few other personal facts submitted through the website. Nevertheless, the Red Devils' media representative, Sin Tong-min, at a post-World Cup forum held on July 9, 2002, was careful to distinguish members and nonmembers. He made the argument that the Red Devils did not mobilize or lead the massive crowds. He insisted that there was a difference between real members of the Red Devils and the fans on the streets. Regardless of this distinction, the web-based fan culture of the Red Devils defined crowd behavior throughout the nation.[9] The participatory culture encouraged by the organization became the hegemonic national culture that was subsequently produced through mainstream media representations.

Even though the Red Devils were named as a major stimulus in producing the crowds, mainstream mass media soon became the most powerful influence as the tournament continued. Various media outlets operated to produce a hegemonic and largely uniform narrative about the crowds. The tournament was a global event, but the primary focus of news was the national team and the crowds of Korean fans. Many mainstream Korean news announcers wore the official Nike-issued Korean team jerseys during the month, thereby proudly displaying their partiality. Furthermore, most news coverage effusively praised the nation's team, the supporters in the stadiums, and the public crowds.

The phrases *uri nŭn han maŭm* (We are of one mind) and *hanaga toenda* (We are becoming one) were repeated at a mind-numbing rate throughout the tournament. Images of the crowds were used to verify the idea that forty-eight million Koreans came together through this event. In Korean America, headlines pronounced that sixty million Koreans around the world became one.[10] A nationalist discourse of oneness infused the entire event and was produced through the language of unity and the visual spectacle of the crimson crowds.[11]

Media outlets and the advertisements that support them dedicated a large proportion of their content to the South Korean national team and the massive crowds of spectators. Even though the event was cohosted, the extent of Korean media coverage on the tournament taking place in Japan was remarkably minimal. The circumstances of the FIFA decision for South Korea and Japan to cohost were rarely discussed.[12] There was some positive coverage on Koreans living in Japan, but the overall treatment of national reception in Japan was hardly positive. The most searing images consisted of a few repeatedly broadcast instances of hooliganism and frightening shots of the fan group Ultra Nippon. The fan members were clad in electric blue, waving the *hinomaru* (Japanese flag; the "circle of the sun") and shouting a shrill "*Nip-pon! Nip-pon!*"

The national representation of the World Cup in South Korea demonstrates an irony about the peculiar joint appointment. For consumers of Korean-language media, the global event was produced and conveyed as an essentially Korean event directed to Korean viewers and readers. Media coverage of stadiums and games was heavily slanted toward the Korean-hosted events. Furthermore, there was a concerted desire on the part of South Korean national media to "show Korea to the world" rather than displaying both Korea and Japan or East Asia to the world.[13] Rarely, if ever, in my interviews with Korean subjects was there an acknowledgment of the shared hosting of the tournament. There was a persistent anxiety over the fact that the Japanese national football team might enter the Round of Sixteen and do better than South Korea in the tournament, but there seemed to be an almost intentional erasure of the fact that Japan was cohosting the event. In South Korea, the entire focus of journalists and even progressive social critics seemed to be on the South Korean national team and the distinctive quality of Korean publics and fan behavior by those on the nation's streets.[14]

In contrast to the Korean responses, the public responses in Japan to the World Cup focused on World Cup fandom as a function of individual preferences for football. There was also an emphasis on the opportunity for regional development and regional pride for cities, such as Yokohama, as the tournament was held in multiple cities throughout the nation (see Cho Han et al. 2004). Furthermore, in contrast to responses in South Korea, there were far more individuals who expressed their enthusiasm for players and teams of other countries in public contexts. There were many Japanese fans of Brazil and England and fans who wore other nations' jerseys and cheered for a variety of national teams throughout the tournament. There were many comparisons between the "individualist" fandom of the Japanese and the "national" fandom of the Koreans, although powerful nationalisms were expressed in both sites.

In many interactions I had with research subjects residing in Seoul, a persistent anxiety was expressed about the insignificance of their country within global contexts. They felt that many people beyond the national boundaries knew little, if anything, about South Korea. Interestingly enough, a version of the following story was told to me over and over again by many respondents. Ku Su-mi, a twenty-three-year-old resident of my kosiwŏn, told me,

> I have a friend of a friend who was studying abroad in Australia, and he told an acquaintance that he was from Korea, host of this year's World Cup. The Australian did not realize that the World Cup was *also* being hosted by Korea, thinking it was the Japan World Cup. He didn't know much about Korea, except that it was a country in Asia and was surprised that an obscure country was going to host the world's largest sporting match.

I was not clear about the origins and pathways of this rumor—whether it was spread by word of mouth, Internet communications, or television—but its constant repetition conveyed a widely shared anxiety about the rest of the world's perceived lack of interest in or knowledge of South Korea. It relayed the hope that South Korea's part in this event would bring it international recognition. This notion of name recognition, as a sort of "name branding" of the country, was a point that came up again and again in my conversations with both policymakers and ordinary citizens. It highlighted the extent to which neoliberal discourses of the nation were subjectively understood and apprehended. It also demonstrated how the project of global Koreanness was internalized through viewing subjects.

Another indication that Korean consumption of the event was heavily focused on the Korean team was the push to sell leftover tickets to games that failed to sell out. Prior to the World Cup, there were leftover tickets to games that didn't include the South Korean team or feature any global superstar players. All games in Japan, on the other hand, were sold out well ahead of the tournament. This caused some public embarrassment, as it seemed to demonstrate a lesser interest on the part of the Korean public and expose South Korean fans as nationalists. They failed to be "good hosts" and "real fans" since the citizenry, as a whole, did not express interest when a match did not involve their own national team. There were also incidents when Korean fans burst out in Korean national chants, such as "*Taehan Min'guk*" and "*Oh! P'ilsŭng Korea*," during games that did not feature the South Korean team. These incidents were met with ambivalence and some embarrassment in the press and among people I questioned. Sin Sŭng-jin, a twenty-eight-year-old self-professed football fanatic, laughed as I mentioned the Korean fans who wore the "Be the Reds" T-shirts and chanted for South Korea's victory in games involving other national teams. "Really, I don't care for [the cheering] that much. It's not good sportsmanship. But, hey, they can't really help it, and when it starts, you can't really exclude yourself." For the most part, these eager fans were excused for their uncouth behavior; they could barely contain their enthusiasm for the South Korean national team, even when it wasn't playing.

Some have noted that the World Cup demonstrated a new openness of Korean society to foreigners, and the Korean team's Dutch coach, Guus Hiddink, became one of the most popular figures of the tournament (Lee et al. 2007). He was hailed as bringing a new cultural paradigm to South Korean society by doing away with "backward" practices of deference to seniority and concerns about "saving face" that were impeding the performance of the national football team. He also brought about a "scientific" management style to the players who were tested, measured, and assessed with the latest technological equipment. Hiddink enforced strict disciplinary regimes for the production of athletic and fit bodies. Given the astounding success of these measures, as demonstrated through the team's victories, there were petitions to make him a South Korean citizen, and there were even (half-joking) calls for him to run in the upcoming presidential race. Hiddink became a metacommodity who was called on to run management seminars, write management books, and star in Samsung credit card commercials.

Bong Sŏng-gyu, a forty-three-year-old father of two, who worked in a white-collar job at a bank, told me that the praise Hiddink received was overblown. Rather than coming from without, he stated that these changes were already taking place in South Korea by DJ (President Kim Dae Jung).

He informed me that he could see through the celebrity bestowed on Hiddink to understand that the changes toward a more democratic and less hierarchical organizational ethos were already happening. Rather than believe a figure such as Hiddink would bring "Western" practices to South Korea, Bong understood that the acceptance of the Hiddink management style was made possible by domestic changes that included the economic contexts of liberalization and "restructuring."

Becoming a Fan The crowd of spectators during the World Cup demonstrated the mobilization of a new fandom culture in South Korea. This new fandom was specifically directed toward producing football fan communities that were distinguished as Korean through "uniquely" Korean language, symbols, and practices. As with other fandom communities, it was based on particular ways of communication among members through modes of speaking; identification with popular icons, events, and images; and the actualization of codified behaviors within highly visible, mass-mediated spaces (see Lewis 1992; Yano 1997). The behavior of most fans, both male and female, during the World Cup was based heavily on practices learned in other fan contexts where largely female crowds gathered for the performances of pop stars. Instead of replicating the sports fandoms of Europe or Latin America, Korean fans during the World Cup evoked the music fandoms that were already a familiar part of South Korean popular culture. Hegemonic narratives of sports in the United States and Europe are said to be based on historical legacies, legendary pasts, and the technical knowledge of the game, but the character of South Korean forms of fandom was not based on relationships between fans and sports mythologies or on the corporeal experience of playing the game and knowing the rules (see Dunning 1988; Elias and Dunning 1986).[15] Instead, this World Cup fan community was one where women came to dominate public spaces with practices of fandom cultures that required little or no technical knowledge of the games, per se, but an adequate ability to perform one's competence as a national media subject—one that would be appropriate in producing and representing the crowds on the streets as well as those watching on national television channels. This does not mean that women didn't understand or know the game, but it does point out that there was little to no technical knowledge of sport required to successfully demonstrate one's competence as a fan. Instead, the feminized practices of consumption came to define fandom cultures of the event.

During the World Cup, the close relationship between the character of the crowd and mediated texts about the crowd expressed a dynamic relationship between media and subjects.[16] The behaviors of the crowd demonstrated forms of sociality produced by Internet fan sites. These fandoms were examples of the power of digital media to produce "online/offline" publics in South Korea. The appropriate symbolic behaviors for the event were discussed and acquired online and then performed offline in public contexts. Evidence of the successful transfer of Internet communications to public performance was presented in newspapers, magazines, television coverage, and websites. With these media texts in circulation, participants went back online to describe their behaviors, encounters, and observations. They also shared the psychological details of their experiences by discussing their emotions, feelings, and opinions about various aspects of the event. The participants assessed the mainstream media coverage of the crowds and weighed the media depictions against their own personal experiences. The debates, discussions, stories, and rumors that occurred through Internet sites demonstrated the ongoing processes by which fans were produced. The public behaviors that came to represent the event were defined through this cycle of online/offline experiences.[17]

Ch'oe He-mi, my fellow kosiwŏn resident, insisted that I accompany her and her Internet moim "gathering" to cheer as a group in the streets and at various venues and, presumably, to remain with the group for celebrations that would last well into the early morning. For her birthday, He-mi had just purchased a brand-new top-of-the-line cell phone with a built-in camera for 300,000 won (approximately $250). Its polyphonic ring had the ubiquitous tune "*Oh! P'ilsŭng Korea!*" set to play with incoming calls. On the day of the match against Portugal, I walked down the hall of the kosiwŏn to meet He-mi in her tiny room. She was still getting ready for the event. Step by step, she flamboyantly demonstrated the process of transformation into a Red Devil. First, she placed black-colored contacts into her eyes. "Isn't it disgusting?" she remarked as she stared at me with bugged-out eyes. "Everyone's doing it. They make your pupils look bigger. You look like a doll . . . or a monster." When I asked her how much they cost, she casually remarked, "About 200,000 won" (which was about $170 at the time). I gasped, as the contacts cost the same amount as her room—a tiny space no larger than one meter by one and a half meters.

She then folded a red "Be the Reds" bandana, tucked it behind her ears, and tied it along the back of her head. She had her face painted earlier that day with the South Korean flag on her right cheek. She carefully rolled up the sleeves of her "Be the Reds" T-shirt to look more like a cap sleeve. As I sat on the mattress in her room, I began to feel impatient as she took extra time to pick the appropriate belt among those hanging over our heads to go with her stretch jeans. Just before she left the room, she wrapped a large *Taegukki* around her waist like a sarong clinging snugly to her hips. As we walked out the door, she slipped on four-inch platform sandals made of hemp and cork. As usual, she tried hard to look "sexy" when going out in public. She took extra care to make particular details stand out on what was, basically, a pre-scribed outfit. She wanted to look like a member of the Red Devils group, yet she still wanted to express a sexualized femininity within the context of this group uniform. It reminded me of the small details, such as sneakers, hair highlights, and hair accessories, that Korean high school students carefully consider in an attempt to supplement their regimented uniforms.

Even with her intensive efforts, Ch'oe He-mi was wearing a variation of the same clothing and accessories I had seen on almost every other spectator-fan. Beyond the official members who attended national games in the stadium and ran the websites, it did not make a difference whether fans in the streets were registered members of the supporters club or not. As long as you claimed to be part of the supporters club and proved it through dress and behavior, you could be considered a Red Devil. Official membership was free, requiring only an easy, straightforward registration on the Red Devils web-site,[18] but unofficial membership was based on how well one could follow the prescribed behaviors and successfully perform the duties of membership.

Due to the hegemonic visions of the appropriate World Cup fan, there was a high degree of uniformity to the World Cup crowds. Nevertheless, some progressive academics were quick to point out the spontaneity and creativity of the crowd (Cho Han 2002a). These observers tended to focus on the individual autonomy of the members of the crowd and the diversity in terms of class, region, gender, and national origin. Despite these diverse elements, the crowd was largely represented as a uniform mass in media depictions and textual renderings of the event. The sheer power of images from that event operated to produce a uniform collective. Members of the crowd were, for the most part, dressed the same way, held the same cheering materials in their hands, and sang the same chants and songs en masse. I am sympathetic to the desire to read this crowd against the grain of the homogenizing narratives of nationalist interest, yet a sociological picture of the red masses has burned an image of pulsing red embers in my mind.

Sexualizing the Crowd During a general conversation about sport in early June, twenty-year-old Kim Sae-hŭi asked playfully, "What are the three topics that Korean men talk about that our country's women hate most?" To my blank stare she replied, "They hate it when men talk about their experiences in the military. They hate it when men talk about playing *ch'ukku*. And they hate it *most* when men talk about playing *ch'ukku* while in the military." Sae-hŭi used the world *ch'ukku* (football) in this statement, but the more accurate term is *chokku*, which is a highly popular game played almost exclusively in the military with a football but on a tennis court with three men on either side, much like volleyball.[19] Nevertheless, the well-known and oft-repeated saying demonstrates the extent to which sports, the military, and masculinity have been linked to the national project of making South Korean men (see chapter 3).

This naturalized connection between the nation, masculinity, and men's sports was challenged by the large number of young women and girls who poured out onto the streets to celebrate the World Cup matches. The densely populated public spaces around City Hall and Kwanghwamun were filled with young females in their teens and twenties. It was reported that females constituted well over half the participants in street celebrations. Though this event did not radically alter the assumption that football matches that feature men, including the FIFA World Cup, are essentially masculinist cultural productions, it did demonstrate the potentiality of a global mega-event to induce new modes of response.

Kim Sae-hŭi told me that she was a member of the Red Devils Supporters Club. She considered herself a "real fan" of football and claimed that she had been since high school. All the other women, she stated, were simply following the trends of the time. "Girls, as you know, are prone to suggestion and trends," she stated in a matter-of-fact manner. She, on the other hand, had been a fan of the Pusan team (featuring the heartthrob Ahn Jung-hwan) for several years. She had spent many Sunday afternoons watching football games with her taxi-driver father who was, she informed me, also a football fanatic. Sae-hŭi's statements reinforced the assumptions about gender and sport consumption by hinting that other women were not as technically proficient as she was in understanding football. As the exception to the rule, she further promoted the naturalization of the relationship between men and sport fandom.

Prior to an evening outing, Kim Sae-hŭi decided to help me become an appropriate fan by instructing me in the basic forms of cheer, clapping the rhythms to the chants, and singing the melodies to songs that would be repeated hundreds of times. After several dozen attempts, I finally picked up the basics, and she felt satisfied that I wouldn't embarrass her. Although she claimed to be a "true" football fan, not once did we talk about the game or the opposing team. She consistently directed our football conversations to non-sports-related issues such as "What are you going to wear?" or "Which football player do you think is the best looking?" We discussed the players that she liked most, particularly her obsession with Ahn Jung-hwan, as well as the two most popular blondes in Asia at the time, British players Michael Owen and David Beckham. Even though Kim Sae-hŭi insisted on her genuine love of football for its own sake, she tended to sway our conversations to matters of personal fashion and romantic persuasion. Herein, she highlighted the contradiction between her diminution of other female fans and her own demonstration of highly feminized behaviors in both her expressions of heterosexual desire for male players and consumer practices that focused heavily on her appearance at sporting events. She may have felt that I would relate to her better as a female myself, but it was clear that she felt no need to demonstrate her sports expertise in my presence.

Throughout the tournament, there were many media accounts commenting on the presence and influence of women in the crowds. Most women in the crowds were well within the modesty standards of Korean grade-school uniforms, but my eye was drawn to a highly visible minority of women who challenged publicly acceptable modes of dress through their risqué clothing and body movements. It was popular to roll up shirt tails to expose midriffs and pierced belly buttons. There was also the transformation of the Korean flag into a versatile fashion fabric with their use as miniskirts, sarongs, tube tops, and halter tops tied around the neck and back with loose ribbon. The application of body paint and temporary tattoos in the form of nationalist symbols were also popular modes of accessorizing. These perfunctory symbols were seductively applied around the belly button or on the cheek, shoulder, shoulder blade, or small of the back.

These scintillating displays of sexuality were enacted by a minority of the women on the streets, but they were highly visible because of their wide circulation in television reports, newspaper articles, and sports tabloids. Representations of women's sexualized bodies were reproduced for consumption by a national public. Mainstream media treated these images like a coming-of-age party for Korean women who were expressing their sexuality

Figure 14. Two female fans cheering during a 2002 World Cup match. Yonhap News, reprinted with permission.

in an appropriate public forum.[20] Sexy women were now a site of national pride as they became examples of the immense beauty, independence, and modernity of Korean women. These women indicated their ability to be frivolous. They displayed a particular pursuit of leisure and entertainment available only to those with the material wherewithal—those who had the time and money to shop and to prepare their "look." They represented a form of cosmopolitanism—urban women whose images were more likely to be captured and circulated by the city-based media.

A particular relationship between Korean women and the nation was articulated through their exhibitionist displays of national signifiers. As Kim Hyun Mee (2002) argues, the national media interpreted the sexualized women in the crowd as demonstrating a form of nation love. In the context of patriarchal nationalist discourses, the "sexy" Korean women of the World Cup demonstrated their loyalty to the nation through their articulations of desire for the national football team. Their energetic and playful bodies were "in the service of the nation." The World Cup crowds were a safe venue for these blunt sexual expressions, and these behaviors could be understood within the context of support for the national team. The behaviors of the young women did not go as far as to subvert existing notions of national allegiance by "misdirecting" that desire toward another nation's players or "self-directing" desire strictly for the sake of personal pleasure (H. Kim 2002). Even though the clothing choices and the all-night revelry of some women challenged the limits of social acceptability, their bold acts were tolerated, even celebrated, in this unique context. They were made appropriate through their appropriation by mass media.

It is important to note that, even though nationalist discourses attempted to appropriate women's public displays of emotion strictly as expressions of nation love, their expressions far exceeded the interests of the patriarchal nationalists. Women's expressions should be understood as important within the context of their struggles for gender and sexual equality in South Korea. Certainly, it can be argued that the crowds indicated objective advances from the blatant repression of women in public contexts during earlier authoritarian regimes. Many women did, in fact, express their personal experiences as ecstatic moments of radical difference. Their experiences offered new visions of future possibilities for their lives. However, even a sympathetic feminist must acknowledge that these shifts in gendered representation and experience lacked a shared vision for social change.[21]

Of course, mainstream media discourses were a primary force in manufacturing notions about the feminized crowd. Mass-mediated narratives operated to induce women to enter the crowds and behave in codified ways. The commercial interests of the media benefited from the significant interest by women. This could be seen as an example of how the "pink dollar" operated in this traditionally male viewer market. In other words, overt displays of male images as sex symbols were used as a way to recruit female consumers (see Bordo 1999; Miller 2002). Furthermore, sexualized female bodies were conveyed through patriarchal media outlets, including the highly sexist sports tabloids discussed in chapter 1. The mainstream media outlets reproduced limited versions of what counted as "sexy."[22] Images of svelte, scantily clad women were used to titillate male readers. Male heterosexual fantasies were piqued through sexualized images of girls and young women. It can be said that men were also compelled to enter into the streets with their own sexualized fantasies. In the interpersonal interactions that took place during long periods of waiting, the embracing of strangers that occurred in moments of intense emotion, and the all-night drunken revelry that took place after the celebrations, men could have interpreted an opportunity for access to young female bodies.

The discourses of national unity worked through gendered contexts that produced the crowds as feminized. Media representations of the event operated to commodify female bodies in a way that left them available to market appropriations. This commodification of female bodies raises important concerns as to whose interests were served through the display of women in the crowds. It is important to detail the limits of the discourses of female liberation and feminist advances, since representations of girls and women were so easily appropriated and reproduced by commercial mass media. The rhetoric of women's empowerment must be tempered by the limits of the event itself to make any significant changes in the social position of women.

Consuming Emotions

Toward the end of the tournament, I watched a game at a large sports bar named South Wales, which took up the entire third floor of a large five-story building in an alley off a major road in Sinch'on, an area of Seoul understood to be a defining center of trendy youth culture in South Korea. I woke up early Sunday morning and met Ch'oe He-mi, who insisted that I get my face painted before we met everyone at the bar. We went to a salon in her neighborhood that was offering free "expert" face painting. She got the name of her second favorite player, Lee Ch'ŏn-su, on her face, and I sheepishly acceded to getting a small *taeguk* mark, the blue and red yin-yang sign, on my left cheek. We got to the bar four hours before the game and waited in the stairwell with nearly thirty other members of her Internet moim. The group had decided to go to South Wales since one member knew the owner and thought it would be a nice alternative to roasting under the hot June sun. We were seated on newspapers along a concrete stairwell that lacked proper ventilation and tried to remain calm within the cramped space. Occasionally, the small crowd would burst into the oft-repeated cheers of *Taehan Min'guk* or the song *Oh! P'ilsŭng Korea*. We were told to come early in order to ensure that our party got seats for the historic match against Spain in the Round of Eight. Given the size of the crowd waiting inside the stairwell and spilling out onto the street, it was obvious that the bar would be filled to capacity.

When we finally entered the bar to watch the important game, there were scores of long tables set with pitchers of beer and platters of finger food. The chairs that lined the tables were facing a large screen covering an entire wall upon which the game would be projected from an LCD projector. We got settled, and I positioned myself between the men and women of the group, rather quiet and reserved as a result of my public shaming for not wearing a red "Be the Reds!" T-shirt. I viewed the game with extra focus, enjoying the hypnotic power of live broadcast coverage. During the game, I felt rather uncomfortable about what I perceived as "questionable" calls that seemed to favor the South Korea team. As I brought up my skepticism about some of the calls, I was given dirty looks and again made to feel like a liability or even a traitor. It was obvious that my personal analyses were not compromised to the interests of a South Korea team win. The vitriolic attitude by members of the moim toward my queries reminded me of the extreme passion that can overtake some sports fans who aggressively silence opposition in their emotional excitement.

I attempted to contextualize this seemingly irrational passion on the part of the fans around me, but I was surprised and angered by the commentators' overwhelming silence about the controversial calls. The decision by MBC not to replay the controversial calls in slow motion more than once was rather dubious.[23] The game was, nevertheless, exciting to watch and reached double overtime in a scoreless tie. The game concluded with a penalty kick shootout. Subsequent kicks by players on each team from the penalty line would determine the outcome of the game. The moment Korean veteran player Hong Myung Bo made the goal that would win the game and send South Korea into the Round of Four, the bar exploded with an overwhelming burst of energy. A roar I had never before experienced was punctuated by women's startling shrieks all around me.

Almost immediately, I picked up the phone to call my parents and their group of Korean friends in the United States before the millions of phone users in South Korea calmed down enough to begin making calls. Throughout the tournament, after each victory by the South Korean team, I called my parents in the United States and the group that had gathered at their home to watch the tournament on *Univisión*, the Spanish-language broadcast network for their regional cable service provider. Through these phone conversations, I could hear the shouts of joy and laughter of Koreans who were watching across the Pacific in the early hours of the morning. As my goal was to engage in a transnational project, I wanted a glimpse into how they were experiencing the World Cup at the same moment. I was hoping to connect with their emotions as Koreans in the diaspora. My father answered my call in an excited tone, and we repeated to each other "*Igyŏtda! Igyŏtda!*" (We won!

We won!). I shouted over the crowd, "Aren't you so proud of the South Korean team? Aren't you so proud of Korea?" My father shot back, "What do you have to be so proud about? You're not Korean." Through this rather startling exchange, I realized that there were assumptions I had made in a transnational context that allowed me to assert Korean ethnic nationalism within a U.S. context, but it made me think this same assertion as supremely dangerous within the Korean context. This contradiction was noted and expressed by my father's retort, causing me to question the shifting constructions of nationalist affect in which I had allowed myself to variously indulge in and critique.

As I shut the phone and returned to the group of men and women with whom I had been watching the game, the members of the group were jumping up and down, slapping high fives, and embracing. Seven women from the moim then moved toward the projection screen, embraced in a group, and collapsed on top of one another. They began to cry loudly and remained on the floor for several minutes wailing. Beside me, my multigame companion, Kim Chang-ho, stood silently and watched the slow-motion replays of the final shots toward victory. He had tears streaming down his face. The other men looked at him obliquely with rather sheepish grins, seemingly a bit embarrassed for him, as they had successfully halted their emotional output within a few moments of victory. I stared at the women and asked a few of the men sitting across from me whether the women were doing okay. No Yŏng-min, a twenty-eight-year-old computer consultant, replied, "Our nation's women just do that because they are competitive. If one woman is crying, they all have to start crying." He continued, "It's trendy to cry, and you know that women follow trends."

I was struck by what seemed to be exaggerated differences in the ways that men and women reacted emotionally to the event. As the women continued to cry in a group, men began to divert their gaze toward the slow-motion replays on television, or they attempted to make phone calls on jammed cellular channels to their friends and family. Eventually, the women got off the floor and returned to rejoin the others in the group. Later in the week, I talked to several participants about the gendered differences in the ways in which women and men reacted. The kinds of pat answers I received seemed to suggest that the gendered differences were due to the emotional and flighty nature of women. "We/They just react that way" seemed to be the dismissive answer to what was taken as my rather irrelevant question.

The naturalization of these differences was based on the expression of gendered forms of public emotion. This display of emotion was deeply in-scribed in gendered modes of media engagement that had been in place for years prior to this event. The outpouring of emotion, particularly the scream-ing, embracing, and the tears, were codified forms of behavior that had been part of adolescent and teen experiences of fandom, if not for most of these young women directly, then for those in their peer groups. These fandom behaviors were personally experienced by many through direct participation in fandoms. If not experienced personally, they likely viewed televised depic-tions of pop fans responding with powerful emotions to performances and public appearances.

These expressions of emotion in response to sports were heavily influ-enced by the cultures of fandom that preceded the event. These forms of emotion were considered a classic example of the *Oppa pudae* (older brother squad), the commonly used and derisive term to describe the culture of adolescent and teenage girls who participate in fandoms of pop stars (such as the all-male pop groups *Sŏtaeji* and H.O.T.).[24] The desire for victory, com-pounded with the intense climax of the game, fueled an emotional reaction in women that followed codified forms of female expression. In contrast to the tears of the women, the "genuine" tears of Kim Chang-ho symbolized his dedication to football and the national team and were understood as a sign of his "sincere nature." For the rest of the evening, the men and women of the group took turns poking fun at his sensitive tendencies. Tears were beautiful because they were a sign of genuine devotion, but Kim's extended crying, albeit muted, surpassed the standard of comfort for public emotion within normative contexts of heterosexuality. The moim reminded him of this by their constant teasing.

Although most men and women with whom I interacted did not play orga-nized sports in any extended way during their lifetimes, there remained the prevailing notion that men's knowledge of sports was legitimated through a closer connection with the experience of playing sports and the acquisition of technical knowledge about the game as part of their education as men. It was thought that men's preferences for sports were more specific to each genre of sport, the technical aspects of play, the history of the sport, and the narratives of personal experiences with the sport. Women's knowledge of sports was not considered technical or constitutive of their female subjec-tivities. Rather, their interests in sports were attuned to the dramatic narra-tive of the games, their sexual desire for particular male players, and the social aspects of being a fan. Instead of the notion that women's subjectivities were shaped through sport, there was the prevailing notion that women's modes of sociality shaped the character of sports spectatorship in an exceptional way during the World Cup.

The above characterizations of women's and men's relationships to sport follow facile stereotypes of gendered relationships to sports, which were defied by the actions of some individuals I met and knew. These assertions, however, reflect dominant ideologies about gender differences that were reproduced in public contexts. The discursive constructions of gendered differences had a significant impact on the social formations of the World Cup. The feminized crowds were not accidental or spontaneous. The crowds had emerged through a combination of nationalist discourses, as promoted within the context of a global sporting event and familiar media-based modes of fandom.

Feminist Interpretations of the Crowd

The role of women in constituting this event as an enormous spectacle was widely debated by feminists in South Korea who attempted to interpret the significance of this event with respect to the present status of women and the history of women's positions in Korean society (see Cho Han et al. 2004). There was also much discussion about the implications of this event for the future possibilities for female empowerment. The sight of women "making history" and privileging their own positions with respect to this global event catalyzed a discourse about the place of women in national narratives. The space made available for the public expression of female sexuality and desire was considered an important aspect of the World Cup (Cho Han 2002b; H. Kim 2002). The power of women to assert themselves as creative and generative actors in the construction of World Cup publics, as well as their ability to dominate representations of these publics, raised the question of how this could work toward shifting the material and social status for South Korean women in general. Did this event work to empower women in their everyday lives by demonstrating the existence of possibilities yet to be explored? Did the event work to reify existing stereotypes and exaggerate differences, thus further impeding the important work still to be accomplished in raising the social status of Korean women? The collective displays of solidarity underscore the possibilities of women coming together to change existing forms of social inequality.

A fifty-six-year-old university administrator, Kang Okhae, announced to

me that Korean women had been oppressed for the entirety of Korean history. Through their shouts during the World Cup, she claimed, they were
breaking out of centuries of Confucian tradition for the first time and letting
go of their deep sense of *han*, the pathos of repressed longing. Without any
mention of the male players or the actual games, she effusively shared the
ways in which she felt that watching the games totally relieved her of the
stress of her job and her family. To her, the acts of screaming, singing, and
dancing were essentially therapeutic. These behaviors, she argued, relieved
Korean women of their pent-up emotions and gave them the opportunity to
let loose in front of the world. "Really, women are the bigger fans," she
stated. "There are more women out there than men, and they are more
energetic about their cheering. Our country's women are finally breaking
out of the Confucian tradition and screaming freely. I see it as a liberating
experience for women. We were always told to be very quiet and to stay inside
when we were young, and now we have the opportunity to move our bodies
and to be loud in public."

Although she expressed several times that she felt far too old for street
cheering, she seemed to be very proud of the fact that she had been invited to
cheer in the streets by some of the students with whom she interacted.
Instead, she told me that she invited friends to her home and screamed
in solidarity with those in the streets. She added that even at home, she
screamed loudly, as though she was screaming for all Korean women. Ms.
Kang joked that she might even venture into the crowds since she was still
quite young at heart and advanced in her thinking. Ms. Kang conveyed the
idea that she saw this tournament as realizing her feminist hopes within
South Korea.

In her assessments of the event, Ms. Kang praised the women of the
World Cup as transforming the event into a feminist event that empowered
women through experiences on the streets as well as through images that
were conveyed in the media. She was moved by the highly visible presence of
women expressing their own pleasure in public. For her, this spectacle resulted in what she claimed to be an incredible catharsis. "As an American," I
was told, "you wouldn't understand the intense amount of repression that
Korean women have had to live through over the years." I acquiesced to the
idea that I was unable to fully understand the oppression of Korean women,
but I was skeptical about her pronouncements about the Korean crowd as a
form of feminist liberation.

Ms. Kang's statements reflected a celebratory interpretation of the feminized publics of the World Cup that understood the crowds as spaces for the expression of personal freedom and liberation. Within the broader spectrum of feminist discussion, Ms. Kang's statements could be located on the extreme celebratory end. Nevertheless, most of the feminist writings and feminists with whom I spoke were quite celebratory in their tone. Kim Hyun Mee (2002; 2004) offers an important discussion about the inability of events such as the World Cup to change material conditions of inequality for women. However, this critique was overshadowed by the emphasis on the spectacular nature of the event and the potential energy of women to shift the character of other entrenched social practices.

I do agree that the pleasure that was experienced in the crowds offered an immense social critique of repressive public cultures. However, it is not clear how these pleasures might be converted to demands for structural changes. Rather than an expression of female freedom, the crowds were the expression of particular gendered modes of consumption and the pleasures experienced through the social practices of consumption. Furthermore, discussions about female participation in the crowds were interpreted within contexts that celebrated national unity rather than understood as expressing personal desires directed toward objects of subjective affection. I believe that the lack of a diverse feminist response should raise questions about the power of nationalist narratives to selectively incorporate feminist narratives of pleasure. How did the women's participation operate to produce ideas of a cosmopolitan nation? How were they used to demonstrate the "modernity" of South Korean women?

These questions connect the concerns raised in this chapter with those of the previous chapter, given that representations of female fans were also interpreted within national discourses of segyehwa. The audience of female fans came to represent a global Koreanness and had little to do with their actual status as women in South Korean society. Furthermore, the audience was praised for its ability to create a global spectacle that then worked to prove the modern status of South Korea in the world. Though the hegemonic interpretations of these publics continued to interpret the actions of women as primarily nationalist in nature, an understanding of the subjective desires that underpinned participation by females helps to challenge this monolithic interpretation. In this chapter, I have established how discourses of nationalism were embedded in the consumer and media responses to the event even prior to the event itself. I have also demonstrated how gender played a central role in connecting the discourses of nation, consumerism, and mass media during this event. Through a discussion of the everyday acts of consumption that created the spectacle, I have attempted to evoke the affective dimensions of media sport consumption. I have shown that the articulations of nation and gender worked within this affective context to generate a new expression of Koreanness that was articulated within the parameters of segyehwa. The place of women in this articulation of nation demonstrates a shift in the visibility of women on the global stage, yet there is little indication that this attention made a difference in changing the material and political conditions for women's lives in South Korea.

In this chapter, I have focused on the ways in which global Koreanness was understood by subjects within Seoul, and the next chapter looks at how Koreanness was articulated within the local contexts of Koreatown in Los Angeles. In addition to the gendered dimensions of the spectacle, the issues of race, U.S. multiculturalism, and ideas of belonging marked Korean/American responses to the event. The analysis in the following chapter continues to focus on the political significance of consumer behaviors by looking at how particular consumer practices operate within national and political contexts. I continue to underscore the importance of understanding how collective modes of consumerism operate to produce new forms of national publics.

Home Field Advantage

NATION, RACE, AND TRANSNATIONAL MEDIA SPORT
IN LOS ANGELES'S KOREATOWN

The 2002 World Cup demonstrated how media sport operates to produce a
sense of Koreanness in Korean America. The month-long event drew attention to the position of Korean America with respect to Los Angeles, the
United States, the Korean diaspora, and the world. As observed through my
field research, the event had a tremendous impact on Korean communities
around the world, including Los Angeles. Even today, the event persists as a
historical monument, a particularly unique moment in Korean history that
was produced through the convergence of many factors: South Korea as the
cohost of the world's most popular media sport event, the formation and
existence of particular fandom cultures in South Korea, the technological
connections forged among Korean communities around the world, and the
processes of *segyehwa* and liberalization in South Korea (see chapter 5). In
this chapter, I discuss the 2002 World Cup as a particularly compelling
manifestation of the transnational dimensions of media sport in Korean
America. I argue that certain political, ideological, and material interests
in U.S. and Korean mainstream media sport constitute the Korean American community as an explicitly transnational community of overseas Korean
nationals. I focus on how the transnational is subjectively experienced, understood, and apprehended through the local and the national (Gupta and
Ferguson 1997).

Through an analysis of subjective Korean American responses to the
World Cup, I demonstrate the multiple locations of Korean Americans as
participants and actors within the transnational social, economic, and political domains of Los Angeles, the U.S. nation-state, the South Korean nation-

state, and the global Korean nation. In doing so, I demonstrate how the subjective experiences of the local, national, and transnational are imbricated and often at odds. My research investigates the place-specific features of Koreanness by focusing on the specific ways that transnationalisms are lived within Koreatown in Los Angeles—a multiethnic and multiracial area that exists as a critical space in representing Korea in America (Abelmann and Lie 1997). I examine discourses of racial difference, spatialized social relations, and national community that are shaped within the contexts of such transnational processes.

In figuring the space of Koreatown as a transnational one, I look at the erasures and appropriations of difference that occurred through the World Cup event. I investigate how dominant Korean apprehensions of space were produced and performed in a way that contrasts sharply with the demographic constitution of Koreatown. By investigating how issues of race and class relations were discussed within the context of the event, I look at how Korean America is produced with respect to racialized and classed others, particularly the Latino majority that constitutes the space of Koreatown. The articulation of Korean America as a transnational space operates within and through these narratives of Koreatown as a space of contested race and class relations.

As argued in previous chapters, productions of transnational media sport that feature Korean players and teams have played a significant role in producing notions of Koreanness for Koreans located around the world. Images of Korean professional baseball players, golfers, and football (soccer) players working in U.S. and European sporting leagues are highly visible in many Korean communities, especially Korean American communities. One factor that contributes to this phenomenon is the substantial Korean population, the largest outside the Korean peninsula, that resides in the United States (Yu and Choe 2003/4).[1] Many members of the Korean diaspora in the United States maintain active material, psychological, and emotional connections to Korea (Abelmann and Lie 1997; Amerasia 2003/4; 2004). Furthermore, a large proportion of the Korean players in baseball and golf who are considered the most popular and talented in their respective fields play in U.S.-based professional leagues, such as MLB and the LPGA.[2] The perceived "cultural proximity" of Korean players to Korean American audiences with respect to national location, hegemonic political ideologies, geography, and cultural experiences as Korean subjects in the United States also might explain this interest (Iwabuchi 2002).

With the emergence of Korean players in mainstream media sport, a new media genre of Korean-language sporting coverage emerged in the United States, and subsequently, new modes of sporting spectatorship developed. Previous decades of Korean-language sport coverage in Korean America had been characterized by episodic reports on the performance of the South Korean national team and athletes at the Olympics or other international tournaments. With the advent of these new stars, Korean Americans began to watch individual players participating in North American and European professional team sports. This resulted in making media sport an object of regular and seasonal interest for many Korean Americans. Certain types of professional and commercial sports—namely golf and baseball—became a considerable part of the Korean-language media programming repertoire. Groups of Korean American fans began showing up at MLB games in visible numbers, waving the *Taegukki*, chanting in *Hankungmal*, eating Korean snacks, and holding up signs in *Han'gŭl* (Korean written language). Korean American spectators attended golf tournaments to eagerly cheer for Korean players, creating a Korean-language ruckus in the galleries. Korean-language news media that circulate in Korean America—including newspapers, radio, and television—began to recruit staff to work on sport features. These media outlets would often (and continue to) prioritize sport features about successful Korean players performing in the United States as front-page, top-of-the-hour news. On newsstands in Koreatown, Korean-language sports dailies increased in circulation and were ubiquitous in and around Korean-owned establishments.

During the 2002 World Cup, Korean Americans expressed their transnational interest in South Korea in spectacular and historically significant ways. This indicates a relatively recent and understudied historical shift in the role of transnationalism in the Korean American community as produced through the circulation of capital, media, and people. At various moments in the twentieth century, transnational connections to Asian nations were considered a dangerous liability. Japanese Americans during and following World War II, as well as Chinese Americans throughout the Cold War, had to assert their Americanness amidst racist accusations of disloyalty. Korean Americans were also subject to this scrutiny, as they were Japanese colonial subjects until the end of World War II (Takaki 1998; D. Yoo 2000; H. Yu 2001).[3] In these cases, being considered *just* American for individuals and groups racialized as Orientals was critical to issues of survival and inclusion in the U.S. national polity. The Asian American movement, even though it was connected to Third World student movements during the 1960s and 1970s, worked to shift popular and academic discourses of Asian Americans toward their apprehension as U.S. national subjects while diminishing transnational ties. Since September 11, 2001, people of South Asian, Middle Eastern, and Islamic heritage have often been subject to suspicion, incarceration, violence, and death as potential terrorists with connections to "foreign" terrorist forces (Grewal 2005). Once again, the public and governmental "sighting/citing" of specific national origins and transnational connections has become highly politicized and dangerous (Puar 2007). Therefore, the effects of transnationalism for different ethnonational groups in Asian America differs, depending on the shifting geopolitical and economic relationships between the particular Asian nation and the United States.

For Korean America, the positive reception of transnationalism indicated by Korean American interest in the World Cup occured within a moment of historical, economic, and political changes in the relationship between South Korea and the Korean American community. This research offers insight into how these changes continue to occur between South Korea and Korean America, and it indicates how popular culture, mass media, and sport work to shape the nature of transnational connections between communities in both places. Furthermore, it highlights how the political contexts that exist between both spaces are mediated through mass consumption and how mass consumption works to shape attitudes and feelings about politics between both spaces. Although the production of an imagined transnational community indicates elements of a shared Koreanness between South Korea and Los Angeles, clearly the articulations of nation in both places are heterogeneous and differentiated. In this chapter, I point out that the production of Korean America in Los Angeles also raises questions about how issues of difference, such as race, class, gender, and age, are articulated in transnational Korean America.

Koreatown Stories: Mediating Korea in the United States

When I arrived in Los Angeles, the excitement of the World Cup could still be felt. Many eating establishments still had posters of the players on their walls next to pictures of customers dressed in red T-shirts with painted faces and wide grins. There were billboards commemorating the event, and many of the advertisements for business in Koreatown continued to evoke the sights, sounds, and feelings of that period in June. I could easily strike up a conversation with a stranger who attended some of the events, and the person would be able to tell me where she or he was during the Korea team games, and how she spent the month. When I shared my own experiences on the streets of Seoul, many of my respondents told me that I was lucky to be in Seoul during the event and stated that they wished they could have been there as well. Others drew comparisons between my experiences in Seoul and theirs in Koreatown; some concluded that they had comparable experiences in Koreatown. Many pointed out that their experiences were marked by a sense of shared Koreanness with others in Korean America, and they could articulate what constituted the Korean community, at least in relation to the media event.

The World Cup demonstrated the power of media in creating a sense of national affect and belonging for the Korean American community. Through an investigation of media texts and interviews about the event, I discovered similarities between mainstream discourses in Korean-language media in South Korea and the United States. Korean media and institutions succeeded in communicating a Korean nationalist rhetoric that operated to suspend significant differences that exist among Korean/Americans, effectively turning the event into a Korean nationalist experience. Though the event did not necessarily inculcate a sense of nationalism in all participants, the publics that emerged as a result of this event were mediated as a national public in mainstream media outlets. Those who expressed a different kind of affiliation with the event were not given a voice within mainstream media outlets, and by their participation in group settings during the World Cup, they were automatically understood to be national fans.

In 2003 and 2004, a two-volume special issue of *Amerasia Journal* was released to commemorate the 2003 centennial of Korean immigration to the United States. The featured articles convey the heterogeneity of Korean America. A number of articles in the second volume (2004) focus more specifically on the social, cultural, and political contours of the Korean American community in Los Angeles, demonstrating that this community is highly diverse with respect to language usage, immigrant generation, educational status, class, political ideology, religion, and age (see Abelmann and Lie 1997; Kim and Yu 1996; Kyeyoung Park 1999). Similarly, in direct response to stereotypical representations of Korean Americans in the wake of the 1992 Los Angeles uprisings, *Blue Dreams* (Abelmann and Lie 1997), a study of the Korean American community in Los Angeles, works to debunk the totalizing myths and generalizations that have been produced or fostered by mainstream U.S. media, government institutions such as immigration and census bureaus, community organizations such as churches and cultural centers, and academic research.

Abelmann and Lie effectively critique the overly homogeneous representation of Korean Americans, but it should also be noted that a dominant understanding of Koreanness is fostered by various powerful Korean institutions and based largely in Los Angeles (centered around media companies, churches, business associations, and centers for culture and arts).[4] With respect to Korean-language mass media, the major media outlets are located in or near Koreatown, and they are, to a large extent, sponsored by parent companies in South Korea.[5] I argue that these media, in many ways, bolster the South Korean government's depiction of the Korean American community as an overseas Korean community. The segyehwa policies of the South Korean government, which were first announced in 1995 (S. Kim 2000b), began a process of building a global Korean network as a way to reach out to Koreans living abroad (see Park and Chang 2005). In 1997, the government installed the nonprofit Overseas Korea Foundation (OKF), based in Seoul, which refers to itself as a "home for the 6 million Koreans overseas."[6] In recent years, an overseas Korean population has been constituted as an important resource to be tapped by the South Korean state. The population in the United States, most commonly represented by Koreatown in Los Angeles, is an important focus of these state interests (S. Kim 2000b; Park and Chang 2005).[7]

The chair of the board of directors for the OKF and well-known Seoul National University anthropologist Lee Kwankyu has stated that the foundation is "committed to carrying out its assignment of helping fulfill national tasks faithfully by bringing together Koreans at home and abroad."[8] On the OKF website in 2004, Dr. Lee, echoing a "clash of civilizations" trope (Huntington 1996), wrote, "The twenty-first century is dubbed as a period wherein races, rather than nations, matter."[9] He then goes on to offer a rags-to-riches story about the history of the Korean race during the past century. The tragedy of colonialism, the victimization of Korea as a "scapegoat" during the Cold War, and the "ugly scar" that has been left by the Korean War and partition offer a melodramatic narrative of Korea's past. The statement then discusses how Koreans bravely responded to these challenges through modern development, thus creating the "miracle of the Han River." Lee writes, "They call us a country of miracles."[10]

Lee proceeds to note how *overseas* Koreans have helped make these national miracles happen. Koreans in Japan sent remittances during postwar rebuilding, Koreans in the United States committed brain power during periods of industrialization, and, in recent years, Koreans in China have contributed their labor. He then concludes with an exhortation for continued support from overseas Koreans to help the North and South reunite and help South Korea achieve a stage of development wherein personal incomes will increase from $10,000 a year to $20,000 a year.[11]

With this assessment, Lee rather bluntly expresses one of the main missions of the OKF: to get those of Korean blood who are located abroad to feel a sense of innate responsibility to South Korea and to express their loyalty by contributing to the financial well-being of the nation. Although Lee points out the historically and nationally distinct character of Koreans' contributions in Japan, the United States, and China, he does so in a way that fails to recognize the often painful histories of political and ideological divisions that have produced real differences among these groups (see Amerasia 2004; Ryang 2000). He ties these groups together through the idea that they all work toward strengthening South Korea's economy. This emphasis on the economic contributions (rather than artistic, intellectual, or other cultural contributions) clearly demonstrates the OKF's practical material imperative.[12]

The Overseas Korea Foundation attempts to unite Koreans under this "race-nation" ideology by sponsoring conferences, cultural events, academic research, and publications that produce knowledge about Korean communities located around the world. In the United States, programs for the cultural promotion of Korea and the academic production of knowledge in Korean Studies are largely funded by the OKF and other government-sponsored nonprofit organizations. These institutions demonstrate the immense investment of the South Korean government in reproducing a sense of Koreanness among Koreans outside South Korea, particularly those residing in the United States and Japan.

For the largely immigrant, Korean-speaking population of Korean America, Korean-language media are a primary means for news and information about the world. Korean-language media institutions represent Koreans in the United States as an overseas population of Korean nationals, rather than as an immigrant group or even a diasporic community. Instead of using the terms *Korean diaspora* or *Korean Americans*, the use of the term *overseas Korean* references a displacement from an original space, a homeland on the Korean peninsula. Furthermore, the assumption of shared blood among

Koreans also underpins the use of this term. As part of the segyehwa policies, the South Korean state's interests in producing discourses of a global Korean network and the overseas Korean emerged at the turn of the century (see Park and Chang 2005).

Transnational media sport featuring Korean players is imbricated with multiple and shifting significations of nationalism and belonging for Korean subjects within U.S. borders. Koreans in the United States are diverse and have a number of different statuses as visitors, students, permanent residents, undocumented residents, and legal citizens.[13] Although Korean-language sports coverage operates to produce an inclusive sense of Korean national belonging through discourses about the shared national essence of Korean players and their Korean spectator-fans, Korean American audiences are also concerned with issues of representation, belonging, rights, and citizenship within the multicultural U.S. nation. The material, legal, psychic, and physical consequences of being considered a foreigner, illegal, or a minority in the United States shape this concern for recognition. There are no simplistic explanations about how individuals apprehend these nationalisms that often locate subjects in spaces of contradiction to the nation. Nevertheless, Korean-language media work to convey relatively conservative ideas about who constitutes the Korean American community. Much of this conservatism comes from the continuing media control by mainstream news outlets based in Seoul. Many of these outlets are funded, at least in part, by the South Korean state. Discourses around Korean Americans follow the dominant nationalist line of the South Korean state, which attempts to interpellate Koreans in the United States as overseas Koreans—that is, loyal Korean national subjects (see Althusser 1971).

Consuming the World Cup in Koreatown

In a manner highly resonant with my interviews with Koreans in Seoul, conversations in Los Angeles half a year after the World Cup were often dominated by personal recollections of the month of June. In most instances, my attempts at some balance among discussions of different sports, such as baseball or golf, were overwhelmed by remembrances of the World Cup. There was a palpable excitement conveyed through vivid recountings of the event. My respondents remarked on the shocking success of the South Korean national team, the personal impact of the event, and the transformation of life for *Hanin Sahoe,* or Korean society, for a month and beyond in Koreatown. Several respondents discussed the event as a moment of exceptional joy within their lives as Korean Americans.

Within community spaces of Koreatown, material remnants of the World Cup operated as persistent memorializations of the event. On Wilshire Boulevard in the heart of Koreatown, there was a highly visible billboard with the painted image of a Korean soccer player engaging in a bicycle kick. This image was posted on the side of the Aroma Wilshire Center, a multistory, multiuse venue for Korean businesses. Many people, including Koreans and Latinos, continued to wear their red T-shirts silk-screened with the words "Be the Reds" in dynamic white lettering. In variety stores, grocery stores, and department stores, leftover piles of World Cup merchandise collected dust—red T-shirts, headbands, scarves, commemorative plaques, key chains, cell phone accessories, and miniature golden statuettes of the official FIFA trophy. Posters of popular South Korean national players, especially heartthrobs such as midfielders Ahn Jung-hwan and Kim Nam-il, were posted in small business establishments, such as beauty supply stores, music stores, beauty salons, and *nore bang* (karaoke rooms). It was obvious that the town, as local Korean speakers and Korean-language media often refer to it, was not ready to let this event fade from memory.

The World Cup was a major historical event in Koreatown for Korean Americans, and the World Cup frenzy was generated in large part through Korean-language media. Through Internet sites, mass media, and word of mouth, Korean American spectators were educated in how to dress and cheer as fans of the South Korean team. Korean-language media also informed Koreans of local programming—game times, channels, and venues —and, in many instances, promoted group viewing. Some fans watched live coverage on ESPN2, which required cable, whereas others watched on the Korean-language station KTE, which also had limited coverage.[14] In addition, a large proportion of Korean Americans enjoyed watching the exciting coverage on KMEX, their local Spanish-language station, *Univisión.*

Korean American viewers consumed the World Cup through multiple forms of media: U.S.-based, Korean-owned media outlets; South Korean media through Internet sites and satellite television; and mainstream, U.S.-based, English-language media. Multilingual Korean Americans often, if not regularly, consume more than one form of media for information about South Korea. It is important to acknowledge that each media form has different effects. However, for the purposes of this analysis, I will focus primarily on the production of and responses to Korean-language media produced in the United States as a powerful and influential genre in the Korean American community in Los Angeles.

When it came to the World Cup, the major Korean-language media outlets in Korean America gathered their sport coverage primarily from parent stations in South Korea and, to a lesser extent, from mainstream U.S. media and international newswires such as the Associated Press. Any original reporting by the affiliate was highly parochial, and focused on the responses of the Korean community in Los Angeles to the sporting events. Therefore, even though Korean-language media coverage of the World Cup was primarily written and produced in Seoul, there were Korean American segments that covered Korean American responses to the event. Korean-language media in Los Angeles covered spaces of collective gathering in private establishments in Koreatown—the Cambridge Hotel; Hamburg Brewery; and Roma Sauna, a twenty-four-hour bath house. Community responses in churches, business associations, and community sporting leagues were also covered. There were stories on how community relations, particularly race relations between Latinos and Koreans, improved during the World Cup. A great amount of attention was also placed on how the event impacted everyday operations of Korean-owned businesses in Koreatown. Many feature stories focused on World Cup sales and free giveaways by local Korean-owned businesses as a way of celebrating wins by the South Korean team.

Inspired by the media coverage of the incredible success of the Korean team and the awe-inspiring images of millions of spectators coloring the Seoul cityscapes red, Korean Americans attempted to create similar media spectacles within Koreatown. For the first few games, crowds of spectators dressed in red T-shirts gathered at mall-like spaces, bars, restaurants, and hotels. By the time the Korean team had advanced to the Round of Sixteen, outdoor venues in parking lots were set up. As a result, large crowds watched the matches on large screens and cheered with thousands of others as fans did in Seoul. The city approved licenses, and the Los Angeles Police Department (LAPD) was deployed to protect businesses, vehicles, and spectators during these late-night and early-morning sessions. During the match for third and fourth place, the Staples Center, a multiuse commercial venue for large-scale sporting and entertainment events, was loaned free of charge to the Korean community. On June 29, 2002, a capacity crowd of 20,000 fans gathered in the early morning to watch the game, which began at 4:30 a.m.

In these gathering spaces, most fans wore the ubiquitous red T-shirts, which were often distributed freely by host establishments. Cheers, derived directly from fan club cultures that emerged in South Korea, were acquired through video on the Internet, televisual media, telephone conversations, and personal interactions.[15] Koreans in the United States cheered the same rhythms, chants, and songs of *Taehan Min'guk, Oh! P'ilsŭng Korea,* and *Arirang* (see chapter 5). In dress and behavior, then, groups in the United States emulated the actions of the millions of spectators on the streets in Seoul. Koreans were engaged in simultaneous acts of media consumption across geographic and national boundaries. As in Seoul, people in Koreatown ran up and down sidewalks waving flags and giving high-fives to strangers after each victory. There were car celebrations, as drivers cruised up and down the streets of Koreatown honking their horns in the rhythm of a popular chant, waving Korean flags out windows, and screaming to pedestrians.

Performing Korea in Koreatown

The 2002 World Cup was a powerful forum for the production of Koreanness in Koreatown and the Korean American community in Los Angeles. Korean Americans' subjective experiences of the World Cup were diverse, taking place in different contexts and at various levels of engagement, but certain dominant representations of Koreanness emerged through media discourses surrounding the event. These representations operated to frame discussions about what it meant to be Korean in the United States. In this section, I investigate the production of Koreanness within the context of racialized spatial relations in Koreatown. In addition to the material, physical, and sensory "evidence" of Koreanness, Koreatown is a space that is defined vis-à-vis race relations between Koreans and other groups. During the period of celebration, Koreatown was produced as a distinctly Korean space that operated in the interests of the South Korean nation. This performance of Korean space failed to acknowledge the multicultural constitution of its geographic area. It also resignified racial difference as important, insofar as it bolstered nationalist claims.

In 1980, the city of Los Angeles designated the area now called Koreatown in a symbolic ceremony (Abelmann and Lie 1997; Yu et al. 2004). Given the contradictory reports and accounts of the area, however, Koreatown still lacks a distinct demographic definition or geographic boundary.[16] Generally, Koreatown is several miles west of downtown Los Angeles and extends from Pico Avenue in the south to Melrose Avenue in the north. It covers approximately six square miles, which stretch from Hoover Boulevard in the east to Fairfax Avenue in the west (Chang and Diaz-Veizades 1999; Yu et al. 2004). Koreatown is adjacent to poor, largely minority neighborhoods, which are heavily Latino and African American (i.e., South Central to the south, Pico-Union to the east, and Echo Park to the north). Wealthier and Whiter neighborhoods border Koreatown to the west and northwest, such as Park La Brea and Hancock Park. There is a sense of precariousness about the position of Korean Americans, who constitute a visible minority in this densely populated area. Many accounts point to the fact that more than 70 percent of the residents in the more densely populated and poorer census tracts of Koreatown are of Latino descent (Chang and Diaz-Veizades 1999; Yu et al. 2004).

Koreatown is produced as a Korean space by the material presence of Koreanness—Korean people, Korean institutions and business, Korean aesthetics, and Korean sensory cues (i.e., sounds, smells, comportment). Following Paulla Ebron's work in *Performing Africa* (2002), I would argue that Korea must be continually reiterated through performances of Koreanness in this space. It is through the enactment of Korea in the United States that both Koreans and non-Koreans alike come to apprehend Korea. Architectural ornaments and embellishments of Koreanness exist, such as Korean-style buildings with tile rooftops, signs in Han'gŭl, and Korean iconography. It is, however, the everyday practices of Koreanness by Koreans and responses to Koreanness by non-Koreans in these contexts that operate to produce the reality of Korea within Koreatown (de Certeau 1984; Williams 2002). These urban spaces are signified as racialized and ethnicized spaces through the shaping of social relations by the irregular effects of private capital and governmental regulation. The spaces are apprehended and lived as such through a "struggle over the meanings" of the social space (Jackson 1989; Massey 1994). Without going into a detailed account of the historical and political struggles over the production of this space, I would like to call attention to the idea that the meaning of the area of Koreatown is continually reproduced in relation to other groups, particularly other racial minorities who also inhabit the geographic area.

Ten years after the 1992 Los Angeles civil unrest, the World Cup came to symbolize a shift in the status of Korean America in Los Angeles.[17] The 1992 Los Angeles civil unrest marked a critical moment in the production of a Korean American identity as a political identity (Amerasia 1993; K. W. Lee 1999; E. Park 1998). This crisis brought to the fore the need for a collective political identity on the part of Korean Americans. During this turbulent time, Koreans were largely depicted in mainstream media as an insular ethnic group that was often racist and absolutely foreign (Abelmann and Lie 1997; Kim-Gibson 1993). Prior to the civil unrest, articles on Korean Americans in mainstream media often focused on the Korean–Black conflict. These narratives tended to focus on the lack of regard by the Korean American community for African Americans, especially in their tendency to open liquor stores in downtrodden neighborhoods. On the other hand, the African American side of the picture was marked by coverage that emphasized "the criminal nature" of African Americans. When the 1992 uprisings occurred, there was a sentiment that Koreans who had suffered major losses had earned their just due for their lack of engagement with the African American and Latino communities in which they opened businesses. By contrast, mainstream media accounts of the World Cup ten years later depicted the Korean American community as a "good minority," still foreign, but well-mannered, self-sufficient, and cheerful. In other words, Koreans in America were engaged in some good, clean fun in their own neighborhoods.[18]

Securing Koreanness in Koreatown

During the World Cup, the space of Koreatown was delimited and reinscribed through discourses of security. As Mike Davis (1992) famously noted, the commercial neighborhoods of Los Angeles have been constructed as militarized spaces to protect the interests of private capital, criminalizing the urban poor in the process. The increasing interests of security, in what Dávila (2004) refers to as the neoliberal city, are central tenets of the production of privatized space in the urban city. Security exists to protect private interests by keeping particular urban zones delimited and designing human use of the space based on particular consumer practices, cultural-linguistic characteristics, and class status. Koreatown, due to its demographic and commercial character, does not allow for such a convenient boundary-making.

In Koreatown, major streets are lined with text-heavy store fronts and strip malls with secured parking lots. The spaces between major thoroughfares are high-density, low-income residential areas heavily populated by Latinos. Security, as it is discussed within the Korean American community, exists to protect Korean business establishments and Korean consumers and businesspeople in the stores and on the streets of Koreatown. This discourse of security, thus, operates to legitimate the existence and protect the movements of the Korean minority in Koreatown. During the World Cup, Korean-language media conveyed the sense that the LAPD's protection of Koreans offered official legitimacy to Koreans as the denizens of the area. Through interviews with journalists and a survey of Korean-language media, I found that police protection and the issue of permits for Korean street cheers were discussed as particularly significant demonstrations of state-sanctioned legitimacy.

One article about the event on June 19, 2002 in the *Korea Daily* or *Joongang* USA is accompanied by a photograph of a White LAPD officer standing on the asphalt, guarding the streets from ecstatic Koreans on the sidewalk as an amused Latino man watches. The caption reads, "On the 18th, as Korea entered the Round of Eight, cheering Koreans spilled out onto the streets. An on-duty police officer from the Rampart Division is waving a South Korean flag cheering in solidarity with Koreans." The article focuses on the outpouring of emotion by Koreans. It goes on to report that, as a response to the commotion, the LAPD's Rampart Division deployed seven cars and about twenty officers. In the article, one officer is reported to have said, "It is a pleasure to work within a context of such joy. This is a rare moment."[19]

Kim Jaeyun, a twenty-eight-year-old Koreatown beat reporter who investigated crimes, human interest stories, and other various news features for a major newspaper in Koreatown, spent the entire month covering one news topic: Koreatown's responses to the World Cup. After passing through security in the lobby of a major Korean-language newspaper located in Koreatown, I joined him for an interview in a small section of the newsroom, separated from the buzzing of the staff by a short cubicle wall. He brought us cups of instant coffee from the vending machine down the hall and sat comfortably across the table from me. Although Kim Jaeyun had been in the United States for fourteen years, he preferred to conduct the interview in Korean.

When I asked about his duties during the World Cup, he exclaimed that he was not able to sleep for the entire month since he was assigned to cover group cheers at different spots throughout the night and was expected to meet demanding deadlines during the day. Smiling as he reviewed the images of the event in his mind, he emphasized the uniqueness of the month, pointing out, "We even had LAPD come to protect us during our early morning street cheering."

I asked if any unfortunate incidents or crime had occurred during that time. He stated, "No, it was absolutely safe. In fact, there were far fewer incidents of drunk driving, altercations, and domestic violence than usual because everyone was watching TV. That made it easier for me as a crime beat reporter [I laughed]. Well, there was one moment during the Italy game in the parking lot on 6th Avenue and Alexandria, and during that group cheer, a man was grazed by a bullet."

"Didn't the gun shots cause major pandemonium? Weren't people scared? Someone could have been killed," I exclaimed.

He replied, "No. The person wasn't really hurt. He was so happy for the success of the Korea team, he just went on and continued to cheer. "

I stared at him incredulously. "Well, what about everyone else?"

He answered, "Well, they continued to celebrate of course."

We then continued to discuss whether he thought this would have been the case in any other "regular situation." He replied, "Of course not." Mr. Kim seemed to think of the shooting as a rather light and humorous incident, easily forgotten in the ecstasy of the moment. He pointed out that the circumstances surrounding the incident were unique and could only be attributed to the fervor of Koreans during this special event. It was important to him that LAPD officers were present to protect the Korean fans watching the game. This emphasis on the LAPD was also reflected in other interviews and media sources.[20] The LAPD, which had abandoned Koreatown during the 1992 Los Angeles uprisings, had arrived to protect, serve, and even celebrate during the World Cup.

Koreatown is an area known to many in the Korean American community for its dangers and its pleasures. Issues of safety and security are major topics of concern for Korean Americans who live, work, shop, and play in Koreatown. Even though they comprise a fraction of its residential population, Koreans are highly visible as business owners and consumers. The concerns over safety are shaped through the narratives of class and race relations, particularly those between Koreans and African Americans, as well as between Koreans and Latinos (Chang and Diaz-Veizades 1999; Chang and Leong 1994). The story of the stray bullet was a testament to the ways that stories of violence and a fear of the streets were superseded during the World Cup by the immense emotional power of the event. During this period of celebration, the area of Koreatown was secured through the participation of the LAPD and signified as an overwhelmingly Korean space.

Race and Space in Koreatown: Korean–Latino Relations

During the World Cup, issues of race and space were raised in a powerful way through discussions about how the event affected Korean–Latino relations. Kim Jaeyun was keen to point out that the crowds were not entirely Korean or Korean American. "There were Latinos and Whites there too," he stated. Much of the Korean-language media attempted to ensure that representations showed that *woeguk in,* or foreigners (i.e., non-Koreans), were also part of the Koreatown crowds. They were careful to note that these woeguk in were, for the most part, cheering for the South Korean team.[21] This particular mention of the "inclusiveness" of the crowds, as evidenced by woeguk in cheering for the South Korean national team, also took place within South Korea. Cho Han Haejong writes that the "passion was generally perceived as progressive and spontaneous, and characterized by the acceptance of diversity" (2004, 16). Some have argued that the inclusion of people of different races in the national celebration indicated the emergence of a new type of Korean nationalism—one that departed from exclusive ethnocentric and race-based notions of the national body (see Pai and Tangherlini 1998; Shin 2006).

Rather than expressing a new and inclusive form of Korean nationalism, it seems to me that these inclusions operated as a preemptive defense against accusations of such exclusionary nationalism. There were, in fact, woeguk in in the crowd, but their function in Korean-language discourse was to expand the significance of what was, essentially, a Korean nationalist spectacle. The representation of the woeguk in was used only when he or she was expressing support for the Korean national team. The crowds were characterized as being absolutely supportive, and they were unified with the Korean fans through dress and comportment. The uniformity of the crowds precluded the possibility of expressing a preference for another team or acting outside of the scripted behaviors of the event. The occasional inclusion of a woeguk in did not operate to diffuse the dominant idea of a race-based notion of "Korea as One"—that during this period, all sixty million Koreans around the world were coming together as one. Rather, it bolstered ideas that even woeguk in wanted to experience the unity all Koreans were experiencing at that moment.

To bolster the idea that there was harmony between Koreans and Latinos during the World Cup, there were many images on television and in newspapers of Koreans and Latinos celebrating together in workplaces and on the streets. About half the Korean population in the city of Los Angeles resides in Koreatown, but Koreans remain a significant minority in the area. The overwhelming majority of residents in the poorer, working-class neighborhoods in Koreatown are of Latino descent. Latinos constitute between 70 and 80 percent of most of the census districts that comprise Koreatown (Chang and Diaz-Veizades 1999; Yu et al. 2004). Driving down major thoroughfares such as Western Avenue or Olympic Avenue, one observes that many of the highly visible establishments are Korean-owned and cater primarily to Korean consumers. However, many of these businesses depend, at least in part, on Latino labor (Min 1996; Kyeyoung Park 1997).

In Korean-language media in Los Angeles, particular attention was paid to the notion that Korean–Latino relations, particularly in Koreatown, had improved through this event. Many Koreans in the United States watched live broadcasts on their local Spanish-language *Univisión* channel. Some of my informants told me that they watched on *Univisión* because it was more widely available on less expensive cable packages than ESPN2. There were also some who said that the announcers were far more exciting and displayed a far greater expertise in calling plays. There were a few football fans who would watch international games beyond the World Cup and were familiar with tuning into *Univisión* to get regular football coverage on weekends. On the Los Angeles affiliate KMEX, special programs featured Korean culture during the World Cup, such as *p'ungmul*, Korean drumming, and, on the day of the Germany—Korea semifinal, Latino news anchors wore "Be the Reds" shirts in solidarity with the Korean team.[22] Through my investigation of the event, I found that there were many personal and media accounts that discussed a sense of mutual goodwill between Latinos and Koreans during this period.

Although there has been quite a bit of media and academic attention on Korean–African American relations, there are relatively few accounts of Korean–Latino relations.[23] An increasing political and academic interest in the relationship between Koreans and Latinos is emerging, particularly with respect to the labor relations between Korean business owners and Latino workers (Kyeyoung Park 1997; I. Yoon 1997). Based on their research in Los Angeles, Lucie Cheng and Yen Le Espiritu (1989) generate an "immigrant hypothesis" to explain the perceived lack of conflict between Koreans and Latinos, in contrast to the highly visible conflicts between Koreans and African Americans. According to this ethnic relations hypothesis, immigrants such as Latinos and Koreans share an ethic of hard work, frugality, and a belief in the American dream. They are also united through their shared experiences of hardships, such as language difficulties and cultural barriers to advancement in U.S. society.

Edward Chang and Jeannette Diaz-Veizades (1999) dedicate a chapter in their text on ethnic peace in Los Angeles to Korean–Latino relations in the adjacent areas of Koreatown and Pico-Union. They support, in part, the "immigrant hypothesis" of Cheng and Espiritu as a way of explaining the appearance of relatively conflict-free relations between Koreans and Latinos in the area. Again, these reports were produced in relation to the documented conflicts between Koreans and African Americans. Chang and Diaz-Veizades found that there were some specific points of conflict, but these conflicts were primarily a result of the economic and political struggles faced by both groups. By contrast, a more recent account by Nadia Kim (2004) discusses the mutually negative attitudes of Koreans, African Americans, and Latinos toward one another, which are based largely on class- and labor-related differences among the various groups in Koreatown and the surrounding areas of Los Angeles. All of these studies conclude that mutual ignorance and a high level of ambivalence seem to characterize the relations between Latinos and Koreans in Los Angeles. At times, conflict and tensions arise, but the limits to political representation and power by the groups involved mean that small-business-owner labor conflicts remain the primary site through which these relations are understood by commentators on race relations in the Koreatown area.

As I sat in an office made of wood-patterned particle board in the KS wholesale produce warehouse, I asked the owner, fifty-six-year-old Cha Dongwŏn, about his response to the World Cup. He remarked that he was most proud of the special "World Cup sales" he had offered as a service to the Korean community. He stated, "My sale was in the newspaper, and it even came out on TV." Outside the office, Latino workers were busily moving boxes of merchandise and running forklifts to move pallets across the warehouse floor.

I asked where he had watched the games.

"We watched the games here, as I have to get here at about 4:00 a.m. anyway," Mr. Cha stated. "I watched with the Mexican *aedul* (boys), and we really had a lot of fun together." (I peered outside at Latino workers, all of whom were adult men and none of whom seemed close to being *boys*.)

Mr. Cha continued, "We even had a wager. I would pay them each $50 if

Korea lost, and they would pay me $50 if Korea won. Well, I made a lot of money." He chuckled and then added, "But even when they were losing money, they still wanted the Korean team to win."

"Really? Why is that?" I asked.

He replied, "They work with Koreans, so they are close to Koreans. That's why."

The patronizing attitude toward Latinos that is apparent in Mr. Cha's remarks was briefly mentioned but ultimately glossed over by Chang and Diaz-Veizades (1999) in their study. Koreans, in their survey, were more likely to think that they were a positive factor in Latinos' lives than that Latinos had been a positive factor in theirs. Nadia Kim (2004) draws a starker picture, identifying an even more negative impression of Koreans by Latinos. Discourses of Koreans and Latino men coming together through this event highlight the gendered and racialized ways this event was apprehended in Korean America. In most of these accounts, Latino men were employees and neighbors to Koreans, who were naturalized as the proprietors of Koreatown. Mr. Cha's comments reflect a dominant attitude that is conveyed through Korean-language media—the assumption that Latino men are crazy about soccer and that their soccer mania would lead them to have warm feelings for the people from the country hosting the World Cup. As indicated by the prior literature, the proximity of Koreans and Latinos, with respect to geography and work, can be seen as both the basis for tension and the reason for good feelings between the two groups. In the opinions of some Koreans, the event marked this proximity as a reason why Latino men had positive feelings for Koreans.

A patronizing attitude toward Latinos was also revealed through initial Korean-language media accounts in which business owners expressed anxiety about whether Latino workers who were crazy about soccer would come in to work during the World Cup. There were also reporters who questioned how Latinos would feel about their Korean employers if South Korea performed better than Mexico (based on the assumption that most Latinos working in Koreatown were of Mexican descent). Furthermore, even though Korean-language media claimed that Latino employees bore goodwill toward their employers during this time, the model status of Koreans in the community was thrown into relief by reports about the disturbance caused by Latinos in the Highland Park area when Mexico lost to the United States. The headline for an article about this disruption called the incident a "riot," stating that rocks and bottles were thrown, people were arrested, and general mayhem ensued.[24]

Bong Chang-sik, a forty-three-year-old sales representative for a Korean food maker, thought that the best thing about the World Cup was that it improved relations between Latinos and Koreans. He stated, "While White people viewed millions of people in red T-shirts with suspicion, Hispanics who really love soccer saw Koreans in a much better light." This suspicion of red T-shirts was based on his understanding of the United States as an anticommunist space and an individualist country. Mr. Bong, who had immigrated from South Korea to the United States eight years earlier, said he loved U.S. sports and did not care much about Korean sports and Korean athletes in general. He made a conscious effort to diminish any ties to South Korea, even though he admitted that he had great interest in the World Cup. Mr. Bong watched *Univisión* in his free time in order to improve his Spanish, and he claimed it was a highly effective means of learning the Spanish language. When I asked him if he thought his own relationships with Latinos had improved, he shook his head and said, "Not really." Mr. Bong seemed to gather from his media experiences that relations had improved, but when asked about how these improvements had changed his everyday relations, he could not name any significant changes.

Rather than directly dealing with some of the underlying causes of tension between these two groups, the World Cup was an opportunity for Koreans to make statements about Latinos in Koreatown. Latino interest in the World Cup was viewed as proof that no bad feelings existed between Koreans and their male Latino workers. In the discursive spaces created through the event, the existence of Korean–Latino tensions could be acknowledged and resolved in the convenient assertion that "Korean–Latino relations have improved." It was particularly significant that the World Cup had already assured that these tensions would be resolved, even though the everyday nature of tensions and conflict, with respect to labor and spatial relations, remained unchanged.

In order to get a more complete picture of Korean–Latino relations, it would be important to investigate the response of the Latino community to the World Cup. Viewership rates of Spanish-language KMEX in contrast to ESPN2 indicate a high level of interest on the part of the Latino community in the World Cup.[25] Although mass media perpetuate the common notion that there is a tight relationship between Latinos and *fútbol* (soccer), the role of fútbol should be understood within the local contexts of viewing for Latinos who are themselves a highly diverse group (see Dávila 2001). In this book, I do not provide critically important Latino perspectives on Korean–Latino relations in Los Angeles, particularly during the World Cup. These limitations highlight the importance of future research into these minority relations by engaging both groups and going beyond economic determinism.

Mainstreaming Korean America

During the World Cup, Korean America was featured in the mainstream U.S. media, which became a major point of interest to many in the Korean American community. Interest and participation in mainstream media sports have increased in frequency; groups of Korean Americans have been sighted in baseball stadiums and golf galleries. As with representations of Korean American baseball and golf fans, Korean America was represented primarily as a community of Korean national sports fans. Similarly, professional Korean players are rarely presented by the U.S. mainstream media as representing Asian America or an Asian American identity.[26] Rather, they are regarded as international athletes—foreign nationals working in the United States as an opportunistic labor force.

In Asian American Studies, there has long been demand for representations in mainstream media that defy a past of invisibility and damaging stereotypes (Hamamoto and Lin 2000; R. Lee 1999). Asian American critics, activists, and artists have worked to critically interpret mainstream representations of the past and promote new cultural productions that create possibilities for "imagining otherwise" (Chuh 2003). Although there has been a significant growth in representations of Asian Americans and Asians in U.S. mass media, these representations should be investigated within political contexts. Mainstream representations of Korean America are politically fraught with questions of citizenship, nation, and transnational capital. Still, it is important to recognize the pleasures of such representations and to understand the desires for mainstream representation (Kondo 1997) In interpreting the significance of mainstream representation, there is a need to question what these pleasures enable and in whose interests they are directed. It is also important to understand the political aspects of pleasure and the power dynamics that produce the contexts for the interpretation of experiences as pleasurable.

The interests in the U.S. mainstream are, in part, Korean American responses to their perceived invisibility, but a strictly U.S. national perspective does not acknowledge the fact that these desires for representation in the U.S. mainstream media were produced within South Korea as well (Won-Doornink 1988). The U.S. engagement in and occupation of South Korea during and after World War II created the military structure for the importation of cultural products such as televisions, household products, and other commodities (C. Choi 1993). The mediation of the United States through such commodities shapes desires in South Korea (see Grewal 2005). This concern with representation in U.S. media, then, may also be understood within the historical experience of consuming U.S. media in South Korea by Korean viewers and consumers. Furthermore, the asymmetrical geopolitical relationship has been defined by trade restrictions and agreements, which in turn has defined the kinds of mass media that move across the two sites. This interest in representation in the U.S. mainstream, therefore, is also a transnational interest developed through a history of postcolonial power relations between South Korea and the United States.

In general, mainstream U.S. media accounts of South Korea and Koreans in America are heavily scrutinized by journalists, politicians, and academics in Korean America. In Korean-language media in particular, there is a high level of sensitivity to the ways that the Korean American community is represented in mainstream U.S. media. This interest is due not only to the invisibility of Koreans in mainstream media generally but also to the fact that representations have often been negative, as in the case of Korean–African American relations, the 1992 Los Angeles uprisings, and Korean–Latino labor conflicts (Amerasia 1993; Kim-Gibson 1993).

During the World Cup, Korean-language media based in Los Angeles were very interested in mainstream media accounts of Korean American responses in Koreatown. For example, the *Korea Times* noted that reporters from *USA Today*, ABC news, NBC news, and *Univisión* were at Rosen Brewery during the U.S.–South Korea game to assess the level of anti-Americanism in Korean America. In various outlets of Korean-language media, there were accounts of how major mainstream news organizations, such as CNN, NBC, and FOX, covered Korean America, particularly the spectacles of street cheering in Koreatown. These stories about the U.S. mainstream media covering the Korean community are examples of a derivative recounting of mainstream coverage. In this practice, Korean-language media simply report on the mainstream U.S. news reporting on Korea or Korean America. At times, entire pages of newspapers, such as the *New York Times* and the *Los Angeles*

Times, are reproduced, in slightly reduced versions of their original format, in Korean-language newspapers.

The Staples Center event, however, is one case in which Korean-language media institutions and mainstream media sport industries worked in direct cooperation to produce a mainstream event for Korean Americans. After the Staples Center event, there were many articles and news segments about how the World Cup had announced the entry of Korean Americans into mainstream U.S. society. The irony of this focus on being *mainstream* was, of course, that this mainstream representation constituted Korean Americans as a group of Korean national fans. Korean America was announced to mainstream society as essentially Korean nationals on U.S. soil. In this case, Korean Americans were the subjects of national representation through mainstream media and private capital interests.

The Korean American gathering at the Staples Center was conveyed as the happy ending to a month-long fantasy. The home of the Los Angeles Lakers, possibly the most popular sports team in Koreatown, was offered to the Korean American community as a venue to celebrate the historical accomplishments of the South Korean national team. It was also an opportunity for Korean Americans to come together in a single place to affirm their existence as a significant ethnic group in the city of Los Angeles. The Staples Center event was a brief yet spectacular visit to the U.S. mainstream by the Korean American community. The Staples Center was made available to the Korean community at no cost to the attendees. About half of the tickets were distributed through Korean media sponsors Radio Korea, *Joonang Ilbo*, and KTE, and the other half were distributed at the Staples Center box office at 10 a.m. on the day prior to the early-morning game.

At the box office, all of the tickets disappeared within two hours, and on the day of the game, the parking lot was at capacity by 2 a.m. Many people were left outside begging for extra tickets. Frankly, in the context of the World Cup tournament, the game didn't mean that much, since it was a consolation match to determine third and fourth place. The big draw was the opportunity to be in the Staples Center with 20,000 other Korean fans dressed in red T-shirts and cheering in unison. It was the unifying nature of the event through dress, language, and comportment, as well as the sheer size of the crowd, that produced an immense sense of pleasure in representation (see Kondo 1997). The emotional pleasure that was structured through the event was intensified by the temporary yet massive sense of inclusion that was produced in this highly mediated and commodified venue.

Korean media in both the United States and South Korea widely hailed this event as a major coming of age in the Korean American community. It announced the arrival of Koreans into mainstream U.S. society. Stephanie Yi, a twenty-two-year-old college student who lived in Fullerton, drove with her friends to the event. They had acquired their tickets through her mother, who worked at a Korean bank in Koreatown.

"I got there at 2 a.m., but I still had to drive around the parking lot for almost an hour to find a space. It was absolutely crazy!" she exclaimed.

When asked what she thought about the event, she said, "It was awesome. I kind of see the Staples Center for rich, high-class, American people. And actually, for the Staples Center to allow 20,000 Koreans to gather together and use their facility, and cheer for their country, was really nice."

Stephanie is a dedicated fan of the Los Angeles Lakers, which added another layer of significance to this, her first visit to the Staples Center. The excitement was produced through the high visibility of the space as a center of mainstream sports and entertainment culture at the cusp of the busy interchange of the I-10 and I-110 freeways. By remarking that she understood the regular visitors to the Staples Center to be "rich, high-class *American*"— in other words, *White*—people, she pointed to her own understanding of the mainstream as constituted through mass-mediated conceptions of race, class, and nation. Her statement points to the multiple social formations that produce the idea of the mainstream for some Korean Americans in Los Angeles.

Before the Staples Center announced its invitation to the Korean community, official plans were made for street cheering on Wilshire Boulevard in Koreatown. These plans included permits to close a section of Wilshire Boulevard with the assurance that the LAPD would protect the area. At the last minute, however, the event was moved away from Koreatown to the Staples Center in downtown as a result of a deal between leaders in the Korean American community, the city of Los Angeles, and the Anshutz Entertainment Group (AEG), owner of the Staples Center.[27] Excited by the level of enthusiasm for Korean soccer in the Korean American community, AEG devised a plan to redirect this enthusiasm to its Major League Soccer (MLS) team, the Los Angeles Galaxy. During the World Cup, they announced a plan to add two to three Korean players to the Galaxy. They also announced their interests in welcoming the Korean community to the Home Depot Center, the home field of the Los Angeles Galaxy, by sponsoring a "Korean Night" during the regular soccer season in July of 2002. Toward this attempt to appropriate Korean interest in soccer, AEG also recruited major Korean-language media outlets as cosponsors of the Staples Center event. These media outlets operated to inform Korean America about the logistics and significance of the event.

Kim Song-sik, a forty-two-year-old editor for a major Korean-language newspaper, stated that he had decided not to watch most of the games live since he was the father of an infant and a two-year-old child. However, he could not pass up the opportunity to go to the Staples Center. He stated, "It was the chance of a lifetime. When do you think this chance will come again, if ever?" Even though he had to wait for several hours to enter the venue, he felt that attending the event was totally worth the experience of feeling a sense of unity with the Los Angeles Korean community. Mr. Kim's enthusiastic interpretation of events reflected the celebratory tone of most reports in the Korean-language media. In both South Korea and Los Angeles, news media offered wholesale support for the South Korean national team and the events celebrating its accomplishments.

The Staples Center event demonstrates how private commercial interests deploy community leaders in the Korean community as well as in local and city governments. All of these groups demonstrated an interest in producing this "Korean" event and came together in complementary ways (see Dávila 2004). The Staples Center event could be seen as a "shameless marketing ploy" on the part of AEG to recruit Korean fans for its Major League Soccer team, but the invitation to use the facility was announced as a triumph by powerful voices in Korean America.[28] It was as though, despite this knowledge of the crassly commercial interests of the AEG, these "business interests" could be overlooked for a more important outcome—that is, the sense of belonging that would be produced as a result of the event.[29]

AEG's attempt to exploit Korean national sentiment in Korean America demonstrates the extent to which media sports industries rely on the assumption that Korean America is largely constituted by a transnational sense of Koreanness. This media sports "business formula" assumes that a popular Korean player equals domestic Korean American interest and, more importantly, the rights to broadcast in South Korea. The payoff, of course, includes all the added benefits of getting an entire nation of nationalist viewers as fans. The presence of Korean American fans at sporting events also becomes a significant aspect of the representation of media sport; their bodies act as evidence of Korean American support for South Korean national players to Koreans elsewhere.

Rather than focusing on some vague notion of multiculturalism, this business practice employs strategic marketing targeted to a transnational audience of Korean consumers. As I mention in chapter 2, multiculturalism has become the mainstream discourse of media sport. This multicultural marketing strategy assumes that Koreans in the United States maintain some sense of loyalty to South Korea through their consumer and media practices, particularly when it comes to media sport. It is also a response to operations of Koreatown as an exclusive ethnic community. This nationally targeted business development strategy can be seen in the practices of MLB and the LPGA, as well. AEG eventually recruited South Korea's "most beloved player"—veteran Hong Myung Bo—to its MLS soccer team. Hong played on the Galaxy for two years, making public appearances and running soccer workshops in the Korean American community, before announcing his retirement in 2004.

The actions of AEG demonstrate how the interests of mainstream media sport are directly involved in the struggle to define Korean America. Media sport industries are highly interested in constituting the Korean community as a transnational one and in connecting the Korean American community with a South Korean market of media consumers. This process of definition occurs through the responses of Korean Americans to the media coverage of these Korean players. Productions of transnational media sport offer powerful spaces through which representations of Korea are apprehended in Korean America. Thus far, the narratives of the South Korean nation conveyed through media sport operate to convey powerful forms of South Korean nationalism within Korean American communities.

Transnational Stakes

Of course, the material realities of living in U.S. society and the power of U.S. nationalism also operate to constitute Korean America. Korean players who play in the United States can symbolize various Korean and U.S. nationalisms. Rather than arguing that all media sports operate in a singular way, I argue that the growing significance of transnational media sport in Korean America raises important questions about how nation, race, gender, and transnationalisms are lived in Korean America. What kinds of investments do Korean Americans have with a sense of Korean nationalism? How are consumer practices shaped by a sense of ethnic identity, and do these consumer identities translate to political identities? Who is excluded in the production of nation in these contexts? How does race play a factor in producing a sense of Korean identity in the United States? The Korean American responses to the World Cup reveal the complicated relationships among the local, national, and transnational produced through media sport.

The World Cup phenomenon demonstrates that there are personal, political, and material interests in constituting Korean America as a transnational community. These interests include desires for capital, community, nation, and belonging. These desires persist beyond the event itself and become one reason why the event has become such a significant historical moment. The discourses of transnationalism indicate a shift in the ways that transnationalisms are conveyed and apprehended in some Asian American communities. The discourses of transnationalism are produced in relation to other local and national discourses of difference to constitute Korean America.

Through my investigation of Koreatown in Los Angeles, I have attempted to demonstrate that questions of the transnational, conveyed through transnational media, are apprehended in local and place-specific contexts of reception. Furthermore, I point out that Korean Americans are directly involved in producing Koreatown as a transnational Korean space through performances of Koreanness. Koreatown exists as physical and mediated evidence of transnational Koreanness in the United States. The production of Koreatown as transnational, however, occurs within and through the erasure and appropriation of racial difference within the space. This chapter discusses some of the erasures and accessions that are deployed to perform this space as Korean.

The promotion of transnational Korean America through corporate mainstream rhetoric raises important issues about the definition of Korean America. Who has the power to define Korean America? In whose interests do these definitions operate? The production of a transnational Korean community is connected to its location within a number of social geographies in Koreatown. I have tried to bring attention to the ongoing struggles over defining the space of Koreatown. In investigating the seductions of mainstream representation for Korean Americans as a minority group in the United States, I have attempted to point out the contingencies and the political stakes of producing national identity within transnational media contexts.

Though this chapter offers a Korean American account of the World Cup national publics, the following chapter focuses on specific connections that make up a transnational Korean public. It looks at how a transnational youth public emerged during the World Cup, as youth culture came to dominate the response to and the mass-mediated representations of the event. I suggest that the connections between South Korean and Korean American youth forged through this event might be seen as particularly powerful evidence of global Koreanness. By looking at the specific discourses around youth, the next chapter attempts to detail the specific processes that give shape to the transnational and brings attention to the stakes for those invested in building and participating in a transnational public.

Generations Connect

DISCOURSES OF GENERATION AND THE EMERGENCE OF
TRANSNATIONAL YOUTH CULTURES

During the World Cup, Korean nationalist discourses in both South Korea and the United States emphasized the idea that 男女老少 *nam nyŏ no so* (men and women, elderly and young) came together during this period of celebration. For Korean communities in Seoul and Los Angeles, the concept of generation was a central mode of understanding the responses of Koreans of all ages to the World Cup. In mainstream Korean-language mass media, the sporting event was said to have improved relations among generations by unifying all Koreans. As with the discourses of race and national difference, the generational divides were said to have been transcended through the event. The discourses of generation during the World Cup demonstrated the critical role of the idea of generation in producing contemporary notions of Korean national identity (H. Song 2003). Although generational differences are often passed off as universal and timeless aspects of human experience, this chapter attempts to detail the contingent and historically specific categories of generation. Through a reading of the transnational publics of the World Cup, this chapter demonstrates how articulations of generation reveal subjective experiences of changing social and historical conditions. The World Cup was understood as a period when the youth—that is, teens and young adults—took the lead in creating a new kind of public culture in Korean communities (Cho Han 2002b; H. Song 2003). A culture of street celebration was characterized by shared acts of media consumption and expressive emotional responses. Mainstream Korean mass media conveyed the idea that young people, who had been largely ambivalent and even disparaging about the nation, were captivated by the national team and drawn back into the nationalist fold. In the largely conservative mass media, the trepidation over increasing individualism in younger generations was quelled momentarily through the massive demonstrations of nation love by the country's youth (see Cho Han et al. 2004; H. Song 2003).

In Korean America, the World Cup was similarly hailed as a moment when young people voluntarily demonstrated their pride in being Korean. Through expressions of support by young Korean Americans, issues commonly articulated as generational conflicts were momentarily suspended by the joy shared between generations. Generational conflicts in Korean America are often attributed to language barriers, cultural misunderstandings, overworked parents struggling to establish themselves, and ambivalent children who turn a blind eye to their parents' efforts. Many of the Korean Americans I interviewed, of all ages, stated that the most important impact of the World Cup in the Korean American community was that it offered the rare opportunity for Koreans in the United States to get together. Koreans of all ages and of all immigrant generations seemed to converge in shared spaces for a single purpose—to cheer for the South Korean national team. The World Cup was understood as a period when all overseas Koreans, particularly those wandering and displaced youth, were reaffirmed as part of the global Korean family. Nevertheless, my fieldwork reveals that there were important refusals to these assertions of unity in both South Korea and Korean America.

The issue of generation has conventionally been an important topic in Asian American studies. Lisa Lowe (1996) argues that generational differences, particularly those between parents and children, have become a master narrative of Asian American "culture." Lowe states that this ubiquitous focus on parent–child relationships in Asian America, as revealed in literary texts, limits understandings of Asian American experiences to the privatized family realm. The problems of Asian America are thus centered on the immigrant generation gap—that is, in the vast differences between recent immigrants and their U.S.-born children. Lowe finds this emphasis on family relations troubling because it obscures critical social and political issues in Asian America, such as class and ideological differences. Though Lowe cites literary examples that express hegemonic discourses of generation, her analysis does not discuss how these discourses are apprehended by Asian American subjects in their everyday lives. In the following pages, I consider how discourses of generation are circulated and become meaningful within a specific Asian American community. The discourses of generation often shape the subjective relationships that individuals have to notions of identity and community. They operate as a means through which national, racial, and ethnic identities are reproduced.

I share Lowe's belief that differences among generations must be viewed within specific historical, social, and political contexts.[1] Moreover, I consider the discourses of generation as categories of difference that are formative and productive of social meanings. Discussions of generation reveal important aspects of how South Koreans and Korean Americans situate themselves in their respective communities. It is also important to understand these discourses of generation as historical instantiations of social categories of difference. Collier and Yanagisako state,

> We do not assume cultural systems of meaning to be timeless, self-perpetuating structures of 'tradition.'" Yet, even when the meanings of core symbols are changing, we can tease apart their different meanings in particular contexts and, thereby, better understand the symbolic processes involved in social change. (1987, 41)

Following Collier and Yanagisako, I am interested in how categories of generation as a cultural system of meaning might bring attention to the human dimensions of social change within and between South Korea and Korean America.

In this chapter, I discuss generational differences as a primary mode of social organization within Korean communities in Seoul and Los Angeles (see Yanagisako 1985). Though I highlight the differences between how issues of generation are apprehended in both contexts, I also draw connections among communities. In South Korea, generation is an important social concept.[2] Therefore, generational differences tend to be considered critically important markers of social difference among South Koreans (H. Song 2003). The discourses about generational differences in mass media, academics, and politics tend to focus on changes in the character of the "youth." By youth, I refer to a rather general and variable category that encompasses teens and young people up to the age of thirty. This variability is reflected in the flexible use of the term in Korean discourses, where it can refer to a broad range of people from adolescents to unmarried adults.[3]

During the World Cup, the critical importance of the topic of youth in Korean society was reflected by the intense focus of Korean national media on youth participation as fans and leaders of fan culture. Angela McRobbie points out that "youth remains a major point of symbolic investment for society as a whole" (quoted in Skelton and Valentine 1998, 9). Indeed, the position of young people in contemporary South Korean and Korean American society is a subject commonly debated by cultural critics and scholars (H. Song 2003; Kibria 2002).[4] Often, stark generational differences are assumed to exist and are passed off as immutable and inescapable facts of life. In discussions of the so-called "generation gap," the divide between age cohorts is said to have grown more pronounced in the digital age. In South Korea, the scale and speed of change wrought by the processes of "compressed modernization" have created immense material differences in the experience of "youth" for children and their parents.[5] For Korean Americans, this difference between age groups is exacerbated by migration to the United States. This is reflected in the linear framework of immigrant assimilation that categorizes immigrants into first, one-point-five, second, and third generations. I believe these terms are in some circumstances useful, as they delimit different historical experiences of migration, settlement, and racialization by specific groups of immigrants. In fact, this framework was itself produced within a particular historical context of U.S. immigration history, and it should therefore be understood as a result of those conditions. However, an overreliance on what Lisa Lowe (1996) refers to as a "vertical" family-based framework prevents a full understanding of the complexity and historical specificity of migration histories and current transnational realities. I interrogate the widespread, uncritical use of these categories as explanatory mechanisms for generational difference in transnational Korean America. I also argue that the obsession with the topic of generations and youth in Korean communities can be understood as an expression of the anxieties around radical social and political change. This idea of generation, therefore, becomes a context through which social and historical changes might be elucidated (see Collier and Yanagisako 1987).

The significance of the multigenerational Korean interest in media sports was raised by many of my interviewees. Generation was an issue of acute and often emotional importance to many I came to know during my fieldwork. This emotional dimension is something that is often missed by studies of generational difference in demographic or sociological analyses. Generational differences are not always determined by conflict, misunderstandings, rebellion, authoritarianism, and abject difference, as connoted by many youth culture studies (see Hebdige 1981; Ross and Rose 1994; Skelton and Valentine 1998). The temporary moment of convergence afforded by the World Cup was a moment of celebration, pleasure, and joy for many of my respondents precisely because the expectations of generational conflict were momentarily suspended. Many experienced through that event an intense emotional bond with those whom they recognized as being connected to themselves in important and intimate ways.

Youth Revolution in South Korea

The notion of generation is a primary mode of social categorization within national culture in South Korea (H. Song 2003). A major narrative of modernity in South Korea concerns the striking differences in experience among those even less than one generation apart. The popular saying "Even twins have a generational difference" describes the inability to track these changes. In current generational narratives, children and youth are often symbols of liberalization and globalization, whereas older generations of Koreans symbolize an authoritarian, isolated, and nationalistic past. The attempts on the part of older Koreans to understand youth experiences, however, do not necessarily reflect a deep nationalist nostalgia for the past. Older generations of Koreans often narrate their lives within antinostalgic frameworks wherein the collective memories of their youth are marked by violent processes of change—colonialism, national division, civil war, the Cold War, developmental nationalism, and military dictatorship. For those who come to the United States, the subjective experiences of social upheaval are compounded with the trauma of migration and settlement.

Differences in national subjectivity are thus often attributed to differences in age and the subsequent experiences of national culture for each age cohort. The generation that comes of age in each political era is seen as so distinct that it is often represented by a number or a letter that corresponds to a series of dates or a descriptive term. The "386 Generation," for example, refers to those in their 30s who went to college in the 1980s and were born in the 1960s (H. Song 2003). Members of the 386 generation are symbolized by their involvement in the student democracy movement of the 1980s and their current power in the national government. There are similarly broad political characterizations of other generations as well, such as the 2030 generation (those in their twenties and thirties, who are considered to be progressive, globally minded, and generally anti-American) and the 5060 generation (those in their fifties and sixties), who are considered to be conservative, isolated, and trapped in a Cold War frame of mind.[6]

In recent years, there has been a general perception that South Korea has undergone dramatic societal change in the wake of its so-called liberaliza-tion, democratization, and globalization. Given these changes, there has been a subsequent rush to place a label on each perceived "new" generation of youth. This fervor to lay claim to the "new generation" has increased at an almost comedic pace. The new generation is often referred to as the Image Generation, the Media Generation, or the Internet Generation, reflected by their world-leading use of the Internet.[7] In the last ten years, I have come across many shorthand labels for today's youth, including *I* for Internet Generation, *N* for Network Generation, *P* for Generation of Passion, and *D* for Generation of Desire. This clamor to name reflects the urge to under-stand and label the rapid processes of social change in South Korea—pro-cesses that are understood to be shaping national subjectivities and the per-ception of one's own life chances in the nation.

During the World Cup, there were discussions of labeling yet another new generation: the *R* generation for Red Devils, or the *Yuwŏl* (June) Generation (see H. Song 2003). Song Ho-gŭn (2003) proposed the name 2002 Genera-tion to reflect the shift in values and ideologies that was dramatically rep-resented in the events of 2002. The civic power of the youth was seen both in the crowds that emerged on the streets during the World Cup and in their participation in electing a progressive human-rights attorney, Roh Moo Hyun, to the presidency. Song Ho-gŭn argues that 2002 marked a demon-stration of youth power to demand and enact social change that was reminis-cent of the 1968 student revolts in Paris or the U.S. antiwar demonstrations of the 1960s.

Youth culture in South Korea has clearly become a significant issue for cultural critics, particularly those dealing with issues of popular culture.[8] Often, youth culture and popular culture are considered one and the same (Skelton and Valentine 1998). The emphasis on issues of the digital society and global media in studies of popular culture brings with it an emphasis on youth who are the primary creators and users of new media and technologies and who are seen as being flexible enough to shift their own subjectivities to the various modes of sociality enabled by new technologies (Lee and Wong 2003).[9] Therefore, it is not surprising that the emergence of a new media sport culture of fandom during the World Cup was associated with youth and technology. Digital technologies and mass media operated together to facili-tate an explosion of youth cultural expression. The overwhelming focus on youth by the mass media can be understood as a result of media interest in the power of youth culture.

Youth Power

Well-known anthropologist and social critic Cho Han Haejong has dedicated her career as a public intellectual to the study and advocacy of South Korean youth. For Cho Han and many South Korean youth advocates, South Korea has been an adult-centered industrializing society that has oppressed the creative, playful, and emotional desires of children and youth (see Cho Han 2002b).[10] In her opinion, the World Cup offered a period for youth to break out of the social binds that constrain these desires. The youth proactively revolutionized public culture in Korean society and produced visions of future possibility for their lives.

In Cho Han's view, South Korean youth earned adult approval for their behavior because it was within the context of a national event. Cho Han writes, "Parents, who once viewed their children as empty-headed and without a worry in the world, were touched to see them leaving their homes waving the Korean flag" (2004, 10). Although Cho Han claims that the youth were having fun on their own terms, she argues that conservative voices attempted to appropriate their enthusiasm toward nationalist interests. "The Korean media lavished praise on young people," writes Cho Han (2004, 10). Rather than expressing a fascist nationalism, she asserts that the collective celebration was a period of spiritual revitalization for the youth.

Cho Han herself evokes a rather nationalist tone when she states, "[The World Cup] served as a healing ritual, able to exorcize the sense of inferiority and self-defeatism that plagues colonial subjects, allowing them to recover the self-love necessary to complete the business of nation building" (2004, 16). Cho Han seems to want to recover a politically progressive and oppositional form of nationalism on the part of the youth, but, unfortunately, she reads it out of context. She writes, "If it was a nationalist movement, it was one of a populist, grassroots and post-colonial kind" (21). Within this national context, Cho Han argues that participants understood themselves for the *first time* as "beings of pleasure" (21). The exaggeration might be understood as an attempt to index a particular moment in South Korean history, but Cho Han understands this shift in subjective apprehensions of nation as having radical effects in transforming the ideological bases of national culture.

Pleasure has immense critical potential, but it cannot alone be the mode through which political issues are transcended or changed. I recognize that the work of Cho Han, *Munhwa Yondae* (Culture Solidarity), *Tto hana ŭi*

Figure 15. Girls in *hanbok* leading the cheers in Seoul.
Yonhap News, reprinted with permission.

munhwa (An Alternative Culture), and other youth culture advocates extends far beyond this event and its commentaries, and this youth advocacy work is critically important. However, I find it necessary to ask what makes pleasure political? How are pleasures themselves structured and produced within ideological domains? It is precisely these political and national contexts that make pleasure an important site of critique.

Pleasure in itself cannot be a solution to the resilient issues of power inequalities ordered along gender, class, and status differences. What is the relationship between pleasure and labor, pleasure and nation, pleasure and gender, pleasure and postcoloniality? How are they produced in relation to each other? What possibilities are imagined by national subjects as an effect of this pleasure? What are the political actions taken as a result of this experience of pleasure? (Kondo 1997).

A major problem with Cho Han's analysis is its inability to deal with issues of class. She claims that the era of ideology represented by "labouring collectivization" has shifted to an era of desire demonstrated by "expressive individuation" (Cho Han et al. 2004, 18). It is not clear, however, how labor issues have been subsumed or assuaged by momentary expressions of pleasure, given the resilient hierarchies of class in South Korea. It seems as though Cho Han assumes these young people and women are not themselves laboring participants in a capitalist market economy faced with extended economic insecurity. In her formulation, the ideas of "labor" and "desire" are separate realms, not clearly tied together in a relational context.

> To many adults of the Cold war generation who suffer, to an extent, from a collective inferiority complex as members of a marginalized nation, the World Cup provided a special moment for overcoming this same complex. This was made possible by the coming together of two very different groups, — the 'generation of ideology' which had grown up struggling with its feelings of inadequacy and marginalization, and the 'generation of desire' which grew up baptized by the holy water of consumer capitalism. Face-to-face with the younger generation, the older generation discovered how different and 'cool' the younger generation was. Gazing at their fresh and sprightly bodies, the members of the 'ideological generation' were able, for the first time in their lives, to feel hopeful about the [sic] future generations, that possess a radically different cultural grammar from their own. (Cho Han 2004, 19)

I do agree with Cho Han that many older people were faced with generational differences in a powerful way, but I'm not convinced that the older generations really thought the behavior of the younger generations was "cool." Furthermore, even though their nationalist anxieties may have been suspended, the class anxieties of the older generations surely were not resolved by the "fresh and sprightly" bodies of the youth.

I am skeptical that consumer identities of youth can be neatly separated from ideology. Therefore, the difference between "the generation of ideology" and the "generation of desire," so commonly evoked in South Korean cultural studies, limits analyses of how desire operates within a capitalist market economy and leads to unfortunate conclusions. For one thing, gender and class inequalities persist within the powerful ideologies of neoliberalism and global capitalism. Furthermore, in my own interviews, youth expressed quite a bit of anxiety about the position of South Korea as a marginalized nation in the context of geopolitics and global economics. In analyses such as Cho Han's, the notion of a binary divide between and among generations is overstated, particularly in its separation of the issues of labor and pleasure. Indeed, the World Cup was a particularly powerful national event because feelings of pleasure were shared by people of various ages. In fact, I believe that it was precisely due to this perceived unity among generations that this pleasure was felt even more intensely by many subjects.

Transnational Visions of Youth

During my fieldwork in Seoul, most articulations of generational issues focused on South Korean youth. The ubiquitous discourses of generation, however, permeated notions of Koreanness that operated beyond the borders of South Korea. In this section, I offer an example of understanding the youth of the nation in transnational terms—that is, of understanding Koreans throughout the world as Korean national subjects.

Kim Chin-hi, a seventy-year-old mother of four and grandmother of eight, lived in Songpa-ku, in an upper-middle-class complex south of the Han River. Her apartment was adorned with classical paintings of fish, lotus blossoms, and bamboo, and large black rocks were placed carefully in every room to direct *ki* (energy) in a balanced way throughout the space. After I offered my formal greetings, I was seated on her green leather sofa. She brought some pale green tea in a delicate British porcelain cup lined with gold trim and speckled with pink flowers. In front of me, she placed slices of a carefully peeled and seeded *ch'amoe*, a yellow Korean melon, along with a tiny fork to spear each slice of fruit.

Kim Chin-hi lived with her husband of the same age and her mother-in-law, whom she shooed to her bedroom once I arrived. She explained that her mother-in-law was going senile and that it was better to do the interview without her lurking about. Three of her children had migrated to the United States and were living in different areas of California. Only her first-born son and his two high school–aged children remained in South Korea—this son, too, had expressed intentions of moving to the United States if his children decided to pursue a college education there.

I reminded Kim Chin-hi that I would be asking her about the World Cup and sports more generally. She claimed to be surprised that I would ask her about these issues, as she was never asked about such matters. "You will have to ask my husband about sports, as he knows much more about this topic," she stated. I assured her that I wanted to hear her story, and, without much goading, she shared her feelings.

> I don't really have too much knowledge about sports, but the first thing I thought about was that through it, our nation, our students, and our children achieved a sense of pride. I was thinking about our nation's children who go to America. They live with such a sense of loneliness. Although they prefer our country, they go to live with difficulty in someone else's country. But this time, through football, they overcame this sense of inferiority. . . .
>
> I went out to see the games myself and without even knowing it, I got so excited my chest started to thump. And I thought to myself, my sons and daughters think that Korean people can't do anything right. There are a lot of tragedies and difficult wounds that [Koreans] have, but this time, the students of *Taehan Min'guk* demonstrated their sense of unity. I think that our country's children will now think of themselves as just as good as the Americans. They will really think of our country as Tae*han Min'guk* [with emphasis on the *tae*, which means "great"]. I was so happy that tears came to my eyes. I was watching it in the same way [as the whole country]. . . . I was so happy.

In her remarks, Kim Chin-hi focused on the nation's youth both within and beyond Korea's national boundaries. Her interpretation was clearly shaped by the experiences of her own family members as migrants to the United States. When she spoke of children who go to the United States, she conflated her own children and grandchildren with *uri nara ŭi chŏlmunidŭl*, or "our country's children." To her, Korean youth was a transnational concept.

Kim Chin-hi also felt that through the World Cup a sense of inferiority to Americans was overcome, not only for her but, more importantly, for her children and the nation's children. Of course, the tournament involved teams representing the United States, South Korea, Japan, and twenty-nine other nations. Nevertheless, she articulated the significance of the event with respect to South Korea's historical relation to the United States. For her, the United States stood for what counts in terms of global contexts. She also understood the event as significant to Korean Americans as a symbolic victory for all Koreans throughout the world. She recognized that issues of racism, inequality, and challenges to the establishment were significant concerns in Korean America.

Kim Chin-hi likened her own understandings of the feelings among Koreans in the United States to Korean athletes in global sports. Indeed, her descriptions often slipped between statements about the athletes and about her own children. She stated that she would prefer it if Korean athletes stayed in South Korea to perform in domestic leagues. Although she understood their need to leave, she expressed concern about the sense of inferiority harbored by those Koreans who work, travel, study, and live abroad.[11] She believed that the World Cup had helped Korean youth discover a sense of pride and self-confidence. "Now, they know they will do well wherever they go," she stated.

Kim Chin-hi understood her own story of a Korean family split between two nations as a familiar experience for many Koreans. Through her discussion, she demonstrated the importance of transnational perspectives in understanding generational differences. Given the tens of thousands of Korean children who go abroad to study and work, how are children and youth abroad understood within this formulation of a global Korean nation? Are Korean youth, who are situated beyond the nation's geographic boundaries, interpellated by South Korean national discussions of generation? How do they respond to the discussions of themselves as overseas Koreans? These are questions that I began to raise as a result of these conversations around family and generation.

Sport Can't Heal All Wounds

In order to guard against conveying an oversimplified picture of generational unity, I want to turn here to an instance in which the World Cup failed to unify generations. It is important to understand that generational differences are also expressed within and through other differences, such as race, class, gender, and sexuality (Skelton and Valentine 1998). Most of the discourses about generation discussed how the World Cup worked to unify the nation by transcending social differences. One young female respondent felt compelled by this structure of feeling, yet she eventually resisted its hegemonic pull.

On the evening of June 18, 2002, Chŏng Chi-hye, a twenty-six-year-old single woman, and I left our residence at the *kosiwŏn* to find a place to watch the South Korean team play the Italian team in the Round of Sixteen. I was exhausted from having spent the last three South Korean games in the streets of Seoul, crowded shoulder to shoulder among hundreds of thousands of fans. I had nearly lost my voice from singing, cheering, and chanting, as well as from the late-night carousing. As a manager of the kosiwŏn, Chŏng Chi-hye had to stay in the area, so we decided to watch at a neighborhood bar. She informed me that my exhaustion was a dead giveaway that I wasn't Korean. "If you were really Korean," she told me, "you would be gaining strength with each win!" I weakly acceded to her assessment.

As we entered various establishments in an attempt to find a spot to watch the game, we were turned away several times. We could hardly believe that there was no space anywhere for two young women. Finally, we climbed up the stairs of a second-story chain snack shop called *Ch'ŏn Ha Il P'um* (Best One Under Heaven) that had a single, dusty ten-inch television precariously dangling from a ceiling corner. In the minutes prior to the game, we talked about the events of the past few weeks, the astounding performance of the South Korean team, and the stunning scale and scope of the celebrations. We also talked about the Korean players, exchanging tidbits of media and Internet-filtered gossip about their backgrounds and personal lives. I could tell that Chŏng Chi-hye was rather annoyed with me for expressing a preference for the "look" of the Italian team, with their skin-tight cobalt jerseys and scruffy hair. As the pregame ceremony began, the card section revealed the message "AGAIN 1966," a reference to the stunning defeat of the Italian team by North Korea in the 1966 World Cup.[12] Our reunification sympathies were sparked for a brief media moment. We mimed expressions of solidarity by squeezing each other's hands and locking our eyes on the screen as the game began.

We remained tense throughout the game, and the many long minutes of anxiety were extended when regulation play ended in a tie at 1–1. The play was fast and aggressive throughout, and it was marked by close shots and colliding bodies. As the midfielder Ahn Jung-hwan headed in a golden goal during overtime, we yelped, bounced up and down, and embraced. Before the cellular networks were jammed, I reached for my phone and called my parents in California, and I could hear a small crowd cheering at three in the morning. "We won," I cried. My parents and their friends in California were weeping, too. Chŏng Chi-hye stood directly in front of the television with her hands locked in a fist under her chin as though she were praying.

After a few minutes, I asked Chŏng Chi-hye if she wanted to use my phone to call her parents, as she was the only person I knew in Seoul who didn't have a phone. She took it in her hands as if it were something very fragile and started to dial. Before anyone could pick up, she snapped it shut suddenly and shoved the phone toward me. I reassured her that I didn't mind if she called. She considered it for a while and then, with watery eyes, said, "This is the first time in two and a half years that I have considered calling my family. I haven't talked to them in two and a half years. I ran away from home."

The emotional charge of the World Cup victory was so powerful that Chŏng Chi-hye felt an intense urge to break a vow she had made to herself when she left home: Never contact her parents again. Later that evening, she told me that her parents had abused her. Her desire for autonomy and self-determination had resulted in intense conflict with her parents who, she claimed, expected her to live a life in service to them and, eventually, a future husband. After a period of immense physical abuse, she ran away from rural Ch'unch'ŏn to live in Seoul. She was working and living in Seoul under an assumed name.

My own desire to call my parents emerged from a desire to connect with them in an emotional way. The event offered a space in which this connection could happen, unencumbered by the usual set of burdensome expectations. I also knew that they would be celebrating, and I wanted to experience the simultaneity of the celebration that was taking place across the Pacific. Though I explained my actions as part of my research impulse, I realized that I myself was interpellated by the emotional narratives of generational unity.

Chŏng had also felt this immense emotional urge for family unity at the moment of victory. We were both overwhelmed by emotions as we watched, rejoiced, and embraced strangers. Nevertheless, she realized that the strife between her parents and herself was great. This moment of nationalist unity could not induce her to bridge that gap. It would not revolutionize the circumstances that positioned her in a contentious relationship with her parents. Ultimately, she did not make the call.

The desires for a better life—of opportunities and personal freedom, cosmopolitanism and technology, glamour and commodities—draw many young women such as Chŏng Chi-hye to Seoul. As a single woman living and working in the kosiwŏn, she became part of a class of young women who were migrants to Seoul, living hand to mouth and dreaming of ever-elusive opportunities. I lived with many such women and came to better understand the potency of the dreams of Seoul for them (see Kendall 1996; Nelson 2000). I also developed an awareness of the precariousness of their residence in the megalopolis. In Seoul, it is nearly impossible to attain a sense of security as an outsider with few financial resources and personal connections.[13]

In the course of the World Cup month, the differences that prevented some people from sensing this feeling of unity were almost entirely absent from the mass media coverage. This celebration did, however, create the opportunity for revealing those very points of dissonance. Chŏng Chihye's own participation in the celebration was selective and strategic, rather than a wholehearted abandonment to the cause of national unity. The issues of gender, class, and national difference were not erased in the frenzy of the World Cup. These attenuating factors were even more apparent for many Koreans who did not exercise the media-prescribed behavior for the event.

Generational Difference in the United States

In Korean America, the terms *il se* (first generation), *il chŏm o se* (one-point-five generation), and *i se* (second generation) are important markers of social categorization. These terms organize differences among immigrant groups at different stages of migration, with respect to age of entry, length of stay, and nation of birth. Il se refers to those who were born in South Korea and have gone through the process of immigration as adults. Il chŏm o se refers to foreign-born immigrants who have had some education in South Korea but migrated to the United States during their school years. I se refers to Korean Americans who are born in the United States or who immigrate at an early age (Kim and Yu 1996).[14] In everyday Korean American contexts, these categories are naturalized and reinforced through mass media, community institutions, and interpersonal communications. Although these terms can mark significant variances in citizenship, education, political subjectivity, and language usage, their widespread use operates to overdetermine crudely configured groups in Korean America. These categories tend to erase from consideration those who do not fall neatly into a "pure-blood" heterosexual family-based model of migration. This model is based on the reproduction of children of Korean blood. For example, this linear understanding of generational succession does not include those who have intermarried, who are adoptees, or biracial Korean Americans. These categories do not recognize the significant number of Koreans who have spent considerable time in other countries (such as Japan, the former Soviet republics, or the countries of Latin America) prior to their entry into the United States (see Amerasia 2003/4; 2004; K. Park 1999).

Furthermore, within each category, there are varying degrees of connection to Koreanness and Americanness. For example, there are Korean Americans who speak American-accented, or "Native-speaker," English who lived most of their lives in South Korea but attended a foreign school or one of the newer English-only schools. There are also many Korean American youth born in the United States who live much of their childhood to adolescence in South Korea and return to the United States for their high school or college education. There are Korean Americans who have lived in the United States most of their lives and yet speak what I perceive as Korean-accented English. Many Korean American youth assert their sense of Korean nationalism in ways that are far more impassioned and explicit than many South Korean youth.[15] There are also many Korean Americans whose parents currently live in South Korea while they attend grade school or college in the United States. They are similar to the "parachute kids" mentioned in reference to Chinese American elites (Chiang-Hom 2004; Ong 1999).[16] In short, the cultural characteristics mapped onto these generational categories, particularly the "second generation" or the youth, tend to erase the complexities of lived experience.

Rather than simply relying on these generational categories as descriptive terms, it is important to historicize the construction of ideas about generation in Korean America. Post-1965 Asian immigration has significant differences from pre-1965 cohorts of migration (Lowe 2001). Newer Asian migration to the United States is largely characterized by higher degrees of transnational connection that is enabled through technologies of travel, media, and communications (J. Park 2004). Transnational connections have, of course, existed since the beginning of Asian migration to North America (Chun 2004; Hsu 2000).[17] Nevertheless, few direct critiques or alternatives have been put forward to this hegemonic generational paradigm.

As the next sections reveal, my research in Korean America not only demonstrates the persistent power of these generational categories in the everyday lives of people but also how subjects negotiate their hegemonic determinations as generational subjects and how a transnational perspective might yield a more accurate and nuanced understanding of generational dynamics.

A Numbers Game

In Asian American Studies and U.S. studies of immigration and race, the dominant terms *first*, *second*, and *third generation* are based on an assimilationist framework for understanding migration to the United States (Portes and Rumbaut 2001).[18] This framework assumes that immigrants who enter the United States will assimilate and eventually obtain U.S. citizenship (Gans 1992; Ngai 2004). The ubiquitous use of these generational categories in Asian America reflects the hegemonic power of the theories of immigration, race, and culture introduced by the Chicago School of Sociology in the early twentieth century (see R. Park 1950; Yu 2001). These theories of immigration and ethnicity promulgate a "straight-line" theory of migration —one that assumes foreigners who enter the United States intend to stay permanently and have no intention of returning to their countries of origin. The longer they and their descendants reside in the United States, the more "American" the family line will become. With each subsequent generation born in the United States, direct ties to their countries of origin loosen and eventually become almost entirely symbolic. According to this framework, the first generation will have substantial difficulties with the foreign culture of the United States, and the second generation will have some sense of biculturalism, as their parents remain living repositories of their countries of origin. By the third generation, participation in ethnicity will be more elective as children will have no direct experience of the homeland themselves or through their parents. It is assumed that, by then, they will have fully assimilated into U.S. life. This straight-line theory also has an optimistic component that assumes each generation will improve on the socioeconomic situation of their parents as they take advantage of the educational and economic opportunities available in the United States.[19]

In their attempt to capture the heterogeneity of experience of second-generation immigrants, immigrant theorists Portes and Rumbaut (2001) espouse a model of "selective acculturation." This theory challenges the usefulness of full cultural assimilation into U.S. dominant culture by suggesting the economic and psychological benefits of a second-generation individual who maintains his or her ties to the first generation and home country. The idea of selective acculturation continues to privilege full citizenship and cultural integration, but it suggests the utilitarian aspects of immigrants and their children to the benefit of the U.S. nation. That is, they believe that the second generation is in a strategic position to further U.S. global hegemony through corporate and diplomatic functions.

These ideas of immigrant generation are integrated into an assimilationist model of immigration that produces a hegemonic vision of U.S. national culture. Lisa Lowe (1996) argues that immigration (rather than assimilation) is a more appropriate analytic to understand Asian America. As a result of many changes to immigration policies, Asian America has become increasingly diverse in terms of national origin, ethnicity, class, religion, and so on. (Zhou 2004). In the past two decades, Asian America has been powerfully affected by the increased visibility of the relationship between Asia and the United States (Palumbo-Liu 1999). Significant improvements in technologies, such as telecommunications and transportation, have made communication and travel between Asia and the United States far easier. Governments now regulate visa and citizenship requirements to ease transnational movement for some Asian migrants (Ong 1999). Furthermore, transnational mass media have enabled new modes of imagining community across borders (Mankekar and Schein 2004). Assimilationist models are thus challenged by the constant flow of people, commodities, and ideas back and forth between national spaces (Appadurai 1996; Grewal, Gupta, and Ong 1999). By opening up the analysis of generation in Asian America to transnational analyses, generational identity itself can be understood beyond the context of assimilation. It can be viewed as a category that moves through and between national boundaries.

As I stated at the beginning of this chapter, generational differences operate as a hegemonic way of discussing differences among Korean communities in Los Angeles and South Korea. The Korean Americans with whom I worked were very invested in discussing issues of generation. Most were more than willing to convey their opinions about these differences and how they played out within their own lives. For my respondents, the issues of generation became a primary mode of talking about their position within Korean America. Nevertheless, the respondents I interviewed interpreted the hegemonic discourses of generational difference in various ways. These hegemonic discourses of generation draw from both U.S. assimilationist rhetoric and the homogenizing narratives of Korean ethnic nationalism. The position of respondents toward these issues of generation often reflected their position with respect to South Korean and U.S. nationalist discourses. My fieldwork demonstrates that there were discrepancies in attitudes about Koreanness and Americanness between and among those of different generations. In the following pages, I attempt to demonstrate the heterogeneity of responses in these generational categories, particularly with respect to discussions about youth.

During the World Cup, Korean nationalist discourses in Korean America focused heavily on the participation by Korean American youth in group celebrations. Powerful images of Korean American youth cheering for the Korean national team were held as proof that Korean American youth possessed a powerful sense of South Korean nationalism. Instead of being a "generation in trouble" (Amerasia 1999), they were demonstrating their cultural citizenship in the Korean American community. In Korean nationalist discourses in the United States, generational discussions were articulated in a similar way to those in South Korea. Somewhat paradoxically, the hegemonic discourses of generation in both places operated to obscure the transnational connections between and within categories of generation in Los Angeles and Seoul.

Celebrating Returns

Many il se pointed to the World Cup as creating an opportunity for what they referred to as the il chŏm o se and i se to participate in something Korean. The association of the il chŏm o se and i se with youth is based on the fact that in 2000 the overwhelming proportion of one-point-five and second-generation Korean Americans—nearly 80 percent—were under the age of eighteen.[20] Therefore, the conflation of categories of one-point-five/second generation with youth reflects a common reality in Korean America. Because so many Korean Americans born or raised from childhood in the United States are not yet adults, they remain a category of speculation by Korean-language media, Korean American adults, and academics.

For many il se, the most important aspect of the World Cup was the opportunity to cheer for the Korean team with their children and other Korean American youth. It was a moment for adults to connect with youth in a way that placed all Korean Americans within mainstream representations in both the United States and South Korea. Jeannie Choi, a fifty-two-year-old mother of two college students, eagerly shared her experience of the World Cup month. She informed me that, since coming to the United States thirteen years prior, she had never felt as much joy in her life—salm mat (literally, "life taste")—as she had during the World Cup. Ms. Choi was divorced and worked as an administrative assistant in a Korean CPA office. She lived in the "ethnoburb" of Hacienda Heights and worked in Koreatown. We decided to meet at her workplace during her lunch break. She had ordered two chicken teriyaki lunches to be delivered. When the lunch arrived, we went into a back storage room and sat on two metal folding chairs. I awkwardly attempted to balance my meal on my lap while I conducted the interview.

When I asked her about her experiences of the event, she began by speaking of her daughters. Her children, whom she refers to as il chŏm o se, were actively involved in street cheering, but she preferred to watch at home with some friends and a few beers. For her, the most important impact of the World Cup was the influence it had on her daughters and their generation of Korean friends. She stated, "Especially for the *il chŏm o se* and *i se*, who don't know our nation, *uri nara,* they were filled with pride through this event." Uri nara, or "our nation," in this case refers to South Korea, and Ms. Choi's statement asserted that it was through this sporting event that her daughters gained some essential knowledge about the country and came to see themselves as part of the South Korean nation. According to her assertions, her daughters had felt enough of a connection with South Korea to feel pride in uri nara through the event. Ms. Choi discussed at length the activities of her daughters and their modes of participation. She did not feel the need to discuss her own participation in the event because its real significance was in the impact it had on Korean American youth.

Ms. Choi's statements reflected a rather conservative Korean nationalist interpretation of the responses by young people to the World Cup. This nationalist discourse hailed the event as producing a unified global Korean nation—"Korea as one." This model of national unity was based on the idea of the family as the model for the nation. Her statements also emphasized the importance of knowledge of South Korea—a consciousness about the homeland—as a critical element in the younger generation's enjoyment of the event.

Chung Seungwon, a thirty-eight-year-old journalist for the largest newspaper in Koreatown, *Korea Times,* also emphasized the importance of national consciousness. He thought the most important aspect of the event was that it caused many Korean American young people, il chŏm o se and i se, to really think about Korea for the first time. Mr. Chung felt that the event created a positive image of Korea in their minds.

I think it had a great impact, especially on the one-point-five and second generation, those who never really think about Korea, those who only think about America. For that age group, I think it had a great impact. They asked, "What is Korea?" For those kids who had a relatively negative image of Korea, this event gave them a chance to think, "I think it's a great thing that there is a place called Korea." When Korea and America played against each other, the kids who said they really didn't know how they would cheer would watch the game and out of their mouths came things like, "Blood is thicker than water," and "Without even realizing it, I came to root for Korea."

Mr. Chung felt that the reactions of the older generations were understandable and predictable. He assumed that older Koreans were nationalist through and through. He noted that older Koreans would say things such as, "My, how Korea has grown!" but the event did not significantly change their attitude toward South Korea. In his opinion, the real importance of this event was its impact on Korean American youth. Like Cho Han, Mr. Chung believed this represented a major breakthrough in the attitude of youth toward South Korea. He stated, "Those young people who didn't care at all about Korea came to think, 'Korea is a good place.' It made them think about Korea." Through this event, Mr. Chung felt that Korean American young people began to consider themselves as *Korean* Americans—that is, not just American but also Korean.

These individuals, who considered themselves the il se, used narratives of loss and recovery to describe the enthusiasm of the il chŏm o se and i se. They believed that the event had a major impact on revolutionizing the position of youth toward South Korea or at least the idea of Korea in their minds. In this way, the interpretations of the event by Korean nationalist discourses in the United States were similar to those of the media in South Korea. However, in the United States, the recovery of Korean nationalism might seem more significant, given the greater distance of Korean American youth from the South Korean nation and the pressures to demonstrate their loyalty to the United States. The il se articulated a sense of relief that uri nara, which had been missing in young Korean Americans' lives, had been rediscovered through this event.

These discourses revealed a desire on the part of il se to recover Korean American youth for the South Korean nation. This desire was shaped by the hegemonic logic of Korean nationalism, which understands Korean American youth as essentially Korean by fact of blood.[21] This hegemonic idea of nation is based on the idea of the essential homogeneity of the Korean race. The ideas of blood, ethnicity, and nation are conflated under the aegis of uri nara. According to this nationalist position, even if Korean youth lose their consciousness of the nation, they are still Korean by the undeniable fact of shared blood. Through the World Cup, they had come to understand this so-called essential blood connection. Therefore, the idea that Korean Americans came to think about Korea did not change an existing reality; rather, it made them aware of it. The idea of Korean American youth returning to Koreanness through this event was celebrated by Korean nationalists. This return fulfilled a desire for national unity, particularly through the recruitment of Korean subjects scattered around the world.

Finding Korea

By contrast, the discussions I had with younger Korean Americans who participated in the street rarely referenced a sense of recovery. Those who participated by going to gatherings in Koreatown talked most about the pleasures of the celebration and the collective experiences of spectatorship. The World Cup was an opportunity for sharing in a unique and festive moment with friends and family. For young people, being Korean was a relatively "cool" thing for the time being. It was a time when the pleasures of mainstream representation united Koreans and Korean Americans in a moment of "temporary coherence" (Massey 1998). It did not, however, revolutionize Korean American culture or the significance of Korea in the minds of the youth. Nor did the event dramatically change their opinions about their position within the United States as Korean Americans.

Sherry Chi, a twenty-year-old receptionist at a Korean dental office on Vermont Avenue, was attending community college at night. We had an interview at a popular snack shop next to the dental office just after she had left work. She was attractive by the contemporary standards of Korean beauty magazines—tall and thin, with a small face and big round eyes framed by long, straight hair. Over the course of our interview, she pulled out a hand mirror several times to make sure that her makeup was properly maintained and to ensure that food particles were not stuck between her teeth.

She explained that she was going to school because she hoped to eventually get a better job. Once she made enough money, she wanted to move out of Koreatown. She had come to the United States at the age of thirteen and had lived in Koreatown with a middle-aged roommate while her parents remained in South Korea. She stated that, initially, during the World Cup, she did not want to go out on the streets at night because: "One, Koreatown was unsafe; and two, I would have rather slept." Her friends dragged her out, though, and they even made her wear a red T-shirt. "I only wore a T-shirt because it was given to me. *For free*," she pointed out. Although she didn't care at all about soccer, or sports for that matter, she really enjoyed feeling the excitement of the crowd. She loved being part of such a big event. As she watched the games and participated in the group cheering, she was drawn into the action. "Everyone was really crazy," she said. "It was just a lot of fun." To Ms. Chi, the World Cup was a unique period of social gathering. Although it was "a lot of fun," her first experience of sports spectatorship on such a massive scale did not bring her together with all of the other Koreans in a feeling of collective unity. Her everyday life was already one in which she felt surrounded by Korean Americans since she worked and lived in the heart of Koreatown. She understood the moment as an isolated incident—a brief moment of ecstatic celebration. It was an instance when the spectacular interrupted her otherwise mundane life.

Some of the young people I interviewed were more proactive about their involvement in the event. Louisa Kim, a nineteen-year-old college student who lived in Glendale, said that her grandmother bought her and her brother red T-shirts to wear. She said, "I don't know why she did that, but she also bought a calendar, scarves, and a bunch of other stuff." She went on, "I wasn't really into soccer, but since the Koreans did so well, I got into it. It was so awesome to be out there with so many other Koreans. We had so much fun." Ms. Kim drove to Koreatown from the suburb of Glendale with several other Korean American friends. They got dressed for the event together and applied face paint and temporary tattoos on one another's bodies. She was totally willing to go "all out" for this event; she became part of the crowds that were represented in the Korean-language media as youthful, loyal, and patriotic.

Many young people who were skeptical about the nationalist frenzy of their elders still experienced the event as an exhilarating, albeit brief, period. However, rather than experiencing it as a spontaneous coming together, the actions of the youth were, in part, a response to Korean-language media, Korean institutions, and Korean adults who encouraged such behavior. Many of the youth I knew were given T-shirts and tickets to the Staples Center event by their parents and relatives. They were strongly encouraged to participate by their parents, who gave them permission to drive to an otherwise dangerous Koreatown, to hang out with their Korean friends, and to stay out all night—all in the interests of the Korean (American) event. In Korean America, the youth did not lead in creating a fan culture as they did in South Korea. They did, however, demonstrate an impressive ability to imitate their counterparts in Seoul.

Of course, there were many Korean American youth in Los Angeles who

Figure 16. Young women in Koreatown, Los Angeles. Photograph by John Lok. *Los Angeles Times* photo, copyright 2002. Reprinted with permission.

didn't care about the World Cup and didn't participate in the spectacle. Ken Nam, a twenty-five-year-old cell phone retailer, made clear his disdain: "I don't like getting together with so many other Koreans. It's so hectic." He added, "They aren't real sports fans; they're just nationalistic." Mr. Nam would often hang out with his Korean American friends in Koreatown on the weekends. He would go to cafés, clubs, and bars in Koreatown because he thought it was more fun than going to some random place in Hollywood. He felt a sense of belonging in Koreatown. He admitted that all of his close friends were Korean American (he grew up in communities with large Korean populations in Garden Grove and Koreatown), but he wasn't going to hang out with a large group of Koreans when it came to sports.

When I asked Mr. Nam about sports, he proclaimed that he was a sports fanatic. He liked all the Los Angeles teams, including the Dodgers, Kings, Lakers, and Angels (based in Anaheim at the time). He felt that Chan Ho Park had betrayed the Korean community, "his base," by leaving the Dodgers to play for the Texas Rangers. Besides Chan Ho, however, Mr. Nam didn't follow or know about many other Korean players in the United States. He knew there were quite a few Korean female golfers, but he didn't really follow golf. He didn't have a problem with Koreans supporting Korean players.

"My problem," he stated, "is with Korean sports fanatics who put their nationalism ahead of sports." When it came to national competitions, he rooted for the United States because he was "American." For example, when we discussed the revival of the Apolo Ohno short-track speed-skating incident during the World Cup, he became indignant.[22] We talked about the e-mail campaign against the U.S. Olympic team and the International Olympic Committee. We even discussed the death threats against Apolo "Anton" Ohno. About the anti-Ohno goal ceremony, Mr. Nam stated, "It was just really stupid to bring that up. It just made the Koreans look stupid." He made generalizations about all Koreans who watched sports. As a Korean American himself, the vehement nationalism of Koreans and Korean Americans made him take a defensive stance as someone who might be misrecognized for a Korean nationalist. He felt that Korean nationalism compromised his own expertise in sports and his belief in the neutrality of sports. He felt the need as a Korean American to distance himself from what he perceived as this non-American way of approaching sports by refusing to take part in large Korean group celebrations during the World Cup and other group outings organized to cheer for Korean athletes.

Regardless of discourses of refusal such as this, Korean-language media repeated again and again that "all two million Koreans in the United States came together as one" during the World Cup. At times, they would include the entire global Korean nation, stating, "All sixty million Koreans around the world came together as one."[23] Rather than feeling some kind of nationalist pressure, most Korean American youth with whom I spoke saw their participation as a matter of personal choice. For those young Korean Americans who did participate, it was time out of the ordinary. It was a uniquely "Korean thing" to do amidst all the other activities from which they could choose. Their consumer identities were tied up in World Cup soccer for a brief period of time, but it was not necessarily a matter of national unity. The unique nature of the responses to this global mega-event by Koreans around the world compelled many younger Korean Americans to articulate a sense of Korean pride that was based on consumer practices and consumer pleasures. Young people were connected to communities around the world through simultaneous viewing and cheering practices.

In many ways, the ideas of Koreanness that were expressed by the youth were left unquestioned. "Being Korean" was often offered as the reason for participation. "I went because I'm Korean," was a common response. However, among the young people I interviewed, there were no nationalist claims of Korea as uri nara. For Korean American youth, Koreanness is often associated with pleasure. The pleasures of Koreatown, the nightclubs, bars, *nore bang* (karaoke rooms), restaurants, and cafés offer many opportunities for fun through consumption. Koreanness is consumed through participation in these commercial contexts of entertainment with other Koreans and Korean Americans. In fact, Koreatown might be considered symbolic of a Korean consumer space that caters to this very fantasy, especially for those who live outside its borders. In the instance of the World Cup, being Korean was once again associated with pleasure.

The Connections across Geographic Spaces

During the World Cup, Korean-language newspapers in the United States ran many photos of the young people filling the streets of Seoul. A photo taken in Koreatown in the *Joonang Ilbo,* or the *Korea Central Daily,* on June 20, 2002, demonstrates the celebration after the victory over Spain in the Round of Eight. The headline reads, "3000 people cheer together, fill the town." The article goes on to state that the people in the picture and the crowd are the il chŏm o se and i se. The scene looks almost identical to the images of young people celebrating on the streets of Seoul. In addition, the picture depicts a feminized crowd, demonstrating that many young females came to watch the sporting event within these crowds. As I argue in Chapter 5, the production of feminized World Cup crowds in South Korea was a widely noted phenomenon, and it is also reflected in pictures of crowds in Koreatown.

I was struck by the resonance of these discourses with the debates over generational differences I encountered while in South Korea. Conservative nationalist discourses in South Korea praised the renewal of national interest in the younger generation. This nation love was proven by the millions of young people cheering for the Korean national team on the streets and even by cleaning up after the massive gatherings. According to these conservative discourses, the younger generation, which had heretofore been characterized by individualism and apathy toward their country, discovered the beauty of the collectivistic spirit of Korean nationalism. Resisting these assertions, youth in South Korea resignified the idea of Korean nationalism by producing it as a festive discourse within the context of this event. In many ways, their behavior sidestepped attempts to appropriate their play in the interests of conservative nationalism (Cho Han et al. 2004).

In Los Angeles, conservative Korean nationalist discourses discussed the interest of young Korean Americans as an il chŏm o se and i se identity crisis that was resolved through the rediscovery of uri nara. Youth were praised for their displays of Koreanness and their orderly conduct. They also cleaned up after the crowd cheers. Much like the youth on the streets of Seoul, young Korean Americans decided to claim this moment for their own interests. Rather than within the parameters of a conservative Korean ethnic nationalism, notions of Korea and Koreanness were discussed within the context of consumer culture, within a commodified realm of entertainment and social interaction.

The extraordinarily high rates of Internet usage by Korean youth in and between Seoul and Los Angeles played a large role in producing transnational spaces of temporary coherence (Massey 1998; J. Park 2004; Woo 2004). The exchange of information in nearly instantaneous contexts enabled the rapid mobilization of youth in Los Angeles and their corresponding celebrations. Korean American youth in Los Angeles were mobilized through connectivities enabled through text messages, cell phones, and Internet communications (see S. Woo 2004). Those in Korean America who participated in the Koreatown celebrations depended on these technologies on a far greater level than those in Seoul who were saturated by the World Cup cultures of celebration nearly every time they turned on their televisions or walked outside.

It would be a mistake to think that media technologies are the only way Korean American youth "discover" a sense of cultural connection. Koreatown is also a site for a large number of community organizations and cultural centers that cater to youth and are sponsored by the Korean government, churches, and nonprofit groups (Chung 2004). These organizations become arenas through which ideas of ethnic identity and ethnic nationalism are produced. Angie Chung (2004) points out that these organizations facilitate the involvement of one-point-five and second-generation Korean Americans in the Koreatown community. They also produce spaces for interactions among the youth. Therefore, the World Cup street cheering might be seen as mobilizing the social networks produced through these existing organizations.

The similarities I found between youth behavior and attitudes in South Korea and the United States call into question the overwhelming dependence on categories of il se, il chŏm o se, and i se to describe differences among Korean Americans of different ages and tenures of migration. These categories are important to the extent that they are still in wide use and are helpful in examining shared experiences between those who have migrated and their children. However, the increasingly transnational dimension to discourses of Koreanness and the connections between Koreans in Seoul and the United States and among age cohorts raise questions about nation-centered approaches to generation. The dependence on il se, il chŏm o se, and i se, particularly with respect to the Korean American community, needs to be reassessed.

The participation and significance of the multigenerational gathering during the World Cup were understood and interpreted in highly disparate ways by participants. The significance of generational discourses demonstrates the desires of Koreans to interpret the radical changes that have upended their lives within the last century. They raise the question of what kinds of futures are imagined by South Koreans and Korean Americans as symbolized by youth. The transnational responses to this event question whether assimilationist dreams are, in fact, a major aspect of everyday life for all youth in Korean America. The so-called Korean American dreams for *anjong* (security), in the terms of Kyeyoung Park (1997), may be just one step in cosmopolitan dreams of "return." In fact, recognition as a Korean success within the current *Hallyu* sweeping Asia may be weighed as a more appealing dream than anjong in the United States.[24] For some, the desire to be highly visible and cosmopolitan in a global context may be, in fact, a desire more powerful than a dream of petty bourgeois success as a minority in the United States.[25]

Conclusion

THE POLITICAL POTENTIALITY OF SPORT

Throughout this book I have focused on how productions of media sport shape ideas around national belonging, identity, and community. As a powerful commercial media context, media sport works to convey hegemonic ideologies of nation, gender, sexuality, and race, and it offers an important context for understanding how these ideologies travel across nation-states. Media sport exists as a complex social arena, and in this conclusion, I suggest that it can be an arena for progressive social change. Media sport can inspire political action by offering people the powerful experience of participating in collective action with a shared purpose. Though there is no necessary political consequence of participation in a sporting public and no completely unifying political purpose, sporting publics exist as realms of political possibility and potentiality. The experience of sporting publics can intensify existing political sentiments and operate as a medium through which these sentiments circulate. The relationship between sport and politics is often linked in discussing sports' fascist potential, but the following discussion suggests a broader political potentiality of sport. It points to the potential of sport to inspire democratic resistance to governmental power and to shape alternative visions of national community.

Through my fieldwork, I witnessed how specific behaviors shaped through participation during a sporting event were again expressed during significant and large-scale political protests. Drawing from experiences of the publics of the 2002 World Cup, progressive groups in South Korea demanding political change at the level of governmental policies successfully initiated mass protests. I suggest that the embodied experiences of being in the mass crowds and the physical memories of participation during the 2002 World Cup event shaped a kind of affective memory that was recalled during large-scale protests in 2002 and 2008. These memories played a part in creating possibilities for large-scale protests and shaping behaviors during the protests. I discuss the protests linked to the "tank incident," which occurred during the 2002 World Cup. The incident involved a U.S. military tank that killed two junior high school girls on their way to a birthday party. Due to mass protests initiated by youth, this incident grew into a significant issue during the 2002 South Korean presidential campaign and influenced its outcome. I then analyze the 2008 mad cow protests that took place in Seoul throughout the months of May, June, and July. These protests once again raised concerns over the role of the United States in South Korea. This protest began as an outcry against the import of U.S. beef and became a general referendum on the policies of President Lee Myung Bak. The mad cow protests were connected to issues of democratic participation, governmental power, and political representation for a number of marginalized groups. Neither event may seem directly related to the World Cup, but I argue that the experiences of the World Cup offered an experience of mass crowd participation that instilled an intimate recognition of the power of collective action.

I conclude this text with a brief discussion of the North Korean–South Korean sporting matches that occurred between 2002 and 2003. These so-called "reunification" events highlight the limits of an analysis that excludes the importance of national division when discussing ideas of Koreanness. Indeed, the role of sport in the contested discursive dance of *t'ongil* (reunification) requires a thorough and book-length project of its own (see Lee et al. 2007). Nevertheless, I do feel that it is important to raise questions about the political potential of sport to transform prevailing ideas of national community. A discussion of the still central question of reunification points to erasures in hegemonic discourses of global Koreanness. Moreover, the issue of reunification highlights the different political stakes for Koreans located in different sites. Do discourses of reunification entail the same political struggles for Korean Americans? Reunification sporting events raise questions about the ethical implications of sport and social responsibilities connected to sport that go beyond commercial profit motivations.

By concluding this book with a discussion of massive protests and reunification events, I hope to demonstrate how the impact of sporting events might be understood well beyond the cultural critique of sport and consumer culture. I aim to raise questions about how issues of media sport might be linked to an ethical and engaged approach to global citizenship.

Waiting for an Uproar

On June 13, 2002, two middle school girls, Sim Mi-sŏn and Sin Hyo-sun, were on their way to a birthday party in Yangju, a town north of Seoul, when they were run over and killed by a U.S. military M60 tank that left giant tracks on their lifeless bodies. The next day, I found a very brief column in the left-leaning *Han'gyŏre* newspaper detailing the circumstances of the incident. Although I searched, I found very little information about this tragedy in the mass media, given that it occurred during the World Cup, a few days after the first-ever South Korean team win against Poland on June 4, following the suspenseful tie against the United States on June 10, and on the eve of the match against Portugal on June 14.

Given the virtual silence around this event, I asked as many people as I could why it was given so little press coverage. Kwŏn Su-mi, a thirty-two-year-old elementary teacher, told me, "Just wait. After the World Cup, people will make a lot of noise. They will hold demonstrations. I'm sure of it." While I was surprised by the lack of public response, I was truly stunned by her predictions. The mass media was so saturated with news about the World Cup that there seemed to be no room to report on this horrible incident. I was dubious about the national public's ability to remember the tragedy.

Toward the close of the event, after South Korea had lost to Germany in the semifinal, and nearly two weeks after the tragedy, media coverage of the incident began to appear. Using this tragedy as a springboard, NGOs started to organize against the U.S. military, the Status of Forces Agreement (SOFA),[1] and the U.S.-led war in Afghanistan. Commercial mass media began to cover this story with regularity. As I witnessed the growing media and public response to the tank incident, I thought of Ms. Kwŏn's assurance that there would be a response and that it would come in due time *after* the World Cup.

The incident became quite politicized, and Hyosuni and Misŏni emerged as household names around which a youth-based, anti-American movement grew (Bong and Moon 2005; Shin 2006; H. Song 2003). It was clear that the U.S. military itself was quite stunned that there would be such a delayed response to this incident. Initially, the driver of the tank, Sergeant Mark Walker, and his associate, Sergeant Fernando Niño, were excused of any wrongdoing in the incident, as it was determined that they were following orders when the accident occurred. The U.S. military also attempted to deal with the event quietly by offering reparations to the families. The delayed public outcry, however, demanded that the drivers of the vehicle be brought to justice in a South Korean court of law and that U.S. president George W. Bush offer a personal apology to the families of the two girls. Only after the stalled uproar did the U.S. military make their apologies public. In an effort to quell the upsurge in anger, the two army personnel were retried and found guilty of negligent homicide.

During the world's most widely watched sporting event, South Korea attempted to showcase its global status to the world, and the national mass media dedicated the bulk of its resources to the event. The discourses of national unity and global success saturated media narratives. Even progressives were swept into the frenzy of the national event. Addressing the tank incident during this time would have soured the mood of the national party. Even if there were some who mobilized against the U.S. military, many (if not most) who later participated in the protests were partying during the month of June. After the global media attention veered away from the nation, activist organizations escalated the issue of Hyosuni and Misŏni.

In November, thousands of youth returned to the center of Seoul, Kwanghwamun, to hold a spectacular candlelight vigil for Hyosuni and Misŏni. They gathered on a cold fall evening, holding signs and lit candles, chanting slogans, and singing in unison. Participants understood the visual impact of a giant mass occupying the area of Seoul City Hall. As during the World Cup, participants gathered to create a highly dramatic media sculpture that would have a dramatic emotional impact in national and global media. The actual protests were clearly related to the World Cup, as the experience of collective convergence—being out in the crowds, taking over major thoroughfares and streets, and moving in unison—was still fresh in the public's memory. The gendered practices of collective singing, gesturing, chanting, and uniform clothing displays appeared again in the mass protests.

Young people, especially young females in junior high and high school, were said to have led the charge in protesting the tank incident. To people like myself and the U.S. military, the protesting groups may have seemed to be expressing a delayed response, yet their own expressions of protests had already been exchanged over the Internet, and their online/offline responses were clearly organized in a way that would garner global media attention in a highly effective way. The groups that gathered in online com-

Figure 17. Candlelight vigil for Hyosuni and Misŏni. Yonhap News, reprinted with permission.

munities debated about the best, most ethical ways to protest, and they then converged on the streets of Seoul on a date decided upon by the groups. It might be easy to argue that particular left-wing groups planned and executed the protests in a way that ensured a uniform message was captured and conveyed in mainstream media, but this argument diminishes the significance of the number of participants who actively participated in online group discussions, debated the appropriate and ethical way to respond, and emerged on the streets. People used personal digital media, including digital cameras, cell phones, and digital recorders, as evidence of their participation and reproduced images and text as personal accounts of their experiences on the streets. The event also evoked a kind of bodily memory—of proprioception— that surely recalled the memory of the World Cup for those who walked through the streets during both events.

Although the massive gatherings in June of 2002 were largely celebratory, the experience of walking through the streets with so many others in the name of national togetherness was again experienced during the protests in November. The collective outcry that emerged during this event might have seemed serious and even somber, when compared to the celebrations of June, but even in the explicit political nature of the event and the presentation of earnestness, the crowd displayed a charisma and energy that transformed a candlelight vigil into an ecstatic event. This event brought together tens of thousands, harnessing the affective potential of a mass gathering to generate shared emotions around national themes of change. The crowd emerged as a sculptural mass ready for circulation in spectacle-driven mass media. The youth who mobilized around the tank incident played a large role in making the U.S. military presence in South Korea and the U.S.-led invasion of Afghanistan a critical issue in the presidential campaign. They became a powerful factor in the election of the progressive, former civil-rights lawyer, Roh Moo Hyun, in December (see H. Song 2003).

Anti-Americanism and Its Legacies

The tank incident brought attention to the complicated relationship between South Korea and the United States (Shin 2006). What I understood as a delayed response demonstrated precisely the contradictions between national dreams of *segyehwa* and the continuing legacy of the Cold War. It is clear that Koreanness continues to be shaped within and through the relations between, but not limited to, South Korea and the United States.

The demonstration was seen by some as another episode in the recent history of anti-American protest. Scholars assert that until the 1980s, most South Koreans regarded the United States favorably as defenders of democratic ideals (Shin 1995). As the South Korean public became aware of the U.S. role in the Kwangju Uprising and its support of authoritarian regimes, anti-Americanism became a key component in dissident nationalisms in the 1980s.[2] Gi-wook Shin states that anti-Americanism was essentially "an ideological struggle over how to define the U.S. role in Korea" (1995, 509). Anti-American rhetoric critiqued the power of the United States in Korea, including its role in the Kwangju Uprising, its support of military dictators, the anticommunist demonization of North Korea, and U.S.-led pressures toward economic liberalization.[3] By the mid-1980s, anti-Americanism was no longer a radical sentiment but part of a popular response to U.S. hegemony and included in the fight for democracy and self-determination.[4] Between the late 1980s and mid-1990s, anti-American rhetoric was less effective as an oppositional strategy because of the democratic transition in 1987 and the collapse of European communism in 1989.[5]

In recent years, however, anti-Americanism has seen quite an upsurge with the growth of civic organizations that protest U.S. hegemony as imposed through its military and economic policies, its North Korea policy, and recent U.S. wars and military aggression in the Middle East.[6] This sentiment grew especially powerful beginning with the election of U.S. president George W. Bush and his foreign policy of preemptive war and unilateralism. The hard-line policies on the part of the United States toward North Korea and the deployment of South Korean soldiers in the Iraq War reminded Koreans of the continuing legacies of the Cold War and their entangled relations with the United States. The anti-American sentiment of recent years has been understood as underpinned by a desire for recognition around the world as a powerful, sovereign state and a state-led policy to pursue closer relations with its Asian neighbors (see Shin 2006; H. Song 2003). In the cultural realm, *Hallyu* has brought an unprecedented level of "global recognition" to media and commodities packaged as "Korean" (Cho Han et al. 2003). This trend has emboldened the South Korean film industry and other cultural industries to lead the cultural fight against an agreement between the United States and South Korea that lifts quotas on Hollywood films.

Embodied Citizenship and the Mad Cow Protests of 2008

With the presidential election of Roh Moo Hyun, there was a turn toward policies that tried to emphasize the relation between South Korea and its East Asian neighbors, even attempting to frame Korea as a "hub" of Asia (Shin 2005). One of the acts of defiance toward the United States was seen in the ban on the import of U.S. beef in 2003. The ban was instituted in 2003 over fears of beef tainted with mad cow disease (bovine spongiform encephalopathy). By 2008, the former governor of Seoul, conservative Lee Myung Bak, was elected president on a platform of economic development and pragmatic diplomatic relations. Part of his platform included improving U.S.– South Korean relations as a way to further develop the sagging South Korean economy. When he took office in early 2008, the Lee administration decided to lift the ban on U.S. beef, and concerns about the safety of U.S. beef became a major point of contention between the Lee administration and several civil society organizations.

The protests were spurred by junior high and high school girls who were protesting U.S. beef primarily for health reasons. The organized opposition to the Lee administration argued that the lifting of the ban was primarily a failure of the government to protect its citizens, and, therefore, Lee should be

Figure 18. Candlelight girl during the 2008 mad cow protests. Photo by author.

impeached and thrown out of office.[7] Harkening back to the 2002 and 2003 protests against the U.S. military, an adolescent girl holding a candle in protest of the government became the symbol of the season of protests. The *ch'ŏtbul sonyo* (candlelight girl) became a symbol around which a large variety of groups converged to protest not only the lifting of the import ban on U.S. beef but also many other issues having to do with the sweeping changes instituted by the Lee administration. A major context for organizing these protests was the online forum Agora, which became a context for leftist activists, marginalized groups, and concerned consumers to debate, share information, and eventually plan protests. By May, groups converged on the streets to protest, and as the protests grew over the course of the month, the police violence against people participating in these mass public gatherings grew.

The protests had the effect of presenting an administration that seemed highly out of touch with the demands of everyday citizens and willing to use violence to quell dissent. President Lee Myung Bak's approval ratings dipped below 20 percent during the course of these protests, and, as a result, his entire cabinet agreed to quit.[8] By June and July, the Seoul protests grew to a massive scale, and they were said to be the largest gathering of people since June 10, 1987, when the democracy movement was successful in overthrowing the dictatorship of President Chun Doo Hwan. The crowds gathering on the streets during the month of July reached, according to some estimates, over one million people. (Official news sources placed the number at around 500,000.) The demonstrators called for the resignation of newly elected Lee Myung Bak and for the retraction of many of political actions, in particular, the further implementation of "free trade" measures between the United States and South Korea, neoliberal policies meant to privatize a variety of state-run industries, widespread cronyism, and his retreat from policies designed to improve relations with the North.

At the beginning of July, I walked with the crowds in several days of massive protests that took place beginning in City Hall plaza, and around Sejŏngno and Chongno. In City Hall plaza, a variety of groups gathered, representing gay and lesbian organizations, immigrant rights groups, Buddhist nuns and monks, Christian organizations, labor unions, well-established nonprofit groups, and citizens consumer groups, among many others. Many of the established groups gathered under their own banners, highlighting the diversity of the crowd. After several hours of open-mic, free-speech time for each group, the crowd mobilized to overtake the streets. With hundreds of thousands of people carrying white candles that were illuminated through small paper cups, the spectacle was breathtaking. Chants and songs marked the peaceful march. The *Han'gyŏre* newspaper stated that the protests turned the streets of Kwanghwamun and Chongno into a "cultural performance space."[9] The crowd was considered open and diverse, characterized by singing, chanting, dancing, and street performances. Because of the immense visual spectacle created through the use of candles, these protests were also referred to as candlelight vigils.

Over the course of the two months of protest, some of the demonstrations were marked by violence between police and protesters. There was damage to property, primarily to police riot buses that were set up as a barrier between the crowd and the road up to the Blue House, the president's residence. However, most of the protests were peaceful and marked by an incredible diversity of interests. These crowds were far more diverse than those of the World Cup and even those that resulted from the tank incident. The protests were largely against Lee Myung Bak's policies, but they could also be considered to have a strong anti-American element. Social movements may use the discourses of anti-Americanism to mobilize, but these struggles cannot be reduced simply to a question of U.S. power in South Korea. Many social movements use anti-American rhetoric as a context to resist other forms of power and inequality. In other national contexts, the United States operates as a symbol for geopolitical, capitalist, and governmental power, and the investment in the discourses of anti-Americanism by prodemocracy groups should be interpreted within the historical and contemporary context of the protests at hand.

As in the case of the World Cup and the 2002 protests, the 2008 mad cow protests demonstrated that media technologies have the power to mobilize people in an almost instantaneous way around a national theme (with global implications). The emotional experience produced through the collective consumption of media and commodities operates to shape Korean subjects as national subjects. The lessons of recent South Korean history have taught us that new media technologies and new forms of sociality produce surprising political results.

Although the cases above detail anti-American protests, I want to avoid privileging the relationship between the United States and South Korea as the all-important narrative, given the hegemonic status of this optic in much scholarship. Many Korean Studies scholars continue to work in and through U.S. institutions where the relationship between the United States and South Korea operates as an ontological and epistemological fact. In other words, the location and funding sources of Korean Studies shape what research looks like. I myself might be accused of being located within this institutional context. Nevertheless, I want to query the kinds of elisions and erasures that are produced through this bilateral scope. Indeed, I am not trying to diminish the significance of geopolitical power relations on scholarship, but I do want to question the relationship between the United States and South Korea as a privileged site of knowledge production. In other words, I want to explore how scholars might "provincialize" the United States (Chakrabarty 2000). This challenge is already taking place because of many historical changes: geopolitical shifts, including China's rise as South Korea's top trade partner; the relaxing of barriers on cultural imports with Japan; the growth of Hallyu; foreign immigration and the movement of migrant workers into South Korea; regional academic dialogues, as represented by the Inter-Asia Cultural Studies movement; and social activist movements for reunification and peace.

Reenvisioning the Nation: Imagining Possibilities and Dreaming of Futures

In these final pages, I point to the legacy of inter-Korean sports that involve athletic teams from both North Korea and South Korea as a way to discuss the political implications of sporting events. I understand these instances as examples of recent attempts by the South Korean state to manufacture cultural exchanges between the North and South. These events are the products of the "sunshine policies" of the Kim Dae Jung presidency that attempted to improve relations between the two countries with the purported goal of eventual reunification. These policies were instituted around the same time as IMF-mandated liberalization measures and the pursuit of globalization as a state goal. These inter-Korean athletic contests raise important questions about Koreanness in an era of globalization. What is the relationship between segyehwa and efforts toward reunification? How do these segyehwa aims variously attempt to involve North Korea while also erasing its existence? What role do mass media and sport have in shaping possibilities of reunification?

I understand these sporting events as staged, yet I ask how the performances of ethnic unity and political difference in these structured contexts shape notions of Koreanness. I believe these contexts are open spaces for imagining and enacting various futures for the nation. During my fieldwork, there were several inter-Korean sporting events that highlighted the central role of sport within North–South cultural exchanges. During the time I was in Seoul, North Korean athletes and supporters came to the South to compete in three major sporting events.[10] The first event was the North–South reunification football (soccer) match in September of 2002. A few weeks later, North Korea sent its largest delegation to the South: 450 athletes and supporters to the 14th Asian Games in Pusan.[11] The third event was the Daegu Universiad Games, which took place nearly a year later from late August to early September of 2003.[12]

On September 22, 2002, I attended a North–South reunification football match in the Seongnam World Cup stadium. The event was interpreted as a palliative gesture, given the inability to create a unified team during the World Cup and the refusal by both sides to hold some of the World Cup events in the North. I obtained tickets for free through some German friends who thought it would be an interesting experience. Although the Germans invited me to sit with them, I declined and decided to watch the game by myself. The volunteers overseeing the crowd were wearing bright orange pullover vests with "believe" printed in white and underlined with a large Nike swoosh. I considered their vests for a while as a potential harbinger of the (post?) neoliberal future, and found the implications of reunification sponsored by corporations such as Nike intriguing indeed.

Many in attendance were wearing their red "Be the Reds" T-shirts. Some began to chant the South Korean soundtrack of the World Cup: "*Taehan Min'guk!*," "*Arirang,*" and "*Oh! P'ilsŭng Korea!*" I found a seat close to a group of young college students who were all wearing T-shirts in the reunification colors—white and sky blue—and carrying white reunification flags painted with a blue icon of a united Korean peninsula. A few in the group began the South Korean national chants, but they were corrected by others in their group who shouted, "*T'ongil! Chikkŭm!*" (Unification Now!) and "*T'ongil! T'ongil!*" (Unification! Unification!). The South Korean team entered the field but without any of the high-profile stars of the World Cup. The North Korean team also entered the field, followed by stares of particular interest from the crowd. Many noted that they were wearing FILA uniforms down to their socks and shoes. "Even the *ppalgaengi* (Reds) like name brands," joked the man next to me.[13]

The game opened with a heartfelt group chorus of "*Arirang,*" the unofficial anthem of reunification. The match proceeded with a high level of ambivalence on the part of the crowd. I gathered that this was because most did not know how to appropriately express enthusiasm for either team, as preference for the North Korean team could be tantamount to treason but cheering too hard for the South Korean team would seem contrary to the goal of reunification. Many around me recognized the highly propagandistic nature of the event, yet they still attended the match. The reasons for participation in this leisure activity, however, varied widely. There were some who came because they earnestly desired *t'ongil* (unification) or wholeheartedly supported the idea, as represented by the group of college students in blue and white T-shirts. Others came because they had family in North Korea and saw it as an opportunity to witness living bodies from the North, possibly as proxies for their own family members. Some, such as the Germans, came because of the novelty factor. A good number of people came to support the South Korean team, show their appreciation for the team's World Cup success, and, possibly, see some of its superstars. Still others attended for the opportunity to watch a sporting match in the state-of-the-art World Cup stadium—a venue they could never dream of entering during a "true" international tournament. The game itself did not offer much in the way of excitement, and it ended without great fanfare, with the South winning. At the close of the game, players from both sides emerged and supported a giant reunification flag. Once again, a swaying crowd broke out into an emotional rendition of "*Arirang.*"

These events offered important representations of human interactions between the North and the South.[14] They were generally regarded as positive forms of interaction by most people I interviewed during my time in Seoul.[15] This sporting exchange, along with many of the other exchanges between the North and South in recent years, were quite remarkable, given the nearly fifty years of absolute separation and intense state demonization on both sides (Shin 2006). Although there have been a few sporting matches between the South and the North throughout the years, they have been largely forgotten (H. Lee et al. 2007). The event demonstrated that there was a general acknowledgment and acceptance of North Koreans as humans, worthy competitors, and fellow ethnics. Of course, the rhetoric of reunification, which is based on a notion of "shared blood," has been a central component of the ideological justification of political regimes on both sides (Grinker 1998; Shin 2006). In other words, each state has proclaimed their mission to rectify the ideological indoctrination of their fellow Koreans on the other side.

I believe that this event operated as a context for the expression of a desire for interaction that did not require the same sort of nationalist compulsion of previous state-sponsored, inter-Korean exchanges. It can be assumed that the relatively young, self-selected crowd was largely sympathetic to the sunshine policies of the Kim Dae Jung regime, but they came to the event for a variety of reasons. No instructions were given to those in attendance as to how they should behave, and they were able to interpret the event in a number of ways. It was a context in which differences in dress and behavior were tolerated. Ultranationalist right-wing extremists were not apparent in this context, although they did emerge to protest the North Korean contingent during the 2002 Asian Games and the 2003 Universiad Games. The fans at the reunification match expressed a variety of reactions to the North Korean team (*within* certain limits), from a sense of ambivalence to one of ethnic affinity.

In many ways, the event highlighted the contradictions inherent in South Korean attitudes toward unification. According to Gi-wook Shin, "It is often assumed, rather than empirically verified, that Koreans' belief in ethnic unity will inevitably bring national unification in the near future" (2006, 185). The actual hard work of reunification—structural and institutional changes, integration of political systems, ideological compromises, and the incorporation of populations—are rarely included in the rhetoric. Shin argues that, contrary to much of the rhetoric by U.S. academics, many Koreans endorse a democratic process of unification. In other words, they support a unified Korea with democratic control from both sides (Shin 2006). Of course, there are concerns by progressives that unification will bring "hegemonic unification" —that is, the domination of one side by the other through economic and political power. This is especially a concern for those who fear capitalist hegemony driven by South Korean capitalist institutions, such as Hyundai, which has already set up shop in North Korea.

In an article for the English-language *Korea Herald* written on January 1, 2003, Kang Seok-jang writes about the possibility of future inter-Korean sporting events. He reports that the head of the Policy Research & Development Division of the Korea Sport Science Institute, Park Young-ok, believed that sports exchanges would be the "most effective means to help restore harmony on the divided Korean Peninsula." The neoliberal ideology driving this political exchange is highlighted when Kang adds, "Park also stressed the importance of greater private-sector sports exchanges, saying government-initiated exchanges have limits."

With Nike as a sponsor of the reunification football match, it became clear that commercial factors on the South Korean side had an interest in promoting a newly popular progressive cause. In what Paulla Ebron calls the "business of identity," (see Ebron 2002), the melodrama of national separation and the dream of unification has been appropriated by Nike's marketing interests in their "BELIEVE" campaign. Of course, this interest raises the question of hegemonic unification led by corporate interests. Although this campaign appeals to the emotions of young, relatively progressive South Korean consumers, it could quite possibly reflect Nike's interest in setting up sneaker sweatshops in North Korea. Furthermore, the North Koreans, rather than denouncing the "capitalist infidels," were wearing stylish FILA outfits (which did not go unnoticed by the fans and commentators). The event demonstrated that unification in the twenty-first century will involve quite a number of interests beyond those articulated by Cold War political ideologues and the tragedy of divided families.

A few weeks after the reunification match, the 14th Asian Games were held in Pusan.[16] The Pusan Asian Games were a ratings disappointment and characterized by a general lack of public interest in the sporting competitions. In contrast to the World Cup, which was staged for a global audience, the Asian Games were directed toward a domestic audience. The mass media coverage focused primarily on domestic interests spurred by the unprecedented number of North Korean visitors and the associated issues of reunification. The Asian Games were distinguished by generally positive, if not voyeuristic, mass media coverage of the North Korean contingent, particularly the female cheerleaders. *Han'gyŏre 21*, the weekly magazine of the left-leaning daily newspaper *Han'gyŏre*, dedicated a cover story to this event. The cover image featured a North Korean cheerleader whose facial expression looked genuine and honest. Her image was approachable and friendly, not saccharine like many of the other images of smiling North Korean women. The cover story exclaimed, "*2002 Gaul Chosŏn nyŏja!*" (The Chosŏn Women of Fall 2002!).[17] It went on to discuss the historic nature of this cultural exchange and the optimistic possibilities the event offered for future exchanges and eventual reunification. The magazine also featured frightening images of violent demonstrations by ultranationalists opposed to the entry of the unprecedented number of North Korean subjects.

Nearly a year later, North Korean athletes and their entourage once again came to the South to participate in the Daegu Universiad Games. This time, however, they were received in a very different way. The media coverage was marked by an entirely different tone. Their depictions as friendly, albeit strange, neighbors shifted dramatically in the wake of deteriorating diplomatic relations. The negative media coverage was catalyzed by what was seen as the unpredictable and frantic behavior of the female cheerleaders. One widely circulated story that seemed to spur this negative opinion involved an instance in which the cheerleaders were riding in their team bus and saw a banner commemorating the first meeting between Kim Dae Jung and Kim Jong Il left hanging in the rain. Crying and screaming, they promptly ran off their bus and pulled down the image of their "dear leader" to protect it from being further defiled by the rain.

The dramatic contrast in public opinion was highlighted by a 2003 cover of *Han'gyŏre 21*.[18] This time, nearly a year after featuring a flattering image of the North Korean woman, the magazine cover featured an image of a crying North Korean cheerleader who seemed masked under a heavy cover of makeup. The cover asked, "*Uri nŭn hana in'ga?*" (Are we really one?). The articles in this issue were dedicated to the deep gulf between the South and North, structured through the North's fascist ideological regime. The Daegu event became a context in which the difficulties of reunification were expressed: Could the North truly be considered part of the same nation? Are they far too different from us after years of ideological indoctrination? Should we really continue to pursue national reunification as a goal in this era of segyehwa?

These North–South sporting contexts became sites around which the possibilities for reunification were mediated, contested, and debated. Sporting contests offered spaces for the expression of the hopes and future possibilities for the nation. They also become contexts for alternative visions of national community. Of course, these possibilities were enacted within the contexts of global asymmetries and capitalist contradictions. They were influenced and framed within geopolitical contexts and multinational political relations. Nevertheless, the responses by members of the Korean public to representations of the North were not altogether predicted. There is a persistent belief that Koreans share an ethnic heritage, yet Gi-wook Shin reminds us that "ethnic consciousness alone cannot facilitate the process of unification" (2006, 203). If reunification is considered a goal that the South Korean state continues to pursue, political change must foreground democratic processes between people in both states, keeping at bay corporate and political interests.

It is debatable whether democratic contexts and practices can be reflected and produced through commercial or government-sponsored sporting events. Nevertheless, I do believe there are moments when the joy induced through sport offers a glimmer of hope and a touch of pleasure within the melodramas of North–South division. It may also offer a forecast of how humans might learn to live together, given the fact that physical togetherness, however fleeting, for North Koreans and South Koreans remains an elusive goal.

Throughout this book, I bring attention to the cultural, social, and political significance of sport by investigating human engagements with productions of transnational media sport. I discuss media representations of Korean athletes as well as subjective experiences of sporting events to detail the role of media sport in shaping meanings of nation, gender, and sexuality in Korean/American communities. The meanings conveyed through media sport travel across national borders to produce ideas of global Koreanness. This book also demonstrates how meanings of transnationalism are conveyed through mass media and popular culture and how media sport as a genre works as a context for the forging of transnational communities through subjective practices of consumption. Maintaining that there exist meaningful social differences within Korean communities, I have also established that the commercial contexts of media sport produce Korean national publics. These publics become a site for the emergence and expression of political ideologies. They also exist as complex social arenas ripe with political potential and possibility.

Notes

Introduction

1. Fédération Internationale de Football Association, the organization that oversees the men's and women's FIFA World Cup.

2. The "mad cow" protests are also referred to as the Candlelight Vigils of 2008. The protests began in April and involved over one hundred days of demonstrations against terms of U.S.–South Korean trade, especially around the import of beef and the rapid onslaught of conservative and corporate-friendly policy transformations enacted by President Lee Myung Bak. See Conclusion.

3. In South Korea, liberalization reforms were installed at an accelerated rate in the aftermath of the Asian financial crisis of 1997 and the subsequent International Monetary Fund bailout in 1998. In chapter 4, I point out that the immense popularity of Se Ri Pak was directly related to the timing of her rookie year success, which coincided with the Asian financial crisis.

4. Also spelled *Hanryu*, the Korean (Han) Wave (ryu). *Hallyu*, as used here, is transliterated using the McCune-Reischauer system. See Cho Han et al. 2003.

5. Rather than regarding globalization as simply economic liberalization, Kim Young Sam's government "decided to keep, not translate, the Korean word *segyehwa*, in its romanized form, as the official name for its globalization drive" (S. Kim 2000a, 2). Kim's decision to emphasize the Korean word demonstrated the nationalist and state-driven nature of South Korea's globalization policies.

6. Korean Japanese are usually divided into two different groups: those connected to the Democratic People's Republic of Korea (North Korea) and those connected to the Republic of Korea (South Korea). This explains the varying relationships between the South Korean government and Korean populations in Japan (Ryang 2000).

7. For more extensive discussions about the place of mass media in generating deterritorialized national communities, see Shohat and Stam (1994) and Ang (1997).

8. Through intensive engagement with subjects, ethnography also has the ability to produce a complex and detailed depiction of how subjects engage with mass media and sporting events. Purnima Mankekar understands "[e]thnography as an *evocative* genre of cultural analysis that aims to represent specific structures of feeling" (1999b, 49). Ethnographies narrate the role of mass media in the context of the worlds that people inhabit and create through their personal experiences and social relations (Ginsburg, Abu-Lughod, and Larkin 2002). They allow for the consideration of the subjective expressions of longing, desire, and belonging in relation to the narratives of mass-mediated texts. Although the audience of mass media research is by no means clear-cut, ethnography's importance is in its ability to constitute a community of viewers within politically-informed categories (Ang 1997). Mankekar notes, "Audiences are actively constructed through careful programming decisions and marketing strategies, as well as transnational flows of information, capital, and commodities, and in some cases, the agendas of the nation-state" (1999b, 49). Mankekar demonstrates how an ethnographic investigation of a specific audience can reveal the particular and varied ways that political subjectivities are constituted through reception to mass-mediated texts.

9. For all the critique of the "culture industry" hypothesis, it brings attention to the challenges of sustaining a rigorous critique of the dominant ideological structures of mass media that "perpetuate modern conditions of domination" (Adorno 1991, 80). Adorno demonstrates the critical importance of maintaining a strong suspicion of mass media as working to reproduce conservative and unoriginal narratives that acquiesce to and strengthen capitalist hierarchies.

10. Stuart Hall, in his "Encoding/Decoding" model of media analysis, categorizes the process of ideological decoding within dominant, negotiated, and oppositional readings. Although Hall acknowledges the possibility of alternative or negotiated readings, he emphasizes the concept of the "preferred" reading as that which the text intends (1980, 134). Hall points out that, though there is "no necessary correspondence, between text and interpretation," there remain "preferred" meanings that work to reproduce hegemonic ideologies (137).

11. Antonio Gramsci's notion of hegemony has been an invaluable tool in understanding how social processes are structured through the power-laden operations of meanings and values in everyday discourses (Gramsci 1992; Williams 1977). Rather than being imposed through state coercion, hegemony is a process that operates through popular consent. Hegemonic ideologies are ideas that everyone "knows" to be true. As "common sense" understandings, hegemonic ideologies constitute relations of domination as "natural" relations.

12. The essays in the collection *Dangerous Women*, edited by Elaine Kim and Choi Chungmoo (1998) offer scathing and subjectively informed critiques of the practices of patriarchal nationalism and androcentrism in South Korea.

13. Koreans engage with media sport within the embedded and interconnected

histories of the two sites. The disciplinary areas of Korean Studies and Asian American Studies inform my investigation of connectivities between the United States and South Korea. I attempt to demonstrate the critical importance of "Area Studies," "Ethnic Studies," and "Diasporic Studies" to framing my project and motivating my work (Chakrabarty 1998). Drawing from these various fields, I highlight the tactical importance of a transnational project and emphasize the salience of intellectual investigations that take seriously fields of knowledge production produced within political geographies (see Price 2003; Rafael 1994). These areal fields help me consider the place-specific features of Koreanness that characterize the reception and production of media sport and how these practices are shaped by interconnected histories and transformations in and between both sites. For example, the coemergence of color television and professional sports in South Korea is better understood within the context of U.S. foreign policy and Cold War politics. Furthermore, the racialization of the twenty-first-century Korean athlete in the United States demonstrates how discourses of race are being transformed in an era of transnationalism.

14. According to Mercer Human Resource Consulting's 2005 cost-of-living survey, Seoul was the fifth most expensive city in the world after Tokyo, Osaka, London, and Moscow. Source: CNNMoney, "World's Most Expensive Cities," http://money.cnn.com/2005/06/21/pf/costliest_cities/index.htm (visited June 1, 2006).

Chapter 1: To Be a Global Player

1. Foucauldian notions of genealogy inform my understanding of the power/knowledge nexus in the articulation and transformation of national discourses and the uneven trajectories in the production of knowledge (see Foucault 1980; 1984).

2. Barbara Keys (2006) points out that a major characteristic of modern sport is its connection with the rise of the modern nation-state and its ability to convey standardized rules and practices for participants internationally. Richard Wilk (1995) refers to "structures of common difference" as a way to explain the ways in which national difference continues to be a salient way of marking distinctions in a global marketplace. Even though there may be a shared structure or format that explains the structural similarities between events such as beauty pageants and *telenovelas* around the world, the narrative content differs from nation to nation.

3. Throughout the modern history of sport in both South Korea and the United States, men have been privileged as producers and consumers of sport. This chapter follows a largely male-centered narrative that can be attributed to the often unexamined and naturalized position of men as central players in media sport. Even though my reading does not assume that women apprehend sports through the gaze of men, it is clear that the assumed viewers of professional media sport in both the United States and South Korea have been and continue to largely be male. Subsequent chapters discuss the production of gendered differences through media sport and how they intersect with the narratives of nation outlined in this first part of this book.

The discussions of gender and sexuality will interrogate how these constructions are expressed and produced through differences in media representations and practices of reception to sporting images.

4. *Chuch'e* is understood to be the official state policy of the Democratic People's Republic of Korea (North Korea), yet Shin, Freda, and Yi (1999) point out that *chuch'e* ideologies played an important role in the founding of the Republic of Korea (South Korea) (see also Shin 2006).

5. By "modern sport," I refer to the sporting practices first introduced to the Korean people as "Western sport" by British and U.S. male administrators and missionaries in the colonial era. In my discussion, modern sport includes institutionalized competitive sport, such as Olympic sport, international sport, and media sport. Following the normative categorizations of current sport scholarship in South Korea, I make a distinction between Korean indigenous, or "traditional," sport and modern sport (H. Lee 2003). Global sports with roots in Asia, such as judo and taekwondo, offer an alternative narrative to this binary division of West and East, but the background offered in this chapter does not discuss these so-called Eastern sports.

6. These assumptions about Korean development are drawn largely from the discipline of Korean Studies. Korean Studies is a rapidly changing, heterogeneous, and interdisciplinary field characterized by differences in methodological, epistemological, and political concerns. The work produced in the field reflects its transnational character, given the unique demands of academic production, the funding structures in place for Korean Studies (see Shin 2006), the breakneck pace of modernization in South Korean society (Amsden 1989; Moon 2005), and the contemporary moment of global flows of information, people, and commodities (see Cho Han et al. 2003). After World War II, the United States attempted to secure relations in Northeast Asia in order to restructure the region's economy with its own developmental agenda (Cumings 1997). With the end of Japanese rule, foreign powers, particularly the Soviet Union and the United States, vied for the opportunity to determine the direction of Korean state formation. As Bruce Cumings famously argued, the U.S. trusteeship in Korea after World War II was a "liberation denied," as the U.S. military and economic strategies reinstituted colonial structures of domination (Cumings 1981). Following the Korean War and subsequent national division, South Korean state leadership was characterized by anticommunist, nationalist rhetoric that promoted U.S.-backed policies of modernization and capitalist development. As a result of its strategic position in the Cold War, South Korea was heavily militarized with aid from the U.S. Army. Furthermore, a great deal of South Korea's modern industrial development can be traced to its substantial "voluntary" participation in the Vietnam War (H. S. Kim 2001; K. Park 2003). The nation was governed by successive authoritarian governments backed by U.S. military, political, and economic support until the country's first democratic elections, which were brought about by the 1987 democracy movement (Moon 2005).

7. Beginning in the latter half of the nineteenth century, competing imperial inter-ests attempted to institute economic relations with Korea, including France, Russia, China, Japan, the United States, Britain, and Germany. Japan emerged as the domi-nant imperial force by compelling the Korean state to sign the Kanghwa Treaty in 1876, thereby instituting asymmetrical relations between the two states. The signing of this treaty is commonly marked as the date for the so-called "opening" of Korea to modern international relations (Cumings 1997). (Interestingly, Cumings demon-strates a penchant for U.S. sporting metaphors throughout his narrative.)

8. See also Mangan 2003. Mangan details how the British colonial project of sport education inculcated so-called Christian values of sportsmanship, fair play, and physi-cal fitness in the colonies.

9. Modern team sports for men, such as baseball, basketball, volleyball, and foot-ball (soccer), emerged at this time. Track and field tournaments were especially popu-lar in Seoul and other growing cities, and they featured student athletes (H. Lee 2003).

10. Between 1906 and 1911, eleven official Korean sports associations appeared. The first organizations were as follows: The *Taehan ch'eyuk kurak pu* (Korean Sports Club) was established on March 11, 1906; the *Hwangsŏng kidok ch'ŏngnyŏn hoe* (Hwangsŏng Christian Youth Association) was established in April; and then the *Taehan kungmin ch'eyuk hoe* (Korean Citizen's Sports Association) began in October (U. Kwŏn 1995; T. Yun 1992).

11. Michael Robinson (1988) details expressions of Korean cultural nationalism during the colonial era through commercial mass media and other forms of public culture.

12. *Dong-A Ilbo* was shut down in 1936 after the Japanese Flag Erasure Incident, and it was reinstated after Liberation.

13. The Japanese colonial government established the *Kyŏngsŏng pangsongguk* or the Kyŏngsŏng Broadcast Corporation (KBC) in 1927. A year later, the first radio broadcast of a sporting event took place. By 1930, two years after the first baseball game was broadcast, at least seventy sporting events were broadcast on radio (T. Yun 1992).

14. A depiction of the distinct public spheres for Koreans and Japanese in colonial Korea comes through in the two novels by Yuasa Katsuei, *Kannani* and *The Document of Flames,* translated by Mark Driscoll (Yuasa 2005).

15. See Shin and Robinson (1999). This edited volume includes essays that discuss various interpretations and contexts of the *naissen ittai* policy, as well as the *kominka* (Movement to Create Colonial Subjects) policy instituted in 1931 and which lasted until the end of colonial rule in 1945.

16. In 2002, a film entitled *YMCA Yagudang* [YMCA Baseball Club], directed by Kim Hyŏnsŏk, was released. The cast, which includes stars Kim Hye-su and Song Kang-ho, performs a lighthearted comedy about "cultural contact" between Koreans and

Americans in the early 1900s against the menacing cloud of Japanese colonialism (Han and Kim 2001; see also P. Kim 2002, 182). In South Korea, the film was received as a mainstream comedy. The film was featured at the San Francisco International Asian American Film Festival in March 2003. The festival catalogue emphasizes the film's portrayal of the colonial impact of foreign nations on Korean society.

17. The Seoul YMCA was founded by a leader of the independence movement, Yun Ch'i-ho, who studied in Japan, Shanghai, and the United States. Cumings points out, "He returned to Korea in 1895 and edited the *Tongnip* while participating in politics of the Independence Club" (1997, 125).

18. See Lee and Patterson (1999) for a discussion of Korean–American relations between 1866 and 1997. Andre Schmid (2002), in *Korea between Empires,* discusses transnational connections during the period between 1895 and 1919.

19. The Berlin Olympics of 1936, or "Hitler's Olympics," is an iconic moment in the global history of sports, since it demonstrated the fascist utilitarianism of specta-tor sports. It has been memorialized in liberal accounts of U.S. sport history since African American Jesse Owens won four gold medals in this Olympics (see Kruger and Murray 2003; Keys 2006).

20. Despite persistent entreaties from the South Korean government to the Inter-national Olympic Committee, the two Korean medal winners are still officially recog-nized as Japanese team members under the Japanese names of Son Kitei and Nan Shoryu. Son Ki-jŏng lit the torch to open the 1988 Seoul Olympics. He passed away in November of 2002 at the age of 90. I was in Seoul when he died and watched numerous televised memorials of the national hero.

21. Bruce Cumings, in *The Origins of the Korean War* (1981), writes about this period after Liberation and prior to the Korean War as a time of fractious internal politics characterized by multiple ideological, regional, and kin-based divisions within the country as well as of immense foreign pressure by the Soviet Union, China, and the United States. Cumings offers a nuanced account of the post-Liberation period that takes domestic politics seriously; most U.S.-based accounts prior to the book's pub-lication in 1981 had reduced this complexity by suggesting that the regime of the North was under the control of the Soviet Union and the regime of the South had the beneficent support of the United States.

22. Cho Hang-je (2003) discusses the emergence of television media with the privately owned commercial station HLKZ-TV in 1956. A year later, in 1957, the first broadcast of a sporting event—a football (soccer) game—occurred. The station be-came DBS in 1957 and ceased operations in 1961. Park Chung Hee's regime estab-lished KBS in 1961, thereby ensuring the stability of television broadcasts. Cho Hang-je also points out that the establishment of both HLKZ-TV and KBS was done in part-nership with RCA. Other U.S., British, and Japanese companies partnered with Ko-rean television and radio stations, including TBC, which was established in 1965, and MBC, which was established in 1969.

23. With the assistance of the U.S. military command, the South sent its first contingent of athletes to the 1948 London Olympics (31 July 1947, MacArthur Papers, Far East Command General Headquarters).

24. After the Korean War, Bruce Cumings notes that Korea was "truncated into half a country, with almost no natural resources, a thoroughly uprooted and aggrieved population, no domestic capital to speak of, a minuscule domestic market, and a work force long claimed to be lazy louts (common Japanese refrain)" (1997, 300). Under the rule of military dictator Park Chung Hee (1961–1979), South Korea embarked on a path to industrialization that was driven by powerful ideologies of state developmental nationalism. From a country devastated by war, its breakneck pace of development transformed it into an industrial force by the turn of the century. This "Miracle on the Han" was due largely to the assistance of U.S. foreign aid and the participation of South Korea in the Vietnam War (Cumings 1997; K. Park 2003).

25. The Mass Games are an important example of the intensive devotion to leader / nation that is expressed through physical discipline, training, and performance in North Korea. The Mass Games take place over several days around the birthday of Kim Il Sung. They feature spectacular performances that involve thousands of youth and spectators of all ages who turn cards to create stadium-sized dioramas. These dioramas are done in a socialist realist style that celebrates the leadership of North Korea and the ideology of the state. The film *A State of Mind* offers a fascinating perspective into the national importance of the Mass Games (Gordon 2005).

26. An official Olympic training center was established by the South Korean government in June 1966 at T'aenŭng (Chong-hŭi Kim 1999). Hwang Pyŏng-ju (2002) discusses the mobilization of South Korean citizens by the Park Chung Hee regime through football tournaments. In the 1966 FIFA World Cup in London, North Korea stunned the global football community by advancing to the Round of Eight. The documentary film *The Game of Their Lives* features the unlikely success of the 1966 North Korean World Cup football team (Gordon and Bonner 2002). As a response, Park attempted to raise the level of football in South Korea, and, in 1971, he instituted the Box Cup, which was the country's first international football tournament (Hwang 2002).

27. From the outset, state-controlled television broadcasts were commercial in nature and depended heavily on commercial advertisements (S. Yoon 1996).

28. Notwithstanding the televisions owned and sold by the American military, national television production increased tremendously over the late 1960s and into the 1970s with the number growing from 10,500 in 1966 to 120,868 in 1970. By 1973, more than one million televisions were produced. Two years later, more than two million were produced (Hang-je Cho 2003).

29. Professional wrestling and boxing were especially popular in early television broadcasts. Cho Hang-je (2003) notes that professional wrestling was extremely popular in Japan as a form of televised entertainment, and its popularity in South Korea is

no coincidence, since NHK was a model for the first South Korean state-sponsored station, KBS.

30. By 1969, there were three major television stations: KBS, MBC, and TBC. In 1980, KBS absorbed TBC, creating a duopoly in the broadcast market between KBS and MBC. Not until 1995 did the market begin to diversify with the nationwide broadcasts of the entirely commercial and privately-owned station SBS.

31. Im Pŏn-jang (1994) notes that the average number of newspaper articles on sport increased from less than one a day in 1946 to two a day in 1960 to almost seven a day in 1965 and to 12.5 a day by the mid 1970s.

32. The first sport daily, called *Ilgan Sŭp'och'ŭ* (Daily Sport), was published in 1963, but its name was changed to *Hyŏndae kyŏngje sinmun* (Modern Economic News) a little over a year later. In 1969, the next sports daily, also named *Ilgan Sŭp'och'ŭ*, began circulation (T. Yun 1992). The next daily sports newspaper was *Sports Seoul* in 1985, then *Sports Chosŏn* in 1990 (Ch'oe and Ch'oe 1998). During the Era of Liberalization, sport dailies exploded in number and circulation, especially in the early 1990s with the spectacularization and sexualization of sport news content.

33. The Kwangju Uprising in May of 1980 and the brute suppression of public dissent by the Chun regime are often referenced as reasons for the turn to the 3-S cultural policies of sports, sex, and screen. The collected essays in *Contentious Kwangju* (Shin and Hwang 2003) offer a number of perspectives on Kwangju. Soon after Chun declared himself president, he was invited to the White House in January of 1981 to meet with Ronald Reagan, thereby cementing the perception that his actions were sanctioned by the United States as this meeting became proof that his military regime was officially recognized by the U.S. government. It was not until the mid-1980s that large-scale civil dissent through aggressive labor organizing was revived (see Koo 1993). In 1996, both Chun Doo Hwan and another former president, Roh Tae Woo, were tried and found guilty as perpetrators of the Kwangju Massacre.

34. The Summer Olympics were awarded to South Korea by the International Olympic Committee in September of 1981 in Baden-Baden, Germany. Kim Chŏng-hŭi (1999) points out that preparation for an Olympic bid began with the Park Chung Hee administration.

35. The Ministry of Sport was restructured and renamed as the Ministry of Sport and Youth during the Roh Tae Woo regime (1988–1992) and then the Ministry of Culture and Sport during the Kim Young Sam era (1993–1997). It was then absorbed into the Ministry of Culture and Tourism during the Kim Dae Jung presidency (1998–2002), and President Roh Moo Hyun (2003–2007) maintained the sport system of the previous government (P. Kang 2001). Lee Myung Bak's administration changed the Ministry of Culture and Tourism to the Ministry of Culture, Sport, and Tourism in February 2008 as part of a broader restructuring of the economy to focus on capitalizing on Hallyu and cultural globalization. See http://www.mct.go.kr. (accessed July 13, 2011).

36. I would like to thank John Duncan for pointing out the importance of the 86–88 rhetoric during a directed reading at UCLA in the winter quarter of 2000.

37. Brohm, in *Sport: A Prison of Measured Time* (1978), offers a Frankfurt School interpretation of the role of sport in modern societies. It focuses on the disciplinary mechanisms of sport, its commercial dimensions, and its ability to produce industrial working subjects.

38. Many of the films discussed by Kim were produced for export and competition in foreign film festivals. Kim even points out that for much of the 1980s, the domestic film market was, in fact, quite bleak and failed to generate a considerable following. Kim does, however, highlight the centrality of the state in producing and promoting these commercial productions.

39. In South Korea, professional sports have been organized in a top-down fashion. In order to ensure their success, teams were associated with corporations, and each represented a particular region. Thus, baseball became a means through which fierce and divisive regionalisms were expressed. This regional rivalry became a major way to promote viewership (S. Lee 2004). Professional baseball, professional football, and *ssirŭm* were all initiated by the state.

40. Ch'oe Chong-sŏn (1983) discusses the massive explosion of sport media viewership that began in 1981. He points out that sports programming primarily aired on the weekends when rates of television viewership were highest.

41. See Amsden (1989), J. Woo (1991), and Lie (1998). The planning for the Olympics was directed by the military government in a top-down fashion, and this approach has been compared to the Chinese state's approach to the 2008 Beijing Olympics (Wasserstrom 2002).

42. Aso notes that the 1964 Olympics in Tokyo turned Japan's capital into a world-class city. She notes, "the Japanese government made Herculean efforts toward improving the mass transportation and sewage systems, as well as athletic facilities" (2002, 15).

43. This tradition was instituted with the founding of the modern Olympics during the 1896 Athens Olympics with the promotion of athletic art and Olympic-associated arts (Keys 2006). With encouragement from Japanese organizers, Olympic arts festivals began in 1964 and showcased the sponsoring country's artistic traditions (Aso 2002).

44. Aso states that the 1964 Tokyo Games "strengthen[ed] mechanisms of domestic mobilization and reaffirm[ed] the position of Japan in the international order born of the Cold War" (2002, 8).

45. As a response to the Soviet invasion of Afghanistan in 1979, the United States and sixty-two allied nations, including West Germany, China, the Philippines, and Canada, boycotted the 1980 Moscow Olympics. In response, the Soviet Union and fourteen other countries, including East Germany, Czechoslovakia, and Cuba, boycotted the 1984 Los Angeles Olympics.

46. Similarly, the 1968 Mexico City Olympics were a stage for protests around social justice issues for residents of Mexico City, and they were also used by African American activists to demand racial equality (Bass 2002).

47. Aso also discusses the national political function of the 1964 Olympics, stating, "the popular democratic energy expressed in the 1960 Anpo protests was rechanneled toward preparations for the Olympics, a focal moment in the high-growth transformation of urban landscape and lifestyle" (2002, 13). Of course, the Mexico City Olympics were also a moment in which demands for racial and economic justice and democracy were powerfully expressed (Bass 2002).

48. Yoon Sug-min (1996) notes that these changes took place as a result of general democratization after the abolition of the Basic Press Law in 1987. The Basic Press Law outlawed any speech considered subversive to the state, especially sympathy for the North Korean regime. The United States began to pressure South Korea to liberalize press markets in 1989. However, the major catalyst for liberalization was a WTO trade order in January of 1995.

49. The Internet was introduced in South Korea in 1994. Major state investments in Internet technologies have made South Korea the most "wired" nation in the world.

50. Chapter 2 investigates how Korean/Americans engage with this symbol of Koreanness and the complex ways that these symbols come to represent both South Korean and U.S nationalisms in an era of globalization.

51. The media focus on particular star players during the 1998 France World Cup offers one powerful explanation of why football became one of the most popular sports in the nation, surpassing baseball for the first time (Chŏn 1998).

52. Barbara Demick, "Many South Koreans See Skating Loss as Part of U.S. Plot," *Los Angeles Times*, February 26, 2002, http://www.latimes.com (accessed February 26, 2002).

53. These protests are mentioned again in chapter 5 and the Conclusion.

54. Kwŏn Uk-dong (1995) argues that the immense level of attention for South Korean players abroad demonstrates that Korean society has not gotten past the 3-S culture and that Korean consciousness continues to be colonized by the need for global recognition.

55. See Lee Kwangkyu's statement on the Overseas Korea Foundation Website, http://www.okf.or.kr (accessed November 11, 2005). See also chapter 2.

56. These controversial noisemakers were invented in South Korea in the 1980s and appeared in U.S. sporting events by the early 1990s.

57. I wrote about the power of colonial memory in shaping the reaction to Chan Ho Park's performance when he first entered Major League Baseball (Joo 2000).

58. Tokdo (Dokdo)/Takeshima is a series of islands between South Korea and Japan also referred to as the Liancourt Rocks in the Sea of Japan. Since Liberation, the

territory has been disputed between the two nations, and the issue is often raised in the context of Korea–Japan diplomatic relations.

59. Jeré Longman, "Balanced on a Skater's Blades, the Expectations of a Nation," *New York Times*, February 22, 2010, http://www.nytimes.com (accessed July 12, 2011).

60. Media outlets understand the benefits of restaging national competitions for the ratings boost that comes with nationalist sentiments. The day South Korea beat Japan in the semifinals in men's baseball during the 2008 Beijing Olympics (August 22, 2008), I listened to call-ins to a popular Korean-language radio program broadcast throughout southern California on Radio Seoul AM 1650. The conversation focused solely on the baseball win. One caller remarked on how beating Japan was better than winning a gold medal, and the two male hosts of the show agreed. During the show, one host stated that he felt that this made up for the *assiŭm* (disappointment) that he felt after the World Baseball Classic. Although the South Korean team went on to beat the Cuban team for their first-ever Olympic gold medal in baseball, the game that received the most media attention and discussion was the semifinal game against Japan.

61. This analysis privileges "first generation" immigrants whose primary language is Korean. It also foregrounds the experience of these immigrants who have had some formal education in South Korea prior to immigrating to the United States. Some Koreans in the United States migrated from Japan, Russia, Mexico, and South America (see Amerasia 2003/2004; Ryang 2000). Although many Korean Americans have ties to North Korea through pre-division migration from the North to the South or family residing in the North, the phenomenon of media sports is understood through a South Korean national lens. Also, the overwhelming number of prominent and successful Korean athletes are South Korean nationals.

62. See *Amerasia* (2003/2004; 2004). This two-volume special issue was published to commemorate the 100th anniversary of the first Korean immigration to the United States in 1903.

63. By Korean-language media, I refer to the U.S. satellites of Korean corporations, such as KBS, MBC, and SBS, but also to Korean American media outlets, which are primarily on the radio. Due to the transnational sponsorship, and the sharing of news media content between the United States and South Korea, these distinctions are difficult to make as news desks in the United States attempt to cater to a Korean American and local, Los Angeles, audience but also to one especially interested in news from the Korean peninsula featuring fellow Koreans. Furthermore, the Korean state plays a powerful role in shaping news content on commercial media outlets that receive funding through state institutions (see M. Kim 1997).

64. This translation process might be compared to the vernacularization of cricket in India (Appadurai 1996).

65. One might argue that, with the emergence of Major League Soccer (MLS), significant internationalization has taken place on U.S. soil. The National Hockey League also displays a transnational dimension, given the significance of Canadian identity and territory in the sport.

66. Mary McDonald (2006) writes about the expectation of nationalism within professional sports following September 11, 2001, and she also discusses the emergence of a new kind of masculinized figure of the nation through sport that emerged in the wake of the attacks.

Chapter 2: A Leveraged Playing Field

1. It is also important to note that U.S.-based commercial interests in sport are often focused on more localized markets and community interests, such as the demonstrated interest of the Los Angeles Dodgers and the Los Angeles Galaxy (Major League Soccer team) in appealing to various "ethnic" populations in Southern California.

2. Although the state played a major role in developing media sport in South Korea, it would be a mistake to think of the sporting industry in the United States as entirely market driven. George Lipsitz points out, "The seeming contemporary eclipse of the state by the power of private capital and transnational corporations hides the crucial role of the state in promoting, protecting and preserving the technologies, social relations, and economic interests of corporate capital and finance" (2001, 240–41). The emergence of television and media sport in the United States should also be understood within the context of state subsidies and regulations. The state certainly subsidized the sporting education for colonial subjects in the Philippines and the movement of U.S. military subjects between the United States and South Korea. In a U.S. domestic sense, the production of U.S. state interests is clearly demonstrated by the subsidization of private sporting facilities by city and state governments (Lipsitz 2002). Furthermore, it is important to recognize the relationship between public schools and sport, as the connection between public schools and private sporting industries begins at a very early educational stage and continues through college (see Shulman and Bowen 2002).

3. This is in contrast to the critical multiculturalism espoused by David Palumbo-Liu in his essay "Multiculturalism Now: Civilization, National Identity, and Difference before and after September 11th" (2002).

4. Elizabeth Povinelli (2002) offers an important critique of multicultural discourse and legislation in an Australian context.

5. Before Jackie Robinson, two notable athletes of color who became nationalist icons were Jim Thorpe and Joe Louis. Jim Thorpe, a Native American, was a gold medal winner in the 1912 Stockholm Olympics. He also played professional football and baseball. Joe Louis, or the "Brown Bomber," was a folk hero to African Americans as the heavyweight champion for over a decade between 1937 and 1949. He was also

widely recognized as a national hero who competed in politicized matches against German Max Schmeling and served the military during World War II mainly as an entertainer and a poster subject in attempts to recruit African American men to the military.

6. Baldassaro and Johnson's collection on baseball (2002) offers a complex portrait of the ethnic and racial diversity of baseball throughout its history in the United States.

7. In the 1936 Berlin Olympics, Jesse Owens and his African American team members represented the United States and famously defied the eugenic racial theories espoused by Hitler's regime. Furthermore, bouts between Joe Louis and German Max Schmeling were often touted as fights between democracy and fascism. These victories of Black Americans have been spun in popular historical accounts as symbolic accounts of the moral superiority of the United States over Nazi Germany. In the United States, however, Jim Crow laws, lynchings, and abject poverty continued to mark the lives of African Americans, including those who had succeeded in the sporting realm (see Keys 2006; Rampersad 1997).

8. Prior to Robinson, several Latino players competed in Major League Baseball, but only those who "passed" for White were allowed to play (Burgos 2007).

9. The politics and life of Jackie Robinson are often placed in contrast with those of Paul Robeson, who was himself a great college athlete turned global star of theater and popular music. Robinson was called to testify against Robeson in front of the House Un-American Activities Committee in 1951 (Rampersad 1997). This instance demonstrates how issues of race in the United States were deployed within the "international" contexts of the Cold War and McCarthyism. The film *Paul Robeson: Here I Stand* portrays the so-called conflict between Robeson and Robinson (Bourne 1999). Federal Bureau of Investigation (FBI) files on Robeson point out the stark contrast between Robeson, as an international socialist, and Robinson, who supported Richard Nixon in his 1960 U.S. presidential campaign against John F. Kennedy (FBI 1987).

10. This integration, however, signaled the demise of baseball's Negro Leagues, whose games acted as important opportunities for leisure and gathering for African Americans. Negro League games functioned as significant consumer entertainments in African American communities at a time of intense segregation and discrimination (Lanctot 2004).

11. The radical demands of social movements were expressed in the realm of sport. The threat of organized boycotts of the 1968 Mexico City Olympics by the U.S.-based Olympic Project for Human Rights, and the public protests that took place prior to and during the Games, exist as important expressions of radicalism in sport. The transformation of Olympic boxer Cassius Clay to heavyweight champion Muhammad Ali offers another well-known and romanticized moment of political resistance in sport (see Farred 2003; Gast 1996). Like Ali, martial arts film star Bruce Lee

connected struggles for liberation in the developing world with racial issues in the United States. Lee became an icon for progressive Asians and Blacks in what Vijay Prashad (2003) refers to as the "polyculturalism" of 1970s progressive social movements. The radical sentiments expressed through these well-known sport-related examples point to the impact of social movements that occurred within broader social arenas. Clearly, the mass-mediated contexts of sport generated opportunities for the expression of and contests around racial, national, gender, and class ideologies. At present, images of sporting luminaries such as Tommie Smith, John Carlos, Muhammad Ali, Roberto Clemente, Billie Jean King, and Bruce Lee have been largely disassociated from the radical politics of the 1960s and 1970s, and they are memorialized as mainstream heroes of sport's progressive past. The images of sporting heroes have been largely commodified to represent ahistorical notions of rebellion, fierce individuality, physical artistry, and triumph over odds—all popular ideas peddled in the marketing strategies of commercial sport industries (Rodriguez 2002; Farred 2003). Moreover, despite these standout examples and the extraordinary lives of these individual athletes, the institutions of mainstream media sport have always tended toward highly conservative, pro-capitalist, and jingoistic rhetoric.

12. This assertion might be challenged by the emergence of African players in the NBA and MLS. In addition, there are other athletes who are considered descendants of the African diaspora and hail from the Caribbean, Europe, or Latin America. The anxieties around policing the boundaries of African Americanness are apparent in many academic contexts and debates around the implementation of affirmative action policies, as many Black immigrant children are seen as benefiting from policies that were meant to alleviate the enduring effects of slavery for those who are the descendants of slaves in the United States.

13. Ethical questions arise when it is quite clear that only a fraction of a percent of athletes become star players. Owners and corporations profit enormously from the commercial value of top players of color, while they stoke the dream of athletic success (Cole 2001b). As government commitments to social welfare issues have rapidly diminished, star athletes of color are hailed as evidence that the underclass has access to economic opportunities in U.S. society. Today, sports are praised as offering positive alternatives to crime and drugs for youth of color and as offering a lift out of racialized and impoverished neighborhoods (Cole 2001b). The contradiction between these narratives of sports uplift and the structural barriers to improving conditions of life among the underprivileged is clearly demonstrated in the lack of equitable access to education for poor minority children (see Darling-Hammond 2000) and in the world-historical incarceration rates for men of color in U.S. society (see Bobo and Thompson 2006).

14. Filipino American athletes might also be understood within this context of the U.S. empire, as both Hawaiians and Filipinos were, on a eugenic hierarchy of races, considered above Blacks (see España-Maram 2006; Willard 2002).

15. The revival of interest in baseball's history is often attributed to Ken Burns's PBS documentary *Baseball*, which premiered in 1994. The fifth installment, entitled "Inning Five: Shadow Ball," focused on the Negro Leagues and had spurred a revival of popular and academic interest in African Americans and other minorities in baseball and other sports.

16. American baseball legend Babe Ruth went on a barnstorming tour of Japan in 1934 to great popular interest and enormous crowds of spectators (Keys 2006).

17. This national correlation is further challenged by the unique baseball traditions that developed within Japan (see W. Kelly 2004).

18. See the children's text, *Sixteen Years in Sixteen Seconds: The Sammy Lee Story*, written by Paula Yoo and illustrated by Dom Lee (2005). This book offers a heroic portrait of Sammy Lee as an American patriot.

19. Richard Lapchnik, "Asian American athletes: past, present, and future," *ESPN*, http://espn.go.com (accessed February 10, 2009).

20. "The Olympic Show: Sammy Lee," narrated by Dan Hicks, http://www.super-cool-products.com/thesammysporttowels/biographydrsammylee.html (accessed June 6, 2008).

21. Gary Okihiro, "Is Yellow Black or White: Revisited," http://www.aaari.info (lecture, Asian American/Asian Research Institute, New York, February 10, 2002) (accessed June 7, 2008).

22. They may also be used to maintain suspicions about the ultimate loyalty of Asian Americans, which can be inflamed in moments of economic or political uncertainty, as in the Wen Ho Lee case (Lee and Zia 2001).

23. In the words of famed sports writer Frank Deford, sport continues to be the "purest form of meritocracy," as it has always allowed entry to talented immigrants and the poor. In an interview with Michael Krasny on Forum, KQED Public Radio FM 88.5, July 18, 2005, 11 a.m., http://www.kqed.org/a/forum/R507181000 (accessed July 11, 2011).

24. David Margolick, "Bearing Kimchi, a Dodger Is a First," *The New York Times*, April 10, 1994, 1.

25. The case of contemporary Japanese players in the United States does not fall as easily into this immigrant narrative. Their foreign status as unassimilated aliens seems to predominate. Ichiro Suzuki is a hero in Japan; he and his Japanese American fans are seen as essentially Japanese (see Mayeda 1999).

26. Lee Jenkins, "For Dawson, a bronze and a chance to find birth parents," *New York Times*, February 16, 2006, http://www.nytimes.com (accessed February 9, 2009).

27. Associated Press, "Sports Briefing: Skiing: Dawson Reunited with Father," *New York Times*, March 1, 2007, http://www.nytimes.com (accessed February 9, 2009).

28. Chuck Finder, "Hines Ward Scores Big for Social Change," *Pittsburgh Post-Gazette*, April 9, 2006, http://www.post-gazette.com (accessed February 9, 2009).

29. Associated Press, "Hines Ward Kicks Off His New Charity," *Pittsburgh Post-Gazette,* May 30, 2006, http://www.post-gazette.com (accessed February 9, 2009).

30. Kim Mi-yŏng, "Insuni yunsuil hamjunga tŏkbune honhyŏl munje haegyŏl toe ŏtna?" *Han'gyŏre,* February 2, 2006, http://www.hani.co.kr (accessed July 13, 2011). Women Migrants Human Rights Center, "Wŏdŭ sindŭrom kwa damunhwa kajŏng ŭi chanyŏdŭl," Han'guk iju yŏsŏng in'kwŏn sentŏ, April 6, 2006. http://www.wmi grant.org (accessed July 13, 2011).

31. *Arli$$* ran from 1996 to 2002 on HBO. The comedy show featured a megalomaniacal sports super agent, Arliss Michaels (played by Robert Wuhl), his multicultural staff, including Rita (played by Sandra Oh), and the challenges they faced as a sports agency. The show featured real athletes and coaches as guest stars.

32. Episode 408: "To Thine Own Self be True." First aired July 26, 1999. Written by Josh Goldstein and directed by Michael Grossman.

Chapter 3: Playing Hard Ball

1. Bi (Rain), Jeong Ji-hoon, was known as one of South Korea's most popular entertainers from 2004 to 2008. In 2006, *Time Magazine* named him one of the "100 Most Influential People Who Shape Our World."

2. *Hallyu,* or Korean wave, refers to the explosion in popularity of South Korean film, pop, and television stars throughout Asia and beyond that began at the turn of the twenty-first century. In many recent Korean films, the sculpted male torso acts as the focus of the shot at the moment of undressing. Sex acts involve the undressing of male and female participants and feature the naked chest, back, and buttocks of the male actor prominently over the eroticized parts of the nude female. The filmic shots invite the viewer to gaze over the male's hardened and contracted muscles as a substitute for his unexposed penis. The naturalistic, yet built, torso reveals and proves a kind of masculinity that demonstrates the strength and power of the Korean man in the context of the global circulation of Korean pop images.

3. Alan Klein's (1993) study of West Coast body-building gyms offers an important ethnographic investigation into the micropolitics and practices that take place in the "hypermasculine" contexts of an elite body-building gym in Southern California.

4. The gym phenomenon I describe here differs from that detailed in Spielvogel's (2003) text about fitness centers in Japan. Whereas Spielvogel focuses primarily on female sociality in the contexts of fitness centers and the ideologies around the attractive feminine body, I focus on the utilitarian uses of the gym for purposes of male body shaping.

5. See *Pumping Iron,* directed by Robert Fiore and George Butler (1977; HBO Home Video, 2003), DVD.

6. Baseball was the first professional sport in South Korea, established in 1982. Arguably, it continues to be the country's most popular sport, although some argue that football (soccer) overtook its popularity in the twenty-first century. Due to its

visibility and the success of Korean players in the United States, baseball has had a significant impact in shaping a media genre of transnational sport.

7. The ability of the commodity image to convey ideas of nation and sexuality has been detailed by William Mazzarella (2003). In his discussion of the introduction of the Kama Sutra brand condom to the Indian market, Mazzarella tracks the image-making practices of advertisers as a way to detail how the branding of the condom imbued the object with erotic signification. With the help of highly recognizable Bollywood stars and Bollywood production qualities, the condom, which was perceived as a state technology of population control, came to symbolize a cosmopolitan sexuality for Indian subjects.

8. Sex-ratio imbalances have been widely reported, and they have resulted in practices to alleviate these population disparities, such as the widespread importation of brides. Furthermore, the national birth rate has plunged in the last decade, but especially in rural areas, resulting in subsidies for families who bear children in certain municipalities and provinces.

9. David Eng (2001) points out that Asian American cultural nationalist projects often engender masculinist attacks against Asian American women for their "treasonous" romantic affiliations with White men.

10. In a 1973 article in *American Anthropologist*, Richard Sipes investigates the power of the war metaphor in sport, but he also disassembles its assumptions.

11. The slogan "Korea Fighting," which is often articulated in the context of international athletic competitions, became very popular in South Korea during the period of the Asian financial crisis. Traveling throughout Seoul in the summer of 1999, I saw painted along the banks of the Han River the statement *Appa him naeseyo!* (Daddy be strong!). This call to Korean fathers by their children was a common nationalist response to the financial crisis. The idea that all Korean fathers had to come to the aid of the nation during the crisis demonstrated the position that Korean men were to assume in global capitalism (see J. Song 2009). This conflation of capital strength, national strength, and masculinity becomes obvious in the discourses that constitute the icon of the Asian male baseball player.

12. Samoans have been recruited as NFL players, and the NFL has finally begun to offer training facilities on American Samoa. See "Samoa, a Football Hotbed, Gets Help," *New York Times*, February 24, 2008, http://www.nytimes.com (accessed July 24, 2008).

13. These stereotypes have no doubt negatively affected Asian American subjects, but Celine Parreñas Shimizu points out in *The Hypersexuality of Race* (2007) that it is important to understand sexual representations within the context of Asian American sexuality, desire, and pleasure, rather than simply saying no to sex.

14. The large number of Asian men who came to the United States as laborers, from the middle of the nineteenth century and into the twentieth century, evoked public anxieties about their sexualities, given the dearth of Asian female partners for

working men. For example, the so-called "bachelor societies" of early twentieth-century Chinatowns were characterized as spaces where the vices of prostitution, homosexuality, and drug use led to disease, moral decay, and miscegenation (Lui 2004; Shah 2001).

15. The depiction of all Asian men as feminized and sexually inferior to White men is challenged by the reception of the transnational film star Sessue Hayakawa. Though he may have acted in primarily villainous and stereotypical character roles, most notoriously in D. W. Griffith's *Broken Blossoms* or *The Yellow Man and the Girl* (1919), Hayakawa emerged as a very popular sex symbol and transnational star in the early twentieth century (Miyao 2007). During World War II, representations of the militarized Asian subject also continued to evoke concern about the Asian male sexual threat to White American women, most bluntly displayed in rape-themed propaganda posters (Westbrook 1990). These fears of Japanese power were again placed in sexualized terms during the 1980s and early 1990s when Japanese economic power was said to be threatening the United States. The Michael Crichton novel *Rising Sun*, which was made into a Hollywood movie, offered a clear depiction of the perverse sexual threat of Japanese men (Kondo 1997).

16. This depiction of the Asian male servant was borne out in a number of popular television shows from the 1950s through the 1970s (Hamamoto 1994).

17. These anxieties are still a large part of the popular literacy of Asian American men, and they are well demonstrated by the controversy over a *Details* April 2004 magazine spread entitled "Gay or Asian," which conveyed the continuing anxieties around Asian male sexuality. The spread evoked an immediate reaction from Asian American media activists, including those at Asian Media Watch and the UCLA Asia Institute, as well as GLBT groups.

18. The Asian male movie star, as represented by Chow Yun Fat, Jet Li, and Jackie Chan, has proven the market profitability of Asian male actors. Furthermore, the popular success of the films *Better Luck Tomorrow* and *Harold and Kumar Go to White Castle* demonstrates the mainstream appeal of Asian American men (in quintessentially American roles) who, unlike the martial artists of Hollywood and Hong Kong action films, lack any transnational connection to Asia. Furthermore, there has been recognition of an Asian male presence in the mainstream music scene as DJs (Mix Master Mike, Babu, Triple Threat DJs), MCs (Jin, The Black Eyed Peas' apl.de.ap), producers (The Neptunes' Chad Hugo and Pharrell), and rock stars (Linkin Park's Mike Shinoda and Joe Hahn and the Smashing Pumpkins' James Iha). Furthermore, the visibility of Asian American men in reality shows, especially in televised poker tournaments, has created an emergence of new kinds of Asian bodies in Asian/American popular culture.

19. Bruce Lee is often seen as exemplifying a period of multiracial alliances and antiracist politics that operated across borders (Prashad 2003).

20. This counterhegemonic masculinity offered an important alternative narrative

at that time period, yet Bruce Lee can also be understood as a precursor to the popularity of Hollywood and Hong Kong martial arts stars such as Jet Li and Jackie Chan. Rather than existing as an alternative form of athletic masculinity, these martial arts stars reflect a movie genre that relies on heavily typecast figures. Although these stars share characteristics with media sport stars in their global commodification, the genre of sport places a heavy emphasis on competition, its assumption of the use of real bodies, and its "liveness," rather than on the staged and choreographed fight scenes of martial arts films.

21. The concern with overcoming the stereotype of the small Asian male is apparent in a few Asian American historical accounts around sport. In the United States, boxing became a site for the development of public cultures that united a divided Filipino American community during the 1930s and 1940s (España-Maram 2006). The size and power of the most famous prizefighter of the time, Ceferino Garcia, was connected to his popularity in the Filipino American community. España-Maram argues that the body itself was treated as a representation of potentiality for the entire group. This focus on the body might seem like an especially exaggerated assertion, given other forms of pleasure and interest in the sporting spectacle itself, but it does demonstrate the importance that Garcia was a welterweight fighter who defied assumptions that all Filipinos were featherweights or lightweights. He also became a champion in what was, at the time, one of the most popular media sports in the United States. This focus on the hard body resonates with the fetish for the hard body in contemporary representations of Asian athletes.

22. Transnationalism has been apparent in the movement of Asian/American athletes across borders. In the early part of the twentieth century, the organized play of Japanese Americans in baseball connected men across transnational borders. Baseball and boxing became popular in the Philippines due to the U.S. military presence, and these sports were instituted as part of the formal educational policies of colonization (España-Maram 2006). Prizefighting and boxing developed spaces for the production of masculinity among Filipino immigrants during the 1920s and 1930s. Sporting policies were used as a way to inculcate "modern" values in their "little brown brothers" through the ideas of sportsmanship, fair play, honesty, and democracy, which were supposedly the hallmarks of U.S. sport (74).

23. Chris Young, "Yao: The Next Big Thing," *Toronto Star*, November 2, 2002, http://waymoresports.thestar.com (accessed March 10, 2004).

24. Jonathan Feigen, "Yao goes to NBA Summit," *Houston Chronicle,* April 2, 2003, http://www.houstonchronicle.com (accessed March 10, 2004). David Stern, commissioner of the NBA, went so far as to suggest that a mutual education was taking place as a result of Yao's successful inclusion: "He is very much an ambassador both ways. America is learning things about the Peoples' Republic of China, and a lot of people in China are learning about America through him" (Feigen 2003). Stern suggested that as the NBA internationalizes, its fans would become more cosmopolitan simply

by seeing the number of foreign nationals playing on the various teams. This assertion demonstrates the extent to which the discourse of multiculturalism has become naturalized as one of the dominant logics of capital in the NBA and other internationalizing sports leagues.

25. Jeré Longman, "Yao's Success Speeds N.B.A's Plans for China," *New York Times*, December 15, 2002, http://www.nytimes.com (accessed June 1, 2011).

26. Alan Shipnuck, "Rededicated Kim Coming Into His Own," *Sports Illustrated*, May 3, 2010, http://www.golf.com (accessed Aug. 10, 2010).

27. Ibid.

28. In January of 2003, there was an online petition that demanded an apology from the Los Angeles Lakers' Shaquille O'Neal for racist language he had uttered against Yao Ming. Once O'Neal made his comments, outrage ensued, and, sure enough, there were petitions circulating on all sorts of Asian American servers. I received many e-mails about this matter through both personal communications and organizational mass mailings. Although I sympathize with the desire for justice within and through the mainstream media and believe there is justifiable outrage in response to O'Neal's racist remarks, I am wary of the choices that Asian American groups make when organizing in self-righteous defense and using arguments that depend upon a narrow definition of Asian American identity politics. Equality for Asian American subjects will not be achieved through a simple increase in positive representations in mainstream media.

Chapter 4: Traveling Ladies

1. Directed by Bong Joon-ho, *Koemul* (2006) was the highest grossing South Korean movie in the history of South Korean film.

2. An earlier and very different version of this chapter, "Sports as Transnational Cultural Current: Politics of Identity seen through Analysis of Discourses on Korean Female Golf Stars of the LPGA," was presented with Kim Hyun Mee at the Yonsei-Stanford conference "Korean Identity: Past and Present" at Yonsei University in Seoul, South Korea, October 28–29, 2004.

3. Anthony Lane, "Down by the River: The Host," *New Yorker,* March 12, 2007, http://www.newyorker.com (accessed June 1, 2011).

4. Anne Allison (2006) describes a similar reception in the United States to the Japanese monster film *Gojira*. Many U.S. critics thought of the film as an entertaining fantasy ride. Rather than simply mindless entertainment, Allison argues that the film evokes a powerful emotional response from postwar Japanese filmgoers by presenting narratives that are connected to political realities. Allison points out that films such as these "grip their audiences with an emotional power that registers as 'True' while remaining a fantasy" (43).

5. Ladies Professional Golf Association, "2009 Tour Roster," http://www.lpga .com (accessed February 22, 2009).

6. See Foucault (1994); see also texts that use biopower as a framework to discuss gendered labor in Asian contexts (e.g., Ong 1987; Rofel 1997).

7. Ladies Professional Golf Association, "2011 International Players," http://www .lpga.com (accessed July 14, 2011).

8. Korean-language media discuss Michelle Wie as essentially Korean, but the U.S. mainstream media highlight her Americanness and her Hawaiianness. Both of her parents were born in South Korea. Although I recognize that differences exist between representations of Korean and Korean American golfers, particularly in relation to Korean and U.S. nationalist discourses, I do not focus on this important issue in this chapter.

9. There are obviously distinctions between a U. S. citizen and a South Korean citizen, but I will refer to all Korean-born and Korean American players as Korean, excluding the areas where I engage in a discussion of national citizenship. The notion of Korean-born is also problematic as several South Korean citizen players were born outside the Republic of Korea, including Aree Song and Naree Song who were born in Thailand and have a Thai mother and Korean father. They changed their Thai surname, Wonglukiet, to a Korean one in 2003. Angela Park, who entered in 2007, is also of Korean ethnicity but was born in Brazil. Furthermore, some South Korean golfers have naturalized to U.S. citizens after entering the tour, and some have claimed dual citizenship.

10. Korean player Ok-Hee Ku won one tournament in 1988. She never reached the status of today's players and subsequently played on the Japanese tour. Michael Arkush, "Asian Golfers at home in L.P.G.A.," *New York Times*, September 1, 2003, Sports, 6. Also, Pearl Sinn-Bonani entered the LPGA in 1991 as the first Korean American on the tour.

11. Thomas Bonk, "Pak Mentality: . . . In a relatively short time, South Korean golfers have become a force on the LPGA Tour," *Los Angeles Times*, June 10, 2004, Sports, D.

12. The number of South Korean players entering their rookie years grew from one in 1998 to thirteen in 2007. The number of Korean American players entering their rookie years rose from two in 2007 to seven in 2011. See http://www.lpga.com (accessed July 13, 2011).

13. Beginning with Japanese colonial rule until the mid-1980s, golf was limited to a small number of the South Korean male ultra-elite. This exclusive realm offered and continues to offer a context for political and economic dealings (Kim and Joo 2004). After Liberation in 1945, only one golf course existed in South Korea. During the Park Chung Hee era (1961–1979), approximately twenty golf courses were built. The golf boom began in the latter half of the 1980s with the construction of sixteen golf courses. Golf courses exploded in the 1990s when eighty-three were built (Shin and Nam 2004).

14. Environmental nongovernmental organizations (NGOs) have mobilized around

this issue of golf construction, demonstrating its undemocratic expropriations of prime property, its displacement of poor people, and its devastating effects on ecosystems.

15. Crosset (1995) points out that this narrative is popular in the LPGA in general, despite the overwhelming number of golfers with wealthy family backgrounds.

16. At the 2008 Olympics, the South Korean team won the team gold, but in the individual competition, Chinese archer Zhang Juan Juan beat three South Korean competitors, including Park Sung-hyun, thereby ending this decades-long streak. Associated Press, "Zhang Dethrones Park," August 14, 2008, http://www.nbcolym pics.com (accessed February 28, 2009).

17. According to 2003 statistics of the United Nations Development Programme, South Korea ranked 30th on the Human Development Index, and ranked 63rd on the Gender Empowerment Measure. The GEM for South Korea was by far the lowest among all top 30 HDI countries. Youkyoung Moon, Soomi Park, Minjung Kang, "Korean National Human Development Report," Seoul: Ministry of Gender Equality, Republic of Korea, United Nations Development Programme, 2005. http://hdr.undp .org/en/reports/national/asiathepacific/southkorea/name,3385,en.html (accessed July 11, 2011).

18. See Graig Dolch, "Foreign Relations," *Palm Beach Post*, November 19, 2003, Sports, 1C.

19. Thomas Bonk, "Pak Mentality: . . . In a relatively short time, South Korean golfers have become a force on the LPGA Tour," *Los Angeles Times*, June 10, 2004; Furman Bisher, "An LPGA surge made in Korea," *Atlanta Journal Constitution*, April 27, 2003, 3D.

20. The case of Kim Yuna and her mother offers another account that challenges the hegemonic narrative of patriarch-led female athlete's career. Coverage around the 2010 Olympics seemed to reproduce the narrative of a patriarchal relationship between Kim Yuna and her Canadian coach Brian Orser. Like Guus Hiddink, Orser became a media sensation as the foreign coach of a national athlete. He was highly praised for Kim Yuna's Olympic success. However, after a well-publicized break with Orser, Kim Yuna's mother emerged in media accounts as the managing force in her career as a celebrity athlete. This mother-daughter narrative offers an important alternative to the patriarchal narrative of father/coach-daughter/athlete narrative I outline in this chapter. Nancy Armour, "Kim Yuna leaves Coach Brian Orser," *USA Today*, August 25, 2010, http://www.usatoday.com (accessed July 11, 2011).

21. This incident is often cited in feature articles on controversies surrounding Korean players. Following the incident, commissioner Ty Votaw called a meeting of all Korean and Korean American players, caddies, and coaches to discuss the rules. See Krista Latham, "Influx of Korean players on LPGA creates challenges," *Detroit Free Press*, August 16, 2003, Sports 1; Associated Press, "Players meeting to discuss claims of cheating Korean dads," *Associated Press Worldstream*, August 5, 2003, Sports.

22. Crosset (1995) emphasizes the individual nature of playing golf in the LPGA with its focus on individual achievement and individual play.

23. Park is quoted as saying "Koreans are more traditional, very conservative. Children stay with their parents until they get married. Until then, they are in their own shell." Joel Boyd, "Seoul Train: Controversy hasn't derailed Korean influx on LPGA Tour," *Chicago Sun Times*, May 30, 2004, 94.

24. Some point to the role of Tiger Woods's late father, Earl Woods, in his career as a counterpoint. There are similarities that might be drawn from a militaristic training standpoint. Nevertheless, I would argue that in the case of Woods, the production of a father figure operates within a U.S. national context that pathologizes the "Black" family. See Henry Yu (2000).

25. Josh Barr, "The New Face of the LPGA Tour," *Washington Post*, May 15, 2003, Sports, D09.

26. There was a 26 percent increase in U.S. domestic television ratings, a 14 percent increase in attendance, and a 43 percent increase in traffic on www.lpga.com from 2001–2004. Bucky Gleason, "LPGA Facing Cultural Divide," *Buffalo News*, June 23, 2004, Sports, D1.

27. The game of golf was introduced in the United States at the turn of the twentieth century and functioned as an arena of leisure and social reproduction for elite Anglo men and women (Crosset 1995). Professional women's golf began in the 1940s, and the U.S.-based LPGA was officially established in 1950. The use of the word *lady* in LPGA evokes a past of White patriarchal exclusivity. The continued use of the term projects a nostalgic sense of genteel domesticity and class privilege (see Feder-Kane 2000).

28. See Jamieson (2000). Women continue to be excluded from private clubs, such as Augusta National Golf Club in Augusta, Georgia, where the PGA Masters Tournament is held annually. This has been a site of contention between women's rights advocates and the male-dominated golfing establishment.

29. Stephenson's now infamous remarks are mentioned in almost every long-form feature article on Korean female golfers. In a *Golf Digest* article, Ron Sirak raises the issue of racism against Asians within the realm of golf, condemns overt racism, and calls for "reason" and acceptance. He also rejects the notion of Korean dominance in the LPGA. "View from the Bunker: On Asians and Racism," *Golf Digest*, August 25, 2005, http://www.golfdigest.com (accessed February 1, 2006).

30. Graig Dolch, "Foreign Relations," *Palm Beach Post*, November 19, 2003, Sports, 1C.

31. Michael Buteau, "Nike signs Park as it hopes to make inroads in LPGA," *Milwaukee Journal Sentinel*, March 2, 2003, 12S.

32. Ibid.

33. Louise Story, "A teenage golfer may also be a marketer's dream," *New York Times*, July 18, 2005, http://www.nytimes.com (accessed July 22, 2005).

34. Lindsey Willhite, "LPGA happy Pak got things rolling," *Chicago Daily Herald*, June 4, 2004, Sports, 1.

35. Quoted in Cecilia Kang, "Cultural conflicts arise on women's golf tour attempts to charge Asian pros criticized," *San Jose Mercury News*, November 1, 2003, http://www.mercurynews.com (accessed August 12, 2004).

36. Bob Harig, "Women's golf; Korean infusion," *St. Petersburg Times*, June 29, 2004, 1C.

37. Quoted in "Pak, Park lead Korean contingent at LPGA Asahi Championship," *Agence France Presse*, May 7, 2003.

38. In Ong's text, flexible citizenship refers to the multiple national affiliations and associations used by Chinese capitalists to maximize their ability to accumulate profit. Through family members in multiple countries, a particular family might be able to take advantage of differentials in wage, knowledge, and technological access. This family might also acquire multiple citizenship advantages such as tax shelters or public education for subsequent generations.

39. Quoted in Cecilia Kang, "Cultural conflicts arise on women's golf tour attempts to charge Asian pros criticized," *San Jose Mercury News*, November 1, 2003, http://www.mercurynews.com (accessed August 12, 2004).

40. Quoted in Vic Dorr Jr., "Country clubbin'/Korean golfers credit success to a cultural propensity for discipline," *Richmond Times Dispatch*, May 5, 2004, Sports, E1.

41. Beth Ann Baldry, "LPGA to demand English proficiency," *Golf Week*, August 25, 2008, http://www.golfweek.com (accessed August 29, 2008). Lorne Rubenstein, "LPGA Puts Its Foot in Its English Speaking Mouth," *Globe and Mail*, August 30, 2008, Sports, S3.

42. See "'Open to All': Title IX at 30, The Secretary of Education's Commission on Opportunity in Athletics," presented in 2003, http://www.ed.gov (accessed February 13, 2006).

43. ABC Television, "Game, Sex Match," on *Nightline*, aired on August, 26, 2002. The description of the piece on the Vanderbilt Television News Archive site states, "Discussion with Ted Koppel (ABC), 'USA Today' columnist Christine Brennan, LPGA Commissioner Ty Votaw, and sports agent Drew Rosenhaus about the promotion of women's professional sports based on the physical attractiveness of its athletes" (http://tvnews.vanderbilt.edu/siteindex/2002-Specials/special-2002-08-26-ABC-1.html) (accessed July 21, 2011).

44. Graig Dolch, "Foreign Relations," *Palm Beach Post*, November 19, 2003, Sports, 1C.

45. Quoted in Cecilia Kang, "Cultural conflicts arise on women's golf tour attempts to charge Asian pros criticized," *San Jose Mercury News*, November 1, 2003, http://www.mercurynews.com (accessed August 12, 2004).

46. This tournament began in 1972 and is held every spring in Rancho Mirage, California, near Palm Springs. It has gone through the following name changes: Col-

gate Dinah Shore (1972–1981), Nabisco Dinah Shore (1982–1999), Nabisco Championship (2000–2001), Kraft Nabisco Championship (2002–current). See http://www.kncgolf.com/history.html (accessed July 13, 2011).

47. See official website for the event: http://www.thedinah.com. Arial Messman-Ruckel, "Q & A with Mariah Hanson," *Curve Magazine,* 2010 Interviews, http://www.curvemag.com (accessed July 14, 2011).

48. Greg Boeck, "Gulbis looks past good looks to winning; Golfer likes being pretty, hates losing," *USA Today,* March 29, 2006, 3C.

49. See "LPGA Player Advertisements," http://www.lpga.com/entertainment_content.aspx?pid=10927 (accessed March 19, 2009).

50. This ad-free website was launched as a hobby by a self-described "White guy" in Seattle named Eric Fleming. Fleming's Korean-born wife helps him translate articles from Korean to English. See Mike Tokito, "'Seoulsisters.com' A (Web) site to behold," *Sunday Oregonian,* June 22, 2003, C04.

51. Juliet Macur, "Olympic Hopes Rest with Skating Favorite Kim Yuna," *The New York Times,* February 13, 2010, http://www.nytimes.com (accessed July 12, 2011). Jeré Longman, "Balanced on a Skater's Blades, the Expectations of a Nation," *New York Times,* February 22, 2010, http://www.nytimes.com (accessed July 12, 2011).

Chapter 5: Nation Love

1. A version of this chapter was previously published as "Consuming Visions: The Crowds of the Korean World Cup," *Journal of Korean Studies* 11 (2006): 41–67.

2. The catchy words and tunes of these cheers were repeated countless times throughout the tournament and offered the soundtrack, so to speak, to the event. The cheers included: *"Taehan Min'guk"* (Republic of Korea or, literally, "Country of the Great Han people"); *"Arirang"* (a traditional folk tune often sung during unification events between North and South Korea); and *"Oh! P'ilsŭng Korea"* (Oh! Korea must win), which was recorded by popular artists the Kim To-hyŏn Band and Crying Nut.

3. See Lewis (1992). The essays in this collection are explorations into various types of media fandoms. Together, they offer a broad definition of fandom.

4. The collection of essays in *Cybersociety 2.0* (Jones 1998) offers an overview of the diverse forms of communication that take place in response to computer-mediated communications.

5. Of course, not all of the articles about the World Cup were celebratory. Hong Seong-Tae (2004) offers a general overview of the various critical positions taken by academics and intellectuals on the World Cup. In my opinion, the celebratory assessments offered by critical academics stand out as particularly distinct and noteworthy, as they mirrored dominant mass media narratives of the event and contributed to the bolstering of hegemonic narratives of national unity.

6. Hong Song-tae also touched on this comparison in his paper during a post–World Cup forum on July 9, 2002 entitled, *"Wŏltŭ k'ŏp ŭn uri sahoe e muŏs ŭl nam-*

gyotna" (What Has the World Cup Left Our Society?) at the Seoul Animation Center. It was sponsored by the Policy Research Institute for Democratic Society, Citizen's Association for Cultural Reform, and the Citizen's Association for Sports.

7. Also known as the Great *Han'guk* Supporters Club: http://www.reddevil.or.kr. See also Lee Tong-yŏn (2002). Ch'oe Won'-gi (2002) argues that the Red Devils Supporters Club is an example of new social formations that have emerged in this period of South Korean political history. In his view, the Red Devils club exists as a new "cultural movement" concerned with improving the cultural landscape of South Korea.

8. For a popular description, see Lee Tong-yŏn (2002). I was able to attend and meet the media representative of the Red Devils, Sin Tong-min, at the post–World Cup forum on July 9, 2002.

9. Lee Tong-yŏn (2002) also discusses the difficulty of distinguishing official members from unofficial members. He raises the issue of whether this distinction is relevant.

10. The figure of sixty million is derived from forty-eight million people in South Korea plus twelve million in the Korean diaspora, estimated by the Overseas Korean Foundation. Importantly, this number did not include the estimated twenty-two million residing in North Korea.

11. Neil Smith (1997) discusses the persistence of nationalism and ethnocentrism in the wake of radical structural economic changes within an era of neoliberal globalization.

12. FIFA did not consider South Korea to be a viable place to host the World Cup on its own. However, with intense lobbying, spearheaded by Korea Football chair and presidential candidate Chung Mong-Joon, FIFA began to seriously consider South Korea. When the World Cup was awarded to both Japan and South Korea in 1996, both World Cup committees were sorely disappointed (Petrov 2004).

13. During the Spain–South Korea match, the card section across an entire section of the crowd read "Pride of Asia." For the most part, however, this brand of "Asian regionalism" was not expressed by any of the three East Asian countries represented. See Leo Ching's (2000) discussion of Asian regionalism as a hegemonic discourse of Japanese nationalism.

14. My own research project could be accused of reproducing the nation-centered investigations, since I limit my discussion to how this event operated to produce notions of Koreanness among Korean subjects.

15. There still exists a male-dominated sport culture that greatly limits the opportunities for females to play most forms of sport, especially team sports, and it continues to privilege the relationship between men and sport.

16. In the first of the series *Culture, Media, and Identities,* du Gay and colleagues (1997) offer an important framework, entitled "Circuits of Culture," that demon-

strates the interactive processes of cultural production through the categories of consumption, representation, identity, production, and regulation.

17. These online/offline cultural movements are now becoming a popular subject of cultural research in South Korea as the impact of the Internet on public culture has begun to shape new forms of sociality in South Korean society (see Yong-sun Kim 2004).

18. I attempted to become a member but was unable to because I did not have a national identification number. I considered "borrowing a membership" but decided against it due to the legal implications of using someone else's national identification number.

19. My thanks to Gi-wook Shin for noting this mistake and also for explaining the game of *chokku* to me.

20. Kim and Choi (1998) offer a strong critique of patriarchal, androcentric Korean culture. They depict Korean public culture as highly sexist and antiwoman.

21. Seungsook Moon (2000) tempers discourses of women's gains toward equality within a liberalizing society with material evidence concerning the obstacles to women's empowerment. Kim Hyun Mee (2002) also points out the inability of the event to offer real alternatives for change.

22. I would like to thank Ki-young Shin for raising this critically important issue during the Stanford Seminar on Korea in June of 2005, which was held at Stanford University.

23. Prior to the game, there had been a loud debate over whether the bar would choose MBC or SBS. It was generally thought that SBS catered to women with their emotionally driven commentary, whereas MBC paid closer attention to the technical aspects of the game since they were called by "experts" and formal players.

24. *Sŏtaeji* formed in the early 1990s and was an enormously popular rock band that spurred the youth cultural phenomenon of pop-star worship. H.O.T., or High-five of Teens, was also an enormously popular boy band in the late 1990s.

Chapter 6: Home Field Advantage

1. The 2000 U.S. census data report 1,076,872 Koreans (http://www.census.gov) (accessed April 1, 2002). The Overseas Korea Foundation and other Korean-language media outlets in South Korea and the United States regularly place this number at approximately two million. It is assumed that these Korean national organizations are also counting long-term visitors, the undocumented, and students, among others.

2. Professional Korean football players aim to perform primarily in European leagues; however, the exodus of South Korean players occurred only after the end of the 2002 World Cup. A popular veteran player, Hong Myong Bo, was the first Korean to play in MLS, beginning in 2002 with the Los Angeles Galaxy. He played for two years before retiring in 2004. At the end of December 2004, the NBA's Phoenix Suns

drafted the first Korean player, 7-foot-3-inch Ha Seung Jin (Liz Robbins, "Size 7 Sneakers are Hard to Fill," *New York Times,* January 5, 2005, Sports, 5). There were also a few Korean female players in the Women's National Basketball Association. The rise of football (soccer) players in Europe challenges the U.S.-Korea connection as Korean players, such as Park Ji-Sung, have risen to fame in professional European leagues.

3. Lili M. Kim (2003/4) discusses the issue of Korean American allegiance during World War II and their negotiations of the transnational throughout this period. She argues that the primary motivation for Korean American allegiance was in liberating the Korean homeland, rather than U.S. victory.

4. Abelmann and Lie (1997) briefly discuss the struggles between Korean American media outlets and the South Korean state.

5. Kil-nam Roh (1983) discusses what he sees as a crisis in Korean American journalism that is due to the control of the Korean state, collaborating media industries, and the Korean Central Intelligence Agency (KCIA). Even though the most egregious forms of intimidation are no longer apparent, many of the complaints about the lack of control and lack of an independent voice for and by Korean Americans remain (Abelmann and Lie 1997). Dávila (2001) discusses the conflicts between the role of the Mexican state and corporate interests of *Univisión* television in the United States, thereby demonstrating the complex state, commercial, and personal connections created among Latino populations between Mexico and the United States.

6. From the homepage of the Overseas Korea Foundation: http://www.okf.or.kr (accessed December 15, 2004). According to Edward Chang, guest editor of the special *Amerasia* issue, Koreans constitute the fourth-largest diaspora, in terms of population, and the first as a proportion of the population of their putative homeland (2003/4). These statistics are questionable, and in the opinion of some, absolutely incorrect. For example, many island nations, including Jamaica, claim that a larger proportion of their population resides outside the country rather than within its borders.

7. The Overseas Korean Act, which granted partial privileges of citizenship to those who had left after the institution of the Republic of Korea in 1948, was passed in 1999. The year of 1948 significantly privileged Korean Americans and those who hailed from U.S.-allied nations while placing Koreans in places like Russia and China at a disadvantage. It was deemed unconstitutional by the Korean Supreme Court in 2001, and it was then redrafted. A revised version was passed in 2003 (Park and Chang 2005). The debate over this act has demonstrated the contested nature of citizenship and the varying understandings of diaspora in South Korea and abroad.

8. See http://www.okf.or.kr (accessed July 3, 2004).

9. There has emerged an entire industry of work that has been produced as a response to Huntington's controversial, yet influential, thesis. His thesis states that,

in the twenty-first century, cultures rather than nations would be the basis for the most significant political and ideological divides around the globe, leading to global conflict among broadly defined cultures. I will not critique Huntington's thesis point by point, but his essentialist and sweeping generalizations about complex and diverse groups of people lend to an inability to understand and engage with salient differences. Furthermore, his Manichean view of the world in good versus bad terms, which places the "West" (especially the United States) in the "good" camp, has been used to justify violence against the "bad." Edward Said (2002) powerfully countered Huntington's thesis and warned of its harmful effects, stating that Huntington's discourse exists as a form of orientalism that works to justify domination by the West of other places in the world, namely the Middle East.

10. See http://www.okf.or.kr (accessed July 3, 2004).

11. Ibid.

12. A Global Korean Network business forum was instituted by the OKF, and I had the opportunity to attend the first annual meeting in July of 2002.

13. I offer a theoretical discussion of such multiple and contesting discourses in my article on Chan Ho Park as a transnational icon (Joo 2000).

14. In the Los Angeles area, KTE is channel 44, or KBS-LA, the global division of the South Korean state-sponsored television station, KBS. The following description of KTE is found on http://english.kbs.co.kr (accessed December 20, 2004): "KTE has acted not only as a medium in introducing KBS programs to Koreans living in the US but also broadcasted KTE-produced programs delivering the essence of Korean culture to expatriates. KTE played a central role in nurturing the identity of the Korean community. In particular, a satellite broadcasting service for the Americas, TV KOREA has been in service for the past two years. And KBS programs can be seen through 25 local Korean Language Broadcasters and found in 13 videotape sales agencies. KTE provided live broadcasting service of the 2002 World Cup, the Busan Asian Games, and the South-North Unification Football Match, *instilling national pride to Koreans all over the world*" (emphasis added).

15. One major, and arguably the most important, site was the webpage of the *Pulgŭn Angma*, or the Red Devils Supporters Club, http://www.reddevil.or.kr.

16. This ambiguity was demonstrated by the controversy around the official naming of the space in 2009. A *New York Times* article detailed the conflict around an application to officially designate the area "Little Bangladesh" by leaders in the Bangladeshi community. This was countered by Korean American community leaders who submitted their own counter-request for an official designation as Koreatown. Mira Jang notes that the lack of an official designation was a surprise to many in the Korean community in Los Angeles. There are official City of Los Angeles signs that state "Koreatown" along Western Boulevard. Mira Jang, "Koreans and Bangladeshis Vie in Los Angeles District," *New York Times*, April 7, 2009, http://www.nytimes .com (accessed April 7, 2009).

17. This was similar to the discussion of the role of the World Cup in assuaging the wounds of the 1997 Asian financial crisis.

18. The following are examples of mainstream media coverage: Daisy Nguyen, "World Cup Is Talk of LA's Koreatown," *Associated Press*, June 8, 2002; KTLA TV, *Morning News Early Edition*, June 25, 2002; KCBS TV, *CBS 2 News this Morning*, June 25, 2002; KNBC TV, *Channel 4 News*, June 25, 2002; KCRW-FM, *Which Way LA?* Santa Monica, June 21, 2002.

19. Jaemin Yu, "*Pulgŭn Angma tŭl ssodajyo nawa kori ch'ukje*," *Korea Daily*, June 19, 2002.

20. See Jang Yun-hwa, "Koreans Display the Best Kind of Cheering: LAPD Stated the Event Finished without Incident," *Korea Daily*, June 20, 2002, and Kim Song-tae, "Wilshire Boulevard Closed, Let's All Cheer," *Korea Daily*, June 27, 2002.

21. Interviews with staff at *Korea Daily*, 2002. In all my interviews with editors, journalists, and reporters, it was noted that the crowds included non-Koreans, particularly Whites ("Americans") and Latinos ("Mexicans").

22. Jang Yun-hwa, "The First Win by Koreans Generates Interest from Mexican TV," *Korea Daily*, June 5, 2002. Other articles about Latino interest in Korean team include: "Noticias," 6 p.m. KMEX-TV, Los Angeles, aired June 22, 2002, and Chu Hyŏn-sok, "A World Cup Event at the Hispanic Festival," Radio Korea AM 1230, aired May 4, 2002.

23. For example, academic texts on Korean–African American relations include the following titles: *No Fire Next Time: Black–Korean Conflicts and the Future of America's Cities* (Joyce 2003); *Civility in the City: Blacks, Jews, and Koreans in Urban America* (J. Lee 2002); *Bitter Fruit: The Politics of Black–Korean Conflict in New York City* (Claire Kim 2000); *Koreans in the Hood: Conflict with African Americans* (Kwang Chung Kim 1999). With respect to Korean–Latino relations, Saito (1993) discusses Asian American and Latino cooperation, and Navarro (1993) discusses a Latino perspective of the Los Angeles uprisings. See also Chang and Leong (1994).

24. Jang Yun-hwa, "Latinos Riot After Loss to America," *Korea Daily*, June 17, 2002.

25. Ellis points out that during the U.S.–Mexico games, KMEX drew 1.5 million viewers, whereas ESPN's entire national audience drew just 1.6 million viewers. Stephen Ellis, "Gringo Corporates take Notice of US Soccer Success," *The Australian*, June 26, 2002, 26.

26. Korean American golfers Christina Kim and Michelle Wie have been given much attention in Korean media, but in the U.S. media, they are presented as U.S. golfers with Korean heritage (see chapter 4).

27. For a fascinating character study of Phil Anschutz and his business strategies, see Graham Bowley, "Goal! He Spends it on Beckham: Phil Anschutz Bets on Star Power, and Everything else," *New York Times*, April 22, 2007, S3: 1, 7.

28. See Corinna Knoll, "Sports Segment," *KoreAm Magazine*, March 2003, http://www.koreamjournal.com (accessed February 13, 2005). The Staples Center has, in the past, opened its doors for other cheer groups to watch games on their enormous screens, for example Lakers fans for away games during the NBA Finals. I recall video of fans in the Staples Center during these games; unlike shots of the seats during home games, there were many minorities in the stands, and the fan composition looked primarily Latino.

29. As opposed to the discourse of all forty-eight million people in South Korea becoming one, the Korean-language media in the United States placed the number at sixty million to include a Korean diaspora of twelve million in the calculation. Importantly, this number excludes the twenty-two million Koreans living in the Democratic People's Republic of Korea (North Korea).

Chapter 7: Generations Connect

1. George Lipsitz (1994) discusses the production of youth within historical and political contexts. He points out that academics who study youth often have agendas shaped through their own nostalgic understandings of youth. Sylvia Yanagisako (1985) offers a historically situated analysis of kinship between Japanese Americans of different age cohorts/immigrant generations in Seattle, Washington.

2. Progressive academics and civic groups, as represented by the collective *Tto hana ŭi munhwa* (An Alternative Culture), have made the issue of youth culture a critical point of social critique.

3. Jennifer Lee and Min Zhou, in *Asian American Youth* (2004), point out that the variability of the category makes it difficult to offer clear boundaries. The category of youth, in their usage, is loosely defined as those who participate in youth culture.

4. For collections that focus on Asian American youth and second-generation issues, see also Lee and Zhou (2004), Ngyuen and Tu (2007), and *Amerasia* (1999).

5. See Amsden (1989) for a discussion of the radical economic changes. See Cho Han (2000) for a discussion on the impact of modernization policies on notions of childhood and family.

6. Song Ho-gŭn (2003) attempts to offer a thorough description of hegemonic values and ideologies of the 2030 generation, based on the framework offered by Robert Bellah's investigation of the American character in his classic text, *Habits of the Heart* (1986).

7. "Broadband Penetration Rates," OECD Science Technology and Industry Scoreboard, 2003, Paris: OECD, 79. South Korea demonstrates, by far, the highest rates of broadband Internet use per household (nearly 20 percent). The closest was Canada at a little over 10 percent, whereas the United States was a little over 5 percent. In 2005, the South Korean ministry of communications stated that seven out of ten Koreans used the Internet regularly. http://www.mic.go.kr/index.jsp (accessed March 22, 2005).

8. The series of texts *Munhwa Yŏn'gu* (Cultural Studies), published in Seoul by *Hyŏnsil Munhwa Yŏn'gu*, offers important original studies of media, youth culture, gender studies, and popular culture in Korea. Issues of youth culture have been at the forefront of research on popular culture in South Korea and in Asian media studies more generally (see Erni and Chua 2005).

9. Kyongwon Yoon (2003) rejects the idea that radical changes take place simply due to the use of new technologies. Yoon demonstrates, somewhat counterintuitively, how cell phones are technological devices for maintaining traditional kin relations between youth and parents.

10. See also Epstein and Tangherlini (2001) and Epstein (2000). In their study and subsequent film of the emergent punk rock scene in South Korea, Epstein and Tangherlini focus on various issues concerning South Korean youth and their position in South Korean national public culture.

11. The number of students studying and traveling has increased exponentially in the fifteen years since liberalization. See Korean Ministry of Culture and Tourism, "2004 Report on the State of Tourism," http://www.mct.go.kr (accessed March 22, 2005).

12. Gordon and Bonner, in their documentary, *The Game of Their Lives* (2002), detail the events of the North Korean success in the 1966 London World Cup.

13. A world cost-of-living survey conducted in 2005 found that the cities with the highest cost of living were: 1. Tokyo; 2. Osaka; 3. Seoul, http://www.mercer.com (accessed July 5, 2006).

14. For more elaborate sociological definitions of the first, one-point-five, and second generations, see Zhou (2004), Gans (1992), and Portes and Rumbaut (2001).

15. Sunaina Maira (2002) demonstrates how South Asian youth cultural spaces in the United States become sites for the reproduction of ethnic nationalism in South Asian communities.

16. "Parachute kids" are understood as children of Asian—especially Chinese—elites who live apart from one or both of their parents to live in the United States or another industrialized nation. Educational opportunities are the primary reason for this divided family structure. For U.S. parachute kids, children are raised in the United States due to the perceived comparative advantage of having U.S. residency and a fluency in English in the global economy. Aihwa Ong (1999) points out that they can become a U.S. "base" for operations by Chinese capitalist families.

17. In fact, this generational model is challenged by studies that demonstrate the transnational connections between "older" cohorts and their countries of origin (see Hsu 2000).

18. In Asian American Studies, this generational model became the predominant paradigm that was based on studies of Japanese Americans after World War II. Given the exclusion acts of the early twentieth century, particularly the Immigration Act of

1924, the Japanese American population could easily be divided into neat generational categories that correlated age with immigrant generation (Ngai 2004; Yanagisako 1985).

19. More recently, the optimism of the straight-line theory has been challenged by the inability of the so-called second generation to improve on the social and economic achievements of their immigrant forebears (Gans 1992).

20. Min Zhou (2004) points out that, according to the 2000 U.S. census, nearly 80 percent of one-point-five and second-generation Korean Americans were younger than seventeen.

21. For a more extended discussion of the characteristics of Korean nationalism, see Pai and Tangherlini (1998); Shin, Freda, and Yi (1999); and Shin (2006). Of course, nationalism is not a singular expression; however, these discussions point to hegemonic conceptions of Korean nationalism as one that understands Korea as a singular and homogeneous group. According to this notion, blood, nation, and ethnicity are one, since they are shared by all Koreans

22. This incident involved the controversial disqualification of Korean speed-track star Kim Dong-sung in the 1500-meter short track during the 2002 Olympics. See chapter 1 for a more detailed account. In 2003, this ongoing defamation resulted in a boycott of a short track World Cup match held in South Korea by Ohno and the U.S. team. Korean commentators saw Ohno as a sacrificial lamb for anti-American hostilities in South Korea. Ohno is quoted as stating, "cyber terrorism is every bit as dangerous and wrong as any other type of terrorism. Without the arrest of the criminals making these threats against me, I see no other choice but to not compete at this World Cup event." In "Ohno Would Rather Be Safe Than Sorry," *USA Today*, November 18, 2003, http://www.usatoday.com (accessed July 21, 2011).

23. This number refers to forty-eight South Koreans and twelve million in the diaspora, excluding North Korea, which, at the time, was estimated to have twenty-two million residents.

24. *Hallyu* refers to a Chinese term for "Korean wave." This term refers to the widespread and growing popularity of Korean popular music, film, dramatic serials, animation, and electronic games throughout Asia (Cho Han et al. 2003). See also Iwabuchi (2002) for a discussion of the processes of transculturation that are brought about by Japanese transnational popular culture in Asia and Asian popular culture in Japan.

25. David Parker (1998) discusses this phenomenon with respect to British Chinese youth who turn to Hong Kong as a cultural center.

Conclusion

1. The Status of Forces Agreement was part of the "Mutual Defense Treaty between the Republic of Korea and the United States of America" and went into effect after the

Korean War in 1954. Essentially, it allowed the U.S. military to use land in South Korea for military bases and maintain its own governance within these spaces and its military. http://www.usfk.mil/usfk/sofa (accessed July 11, 2011).

2. The Kwangju Uprising (May 18–27, 1980)—also referred to as the Kwangju Massacre—is considered a landmark in the struggle for democracy (Shin and Hwang 2003). During massive civilian uprisings for democracy, around five hundred people were killed in violent clashes with the military police. It has been understood that the use of deadly force was approved by the U.S. commander who led the UN forces in South Korea. The United States denied all involvement, but popular suspicion was confirmed with the "U.S. invitation of then President Chun to President Reagan's White House in 1981" (Shin 1995, 513). Helen Jun states, "the Kwangju massacre became a period when democracy and national liberation seized the consciousness of the Korean people with new historical urgency" (1997, 330).

3. Radical intellectuals promoted a sympathetic reading of North Korean *chuch'e* (self-reliance) ideology as one rooted in struggles for national liberation from feudal-ism and colonialism. They emphasized reunification and resistance to U.S. imperial-ism. It was in the interests of Korean radicals to construct a new kind of democratiza-tion movement that was not based on U.S. liberal democracy (Shin 1995).

4. Min-Jung Kim argues that although anti-Americanism in South Korea was a crucial organizing discourse of *minjung* nationalism, it has since had "contradictory articulations as an official South Korean cultural/economic nationalism in which the critique of American imperialism works simultaneously to consolidate capitalist de-velopment and mass consumption in the interests of the South Korean state" (1997, 379). Therefore, she argues, anti-Americanism can't be categorically understood as expressions of Korean dissident nationalism.

5. In 1987, the prodemocracy movements culminated in the "June Popular Upris-ing." Leading up to this period of civil demonstrations, social movements repre-senting a diversity of groups constituted a growing democratization movement that demanded many reforms, including constitutional revision, direct presidential elec-tions, labor rights, and the guarantee of basic human rights (Koo 1993). This mass mobilization of the public, the largest in South Korean history prior to the World Cup, eventually compelled the regime to accede to many of its demands with the June 29 Declaration.

6. With democratic reforms, there has been an emergence of a growing "civil society" (Armstrong 2002). Armstrong argues that the former opposition between state and society is no longer useful for understanding Korea today. He states that the relationship is an "increasingly complex and rapidly changing constellation of forces within, as well as between, the government and various kinds of social groups" (2002, 3). Throughout the 1990s, new forms of social movements proliferated with diversified issues, including the environment, economic justice, consumers' rights, and gender equality (W. Park 2000).

7. A documentary on U.S. beef from the popular documentary program *PD Diary*, which aired in April (on the major network MBC), is said to have led to the widespread belief that much of U.S. beef remained dangerous and potentially infected with mad cow disease. The network was forced to apologize for inaccuracies in its reporting, and it has been subject to ongoing investigations and prosecutions.

8. Choe Sang-hun, "Cabinet Offers to Quit after Beef Protests," *New York Times*, June 20, 2008, http://www.nytimes.com (accessed June 20, 2008).

9. *Han'gyŏre* Staff, " '50 man ch'ŏtbul' kwangjange tasi moyŏtda," July 6, 2008, http://www.hani.co.kr (accessed July 6, 2008).

10. Kang Seok-jae, "Two Koreas seen to up tempo of sports exchanges," *Korea Herald*, January 1, 2003, http://www.koreaherald.com (accessed July 11, 2011). Kang reports that the first friendly matches began in 1990 and 1991, taking place in both Seoul and Pyongyang. Then, after an eight-year hiatus, they began in earnest again in 1999. In 2000, the North Korean and South Korean delegations to the Olympics marched together in the opening and closing ceremonies.

11. Pak Sung-hwa, "Miingye esŏ p'yŏnghwa ŭi sangjing kkaji . . . Puk Han minyo ŭngwŏndan ŭl po nŭn tach'aeroŭn sigak," *Han'gyŏre 21*, October 17, 2002, 34–38.

12. Kwŏn Hyŏk-ch'ŏl, "Kkurŏ an'go hanaro hwangdanghan ch'a'i," *Han'gyŏre 21*, September 18, 2003, 16–19.

13. FILA is a brand of designer sportswear.

14. As a precursor to the World Cup, a British-made documentary entitled *The Game of their Lives* (Gordon and Bonner 2002), about the North Korean football team of the 1966 Olympics, was aired both on South Korean and North Korean television in the winter/spring of 2002. It was the first such media event to air on both sides without censorship (personal communication). The film detailed the astounding rise of the North Korean team to the 1966 World Cup and their entry into the Round of Sixteen. Knowledge of this event was largely censored in South Korea, whereas in the North it became instantly memorialized as part of the nationalist sporting lore.

15. This was not the case with Korean Americans or many Koreans older than sixty. For Korean Americans in Los Angeles, there was generally a suspicion of North Korea or total ignorance of these sporting events.

16. Kang Seok-jae, "Two Koreas seen to up tempo of sports exchanges," *Korea Herald*, January 1, 2003, http://www.koreaherald.com (accessed July 11, 2011).

17. Pak Sung-hwa, "Miingye esŏ p'yŏnghwa ŭi sangjing kkaji . . . Puk Han minyo ŭngwŏndan ŭl po nŭn tach'aeroŭn sigak," *Han'gyŏre 21*, October 17, 2002, 34–38.

18. Kwŏn Hyŏk-ch'ŏl, "Kkurŏ an'go hanaro hwangdanghan ch'ai," *Han'gyore 21*, September 18, 2003, 16–19.

References

Abelmann, Nancy, and John Lie. 1997. *Blue Dreams: Korean Americans and the Los Angeles Riots.* Cambridge, Mass.: Harvard University Press.

Adams, Ansel. 1944. *Born Free and Equal: The Story of Japanese Americans.* New York: U.S. Camera.

Adorno, Theodor W. 1991. *The Culture Industry: Selected Essays on Mass Culture.* Ed. J. M. Bernstein. London: Routledge.

Ahmed, Sara. 2004. Affective Economies. *Social Text* 22 (2): 117–39.

Allison, Anne. 2006. *Millenial Monsters: Japanese Toys and the Global Imagination.* Berkeley: University of California Press.

Alter, Joseph S. 1992. *The Wrestler's Body: Identity and Ideology in North India.* Berkeley: University of California Press.

Althusser, Louis. 1971. Ideology and Ideological State Apparatuses (Notes Towards an Investigation). In *Lenin and Philosophy and Other Essays*, 127–86. New York: Monthly Review Press.

Amerasia. 1993. Los Angeles Struggles toward Multiethnic Community. Special Issue. *Amerasia Journal* 19 (2).

———. 1999. Second Generation Asian American Ethnic Identity. Special Issue. *Amerasia Journal* 25 (1).

———. 2003/4. What Does It Mean to Be Korean Today?: Part I. Across Nations, Generations, and Identities. Special Issue. *Amerasia Journal* 29 (3).

———. 2004. What Does It Mean to Be Korean Today?: Part II. Community in the 21st Century. Special Issue. *Amerasia Journal* 30 (1).

Amis, John, and Bettina Cornwell, eds. 2005. *Global Sport Sponsorship.* New York: Berg.

Amsden, Alice H. 1989. *Asia's Next Giant: South Korea and Late Industrialization.* New York: Oxford University Press.

An, Min-sŏk, Chŏng Hong-ik, and Im Hyŏn-jin. 2002. *Saeroun sŭp'och'ŭ sahoehak*. Seoul: Paeksansotang.

Anderson, Benedict. 1991. *Imagined Communities: Reflections on the Origin and Spread of Nationalism*. New York: Verso.

Andrews, David L. 2000. Excavating Michael Jordan's Blackness. In *Reading Sport: Critical Essays on Power and Representation*, ed. Susan Birrell and Mary G. McDonald, 166–205. Boston: Northeastern.

———, ed. 2001. *Michael Jordan, Inc.: Corporate Sport, Media Culture, and Late Modern America*. Albany: State University of New York Press.

Ang, Ien. 1997. *Living Room Wars: Rethinking Media Audiences for a Postmodern World*. New York: Routledge.

Appadurai, Arjun. 1996. *Modernity at Large: Cultural Dimensions of Globalization*. Minneapolis: University of Minnesota Press.

Armstrong, Charles K. 2002. Civil Society in Contemporary Korea. In *Korean Civil Society: Social Movements, Democracy, and the State*, ed. Charles K. Armstrong, 1–15. New York: Routledge.

Aso, Noriko. 2002. Sumptuous Re-Past: The 1964 Tokyo Olympics Arts Festival. *positions: east asia cultures critique* 10 (1): 7–38.

Baldassaro, Lawrence, and Richard Johnson, eds. 2002. *The American Game: Baseball and Ethnicity*. Carbondale: Southern Illinois University Press.

Bass, Amy. 2002. *Not the Triumph but the Struggle: The 1968 Olympics and the Making of the Black Athlete*. Minneapolis: University of Minnesota Press.

Bellah, Robert. 1986. *Habits of the Heart: Individualism and Commitment in American Life*. Berkeley: University of California Press.

Berlant, Lauren, ed. 2000. *Intimacy*. Chicago: University of Chicago Press.

———. 2008. *The Female Complaint*. Durham, N.C.: Duke University Press.

Bloom, John, and Michael Nevin Willard, eds. 2002. *Sports Matters: Race, Recreation, and Culture*. New York: New York University Press.

Bobo, Lawrence, and Victor Thompson. 2006. Unfair by Design: The War on Drugs, Race, and the Legitimacy of the Criminal Justice System. *Social Research* 73 (2): 445–72.

Bong, Joon-ho. 2006. *Koemul* (The Host). South Korea: Showbox.

Bong, Youngshik, and Katherine Moon. 2005. What's Youth Got to Do with It? Nationalism and Anti-Americanism in South Korea. Paper presented at the Yonsei University Conference on Korean Identity: Past and Present, Seoul, South Korea.

Bordo, Susan. 1999. *The Male Body: A New Look at Men in Public and in Private*. New York: Farrar, Straus and Giroux.

Bourne, St. Clair. 1999. *Paul Robeson: Here I Stand*. USA: WinStar Home Entertainment.

Brohm, Jean-Marie. 1978. *Sport, a Prison of Measured Time: Essays*. London: Ink Links.

Brownell, Susan. 1995. *Training the Body for China: Sports in the Moral Order of the People's Republic*. Chicago: University of Chicago Press.

Burgos Jr., Adrian. 2007. *Playing America's Game: Baseball, Latinos, and the Color Line*. Berkeley: University of California Press.

Burns, Ken. 1994. *Baseball: A Film by Ken Burns*. USA: PBS.

Cashmore, Ellis. 2006. *Celebrity/Culture*. New York: Routledge.

Chakrabarty, Dipesh. 1998. Reconstructing Liberalism? Notes toward a Conversation between Area Studies and Diasporic Studies. *Public Culture* 10 (3): 457–81.

———. 2000. *Provincializing Europe: Postcolonial Thought and Historical Difference*. Princeton, N.J.: Princeton University Press.

Chan, Sucheng, ed. 2005. *Chinese American Transnationalism: The Flow of People, Resources and Ideas between China and America During the Exclusion Era*. Philadelphia: Temple University Press.

Chang, Edward Taehan, and Jeannette Diaz-Veizades. 1999. *Ethnic Peace in the American City: Building Community in Los Angeles and Beyond*. New York: New York University Press.

Chang, Edward Taehan, and Russell Leong, eds. 1994. *Los Angeles—Struggles toward Multiethnic Community*. Seattle: University of Washington Press.

Cheng, Lucie, and Yen Le Espiritu. 1989. Korean Business in Black and Hispanic Neighborhoods: A Study of Intergroup Relations. *Sociological Perspectives* 32: 521–34.

Chiang-Hom, Christy. 2004. Transnational Cultural Practices of Chinese Immigrant Youth and Parachute Kids. In *Asian American Youth: Culture, Identity, and Ethnicity*, eds. Jennifer Lee and Min Zhou, 143–58. New York: Routledge.

Ching, Leo. 2000. Globalizing the Regional; Regionalizing the Global: Mass Culture and Asianism in the Age of Late Capital. *Public Culture* 12 (1): 233–57.

Cho, Haejoang (Cho Han, Haejong). 1998. Male Dominance and Mother Power: The Two Sides of Confucian Patriarchy in Korea. In *Confucianism and the Family*, ed. W. H. Sloate and G. A. De Vos, 187–208. Albany: State University of New York Press.

Cho, Hang-je. 2003. *Han'guk pangsong ŭi yŏksa wa chŏnmang*. Seoul: Hanul Academy Press.

Cho Han, Haejong. 2000. "You Are Entrapped in an Imaginary Well," the Formation of Subjectivity within Compressed Development—a Feminist Critique of Modernity and Korean Culture. *Inter-Asia Cultural Studies* 1 (1): 49–69.

———. 2002a. P'ip'a ŭi wŏltŭ k'ŏp ŭl nŏmŏsŏ; Ilsijŏk chayul konggan, chŏnbokjŏk sigan ch'ehŏm. *Tangdae Pip'yŏng* 5 (1): 24–47.

———. 2002b. Beyond FIFA's World Cup: Temporary Autonomous Zone and the Subversive Experience of Disciplinary Modern Time. Paper presented at the inside/out: 2002 Korea—Japan Symposium, Seoul Women's Plaza.

Cho Han, Haejong, Sang-min Hwang, Koichi Iwabuchi, Tong-hu Lee, and Hyun Mee Kim, eds. 2003. *Hanryu and Asian Popular Culture*. Seoul: Yonsei University Press.

Cho Han, Haejong, Yoshitake Mori, Toshiya Ueno, and Hiroki Ogasawara, eds. 2004. Beyond FIFA's World Cup: Shared Event, Different Experiences. Special Issue. *Inter-Asia Cultural Studies* 5 (1).

Ch'oe, Chong-sŏn. 1983. *Sŭp'ochŭ pangsong p'yŏnsŏng e kwanhan punsŏkjŏk yŏn'gu*. Seoul: Dongdok University Press.

Ch'oe, Han-su, and Ch'oe Yong-hwan. 1998. *TV nŭn sŭp'och'ŭ ro mŏkgo sanda?* Seoul: Pobwonsa.

Ch'oe, Won'-gi. 2002. Pulgŭn Angma kŭ sahoe munhwajŏk ŭimi. In *Wŏltŭ k'ŏp, sinhwa wa hyŏnsil*, ed. An Min-sŏk. Seoul: Hanul Academy Press.

Choi, Chungmoo. 1993. The Discourse of Decolonization and Popular Memory: South Korea. *positions: east asia cultures critique* 1 (1): 77–102.

Choi, Jang Jip. 1993. Political Cleavages in South Korea. In *State and Society in Contemporary Korea*, ed. Hagen Koo, 13–50. Ithaca, N.Y.: Cornell University.

Choi, Yoon Sung. 2004. Football and the South Korean Imagination: South Korea and the 2002 World Cup Tournaments. In *Football Goes East: Business, Culture, and the People's Game in China, Japan, and South Korea*, ed. John Horne and Wolfram Manzenreiter, 133–47. New York: Routledge.

Chŏn, Sang-don. 1998. Sŭp'och'ŭ podo ŭi hyŏnhwang kwa munjejŏm. *Chŏnŏllijŭm Pip'yŏng* 26: 60–65.

Chŏng, Tong-su. 1999. Sŭp'och'ŭ ipaent'ŭ ka kaech'oe chiyŏk ŭi hwan'gyŏng e mich'in yŏnghyang: '88 Sŏul Ollimp'ik taehoe rŭl chungsim ŭro. Master's Thesis, Hanyang University.

Chu, Chin-suk. 1991. Sŭp'och'ŭsinmun ŭi sŏnchŏngjŏk manhwa e daehan ilgo. *Chŏnŏllichŏm Pip'yŏng* 3: 48–53.

Chuh, Kandice. 2003. *Imagine Otherwise: On Asian Americanist Critique*. Durham, N.C.: Duke University Press.

Chuh, Kandice, and Karen Shimakawa, eds. 2001. *Orientations: Mapping Studies in the Asian Diaspora*. Durham, N.C.: Duke University Press.

Chun, Gloria Heyung. 2004. Shifting Ethnic Identity and Consciousness: U.S.-Born Chinese American Youth in the 1930s and 1950s. In *Asian American Youth: Culture, Identity, and Ethnicity*, ed. Jennifer Lee and Min Zhou, 113–28. New York: Routledge.

Chung, Angie Y. 2004. Giving Back to the Community. *Amerasia Journal* 30 (1): 107–24.

Cole, C. L. 2001a. Close Encounters: Sport, Science and Political Culture. In *A Companion to Cultural Studies*, ed. Toby Miller, 341–56. Malden, Mass.: Wiley-Blackwell.

——. 2001b. Nike's America/America's Michael Jordan. In *Michael Jordan, Inc.*, ed. David L. Andrews, 65–103. Albany: State University of New York Press.

——. 2008. Race Women: The Us-Chi Cheng Encounter. Paper presented at the conference of the Asian American Studies Association, Chicago, Ill.

Cole, C. L., and David Andrews. 2001. America's New Son: Tiger Woods and America's Multiculturalism. In *Sports Stars: The Cultural Politics of Sporting Celebrity*, ed. David Andrews and Steven Jackson, 70–86. New York: Routledge.

Collier, Jane Fishburne, and Sylvia Junko Yanagisako. 1987. Toward a Unified Analysis of Gender and Kinship. In *Gender and Kinship: Essays toward a Unified Analysis*, ed. Jane Fishburne Collier and Sylvia Yanagisako, 14–50. Stanford, Calif.: Stanford University Press.

Condry, Ian. 2006. *Hip-Hop Japan*. Durham, N.C.: Duke University Press.

Connell, R. W. 2005. *Masculinities*. 2nd ed. Berkeley: University of California Press.

Constable, Nicole. 2003. *Romance on a Global Stage: Pen Pals, Virtual Ethnography, and "Mail Order" Marriages*. Berkeley: University of California Press.

Crosset, Todd W. 1995. *Outsiders in the Clubhouse: The World of Women's Professional Golf*. Albany: State University of New York Press.

Cumings, Bruce. 1981. *The Origins of the Korean War*. Princeton, N.J.: Princeton University Press.

——. 1997. *Korea's Place in the Sun: A Modern History*. New York: Norton.

Darling-Hammond, Linda. 2000. School Contexts and Learning: Organizational Influences on the Achievement of Studies of Color. In *Addressing Cultural Issues in Organizations*, ed. Robert T. Carter, 69–86. Thousand Oaks, Calif.: Sage.

Dávila, Arlene. 2001. *Latinos Inc.: The Marketing and Making of a People*. Berkeley: University of California Press.

——. 2004. *Barrio Dreams: Puerto Ricans, Latinos, and the Neoliberal City*. Berkeley: University of California Press.

Davis, Mike. 1992. Fortress L.A. In *City of Quartz: Excavating the Future in Los Angeles*, 221–63. New York: Vintage.

de Certeau, Michel. 1984. *The Practice of Everyday Life*. Trans. Steven Randall. Berkeley: University of California Press.

Debord, Guy. 1995. *Society of the Spectacle*. New York: Zone Books.

Deloria, Philip. 1996. I Am of the Body: Thoughts on My Grandfather, Sports, and Culture. *South Atlantic Quarterly* 95 (2): 321–38.

du Gay, Paul, Stuart Hall, Linda Janes, Hugh Mackay, and Keith Negus. 1997. *Doing Cultural Studies: The Story of the Sony Walkman*. Vol. 1, Culture, Media, and Identities. Thousand Oaks, Calif.: Sage.

Dudziak, Mary. 2000. *Cold War Civil Rights: Race and the Image of American Democracy*. Princeton, N.J.: Princeton University Press.

Dunning, Eric. 1988. *The Roots of Football Hooliganism: A History and Sociology Study*. New York: Routledge.

Dyer, Richard. 1982. Don't Look Now. *Screen* 23 (3–4): 67–68.

Dyson, Michael Eric. 1993. Be Like Mike?: Michael Jordan and the Pedagogy of Desire. *Cultural Studies* 7 (1): 64–72.

Ebron, Paulla A. 2002. *Performing Africa*. Princeton, N.J.: Princeton University Press.

Elias, Norbert, and Eric Dunning, eds. 1986. *Quest for Excitement: Sport and Leisure in the Civilizing Process*. Oxford: Blackwell.

Eng, David. 1997. Out Here and Over There: Queerness and Diaspora in Asian American Studies. *Social Text* 52/53 15 (3/4): 31–52.

———. 2001. *Racial Castration: Managing Masculinity in Asian America*. Durham N.C.: Duke University Press.

Epstein, Stephen. 2000. Anarchy in the UK, Solidarity in the ROK: Punk Rock Comes to Korea. *Acta Koreana* 3: 1–34.

Epstein, Stephen, and Timothy Tangherlini. 2001. *Our Nation: A Korean Punk Rock Community*. New York: Filmakers Library.

Erni, John Nguyet, and Siew Keng Chua, eds. 2005. *Asian Media Studies*. Malden, Mass.: Blackwell.

España-Maram, Linda. 2006. *Creating Masculinity in Los Angeles's Little Manila: Working-Class Filipinos and Popular Culture, 1920s–1950s*. Chichester, N.Y.: Columbia University Press.

Farquhar, Judith. 2002. *Appetites: Food and Sex in Postsocialist China*. Durham, N.C.: Duke University Press.

Farred, Grant. 2003. *What's My Name? Black Vernacular Intellectuals*. Minneapolis: University of Minnesota Press.

Federal Bureau of Investigation (FBI). 1987. FBI File on Paul Robeson. Wilmington, Del: Scholarly Resources.

Feder-Kane, Abigail. 2000. "A Radiant Smile from the Lovely Lady": Overdetermined Femininity In "Ladies" Figure Skating. In *Reading Sport: Critical Essays on Power and Representation*, ed. Susan Birrell and Mary G. McDonald, 206–33. Boston, Mass.: Northeastern University Press.

Foucault, Michel. 1994. The Birth of Biopolitics. In *Essential Works of Foucault: Ethics: Subjectivity and Truth*, ed. Paul Rabinow, 73–80. New York: New Press.

Foucault, Michel. 1980. *Power/Knowledge: Selected Interviews and Other Writings, 1972–1977*. Ed. and trans. Colin Gordon. New York: Pantheon Books.

Foucault, Michel. 1984. *The Foucault Reader*. Ed. Paul Rabinow. New York: Pantheon Books.

Franks, Joel S. 2000. *Crossing Sidelines, Crossing Cultures: Sport and Asian Pacific American Cultural Citizenship*. Lanham, Md.: University Press of America.

Fraser, Nancy. 1995. Politics, Culture, and the Public Sphere: Toward a Postmodern Conception. In *Social Postmodernism: Beyond Identity Politics*, ed. Linda Nicholson and Steven Seidman, 287–312. Cambridge: Cambridge University Press.

Gans, Herbert J. 1992. Second-Generation Decline: Scenarios for the Economic and Ethnic Futures of the Post-1965 American Immigrants. *Ethnic and Racial Studies* 15 (2): 173–92.

Gast, Leon. 1996. *When We Were Kings*. USA: MCA Home Video.

Ginsburg, Faye D., Lila Abu-Lughod, and Brian Larkin, eds. 2002. *Media Worlds: Anthropology on New Terrain.* Berkeley: University of California Press.

Gitlin, Todd. 2003. *The Whole World Is Watching: Mass Media in the Making and Unmaking of the New Left.* Berkeley: University of California Press.

Gopinath, Gayatri. 2005. *Impossible Desires: Queer Diasporas and South Asian Public Cultures.* Durham, N.C.: Duke University Press.

Gordon, Dan. 2005. *A State of Mind.* New York: Kino Video.

Gordon, Dan, and Nicholas Bonner. 2002. *The Game of Their Lives.* United Kingdom: Passion Pictures.

Gramsci, Antonio. 1992. *Prison Notebooks.* Ed. Joseph A. Buttigieg. New York: Columbia University Press.

Green, Alfred A., ed. [1950] 2001. *The Jackie Robinson Story.* Santa Monica, Calif.: MGM Home Entertainment.

Gremillion, Helen. 2003. *Feeding Anorexia: Gender and Power at a Treatment Center.* Durham, N.C.: Duke University Press.

Grewal, Inderpal. 2005. *Transnational America.* Durham, N.C.: Duke University Press.

Grewal, Inderpal, Akhil Gupta, and Aihwa Ong. 1999. Introduction: Asian Transnationalities. *positions: east asia cultures critique* 7 (3): 653–66.

Grinker, Roy Richard. 1998. *Korea and Its Futures: Unification and the Unfinished War.* New York: St. Martin's Press.

Gupta, Akhil, and James Ferguson. 1997. Beyond "Culture": Space, Identity, and the Politics of Difference. In *Culture, Power, Place: Explorations in Critical Anthropology,* ed. Akhil Gupta and James Ferguson, 33–51. Durham, N.C.: Duke University Press.

Ha, Nam-gil, and J. A. Mangan. 2003. Ideology, Politics, Power: Korean Sport-Transformation, 1942–92. In *Sport in Asian Society: Past and Present,* ed. J. A. Mangan and Fan Hong, 174–97. London: Frank Cass.

Hall, Stuart. 1980. Encoding/Decoding. In *Culture, Media, Language,* ed. Stuart Hall, Dorothy Hobson, Andrew Lowe, and Paul Willis, 128–38. New York: Routledge.

———. 1985. Signification, Representation, Ideology: Althusser and the Post-Structuralist Debates. *Critical Studies in Mass Communication* 2 (2): 91–114.

———. 1986. The Problem of Ideology: Marxism without Guarantees. *Journal of Communication Inquiry* 10 (2): 28–44.

———, ed. 1997. *Representation: Cultural Representations and Signifying Practices.* Thousand Oaks, Calif.: Sage.

Hamamoto, Darrell. 1994. *Monitored Peril: Asian Americans and the Politics of TV Representation.* Minneapolis: University of Minnesota Press.

Hamamoto, Darrell, and Sandra Lin, eds. 2000. *Countervisions: Asian American Film Criticism.* Philadelphia: Temple University Press.

Han, Hŭi-chŏng. 2002. Ollŏ nŭn sŭp'och'ŭ chŏngsin kwa kongik ŭl saenggak haeya. *Chŏnŏllichŭm Pip'yŏng* 33: 59–66.

Han, Kwang-kŏl, and Kim Tong-kyu. 2001. *Sŭp'och'ŭ ŭi sahoehakjŏk ihae.* Kyongsan: Yongnam Daehakgyo.

Hargreaves, John. 1986. *Sport, Power, and Culture: A Social and Historical Analysis of Popular Sports in Britain.* New York: St. Martin's Press.

Hebdige, Dick. 1981. *Subculture: The Meaning of Style.* New York: Routledge.

Hessler, Peter. 2003. Home and Away: Yao Ming's Journey from China to the N.B.A., and Back. *The New Yorker,* December 1, 65–74.

Hong, Seong-Tae. 2004. The World Cup, the Red Devils, and Related Arguments in Korea. *Inter-Asia Cultural Studies* 5 (1): 89–105.

Honig, Bonnie. 1998. Immigrant America? How Foreignness "Solves" Democracy's Problems. *Social Text* 56 16 (3): 1–27.

Horne, John, and Wolfram Manzenreiter, eds. 2002. *Football Goes East: Business, Culture, and the People's Game in China, Japan, and South Korea.* New York: Routledge.

Hsu, Madeline. 2000. *Dreaming of Gold, Dreaming of Home: Transnationalism and Migration between the United States and South China, 1882–1943.* Stanford, Calif.: Stanford University Press.

Huh, Hyun-Joo. 2004. Passion & Fashion. *Inter-Asia Cultural Studies* 5 (1): 124–29.

Huntington, Samuel P. 1996. *Clash of Civilization and the Remaking of World Order.* New York: Simon and Schuster.

Hwa, Yong-dŭk. 2000. The Ideology of the Development of Sport in Korea. Master's Thesis, Gyeongsan National Unviersty.

Hwang, Pyŏng-ju. 2002. Pak Chŏnghŭi sidae ch'ukku wa minjŏkjuŭi. *Tangdae Pip'yŏng* 19.

Im, Pŏn-jang. 1994. *Sŭp'och'ŭ sahoehak kaeron.* Seoul: Munhwa.

Im, Tae-sŏng. 1994. Sŏul ollimp'ik i han'guk ŭi sahoe pyŏndong e mich'in yŏnghyang. Ph.D. Dissertation, Hanyang University.

Iwabuchi, Koichi. 2002. *Recentering Globalization: Popular Culture and Japanese Transnationalism.* Durham, N.C.: Duke University Press.

Jackson Jr., John L. 2008. *Racial Paranoia: The Unintended Consequences of Political Correctness.* Philadelphia: Basic Civitas.

Jackson, Peter. 1989. *Maps of Meaning.* New York: Routledge.

James, C.L.R. 1983. *Beyond a Boundary.* New York: Pantheon Books.

James, Steve. 1994. *Hoop Dreams.* USA: Turner Home Entertainment.

Jameson, Fredric. 1989. Nostalgia for the Present. *South Atlantic Quarterly* 88 (2): 527.

Jamieson, Katherine M. 2000. Reading Nancy Lopez: Decoding Representations of Race, Class, and Sexuality. In *Reading Sport: Critical Essays on Power and Representation,* ed. Susan Birrell and Mary G. McDonald, 144–65. Boston: Northeastern University Press.

Jhally, Sut. 1989. Cultural Studies and the Sports/Media Complex. In *Media, Sports, and Society,* ed. L. A. Wenner, 41–57. Thousand Oaks, Calif.: Sage.

Johnson, Leola, and David Roediger. 2000. Hertz, Don't It? In *Reading Sport: Critical*

Essays on Power and Representation, ed. Susan Birrell and Mary G. McDonald, 40–73. Boston: Northeastern University Press.

Jones, Steven G., ed. 1998. *Cybersociety 2.0: Revisiting Computer-Mediated Communication and Community: New Media Cultures.* Thousand Oaks, Calif.: Sage.

Joo, Rachael Miyung. 2000. (Trans)National Pastimes and Korean American Subjectivities: Reading Chan Ho Park. *Journal for Asian American Studies* 3 (3): 301–28.

Joyce, Patrick. 2003. *No Fire Next Time: Black-Korean Conflicts and the Future of American Cities.* Ithaca, N.Y.: Cornell University Press.

Juffer, Jane. 2002. Who's the Man? Sammy Sosa, Latinos, and Televisual Redefinitions of The "American" Pastime. *Journal of Sport and Social Issues* 26 (4): 337–59.

Jun, Helen Heran. 1997. Contingent Nationalisms: Renegotiating Borders in Korean and Korean American Women's Oppositional Struggles. *positions: east asia cultures critique* 5 (2): 325–55.

Kang, Laura Hyun Yi. 2002. *Compositional Subjects: Enfiguring Asian/American Women.* Durham, N.C.: Duke University Press.

Kang, Pok-chang. 2001. *Sŭp'och'ŭ sahoehak kaeron.* Seoul: Taegŭn.

Kang, Su-tol. 2002. Wŏltŭ K'ŏp 4 kang kwa 'kyŏngje 4 kang' sinhwa. *Tangdae Pip'yŏng* 20: 90–128.

Kaplan, Caren, Norma Alarcón, and Minoo Moallem, eds. 1999. *Between Woman and Nation: Nationalisms, Transnational Feminisms, and the State.* Durham, N.C.: Duke University Press.

Kelly, John D. 2006. *The American Game: Capitalism, Decolonization, World Domination, and Baseball.* Chicago: Prickly Paradigm Press.

Kelly, William. 2004. Sense and Sensibility at the Ballpark. In *Fanning the Flames: Fans and Consumer Culture in Contemporary Japan,* ed. William Kelly, 79–108. Albany: State University of New York Press.

Kendall, Laurel. 1996. *Getting Married in Korea: Of Gender, Morality, and Modernity.* Berkeley: University of California Press.

Keys, Barbara J. 2006. *Globalizing Sport: National Rivalry and International Community in the 1930s.* Cambridge, Mass.: Harvard University Press.

Kibria, Nazli. 2002. *Becoming Asian American: Second-Generation Chinese American and Korean American Identities.* Baltimore, Md.: Johns Hopkins University Press.

Kim, Chin-song. 1999. *Sŏul e ttansŭhol ŭl hŏhara.* Seoul: Hyŏnsil Munhwa Yŏn'gu.

Kim, Chong-hŭi. 1999. Pak chŏnghŭi chŏngkwŏn ŭi chŏngch'i inyŏm kwa ch'eyuk chŏngch'ek e kwanhan yŏn'gu. Master's Thesis, Hanyang University.

Kim, Claire Jean. 2000. *Bitter Fruit: The Politics of Black-Korean Conflict in New York City.* New Haven, Conn.: Yale University Press.

Kim, Elaine H., and Chungmoo Choi. 1998. *Dangerous Women: Gender and Korean Nationalism.* New York: Routledge.

Kim, Elaine H., and Eui-Young Yu. 1996. *East to America: Korean American Life Stories.* New York: New Press.

Kim, Eleana. 2001. Korean Adoptee Auto-Ethnography: Refashioning Self, Family, and Finding Community. *Visual Anthropology Review* 16 (1).

Kim, Hyun Mee. 2001. Work, Nation, and Hypermasculinity: The "Woman" Question in the Economic Miracle and Crisis in South Korea. *Inter-Asia Cultural Studies* 2 (1): 53–68.

———. 2002. 2002 nyŏn wŏltŭ k'ŏp ŭi yŏsŏnghwa yŏsŏng paendŏm. *Tangdae Pip'yŏng* 20: 48–61.

———. 2004. Feminization of the 2002 World Cup and Women's Fandom. *Inter-Asia Cultural Studies* 5 (1): 42–51.

Kim, Hyun Mee, and Rachael Joo. 2004. Sports as Transnational Cultural Current: Politics of Identity Seen through Analysis of Discourses on Korean Female Golf Stars of the LPGA. Paper presented at conference, Korean Identity: Past and Present, Yonsei University.

Kim, Hyun Sook. 2001. Korea's "Vietnam Question": War Atrocities, National Identity, and Reconciliation in Asia. *positions: east asia cultures critique* 9 (3): 620–49.

Kim, Kwang Chung, ed. 1999. *Koreans in the Hood: Conflict with African Americans.* Baltimore, Md.: Johns Hopkins University Press.

Kim, Kyung Hyun. 2004. *The Remasculinization of Korean Cinema.* Durham, N.C.: Duke University Press.

Kim, Lili M. 2003/4. The Limits of Americanism and Democracy: Korean Americans, Transnational Allegiance, and the Question of Loyalty on the Homefront During World War II. *Amerasia Journal* 29 (3): 79–96.

Kim, Min-Jung. 1997. Moments of Danger in the (Dis)Continuous Relation of Korean Nationalism and Korean American Nationalism. *positions: east asia cultures critique* 5 (2): 357–89.

Kim, Nadia. 2004. A View from Below: An Analysis of Korean American's Racial Attitudes. *Amerasia Journal* 30 (1): 1–24.

Kim, Pŏm-sik. 2002. *Hyŏndae sahoe wa sŭp'och'ŭ.* Seoul: Doso Ch'ulp'an Hongkyŏng.

Kim, Samuel S. 2000a. Korea and Globalization (*Segyehwa*): A Framework for Analysis. In *Korea's Globalization*, ed. Samuel Kim, 1–28.New York: Cambridge University Press.

———, ed. 2000b. *Korea's Globalization.* New York: Cambridge University Press.

Kim, Tae-gwang. 2003. Han'guk ch'eyuk chŏngch'aek ŭi pyŏnch'ŏn kwachŏng kwa panghyang sŏljŏng. Ph.D. Dissertation, Korea School of Physical Education.

Kim, Tal-u. 1992. Haebang ihu hakkyo ch'eyuk ŭi chaepyŏn mit chŏngch'ak kwachŏng e kwanhan yŏn'gu. Ph.D. Dissertation, Seoul National University.

Kim, Yong-hwan. 1988. Ollimp'ik ŭi kukkapaljŏn e mich'i nŭn yŏnghyang. Master's Thesis, Kungmin Daehakgyo.

Kim, Yong-sun, ed. 2004. *Munhwa, midiŏ ro sot'onghagi.* Seoul: Nonhyŏng Haksul.

Kim-Gibson, Dai Sil. 1993. *Sa-i-gu. 4.29.* San Francisco: National Asian American Telecommunications Association.

Klein, Alan. 1991. *Sugarball: The American Game, The Dominican Dream*. New Haven, Conn: Yale University Press.

——. 1993. *Little Big Men: Bodybuilding Subculture and Gender Construction*. Albany: State University of New York Press.

Kondo, Dorinne. 1997. *About Face: Performing Race in Fashion and Theater*. New York: Routledge.

Koo, Hagen, ed. 1993. *State and Society in Contemporary Korea*. Ithaca: Cornell University Press.

Koshy, Susan. 2004. *Sexual Naturalization: Asian Americans and Miscegenation*. Stanford, Calif.: Stanford University Press.

Kruger, Arnd, and William Murray, eds. 2003. *The Nazi Olympics: Sport, Politics, and Appeasement in the 1930s*. Champaign: University of Illinois Press.

Kwŏn, Hyŏk-bŏm. 2002. Woltŭ k'ŏp kukmin ch'ukche pŭllaek hol e ppallyo, tŭrogan taehan min'guk -tongnipjŏk chisŏng ŭn ŏdi e it nun ga? *Tangdae Pip'yŏng* 20: 48–61.

Kwŏn, T'ae-yun. 2003. Haeoe hwaltong sŭp'och'ŭ sŏnsudŭl e taehan chinach'in kwansim. *Inmul kwa sasang* 63.

Kwŏn, Uk-dong. 1995. Han'guk sinmun e nat'anan sŭp'och'ŭ ŭi munhwajŏk hyŏnsang. Master's Thesis, Yonsei University Graduate School.

Lanctot, Neil. 2004. *Negro League Baseball: The Rise and Ruin of a Black Institution*. Philadelphia: University of Pennsylvania Press.

Lee, Hang-nae. 1985. Han'guk kundae ch'eyuksa yŏn'gu. Ph.D. Dissertation, Dongguk University.

——. 2003. *Han'guk ch'eyuksa yon'gu*. Seoul: Han'guk Charyowŏn.

Lee, Hang-nae, Kim Tong-sŏn, Kim Hyŏn-sŏk, Lee Hŭi-gŭn, and Park Sŭng-bŏm. 2007. *Nam-Puk Han ch'eyuk haengjŏng pikyo yŏngu*. Seoul: Kwalim Book House.

Lee, Jennifer. 2002. *Civility in the City: Blacks, Jews, and Koreans in Urban America*. Cambridge, Mass.: Harvard University Press.

Lee, Jennifer, and Min Zhou, eds. 2004. *Asian American Youth: Culture, Identity, and Ethnicity*. New York: Routledge.

Lee, K. W. 1999. Legacy of *Sa-Ee-Gu*: Goodbye *Hahn*, Good Morning Community Conscience. *Amerasia Journal* 25 (1): 42–64.

Lee, Kwang-kyu. 2000. *Overseas Koreans*. Seoul: Jimoondang.

Lee, Nammi, Steven J. Jackson, and Keunmo Lee. 2007. South Korea's "Glocal Hero": The Hiddink Syndrome and the Rearticulation of National Citizenship and Identity. *Sociology of Sport Journal* 27: 283–301.

Lee, Rachel C., and Sau-ling Cynthia Wong, eds. 2003. *Asian America.Net : Ethnicity, Nationalism, and Cyberspace*. New York: Routledge.

Lee, Robert G. 1999. *Orientals: Asian Americans in Popular Culture*. Philadelphia: Temple University Press.

Lee, Sŏng-jin. 2004. *Ch'eyuksa*. Seoul: Kyohak yŏn'gusa.

Lee, Tong-yŏn. 2002. Pulgŭn angma wa chuch'e hyŏngsŏng: naesyŏnŏllijŭm in'ga sŭtail ŭi ch'wihyang inga. *Munhwa/Kwahak* 31: 163–77.

Lee, Tŭk-jae. 1995. Sŭp'och'ŭ sinmun, yokmang ŭi yongsanghwa. *Journalism Review* 17: 18–23.

Lee, Wen Ho, and Helen Zia. 2001. *My Country Versus Me: The First-Hand Account by the Los Alamos Scientist Who Was Falsely Accused of Being a Spy.* New York: Hyperion.

Lee, Yur-Bok, and Wayne Patterson, eds. 1999. *Korean American Relations, 1966–1997.* Albany: State University of New York Press.

Lewis, Lisa, ed. 1992. *The Adoring Audience: Fan Culture and Popular Media.* New York: Routledge.

Lie, John. 1998. *Han Unbound: The Political Economy of South Korea.* Stanford, Calif.: Stanford University Press.

Ling, L. H. M. 1999. Sex Machine: Global Hypermasculinity and Images of the Asian Woman in Modernity. *positions: east asia cultures critique* 7(2): 277–306.

Lipsitz, George. 1994. We Know What Time It Is: Race, Class and Youth Culture in the Nineties. In *Microphone Fiends: Youth Music and Youth Culture*, ed. Andrew Ross and Tricia Rose, 17–28. New York: Routledge.

——. 2001. In the Sweet Buy and Buy: Consumer Culture and American Studies. In *American Studies in a Moment of Danger*, 234–68. Minneapolis: University of Minnesota Press.

——. 2002. The Silence of the Rams: How St. Louis School Children Subsidize the Super Bowl Champs. In *Sports Matters: Race, Recreation and Culture*, ed. John Bloom and Michael Nevin Willard, 225–45. New York: New York University Press.

Lowe, Lisa. 1996. *Immigrant Acts: On Asian American Cultural Politics.* Durham, N.C.: Duke University Press.

——. 2001. Epistemological Shifts: National Ontology and the New Asian Immigrant. In *Orientations: Mapping Studies in the Asian Diaspora*, ed. Kandice Chuh and Karen Shimakawa, 267–76. Durham, N.C.: Duke University Press.

Lui, Mary Ting Yi. 2004. *The Chinatown Trunk Murder Mystery: Murder, Miscegenation, and Other Dangerous Encounters in Turn-of-the-Century New York.* Princeton, N.J.: Princeton University Press.

Maguire, Joseph. 1999. *Global Sport: Identities, Societies, and Civilizations.* Malden, Mass.: Blackwell.

Maira, Sunaina. 2002. *Desis in the House: Indian American Youth Culture in New York City.* Philadelphia: Temple University Press.

Manalansan IV, Martin F. 2003. *Global Divas: Filipino Gay Men in the Diaspora.* Durham, N.C.: Duke University Press.

Mangan, J. A. 2003. Imperial Origins: Christian Manliness, Moral Imperatives and Pre-Sri Lankan Playing Fields—Consolidation. In *Sport in Asia: Past and Present*, ed. J. A. Mangan and Fan Hong, 29–55. Portland, Ore.: Frank Cass.

Mangan, J. A., and Nam-gil Ha. 2001. Confucianism, Imperialism, Nationalism: Modern Sport, Ideology and Korean Culture. In *Europe, Sport, World: Shaping Global Societies*, ed. J. A. Mangan, 49–76. Portland, Ore.: Frank Cass.

Mani, Lata, and Ruth Frankenberg. 1996. Crosscurrents, Crosstalk: Postcoloniality and the Politics of Location. In *Displacement, Diaspora, and Geographies of Identity*, ed. Smadar Lavie and Ted Swedenberg, 273–93. Durham, N.C.: Duke University Press.

Mankekar, Purnima. 1999a. Brides Who Travel: Gender, Transnationalism, and Nationalism in Hindi Film. *positions: east asia cultures critique* 7: 731–61.

———. 1999b. *Screening Culture, Viewing Politics: An Ethnography of Television, Womanhood, and Nation in Postcolonial India*. Durham, N.C.: Duke University Press.

———. 2002. India Shopping: Indian Grocery Stores and Transnational Configurations of Belonging. *Ethnos* 67 (1): 75–98.

Mankekar, Purnima, and Louisa Schein. 2004. Introduction: Mediated Transnationalism and Social Erotics. *Journal of Asian Studies* 63 (2): 357–65.

Markovitz, Andrei, and Steven Hellerman. 2001. *Offside! Soccer and American Exceptionalism*. Princeton, N.J.: Princeton University Press.

Martin, Randy, and Toby Miller, eds. 1999. *Sportcult*. Minneapolis: University of Minnesota Press.

Massey, Doreen. 1994. *Space, Place, and Gender*. Minneapolis: University of Minnesota Press.

———. 1998. Spatial Construction of Youth Cultures. In *Cool Places: Geographies of Youth Cultures*, ed. Tracey Skelton and Gill Valentine, 121–29. New York: Routledge.

Massumi, Brian. 2003. *Parables for the Virtual: Movement, Affect, and Sensation*. Durham, N.C.: Duke University Press.

Mayeda, David Tokiharu. 1999. From Model Minority to Economic Threat: Media Portrayals of Major League Baseball Pitchers Hideo Nomo and Hideki Irabu. *Journal of Sport and Social Issues* 23 (2): 203–17.

Mazzarella, William. 2003. *Shoveling Smoke: Advertising and Globalization in Contemporary India*. Durham, N.C.: Duke University Press.

McDonald, Mary G. 2006. Imagining Benevolence, Masculinity, and Nation: Tragedy, Sport, and the Transnational Marketplace. In *Sport and Corporate Nationalisms*, ed. Michael Silk, David Andrews, and C. L. Cole. New York: Berg.

Miller, Toby. 2002. *Sportsex*. Philadelphia: Temple University Press.

Min, Pyong Gap. 1996. *Caught in the Middle: Korean Merchants in America's Multiethnic Cities*. Berkeley: University of California Press.

Miyao, Daisuke. 2007. *Sessue Hayakawa: Silent Cinema and Transnational Stardom*. Durham, N.C.: Duke University Press.

Mochizuki, Ken, and Dom Lee. 1995. *Baseball Saved Us*. New York: Lee and Low.

Moon, Seungsook. 2000. Overcome by Globalization: The Rise of a Women's Policy in South Korea. In *Korea's Globalization*, ed. Samuel Kim, 126–46. New York: Cambridge University Press.

———. 2005. *Militarized Modernity and Gendered Citizenship in South Korea*. Durham, N.C.: Duke University Press.

Morley, David. 1992. *Television, Audiences, and Cultural Studies*. London: Routledge.

Morley, David, and Kevin Robins. 1995. *Spaces of Identity: Global Media, Electronic Landscapes, and Cultural Boundaries.* New York: Routledge.

Morrison, Toni, and Claudia Brodsky Lacour, eds. 1997. *Birth of a Nation'hood: Gaze, Script, and Spectacle in the O.J. Simpson Case.* New York: Pantheon Books.

Muñoz, José Esteban. 1999. *Disidentifications: Queers of Color and the Performance of Politics.* Minneapolis: University of Minnesota Press.

Natividad, Irene, and Susan B. Gall, eds. 2004. *U-X-L Asian American Almanac.* 2nd ed. San Diego, Calif.: Thompson-Gale.

Navarro, Armando. 1993. The South Central Los Angeles Eruption: A Latino Perspective. *Amerasia Journal* 19 (2): 69–85.

Nelson, Laura. 2000. *Measured Excess: Status, Gender, and Consumer Nationalism in South Korea.* New York: Columbia University Press.

———. 2004. Who's Buying Now: South Korean Consumer Nationalism before and after 1997. Paper presented at the Korean Seminar Series, A/PARC Stanford University.

Ngai, Ming. 2004. *Impossible Subjects: Illegal Aliens and the Making of Modern America.* Princeton, N.J.: Princeton University Press.

Nguyen, Mimi, and Thuy Linh Nguyen Tu, eds. 2007. *Alien Encounters: Popular Culture in Asian America.* Durham, N.C.: Duke University Press.

Nguyen, Viet Thanh. 2002. *Race and Resistance: Literature and Politics in Asian America.* New York: Oxford University Press.

No, Ch'i-chun. 1987. Ilje ha han'guk YMCA ŭi kidokkyo sahoejuŭi sasang yŏn'gu. *Sahoe wa Yŏksa* 7: 104–31.

Ok, Ch'i-il. 1995. Influences of Sports Policy on the Changes in Urban Development. Master's Thesis, Hanyang University.

Omi, Michael, and Howard Winant. 1994. *Racial Formation in the United States: From the 1960s to the 1990s.* 2nd ed. New York: Routledge.

Ong, Aihwa. 1987. *Spirits of Resistance and Capitalist Discipline: Factory Women in Malaysia.* Albany: State University of New York Press.

———. 1999. *Flexible Citizenship: The Cultural Logics of Transnationality.* Durham, N.C.: Duke University Press.

———. 2007. *Neoliberalism as Exception: Mutations in Citizenship and Sovereignty.* Durham, N.C.: Duke University Press.

Oppenheim, Robert. 2008. *Kyŏngju Things: Assembling Place.* Ann Arbor: University of Michigan Press.

Pai, Hyung Il, and Timothy Tangherlini, eds. 1998. *Nationalism and the Construction of Korean Identity.* Berkeley: University of California Press.

Palumbo-Liu, David. 1999. *Asian/American: Historical Crossings of a Racial Frontier.* Stanford, Calif.: Stanford University Press.

———. 2002. Multiculturalism Now: Civilization, National Identity, and Difference before and after September 11th. *Boundary 2* 29 (2): 109–27.

Park, Edward J. W. 1998. Competing Visions: Political Formation of Korean Americans in Los Angeles, 1992–1997. *Amerasia Journal* 24 (1): 41–57.

Park, Jung-Sun. 2004. Korean American Youth and Transnational Flows of Popular Culture across the Pacific. *Amerasia Journal* 30 (1): 147–69.

Park, Jung-Sun, and Paul Y. Chang. 2005. Contention in the Construction of a Global Korean Community: The Case of the Overseas Korean Act. *Journal of Korean Studies* 10 (1): 1–27.

Park, Keunho. 2003. The Vietnam War and the "Miracle of East Asia." *Inter-Asia Cultural Studies* 4 (3): 372–99.

Park, Kyeyoung. 1997. *The Korean American Dream: Ideology and Small Business in New York City*. Ithaca, N.Y.: Cornell University Press.

——. 1999. "I Am Floating in the Air": Creation of a Korean Transnational Space among Korean-Latino American Remigrants. *positions: east asia cultures critique* 7 (3): 667–95.

Park, Robert. 1950. *Race and Culture*. Glencoe, Ill.: Free Press.

Park, Won-soon. 2000. NGO Development in Korea. *Songgonghoe taehak nonch'ong* 15: 49–84.

Parker, David. 1998. Rethinking British Chinese Identites. In *Cool Places: Geographies of Youth Cultures*, ed. Tracey Skelton and Gill Valentine, 66–81. New York: Routledge.

Petrov, Leonid A. 2004. Korean Football at the Crossroads: A View from Inside. In *Japan, Korea and the 2002 World Cup*, ed. Jorn Horne and Wolfram Manzenreiter, 106–20. New York: Routledge.

Portes, Alejandro, and Ruben G. Rumbaut. 2001. *Legacies: The Story of the Immigrant Second Generation*. Berkeley: University of California Press.

Pound, Richard W. 1994. *Five Rings over Korea: The Secret Negotiations Behind the 1988 Olympic Games in Seoul*. New York: Little, Brown.

Povinelli, Elizabeth. 2002. *The Cunning of Recognition: Indigenous Alterities and the Making of Australian Multiculturalism*. Durham, N.C.: Duke University Press.

Povinelli, Elizabeth, and George Chauncey. 1999. Thinking Sexuality Transnationally. Special Issue. GLQ 5 (4).

Prashad, Vijay. 2003. Bruce Lee and the Anti-Imperialism of Kung Fu: A Polycultural Adventure. *positions: east asia cultures critique* 11 (1): 51–90.

Price, David H. 2003. Subtle Means and Enticing Carrots: The Impact of Funding on American Cold War Anthropology. *Critique of Anthropology* 23 (4): 373–401.

Puar, Jasbir. 2007. *Terrorist Assemblages: Homonationalism in Queer Times*. Durham, N.C.: Duke University Press.

Rafael, Vicente. 1994. The Cultures of Area Studies in the United States. *Social Text* 41: 91–112.

Rampersad, Arnold. 1997. *Jackie Robinson: A Biography*. New York: Knopf.

Regalado, Samuel O. 2002. Baseball along the Columbia: The Nisei, Their Community, Their Sport in Northern Oregon. In *Sport Matters: Race, Recreation and Culture*, ed. John Bloom and Michael Nevin Willard, 75–85. New York: New York University Press.

Robinson, Michael Edson. 1988. *Cultural Nationalism in Colonial Korea, 1920–1925*. Seattle: University of Washington Press.

Rodriguez, Julio. 2002. Documenting Myth: Racial Representation in Leon Gast's *When We Were Kings*. In *Sports Matters: Race, Recreation and Culture*, ed. John Bloom and Michael Nevin Willard, 209–22. New York: New York University Press.

Rofel, Lisa. 1997. Rethinking Modernity: Space and Factory Discipline in China. In *Culture, Power, Place: Explorations in Critical Anthropology*, ed. Akhil Gupta and James Ferguson, 155–78. Durham, N.C.: Duke University Press.

———. 2007. *Desiring China: Experiments in Neoliberalism, Sexuality, and Public Culture*. Durham, N.C.: Duke University Press.

Roh, Kil-nam. 1983. Issues of Korean American Journalism. *Amerasia Journal* 10 (2): 73–102.

Ross, Andrew, and Tricia Rose, eds. 1994. *Microphone Fiends: Youth Music and Youth Culture*. New York: Routledge.

Rouse, Roger. 1995. Thinking through Transnationalism: Notes on the Cultural Politics of Class Relations in the Contemporary United States. *Public Culture* 7 (2): 353–402.

Ryang, Sonia, ed. 2000. *Koreans in Japan: Critical Voices from the Margin*. New York: Routledge.

Said, Edward. 1978. *Orientalism*. New York: Vintage.

———. 2002. *The Myth Of "The Clash of Civilizations": Professor Edward Said in Lecture*. Northampton, Mass.: Media Education Foundation.

Saito, Leland T. 1993. Asian Americans and Latinos in San Gabriel Valley, California: Ethnic Political Cooperation and Redistricting 1990–92. *Amerasia Journal* 19: 55–68.

Sassen, Saskia. 2001. *The Global City: New York, London, Tokyo*. 2nd ed. Princeton, N.J.: Princeton University Press.

Schein, Louisa. 1999. Diaspora Politics, Homeland Erotics and the Materializing of Memory. *positions: east asia cultures critique* 7 (3): 697–729.

Schmid, Andre. 2002. *Korea between Empires, 1895–1919*. New York: Columbia University Press.

Shah, Nayan. 2001. *Contagious Divides: Epidemics and Race in San Francisco's Chinatown*. Berkeley: University of California Press.

Shimizu, Celine Parreñas. 2007. *The Hypersexuality of Race: Performing Asian/American Women on Screen and Scene*. Durham, N.C.: Duke University Press.

Shin, Eui Hang, and Edward Adam Nam. 2004. Culture, Gender Roles, and Sport: The Case of Korean Players on the LPGA Tour. *Journal of Sport and Social Issues* 28 (3): 223–44.

Shin, Gi-wook. 1995. Marxism, Anti-Americanism, and Democracy in South Korea: An Examination of Nationalist Intellectual Discourse. *positions: east asia cultures critique* 3 (2): 508–34.

——. 2005. Asianism in Korea's Politics of Identity. *Inter-Asia Cultural Studies* 6 (4): 616–30.

——. 2006. *Ethnic Nationalism in Korea: Genealogy, Politics, and Legacy.* Stanford, Calif.: Stanford University Press.

Shin, Gi-wook, James Freda, and Gihong Yi. 1999. The Politics of Ethnic Nationalism in Divided Korea. *Nations and Nationalism* 5 (4): 465–84.

Shin, Gi-wook, and Kyung Moon Hwang. 2003. *Contentious Kwangju: The May 18 Uprising in Korea's Past and Present.* New York: Rowman and Littlefield.

Shin, Gi-wook, and Michael Robinson, eds. 1999. *Colonial Modernity in Korea.* Cambridge, Mass.: Harvard University Asia Center.

Shohat, Ella, and Robert Stam. 1994. *Unthinking Eurocentrism: Multiculturalism and the Media.* New York: Routledge.

Shulman, James, and William G. Bowen. 2002. *The Game of Life: College Sports and Educational Values.* Princeton, N.J.: Princeton University Press.

Sipes, Richard G. 1973. War, Sports, and Aggression: An Empirical Test of Two Rival Theories. *American Anthropologist* 75 (1): 64–86.

Skelton, Tracey, and Gill Valentine, eds. 1998. *Cool Places: Geographies of Youth Cultures.* New York: Routledge.

Smith, Neil. 1997. The Satanic Geographies of Globalization: Uneven Development in the 1990s. *Public Culture* 10 (1): 169–89.

Song, Hae-ryong, and Ch'oe Tong-ch'ŏl. 1999. *Midiŏ sŭp'och'ŭ wa sŭp'och'ŭ k'ŏmyunik'eisyŏn.* Seoul: Communication Books.

Song, Ho-gŭn. 2003. *Han'guk, musun iri irŏnago inna?* Seoul: Samsŏngkyŏngje yŏn'guso.

Song, Jesook. 2009. *South Korea in the Debt Crisis: The Creation of a Neoliberal Welfare Society.* Durham, N.C.: Duke University Press.

Spalding, Albert G. [1911] 1992. *America's National Game.* Lincoln: University of Nebraska Press.

Spielvogel, Laura. 2003. *Working out in Japan: Shaping the Female Body in Tokyo Fitness Clubs.* Durham, N.C.: Duke University Press.

Starn, Orin. 2006. Caddying for the Dalai Lama. *South Atlantic Quarterly* 105 (2): 447–63.

Takaki, Ronald. [1989] 1998. *Strangers from a Different Shore.* Boston: Back Bay.

Tasker, Yvonne. 1997. Fists of Fury: Discourses of Race and Masculinity in the Martial Arts Cinema. In *Race and the Subject of Masculinities,* ed. Harry Stecopoulos and Michael Uebel, 315–36. Durham, N.C.: Duke University Press.

Tomlinson, Alan. 2006. The Making of the Global Sports Economy: ISL, Adidas, and the Rise of the Corporate Player in World Sport. In *Sport and Corporate Nationalisms*, ed. Michael Silk, David Andrews, and C. L. Cole, 35–65. New York: Berg.

Tsing, Anna. 2000. The Global Situation. *Cultural Anthropology* 15 (3): 327–60.

———. 2005. *Friction: An Ethnography of Global Connection*. Princeton, N.J.: Princeton University Press.

Tygiel, Jules. 1997. *Baseball's Great Experiment: Jackie Robinson and His Legacy*. 3rd ed. New York: Oxford University Press.

United Nations Division for the Advancement of Women. 2007. Women, Gender Equality, and Sport. In *Women 2000 and Beyond*. New York: United Nations Division of the Advancement of Women of the United Nations Secretariat. December.

Wang, Chi-ming. 2004. Capitalizing the Big Man: Yao Ming, Asian America, and the China Global. *Inter-Asia Cultural Studies* 5 (2): 263–78.

Warner, Michael. 2002. Publics and Counterpublics. *Public Culture* 14 (1): 49–90.

Wasserstrom, Jeffrey N. 2002. Using History to Think about the Beijing Olympics: The Use and Abuse of the 1988 Analogy. *Harvard International Journal of Press/Politics* 7: 126–29.

Westbrook, Robert. 1990. "I Want a Girl, Just Like the Girl That Married Harry James": American Women and the Problem of Political Obligation in World War II. *American Quarterly* 42 (4): 587–614.

Whang, Soon-Hee. 2004. Football, Fashion and Fandom: Sociological Reflections on the 2002 World Cup and Collective Memories in Korea. In *Football Goes East: Business, Culture, and the People's Game in China, Japan, and South Korea*, ed. John Horne and Wolfram Manzenreiter, 148–64. New York: Routledge.

Wilk, Richard. 1995. Learning to Be Local in Belize. In *Worlds Apart: Modernity through the Prism of the Local*, ed. Daniel Miller, 110–33. New York: Routledge.

Willard, Michael Nevin. 2002. Duke Kahanamoku's Body: Biography of Hawai'i. In *Sports Matters: Race, Recreation and Culture*, ed. John Bloom and Michael Nevin Willard, 13–38. New York: New York University Press.

Williams, John, Eric Dunning, and Patrick Murphy. 1984. *Hooligans Abroad: The Behaviour and Control of English Fans in Europe*. Boston: Routledge.

Williams, Raymond. 1977. *Marxism and Literature*. Oxford: Oxford University Press.

———. 2002. Culture Is Ordinary. In *The Everyday Life Reader*. New York: Routledge.

Won-Doornink, Myong Jin. 1988. Television Viewing and Acculturation of Korean Immigrants. *Amerasia Journal* 14 (1): 79–92.

Woo, Jung-en. 1991. *Race to the Swift: State and Finance in Korean Industrialization*. New York: Columbia University Press.

Woo, Susie. 2004. Online and Unplugged: Locating Korean American Teens in Cyberspace. *Amerasia Journal* 30 (1): 171–87.

Yanagisako, Sylvia. 1985. *Transforming the Past: Tradition and Kinship among Japanese Americans*. Stanford, Calif.: Stanford University Press.

Yano, Christine. 1997. Charisma's Realm: Fandom in Japan. *Ethnology* 36 (4): 335–49.

Yoo, David. 2000. *Growing up Nisei: Race, Generation, and Culture among Japanese Americans of California, 1924–49.* Urbana: University of Illinois Press.

Yoo, Paula, and Dom Lee. 2005. *Sixteen Years in Sixteen Seconds: The Sammy Lee Story.* New York: Lee & Low.

Yoon, In-Jin. 1997. *On My Own: Korean Business and Race Relations in America.* Chicago: University of Chicago Press.

Yoon, Kyongwon. 2003. Retraditionalizing the Mobile: Young People's Sociality and Mobile Phone Use in Seoul, South Korea. *European Journal of Cultural Studies* 6 (3): 327–43.

Yoon, Sug-min. 1996. The Liberalization of Broadcasting and Telecommunications in Korea. *Korean Social Science Journal* 22: 95–119.

Yu, Eui-Young, and Peter Choe. 2003/4. Korean Population in the United States and Reflected in the 2000 Census. *Amerasia Journal* 29 (3): 2–21.

Yu, Eui-Young, Peter Choe, Sang Il Han, and Kimberly Yu. 2004. Emerging Diversity: Los Angeles' Koreatown 1990–2000. *Amerasia Journal* 30 (1): 25–52.

Yu, Henry. 2000. How Tiger Woods Lost His Stripes: Post-Nationalist American Studies as a History of Race, Migration, and the Commodification of Culture. In *Post-Nationalist American Studies*, ed. John Carlos Rowe, 223–48. Berkeley: University of California Press.

——. 2001. *Thinking Orientals: Migration, Contact, and Exoticism in Modern America.* New York: Oxford University Press.

——. 2002. Tiger Woods at the Center of History: Looking Back at the Twentieth Century through the Lenses of Race, Sports, and Mass Consumption. In *Sports Matters: Race, Recreation, and Culture*, ed. John Bloom and Michael Nevin Willard, 320–53. New York: New York University Press.

Yuasa, Katsuei. 2005. *Kannani and the Document of Flames: Two Japanese Colonial Novels.* Trans. Mark Driscoll. Durham, N.C.: Duke University Press.

Yun, Hoe-ch'ŏn. 1999. Sŭp'och'ŭ wa taechung minjŏk chuŭi. *Sahoe Pip'yŏng* 20: 194–202.

Yun, Pyŏng-kŏn. 2001. Sŭp'och'ŭ p'ŭrokŭraem ŭi pop'yŏnjŏk sŏpisŭ wa chŏpkŭn'gwŏn e kwanhan yŏn'gu. Master's Thesis, Yonsei University Graduate School.

Yun, Tŭk-hŏn. 1992. Sŭp'och'ŭ wa maesŭ midiŏ ŭi sanghoewichŏndo kwanhan chosa yŏn'gu. Master's Thesis, Korea University Graduate School.

Zhou, Min. 2004. Coming of Age at the Turn of the Twenty-First Century: A Demographic Profile of Asian American Youth. In *Asian American Youth: Culture, Identity, and Ethnicity*, ed. Jennifer Lee and Min Zhou, 33–50. New York: Routledge.

Index

Rachael Miyung Joo is an assistant professor
of American Studies at Middlebury College.

Library of Congress Cataloging-in-Publication Data
Joo, Rachael Miyung, 1975–
Transnational sport : gender, media, and global Korea /
Rachael Miyung Joo.
p. cm.
Includes bibliographical references and index.
ISBN 978-0-8223-4842-9 (cloth : alk. paper)
ISBN 978-0-8223-4856-6 (pbk. : alk. paper)
1. Sports—Social aspects—Korea. 2. Sports—Social
aspects—United States. 3. Nationalism and sports—
Korea. 4. Nationalism and sports—United States. 5. Mass
media and sports—Korea. 6. Mass media and sports—
United States. I. Title.
GV706.34.J66 2012
306.483—dc23
2011027456